The Christian College and the Meaning of Academic Freedom

The Christian College and the Meaning of Academic Freedom

Truth-Seeking in Community

William C. Ringenberg

First published 2016 by
PALGRAVE MACMILLAN

The author has asserted his right to be identified as the author of this work in accordance with the Copyright, Designs and Patents Act 1988.

Palgrave Macmillan in the UK is an imprint of Macmillan Publishers Limited, registered in England, company number 785998, of Houndmills, Basingstoke, Hampshire, RG21 6XS.

Palgrave Macmillan in the US is a division of Nature America, Inc., One New York Plaza, Suite 4500, New York, NY 10004-1562.

Palgrave Macmillan is the global academic imprint of the above companies and has companies and representatives throughout the world.

Hardback ISBN: 978–1–137–39832–1
E-PUB ISBN: 978–1–137–39834–5
E-PDF ISBN: 978–1–137–39833–8
DOI: 10.1057/9781137398338

Distribution in the UK, Europe and the rest of the world is by Palgrave Macmillan®, a division of Macmillan Publishers Limited, registered in England, company number 785998, of Houndmills, Basingstoke, Hampshire RG21 6XS.

Library of Congress Cataloging-in-Publication Data

Names: Ringenberg, William C., 1939–
Title: The Christian college and the meaning of academic freedom : truth-seeking in community / William C. Ringenberg.
Description: New York : Palgrave Macmillan, 2016. | Includes bibliographical references and index.
Identifiers: LCCN 2015024364 | ISBN 9781137398321 | ISBN 1137398329
Subjects: LCSH: Academic freedom. | Christian universities and colleges.
Classification: LCC LC72 .R56 2016 | DDC 378.1/213—dc23
LC record available at http://lccn.loc.gov/2015024364

A catalogue record for the book is available from the British Library.

Dedicated with gratitude to
Six Colleagues in Community:
Dan Bowell
Stan Burden
Jay Kesler
Dave Neuhouser
Todd Ream
Alan Winquist

Contents

Section III Testing the Limits: Recent Case Studies in Christian Higher Education

Tables

Foreword

The Christian College and the Meaning of Academic Freedom provides an impressively comprehensive overview of the state of the argument regarding one of the most pressing issues facing Christian higher education today. William Ringenberg, moreover, does not address these matters as merely a detached observer. Rather, he offers his wisdom drawn from his own experience as a Christian college professor and a distinguished career of study of the history of American Christian colleges. As his subtitle *Truth-Seeking in Community* suggests, the place to start is to see Christian colleges as communities that cultivate a healthy set of virtues that provide the context for fostering a truly constructive freedom.

The Christian College and Academic Freedom is a timely book in part because Christian colleges and universities are doing so well. Most of them, especially most of the more than a hundred associated with the Council of Christian Colleges and Universities, are stronger academically then they ever have been. During the past two generations there has been a renaissance in thought and scholarship in the American evangelical and traditionalist Protestant religious communities. People from such communities tend to be interested in truth-seeking and in using their talents for service. As a result, substantial numbers have gone into academia and made it possible for Christian colleges to assemble truly outstanding faculties and administrators. Such colleges offer high-caliber versions of classic collegiate education. By way of contrast, there has been a spate of books in recent years lamenting the decline of mainstream American university education, even at the best schools such as in the Ivy League. The liberal arts are in decline. There is no coherence to the curriculum. Education turns into learning skills for career training. Professors are interested only in their own careers, specialization, and advancement. Very little in the experience is oriented toward building the characters of 18- to 22-year-olds. Truth-seeking comes only in fragments and imparting wisdom is a rarity. In contrast to the state of mainstream higher education that these complaints point to, Christian colleges and universities appear as coherent intentional communities in which teachers and students can gather together around common ideals, goals, and aspirations. Truth-seeking and service are seen as at the heart of the enterprise. Parts of the curriculum are related to each other or at least by common goals of helping students to make wise vocational choices. Student life, welfare, and spiritual concerns are interrelated with classroom experiences. Such schools, while not without flaws, offer rare opportunities to spend formative years in intentional communities built around a purpose. Despite the costs of private education, many parents and students see the value of sustaining such communities.

At the same time that such communities are flourishing, they have to grapple with major issues regarding academic freedom. As the present volume makes clear, that is nothing new. Such challenges have been present from the beginning. Further, as Ringenberg's far-reaching presentation is especially helpful in clarifying, academic freedom issues come in many varieties. Some have to do with the relationships between academic institutions and the churches/religious constituencies that support them. How much freedom should faculty have to go beyond, refine, or criticize church teachings? American Christian colleges and universities reflect a wide spectrum in degrees of doctrinal flexibility. Such issues intersect with, sometimes in uncomfortable ways, issues of the relationships between Christian colleges and universities and standards for higher education in the secular culture. Christian colleges and universities have not only to relate to standards of their supporting religious constituencies but also to the secular standards for academic freedom as reflected in accrediting agencies, the American Association of University Professors, or government regulations. Pressures from secular agencies most often relate to issues regarding academic freedom for individual professors at Christian institutions. But as Ringenberg also points out, outside efforts to regulate Christian institutions also inevitably raise questions of *institutional* academic freedom or the rights of religious institutions to follow distinctive religious teachings or standards.

The focal points for tensions regarding the standards of Christian and secular communities seem always to be changing. For much of the twentieth century secular agencies generally acknowledged the rights of Christian institutions to teach according to sectarian doctrinal standards, but typically regarded them as necessarily second rate for doing so. During the past generation, with the rise of multiculturalism and post-modernism there is greater (though far from universal) recognition that there is not one standard of rationality that all fair-minded people can be expected to agree to. There is more recognition that intellectual inquiry always takes place within the context of particular communities, traditions, and unproven assumptions. Progress in recognizing that point, combined with excellence of academic work by many scholars working within traditional Christian communities and assumptions, has helped Christian institutions and scholars to gain recognition that their outlooks are not second rate simply because they are based on prior confessional assumptions. Everyone starts with some unproven assumptions. The irony is that just as that point has been gaining ground in the intellectual communities, Christians are facing even more intense challenges to their institutional freedom to follow their distinctive religious teachings on another front: regarding sexual behavior and especially regarding issues of acceptance and nondiscrimination regarding lesbian, gay, bisexual, and transgender (LGBT) behavior. Once again, Ringenberg provides a fine overview of the state of that major debate which is ongoing and not likely to be soon resolved.

One reason why such academic freedom issues are so intractable is that "freedom" itself is such an elusive concept. Practically everyone in our culture celebrates the value of freedom. Yet the simple fact is that one person's freedom is often another person's enslavement. Basic Christian teaching reflects that principle. Christians believe that we are "free" in Christ, or else we are enslaved to sin. But to be free in Christ means to serve Christ and follow God's will, something that secularists may find oppressive. Everyday experience illustrates the same principle. Addicts insist that they must be free to indulge their pleasures. Everyone else sees that they are enslaved to their addictions. Or at the intellectual level, secularist scientific naturalists see themselves as free to seek the truth wherever it may be found and think of committed Christians as unduly restricted by the blinders of their creed. Christians, by contrast, see naturalistic assumptions that limit human inquiry to empirically observable natural phenomena as unduly restrictive of freedom for truth-seeking since it excludes investigation into the possibility that the higher truths may be found in the vast realms of the spiritual and the supernatural. Once again, one person's freedom is another person's enslavement to a narrow point of view.

If we recognize that principle, then we will recognize that we cannot get very far in dealing with our differences if we talk simply about freedom. Rather, we need to recognize that freedom, while unquestionably a value, is never an absolute. It is always subordinate to something higher that people value their freedom for. As Ringenberg says well in his helpful epilogue regarding freedom in academia: "Freedom is not an end in itself. Truth is. Freedom does not exist in a vacuum; it always exists in context." What matters, then, is who or what determines the context of what we want to be free for. Once we recognize that what differing American communities differ about is not likely to be about the value of freedom itself, but rather about the standards, authorities, and ideals that ought to shape the context of our freedom, we will have taken a step in the direction of getting to the heart of the issues involved. This volume is an excellent guide to sorting out and understanding such issues.

George M. Marsden
Francis A. McAnaney Professor of History Emeritus,
University of Notre Dame

Preface

Christian college leaders long have held mixed thoughts about the concept of academic freedom. They have embraced the idea in general; in fact they have believed that in a holistic sense they come closer to realizing its ideals than do the secular institutions. Their hesitancy stems from the manner in which the general academy has defined and measured academic freedom during the past century. Thus the Christian college view of academic freedom both overlaps with and stands in contrast to the secular concept of academic freedom.

The American Association of University Professors (AAUP) arose in the early twentieth century when the secular mode of higher education was eclipsing the traditional Christian model as the dominant force in the academy. Most of the leadership of the AAUP then and since has reflected a naturalistic philosophy of education. The primary specific incident which led to the formation of the AAUP in 1915 was the dismissal of Stanford economist and sociologist Edward Ross because of trustee Mrs. Leland Stanford's objections to his outspoken advocacy of eugenics theory and criticism of the railroad industry. While early AAUP leaders such as Arthur Lovejoy of Johns Hopkins and John Dewey of Columbia wanted to protect the right of professors to speak freely on political, economic, and social issues, they also were aware of the not-too-distant past when the instruction in most colleges operated from a Christian frame of reference, a situation they did not wish to see return.

Over the years the AAUP has established itself as the watchdog and arbiter of faculty free speech issues in the academy. As such it has served the Christian colleges well by insisting that religious institutions explicitly identify to prospective faculty members the religious conditions for an instructional appointment and also that they give careful attention to operating with well-developed due process procedures for use when there is reason to believe that a faculty member may have violated an original agreement. By contrast, the AAUP has served the Christian colleges poorly—even prejudicially—by the disdain with which it has viewed those institutions that wished to continue to operate with a Christian worldview after the Secular Revolution in higher education. Prior to that revolution when the locus of power in academe lay with the religious interests, the latter were reluctant to share it with the secularists, even those in the state universities. When the situation reversed after World War I, the secularists, often without completely realizing it, became as illiberal as they thought their rivals had been in their quest for control. Alas, in the long history of American higher education, the search for intellectual openness and fairness often has been honored more as stated ideal than by regular practice.

Today the secular institutions understand the Christian institutions less well than the Christian institutions understand them. This is so largely because the Christian colleges depend heavily upon the secular universities to provide the graduate training for their faculty. One of the major purposes of this book then is to help explain the ethos of modern Christian higher education—including especially its approach to truth-seeking—to those in the academy who know the Christian college only vaguely. A second major purpose of the book is to discuss the long history of how the Christian college has attempted, with varying degrees of success, to realize its lofty goals of intellectual honesty in truth-seeking within the context of Christian theism. A third goal is to show how academic freedom aims of both secular and Christian universities can and should be complementary, how each has recently improved in the effort to realize these aims, and to encourage each type in their continuing quest for intellectual integrity.

The primary difference between a Christian and secular institution is less that of methodology than that of worldview. At their best both institutions are intellectually open in the search for truth. At its worst, the Christian college is not fair in its consideration of alternative worldviews, while the secular institution at its worst, formally or informally, excludes from classroom consideration the spiritual dimension of the human condition even while subtly promoting a naturalist way of thinking. A public institution, by definition, must not institutionally favor nor disfavor a specific religion or interpretive mode, although individual professors may and probably should share, in an even-handed manner, their best personal conclusions on the subject under consideration. Methodologically, there need be no difference between the Christian college instructors and the secular university instructors. Ideally both seek the truth and present their best insights with integrity, fairness, and humility.

The worldview of the public institution is that institutionally there should be no worldview—thus it might better be called a multiversity than a university. While, as an institution for the citizenry in general, it may not formally hold a religious test for hiring, for the sake of exposing its students to a variety of perspectives it must be diligent to assure that its hiring policy results in a teaching staff that is ideologically pluralistic. The suspicion of the Christian college community is that this does not sufficiently happen in the state school, particularly with regard to instruction in the religious and moral domain. Private secular colleges, of course, are not legally so obligated.

A second major difference between a secular institution and a Christian university lies in their respective understandings of freedom. The secular institution thinks primarily in terms of individual freedom for professors while the Christian college thinks in terms of institutional freedom to hire professors who have freely chosen to seek the freedom that comes from uniting their minds and entire personas with the mind and purpose of the Creator. The one is a "freedom from" (outside human restraints); the other is a "freedom to" something greater and wiser than the best human understanding. The "freedom from" and the "freedom to" emphases are not necessarily in conflict, but in practice they often are.[1]

One relationship in which a Christian college sometimes wishes that it possessed greater "freedom from" is its partnership with the sponsoring denomination. Many denominational officials lack sufficient understanding of the differences between a Christian church and a Christian college. The college president together with the governing board have as one of their most important responsibilities that of educating the leadership and even the laity of the sponsoring denomination on the vitally complementary roles of the Christian church and Christian college. The church has an educational program although of necessity operates at a narrowly focused and elementary or intermediate level. The college has a worship program but that is not its primary activity. The purpose of the church is to catechize the children and celebrate the good news of the Gospel with all, while the purpose of the college is to explore all of creation and to seek the mind of the Author of Truth in all things. The one focuses upon loving God with the heart and the other upon loving God with the mind. The church proclaims the truth that it has found, while the college assumes that there is more truth to be found and seeks it. The church sometimes needs to watch the orthodoxy of the college, while the college sometimes needs to speak prophetically to the church. Each needs to listen to the other; neither should seek to dominate the other.

A major question in this discussion is this: does defining an institution as a Christian college in and of itself place limits on the search for truth? It need not; indeed it should not. An individual in a free society must be able to seek truth wherever it leads him or her. Some individuals who on their own reach the conclusion that the key to understanding the human condition is the incarnational idea that God has come to us in Christ are free to assemble themselves together into an educational community to engage in further truth-seeking. Should any such individuals decide to no longer believe the central premise of the Christian faith, then they are free to leave the voluntary educational community; indeed that would be the natural thing to do.

When I have mentioned to my scholar friends that I was working on this project on the Christian college and academic freedom, a typical response has been, "Oh, there is a need for that?" If such is the case, why is it so? The reasons are several.

More than any time since the Secular Revolution, Christian colleges encourage and even expect their faculty to conduct research and publish their findings. As the case studies in Section III demonstrate, publishing more than teaching alone places faculty members at a greater risk of receiving challenges to their academic freedom. Also, the nature of the scholarship coming from the continuing Christian colleges, with their major emphasis on faith and learning integration subjects, gives more emphasis, directly or indirectly, to religious themes—the very subjects most sensitive to those in the larger college constituency who most closely watch the continuing orthodoxy of the faculty. Continuing Christian Protestant colleges tend to produce more ideologically oriented academic freedom cases than do historically Christian mainline schools.[2] The primary umbrella organization of the evangelical colleges, the Council of Christian Colleges and Universities (CCCU), lists academic freedom ("How is academic freedom negotiated in the context of institutional commitment at CCCU schools?") as one of the 16 items on its research agenda. Former CCCU director of research Ronald Mahurin states that the member schools are showing greater interest in academic freedom. The parallel organization for Bible colleges, the Association for Biblical Higher Education (ABHE), identifies the development and publication of an institutional statement of academic freedom as a condition for membership.[3]

Then there is the still widespread belief in the academy that Christian colleges do not practice academic freedom. Here is an illustrative anecdote that is all too representative. A long-time colleague in our Christian college told me recently of his experience at a conference of English scholars. In an informal conversation a professor in a secular college upon learning of his institutional identity remarked, "So you teach in a college that doesn't practice academic freedom?" His response was, "I have never had anyone tell me what books I could assign. Furthermore, I have a freedom to discuss the religious dimensions of the subject matter, even talking about God. You, as I understand, in your public institutions don't possess the same degree of liberty. So who has the most academic freedom?" His English colleague responded, "I never thought of it that way."[4] This scenario nicely illustrates two points, namely

(1) the aforementioned need for the secular academy to better understand the Christian college and (2) the truism that the optimum practice of academic freedom is heavily dependent upon achieving a good fit between institution and scholar. While my friend possesses greater freedom in our college than he would have possessed in a public institution, just the opposite would likely be true for his interlocutor. Hiring for fit is so important! The college must hire as if its future depended on it—for it does; and the scholars must work as hard as possible to find a place where they can most fully and freely act out who they are—a place where there can be harmony between inner thoughts and the public expression of those inner thoughts.

A very practical reason for Christian colleges to be increasingly sensitive to operate with well-developed and implemented academic freedom procedures is that this is the age of the Internet with both careful journalists and less careful bloggers and chat room commentators easily and quickly disseminating accurate and erroneous stories about what professors do and say. Christian colleges are heavily financed by tuition and constituency contributions, and thus are dependent upon a continual flow of positive public reports. There is no better defense from external attack for a Christian college than the mutual commitment and goodwill displayed by the several components of its internal community. A strong and equitable academic freedom statement should be a vital part of this commitment.

Fortunately both the secular institutions and the Christian colleges in the twenty-first century have made progress in remedying their worst academic freedom violations of the previous century. Secular scholars "have begun to recognize that secular rationalism itself is not a neutral, absolute position, rising above all faith commitments," notes C. John Sommerville in his major study, *The Decline of the Secular University*. "Secularism is seeming more and more like a stage within history, rather than its final goal. We can see it as one way of thinking among others . . . . The secularism that looked vital and self-sufficient in 1900 has exhausted itself before reaching its goals of offering wisdom and leadership to American life." In recognition of their previously dismissive and even discriminatory attitude toward religion, some of the secular institutions have begun to again accept religion as a legitimate area of academic inquiry. Douglas and Rhonda Jacobsen over a five-year period visited over 50 colleges of various types to find how higher educational institutions were engaging religion in the post-secular age. What they found was a slow but steady reversal of the earlier dominant secularization model. Arguably it will be pluralism rather than secularism that will characterize the future of higher education. All of this is not to say that the academy in general and its professors in particular do not continue to be considerably more secular than does society in general, but the tide has turned. Meanwhile the

Christian colleges have become more moderate in tone, spirit, and practice as they move toward the academic mainstream. Bible institutes and Bible colleges are becoming more like Christian liberal arts colleges, and the most conservative colleges are deemphasizing their earlier separationist rhetoric and anti-intellectualism.[5]

Table 1 identifies four classic models of how colleges and universities practice academic freedom. Two are religious and two are secular. Two are extreme

Table 1 The practice of academic freedom: higher education models

	Religious college no. 1	Religious college no. 2	Secular college no. 1	Secular college no. 2
	Polar	Moderate	Moderate	Polar
Religious orientation of campus membership	Favorable to a specific religion	Favorable to a specific religion	Widely diverse	Skeptical
Campus intellectual mind-set toward religion	Defender of the faith	Seeker of the truth	Seeker of the truth	Discourager of the faith
Openness to discussing religion	Open to one religion; either avoid or discuss other religions so as to "know the enemy"	Open; privileging one religion but fair to all; seeking truth where it may be found	Open; fair to all	Limited but discouraging especially of traditional religion
Orientation toward the general academy	Skeptical	Sympathetic but discerning	Sympathetic but discerning	Sympathetic but not discerning
Religious curriculum	Extensive; heavily oriented toward study of one faith	Extensive; considerably oriented toward the study of one faith, but with a fair amount of breadth	Proportionate recognition of the importance of religion in a study of human history and the human condition	Limited, even ignoring
Teaching ethos	Considerable indoctrination	Intellectually open	Intellectually open	Considerable indoctrination, even if not recognizing it as such

and two are moderate. Two are presented as desirable and two as not. Obviously there are many intermediate models. The moderate secular model is the ideal for a public institution which is under Constitutional mandate to neither favor nor disfavor religion. The moderate religious model is the ideal for a Christian institution of learning which operates from the principle that all truth is God's truth and that a scholar should seek truth wherever it may be found, even in secular sources and those of other religions.

In a sense I have been preparing for this book all of my professional life. My doctoral dissertation at Michigan State University was a study of *The Protestant College on the Michigan Frontier* (1970). When I returned to teach at my undergraduate alma mater and discovered that it had no full-length history, I wrote *Taylor University: The First 125 Years* (1974) which was updated later as *Taylor University: The First 150 Years* (1996). Then I wrote the history of the Protestant college movement in general, *The Christian College: A History of Protestant Higher Education* (1984, 2006).

With the completion of my autobiography in 2013, I thought that I was done writing books. Then Burke Gerstenschlager of Palgrave Macmillan invited me to pursue this work. I could not refuse. The history of Christian higher education had been my primary research area and there was a need for the general academic community to better understand the Christian college and for the Christian college community to better appreciate the value of academic freedom.

The present book appears in three major parts. The first section seeks to describe many of the Christian virtues that provide the basis for much of the Christian college thinking about academic freedom. The second section traces the history of the thought about the practice of academic freedom in Christian and secular institutions beginning before the relatively recent emergence of the AAUP and continuing to the present. Then the final section reviews by principal categories a cross section of major case studies in the modern period and primarily in the Christian college.

While the Christian virtue section is shorter than the other two sections, it is not less important. For the Christian scholar is a Christian first and a scholar second. "Christian" is his essence; "scholar" is her vocation. Accordingly the Christian college looks first to the Christian virtues to inform the campus ethos, while finding much in the AAUP Redbook that is exemplary as well. It seeks to embrace as much of the latter as it can.

Of the number of people contributing directly and indirectly to the making of a book there is no end. Each work has its own history. The footnotes themselves attest to how the named author builds upon the work of prior scholars. Others freely share their thoughts and counsel verbally, and they in turn were influenced by countless others before them. Still others participate in the composition process. Often benefactors share with the expenses.

With this present work the collaborating scholars include Randall Bell, Daniel Bowell, Joel Carpenter, Edward Davis, Anthony Diekema, Ralph Enlow, Eugene Habecker, Lowell Haines, Barry Hankins, Stephen Hoffman, Richard Hughes, Dwight Jessup, Tom Jones, Robert Linder, Shapri LoMaglio, Ronald Mahurin, David Meadors, Drew Moser, Jeffrey Moshier, Todd Ream, Matthew Ringenberg, Michael Smith, Kenneth Swan, Skip Trudeau, and Henry Voss. Todd Ream read the entire manuscript, contributing his careful editorial skills. Burke Gerstenschlager, Phil Getz, Jeff LaSala, and Alexis Nelson served as my editors at Palgrave Macmillan. Carli Stewart typed and managed the manuscript through its many stages. As usual, my wife, Becky Ringenberg, shared gladly with her English teacher proofreading skills.

The Taylor librarians and staff including specifically Daniel Bowell, Jo Ann Cosgrove, Lana Wilson, Carli Stewart, Alex Moore, and Jeffry Neuhouser provided facilities as well as their generous services. Kelsey Mitchener contributed late-stage editorial assistance. The office of Taylor President Eugene Habecker funded clerical expenses.

Finally, let me offer a few explanations about the text. Parts of Section I appeared previously in my *Letters to Young Scholars: An Introduction to Christian Thought* (2003), with reproduction here by concurrence of the Taylor University Press. Occasionally I will reference an incident in a theological seminary or Catholic college when it has important implications for religious higher education in general. On the issue of gender-related phrasing usually I will use alternate word forms (sometimes "he," sometimes "she") when speaking generically or plural expressions (e.g., "people" . . . "their") rather than "he or she."

SECTION I

Christian Values as Context for the Idea of Academic Freedom

The modern college idea of academic freedom began to develop long before the emergence of the American Association for University Professors (AAUP) in the twentieth century. The teachings of Jesus and his early followers, together with the Hebrew tradition from which they emerged, informed the approach to learning which has influenced significant parts of the academic community from the Middle Ages to the present. This section then discusses some of the most important of these concepts.

CHAPTER 1

Freedom

Human freedom as well as the sovereignty and love of God are at the heart of the Christian worldview. What is arguably the central verse of the Bible (John 3:16) states that "whosoever will" may unite with the One God. This phrase, of course, assumes that humans possess the freedom to choose for good or for evil. If God so valued human freedom and thus our ability to choose to align our ways with His, how dare we seek to violate the freedom of our fellow creatures? And yet we do this so easily and so frequently!

Much of human history could be told as one group of people seeking to control another group of people and the second group seeking to resist that effort. And the story repeats and repeats. For no other reason than to protect themselves from human threats to their God-given freedom have people been so willing to die prematurely. This passionate valuing of freedom by people everywhere at all times is the best proof of its existence as a prime factor in the human condition.

The control/resist dynamic is a significant factor, if not the dominant one, in arguably the majority of wars, internal revolts, church fights, husband–wife arguments, parent–child struggles, and labor–management conflicts. Why is humanity's need to control so consuming? Part of the desire to control stems from our intuitive belief that there are right and wrong ways of doing things, and, wanting others to choose rightly, we therefore seek to assure that they will do so by controlling their circumstances. With few exceptions such as the appropriate parental direction in the development of children and governmental restraint of the wicked, this control is usually self-defeating in that it is contrary to the principle of individual choice with which God endowed us. Additional reasons for seeking to control others are less noble: to exercise willfulness, to demonstrate authority, or to act out sadistic feelings.

If the desire to control others is due largely to sinfulness, including perhaps a quest to be like a false image of God or even to replace God, the desire to be free from control stems from the way God made us all not merely as free moral beings but as creatures who value this freedom to an inestimable degree. But freedom, no less than power, can be misused. A person abusing power seeks to control others; a person abusing freedom ignores others and their needs. Freedom is never an end in itself, but is a gift to allow us to choose voluntarily the collective good for ourselves and others, namely, union with God and one another. In exercising our freedom, we can ignore people one by one or as collective entities. If, in the twentieth century, Communist and Fascist systems often sinned in exercising tyranny over their subjects, then Western systems of capitalism have often erred by emphasizing the importance of production and industrialism over assuring minimum security for large numbers of their people. As Richard Emrich reminds us,

> Our responsibility does not cease when our neighbor confronts us, not as an individual, but in the shape of millions of slum dwellers and tenant farmers, To love God means to . . . never . . . rest content while a social order condemns millions to insecurity. Christian individualism then, is a social individualism, and we can only be bound to God if we are bound to our fellows with their very practical needs.[1]

We humans passionately seek and need both large amounts of freedom and large amounts of security. God gives us love and freedom, and, as needed with it, security; we best act out Jesus' commandments to love God and our neighbors when we give the same to others. When Christians debate theology, perhaps the greatest point of agreement is the idea of discipleship—we are to seek to be as much as possible like the God-man Himself. This concept is expressed in the title of two of the most read Christian classics, Thomas á Kempis's *The Imitation of Christ* and Charles Sheldon's *In His Steps*. The heart of imitating Christ is this: Just as He emptied Himself of some of His power to create and empower us as free moral agents, so also we are to use this freedom and power to both give ourselves back to Him and to freely empower those fellow creatures who, in some way, need part of our strength. Historically, humans have less clearly seen the idea of a God who lovingly shares His power and calls His followers to do the same than they have the idea of a God who exerts His power to the maximum. Truly loving, giving, Christian individuals, churches, and even states use their power to help people move away from an immature dependence to the appropriation of the self-respect given to us all by a loving God. By contrast, the drive for power over others stands in contrast to both the example and formula given to us by the Son of Man.

Empowering my neighbor then is loving him as myself, thus fulfilling one of the two commandments that Jesus has given to us.[2] Loving God, of course, is the other commandment and we do this by walking in union or fellowship with God, thus obeying Him ("If you love me you will obey my commandments"[3]). We choose to use our freedom to fulfill that for which we are created. By contrast, to choose freedom as license to sin and follow our sinful tendencies is to choose to not be free but to be bound in our sinfulness.

French philosopher and lawyer Jacques Ellul describes the radical nature of Christian freedom,

> I want to affirm as strongly as I can that the freedom given by Christ is in effect this: "All things are lawful"[4]—absolutely all things. There is no specifically Christian way of life which imposes this or that conduct or focuses us not to choose certain things, . . . It is so to the point where Christians may take up contradictory attitudes . . . Any lifestyle then, can be an expression of freedom . . . "Do as you like" is the second part of the celebrated formula[5] of Augustine. The death of Christ has snatched us from the fatal grip of sin. It has liberated us from the powers . . . . The Holy Spirit dwells within us. I live, yet not I, but Christ lives in me. There has thus been a tremendous reversal which has changed the very root of our being and made us free. Hence, when we act, we no longer express the evil one; we express the Holy Spirit . . . . We may use all things if we do so in prayer, if we do so in the action of grace, if we bring these things into the world of grace that God confers upon us.

By contrast, the world without Christ needs many rules to control conduct. Sometimes even the church itself can seem so controlling. The extent to which this is true, Ellul contends, is the extent to which it has, "lost the basic meaning of the Christian life, which is freedom."[6]

CHAPTER 2

Seeking

For the Christian, including the Christian scholar, seeking truth is the same as longing for God. Like the Psalmist, he proclaims, "my soul pants for you, O God"[1]; like Augustine she acknowledges, "Thou madest us for thyself, and our heart is restless until it reposes in Thee"[2]; and like the prophet and the Savior, he is confident that sincere seeking leads to ultimate finding.[3]

For the Christian, truth is one of the names of God. There are only two places in the Bible where the text reads, "God is (something)"; one states that God is light (a synonym for truth) and the other proclaims that God is love.[4] In his classic study of near-death experiences (NDEs), Raymond Moody found that the most common interests of people who return from nearly dying are, not surprisingly, knowledge and love.[5] As beings made in the image of God, all of us creatures have as our highest purpose to seek, value, and share truth and love; other good things such as academic freedom possess their value in derivation from these.[6]

We seek because we long for something greater than ourselves or any other temporal thing in the mortal world. We long for the Ultimate. Knowingly or otherwise, everyone is lonely, everyone feels inadequate, and everyone longs for something more. This universal sense bespeaks a human separateness, an existence of partiality rather than unity. We are made for God, but we are not totally united to Him. This inherent need for passionate attachment to something greater than ourselves is one of the most empirically verifiable evidences for the existence of God. Those who deny or reject this basic desire are fighting against their basic instincts. Those who embrace this longing are blessed because of that to which the longing can lead.

Longing is so universal and intense that we seek to find a solution to it somewhere, somehow, even when our seeking is misguided (i.e., directed toward objects that are only imitations—and sometimes very cheap ones—of the real solution). While these substitutions can provide some fulfillment, they are always incomplete and even disappointing in the end.

Many of the substitute solutions involve things that are not bad in and of themselves but become false gods when we seek to find ultimate happiness through them. They are incapable of giving this to us, and we are foolish to place such high expectations upon them. Many of these are gifts of God (e.g., key people in our lives like family members, friends, or inspiring political or cultural figures; financial resources; personal influence or even power; personal talents; a fulfilling career; or an able mind). Of course, only the giver of these gifts can provide us with the ultimate gift, that fulfillment which comes not only from Him but in Him.

Sometimes we pursue noble causes that seek to promote the divine purposes of peace, justice, and human dignity in the world but then come to identify with an associated movement or organization and its humanly defined success more than the One who gives meaning to the cause. Specific examples of these causes could include economic opportunity for the deprived, world hunger, world peace, relief and development, political liberation, the sacredness of life, and even the local church or institutional religion in general.

Then there are the ways of seeking satisfaction that appear blatantly evil. In many cases, however, even these are less inherently wicked than representing the pursuit of good (i.e., fulfillment) in counterproductive ways. Prostitution and promiscuity often represent a search for love, acceptance, and meaning; the active pursuit of power and popularity for their own sake frequently stems from a quest for acceptance; the focus on the acquisition of large sums of money sometimes reflects the search for security. Of course, love, acceptance, dignity, meaning, and security are good things, and the desire for them is a God-given blessing designed to draw us to Him. So often, however, we take the wrong path in our search for Him.

The practitioners of non-Christian religions often have an advantage over those followers of the aforementioned substitute solutions to the problem of longing, for they are more likely to be sincere seekers of God, a status to which Jesus offers great hope (Matthew 7:7; also see Deuteronomy 4:20). We must not too quickly judge people on the basis of their organizational affiliation. Jesus also tells us that Judgment Day will offer many surprises (Matthew 7:21–23, 8:11–12).

Another non-Christian view that has much to commend is the pessimist variety of existential philosophy. Its primary virtue is its commitment to intellectual honesty, yet it is a very courageous half-truth. It clearly sees the problem of human loneliness and the barrenness of the previously discussed substitute solutions, but it stops short of finding and embracing the ultimate solution. The natural consequence is despair. The near greatness of this view is also its awfulness. Few can tolerate facing with honesty the misery of our fallen state unless this is coupled with an immediate prospect of relief and redemption. The logical consequence of the intolerable pain of the ideas of a non-Theistic existentialism is insanity or suicide.

The ultimate solution to the problem of loneliness is to recognize and fully embrace the idea that we were made for nothing less than intimate fellowship with God both now in this imperfect order and eternally in His new order. In our present search for God, it is of great comfort to know that God is also searching for us (e.g., see Revelation 3:20). He wants us to find Him; He is not hiding. However, He wants us to seek Him freely because He respects and values our freedom. To help us in the search for Him in this life, He has come to us in the second and third members of the Trinity. Jesus in the Incarnation not only provided for our restoration to God but also revealed to us more fully the nature of God (He who has seen me has seen the Father . . . "[7]). Then as He prepared to leave this earth, He promised that the Holy Spirit would come in a new way as a permanent divine Helper and Comforter.

Nevertheless, even Christians long for something more, and well they should. God has revealed Himself progressively, and we modern believers have a fuller understanding of the nature and purposes of God than did the pre-Christian era people. Thus our knowledge of the New Testament record can mitigate our sense of void and help us to see it as a sign of love and as a promise of a future era of ultimate fulfillment. Thus, ironically, the people who have found God continue to pursue Him.

As Peter Kreeft states so eloquently in his classic study on the universal search for God, *Heaven: The Heart's Deepest Longing,*

> We have a homing instinct, a 'home detector,' and it doesn't ring for earth. That's why nearly every society in history . . . instinctively believes in life after death. Like the great mythic wanderers, like Ulysses and Aeneas, we have been trying to get home. Earth just doesn't smell like home. However good a road it is, however good a motel it is, however good a training camp it is, it is not home. Heaven is . . . . It is our final home because we receive there our true identity. [8]

CHAPTER 3

Honesty

The problem of the closed mind has been with us since the Fall when humankind first had something to hide. Jesus compared the closed mind to impacted soil in His parable of the sower.[1] In the story the seed represented the light of the Kingdom of God. When the farmer planted it, there were four results, three of which were negative. In two cases it found short-term reception until the rocky soil (i.e., belief that the cost of maintenance is too high) or competition with the weeds (i.e., the perception that the side shows are more appealing than the central reality) prevented it from growing. The hardest soil, by contrast, didn't even allow the seed to germinate.

It is a dangerous thing to reject light. Physically, without light we could not see and would have no food to eat, air to breathe, nor heat to keep sufficiently warm. Intellectually, without light we would have no knowledge, no awareness of truth, and no ability to perceive God.

Closed-mindedness is a result of willfulness or fear. The former involves a rejection of the sovereignty of God, at least for the person. The latter involves inadequate or incomplete knowledge, with the solution being more light regarding the love, goodness, or power of God. Surely God looks more approvingly at the person who is very slow to embrace new light because of a fear of displeasing Him than the one who is open to change merely because of an admiring enjoyment of engaging one's mind. Open-mindedness in the abstract is not necessarily helpful; it is meaningful only inasmuch as it indicates that we are pursuing truth, which, to the degree that it is done purely, means that we are pursuing God.

Lies and the human insistence on believing them are the ultimate explanation of the human malaise. We seek to convince others and ourselves that we are more noble and whole than we actually are. There are people who are brilliant at hiding themselves from seeing truth they don't want to see; it is amazing to hear the logical constructs that can come out of their mouths.

By contrast we tend to view others in lower esteem than is realistic. "Putting down" others helps to elevate us, we think, in the scale of values. This competition for psychological supremacy leads to many of the ills of society; "I win only as you lose" is the thinking, and then when you "lose," you strike back.

Another form of lying works another form of havoc. Some neurotics tend to underestimate their abilities and dignity with respect to others and to believe themselves responsible when they are not. Their misperceptions are more likely to harm themselves than others. Oftentimes their intellectual "disease" leads to physical illness or other troublesome symptoms.

Unfortunately society encourages our individual predisposition toward unreality. Much of business is based upon a form of advertising more designed to deceive than inform; and much of politics is based upon a distortion of the character, proposals, and programs of other people. Even such fields as education, psychotherapy, and religion, which purportedly are designed to help people overcome the lies they believe, all too often promote a specific school of thought rather than a genuine intellectual openness.

The truth, however, is always healing. The ultimate truth is that God loves each of us supremely and wants to give us His grace as we are willing to receive it. We shrink from truth because it is often very painful; but if it is painful initially, it then leads to pleasure—indeed, to the only ultimate pleasure.

In academe, intellectual honesty in teaching and research is heavily dependent upon honesty within the person of the scholar. In one of Shakespeare's famous lines from *Hamlet*, royal counselor Polonius, in confession of his weakness, advises his son Laertes "To thine own self be true, and it must follow as the night follows the day, thou canst not then be false to any man."[2] In other words, one best judges other people when one possesses personal understanding and integrity. So much is this the case, argued Peter Kreeft, that "It is better to be an honest atheist than a dishonest theist, for honesty seeks truth and when the honest atheist sees that God is the truth, the atheist will embrace Him and be embraced . . . but the God sought by rejecting truth is not the true God."[3]

Psychologist Scott Peck sees the lack of personal honesty as lying at the heart of evil. In the Judeo-Christian story, he notes that Satan, the father of lies, originally served the function of "light bearer" to test mankind to facilitate spiritual growth. Then when he fell from God, he changed his purpose to tempt people toward spiritual regression, beginning with his successful effort to convince Adam and Eve of the Big Lie that God could not be trusted to give them what was best for them. Peck characterizes the "people of the lie" as being consistent in their refusal to see the sin within themselves, as projecting their evil onto others, as dedicated to preserving a self-image of perfection, and by an extraordinary willfulness.[4]

Finally, here are some concluding thoughts on the importance of being intellectually honest about being intellectually honest.

1. As St. Paul ("we see in a mirror dimly"),[5] Karl Popper (there is no certainty in science),[6] Søren Kierkegaard (we need to make an intelligent leap into the dark),[7] and others remind us, our minds are a limited affair in this world. At some point faith needs to succeed the hard data.

2. Given the limits of the human mind and the vast unknown beyond it, we must remain utterly humble as we seek as we can.

3. We must be gracious in our posture toward other seekers, sharing rather than competing in our understandings. When we differ, as differ we must, we can be respectful rather than argumentative.

4. In the pursuit of truth, it is rarely wise to abandon a position—and the community which may be associated with it—which is functionally and psychologically viable but involving intellectual difficulties, unless and until one finds an alternative perspective that on balance is clearly better. There is no such thing as a worldview with no accompanying intellectual difficulties.

5. Truth is wherever you find it. Just as one can find falsity in anyone, so also one can learn from any person and any situation. Even evil is in part truth or it would not be so attractive. Avoid tying your worldview too closely to any single human system; look for truth everywhere.

6. A meaningful test of one's intellectual openness is the capacity to reflect with honesty upon the best arguments against one's position and the best arguments for competing perspectives. Note the counsel of Ralph Waldo Emerson ("no man thoroughly understands a truth until he has contended against it")[8] and John Stuart Mill ("He who knows only his side of the case knows little of that").[9] The scholar with integrity earns her right to believe what she does.

7. Truth-seeking facilitates intellectual fellowship and witness between Christians and non-Christians. If both you and your friend are, at least to a meaningful degree, focused on seeking truth, you have much in common. If the friend sees you looking for whatever truth exists in his system of thought, then he will more likely be open to seriously considering your best understanding. If she sees you as less focused on telling her what truth is than in convincing her to ask God for herself, then she is more likely to be willing to hear the truth. Indeed, for all of us, no search for truth is complete without asking God to reveal, whether

on a specific issue or in an open-ended manner, what understanding He wishes us to receive.

Truth-seeking facilitates intellectual fellowship between Christians. What more lovely scene can there be among humans than that of a group of believers frankly acknowledging and celebrating the gifts of thoughtful discourse, mutual learning, transparency, humility, and openness?[10] Whether among Christians or between a Christian and a non-Christian, dogmatism repels whereas honesty and charity compel.

CHAPTER 4

Humility

If humility is not unique to the Judeo-Christian tradition, it is arguably more prominent there than among other worldviews. Secular philosophies tend to ignore it or view it as weakness. Aristotle promotes the development of self-sufficiency while Nietzsche vigorously opposes humility in favor of a striving toward a demigod-like, elite, Superman type of state.

By contrast the Judeo-Christian worldview offers many models of humility such as Abraham (I am "nothing but dust and ashes"[1]); Moses ("a very humble man, more humble than anyone else on the face of the earth"[2]); Solomon ("He mocks the proud but gives grace to the humble"[3]); Micah ("He has showed you, O man, what is good. And what does the Lord require of you? To act justly and to love mercy and to walk humbly with your God"[4]); Mary ("And Mary said: 'My soul glorifies the Lord and my spirit rejoices in God my Savior, for he has been mindful of the humble state of his servant' "[5]); Isaiah ("The Spirit of the Lord is upon me, to bring good tidings to the humble"[6]); Jesus ("blessed are the poor in spirit, for theirs is the Kingdom of heaven"[7]); and Augustine ("should you should ask me: what is the first thing in religion? I should reply: the first, second, and third thing therein is humility").[8]

Many Christian theologians describe both pride as "the great sin" (because, in the words of C.S. Lewis, "it leads to every other vice: it is the complete anti-God state of mind")[9] and humility as its moral opposite. While this does not mean that humility is the greatest virtue, it does suggest that it is at least a necessary one, a precondition to saving faith and spiritual maturity.

Humility is best understood as a realistic view of one's position in the universe. It recognizes that we are not of our own creation, possess nothing that we did not receive, and cannot do one thing nor continue one second on our own resources. Yet it also understands that we humans—all of us—are the culminating act of God's creation, supremely and personally beloved of the Father. Each individual human who possesses humility perceives clearly both that there is no one in the whole world who is any more important in God's sight than is he, and also that there is no one in the whole world who is any less important in God's sight than is he. The former realization reduces the tendency toward self-disparagement; the latter one reduces the tendency toward arrogance. How many of the problems of the world would be reduced to insignificance if we would become fully aware of how highly God values each of us!

In their thinking on pride and humility, Christians and non-Christians alike frequently confuse self-love (i.e., pride) with self-respect and self-disparagement with humility. The differences are profound in each case. Self-love is essentially self-centered to the exclusion of God-centeredness and concern for others. Of one such self-loving person popular lore states, "Mary's world was bound on the north, south, east, and west by Mary." This type of person interprets all incidents and comments with almost exclusive reference to himself or herself. Self-respect, by contrast, has a larger worldview. It sees both oneself and all others as possessing supreme value because that is their endowment from their Creator; it also understands that fulfillment for each is realized only by continuously drawing upon the unlimited Divine resources.

Apparently, many Christians sincerely believe that self-deprecation is the same as humility and thus a great virtue. They constantly talk about how they are not good and everybody is better than they are. Following this false logic, if self-deprecation is good, then masochism in general and even ultimately suicide must be very good things. Even worse than a sincere self-deprecation is a pretended one. This is often done to protect oneself from criticism (from oneself as well as from others).

Why is the self-deprecation view of humility so widely believed to be true? Some biblical verses seem to suggest it ("let each esteem others as better than himself" and "sinners, of whom I am chief").[10] So do the writings of some prominent Christian mystics (e.g., Thomas á Kempis: "Do not think that thou hast made any progress unless thou esteem thyself inferior to all").[11] These passages are probably best understood as dramatic overstatements for corrective effect. Most of the time most people are hard on others and easy on themselves. These writers call for the opposite approach, emphasizing how it is important to see your own weaknesses (not just your strengths) and the strengths of others (not merely their weaknesses). Also helpful on this subject is the balance provided by Paul in Romans 12 where he says that we should *think of ourselves* (verse 3) with sober judgment but *treat others* (verse 10) with higher priority.

True humility thanks God for life, recognizes the gifts God has given and not given to oneself, accepts what one has and does not have to work with, dedicates them to God, and then goes about the service of God and humanity as well as one can without calling undo attention to it.

The teaching and example of Jesus—and the record of history—show that for us humans, humility is often strengthened by suffering and enhanced by service. Jesus, the ultimate "suffering servant," humbled Himself through the Incarnation to suffer with and for us.[12] In His providence, God gives us humbling circumstances (trials) to sharpen our sense of dependency on Him and nothingness apart from Him that we might more effectively serve Him and others. Countless numbers of people have testified to the development of a humbler spirit through the fire of personal pain. The spirit and action of service not only follow humility; they also lead to humility.

The ultimate significance of humility, then, is to acknowledge and embrace rather than to deny or even defy one's creatureliness with all of the implications that derive from the acceptance of one's identity.

Wheaton philosopher Jay Wood and Baylor ethicist Robert Roberts have studied how the virtue of humility when applied to academic investigation enhances the achievement of understanding. The humble mind is continuously open to new insight, whereas "intellectual pride fosters closed-mindedness that risks cutting us off from persons and ideas 'that can' contribute to our growth in intellectual goods."[13]

Similarly a focus upon professional status as opposed to pure truth-seeking can limit one's acquisition of knowledge. Often early success in knowing tempts one to celebrate one's reputation for acquiring a new insight to the exclusion of receiving later insights that might improve upon one's understanding even while forcing one to admit the partiality of one's earlier view. Pride gets in the way of new discovery. It limits one's ability to listen to others and to be open to the possibility that one's views could be improved. It is important to replace a focus on ego with a concentration upon a greater goal such as love of God, love of humanity, love of truth, and love of understanding. "Humility, then," states Roberts, "is a non-preoccupation or unconcern about one's rank and status and worth, but not ignorance of it."[14]

To return to the important parable of the sower and the seed mentioned in the previous chapter, Jesus, in arguably what was his first parable, compared closed-mindedness to hard soil in which seeds could not grow. Most gardens of any size have a path in which the gardener can walk while cultivating the plants. I recall one such pathway in my parents' backyard plot. Nothing grows on such hard walkways. Jesus' point was obvious—the hard heart and the hard mind, like the hard ground, cannot grow toward virtue and understanding because of the choice to be closed to anything new.[15]

CHAPTER 5

Courage

Courage is the mental or moral ability to persevere under difficulty, danger, or fear. Courage in the Judeo-Christian tradition usually involves a determined resolve to follow God's leading, while in an explicitly Christian sense it most frequently refers to faithfulness to Christian witness in the face of opposition by a competing religious or political force. Needless courage or courage in a misguided cause is not a virtue and can be seen as foolhardy. Thus, for example, sixteenth-century English chancellor Thomas More ("the man for all seasons") expressed great concern to know the exact wording of Henry VIII's required oath of allegiance during the crisis with the Pope over the King's desired divorce from Catherine. More hoped that he could take the oath conscientiously rather than face dismissal and possible execution.

Christians have always celebrated their heroes of faith and courage, especially including martyrs and missionaries, most notably pioneer missionaries. Every denomination has its celebrated story, often—even usually—related to the path-breaking efforts of their founding fathers. Even when part legend and part hagiography, it still celebrates the virtue of courage.

Biblical prototypes of courage include Moses (who stood up to Pharaoh), Joshua (who led the military effort to conquer the Holy Land), Jesus (the perfect model), Stephen (the first martyr), and Paul (the relentless missionary).[1]

Moses, who was not allowed to cross the Jordan River into the Promised Land, urged Joshua who led the invasion, "Be strong and courageous, for you must go with this people into the land that the Lord swore to their forefathers to give to them . . . the Lord your God goes with you; He will never leave you nor forsake you."[2] A part of what Joshua understood to be his mandate involved savage violence: "completely destroy them—men, women, and children."[3]

Similarly, the celebrated Judas Maccabees led a successful Jewish military campaign this time against their despised Hellenistic ruler, Antiochus IV Epiphanes. The Jews still commemorate his exploits in the annual Hanukkah celebration, also known as the Festival of Lights, which takes place near the Christian Christmas.[4]

By contrast, Jesus introduced a revolutionary form of courage in opposing evil, namely nonviolent prophetic resistance. He declared that as His Kingdom was not of this world, so also would His tactics not be those of the rulers of the world. Calling His followers to "put up their swords" and employ the weapons of the Spirit, He provided, through the example of His own death as the suffering servant, the ultimate model for patience and forgiving forbearance in the midst of suffering for righteousness sake.[5]

Stephen as the first Christian martyr and Paul as the theologian of Christian discipleship provided the early Christian models of how the followers of Jesus must be prepared to suffer like He did for their testimony of the Gospel. Jesus had warned that His followers would be treated as He was: "If they persecute me, they will persecute you also."[6] Even while Stephen was giving his lengthy testimony to the Sanhedrin, including describing his accusers as "Stiff-necked people with uncircumcised hearts and ears," they were preparing to stone him to death as he, seeing a heavenly vision, asked God to forgive them.[7] The historian Luke in Acts describes Paul as receiving encouragement from Jesus to be a witness not only in Jerusalem but also in Rome, where reportedly he ultimately suffered martyrdom at the hands of the imperial authorities. Throughout his ministry, Paul encouraged the Christian community to be strong and courageous, like a devoted soldier, a disciplined athlete, or an industrious farmer, in serving Christ and His cause and His message even if it meant death. To do so would bring the reward of eternal life, while to fail in the effort would mean that all would be lost ("if we disown Him, He will also disown us").[8]

The classic period of Christian martyrdom continued beyond the New Testament period until 313 A.D. when Emperor Constantine lifted the ban on faithful Christian witness. Persecution by the government was sporadic; it was also local in implementation before 250 A.D. when Decius (249–251 A.D.) and then Diocletian (284–305 A.D.) engaged in empire-wide efforts to counter the growing strength of Christianity and the declining power of the Empire. Their fear was that the traditional Roman gods were angry at the growing influence of the Christian superstition with the imperial decay being the resultant punishment. Porphyry, the third-century philosopher, respected Jesus but despised his followers, considering the latter to be atheists: "How can people not be in every way impious and atheistic who have apostatized from the customs of our ancestors through which every nation and city is sustained? . . . What else are they than fighters against God?" Until Diocletian, the emperors had been willing to tolerate the Christian faith as one more religion as long as the Christians were also willing to sacrifice to the gods of the state, including emperor worship.[9]

The prevailing Christian belief was that to sacrifice to Roman gods was forbidden for it may have been the unpardonable sin. Under pressure of heavy persecution, the response of Christians varied. Many refused to compromise and lost their lives. Among the more celebrated of the early martyrs, tradition counts the 12 apostles and other New Testament apostles Matthias, Paul, Barnabas, Mark, James the Just, Luke, and Timothy; Ignatius of Antioch, Polycarp of Smyrna, Justin Martyr of Samaria, and Blandina of Lyon of the second century; and Perpetua, Felicity, and Origen of the third century. Many others either sacrificed or bought certificates that stated that they had done so. When the intense periods of persecution ended, the Christian community struggled to decide how to deal with those who had compromised. Some, such as Tertullian and the North African Donatists, insisted that the sacrificing Christians not be readmitted to the church. More moderate was Hermas who favored a one-time forgiveness. Ultimately the consensus of the Western Church was to adopt a generous re-admittance policy.[10]

Ironically, when the Christians gained freedom of worship and then political power, they changed from being the persecuted to being the persecutors. In 300 A.D. it was illegal to be a Christian in the Roman Empire. By 400 A.D. it was illegal to not be a Christian, with the established religion of Catholic Christianity oppressing the remaining pagans and dissenting Christian groups.[11]

It is important to view the early Christian persecution in the larger context of the overall Christian persecution to the present and the persecution of all major world religions throughout their histories. Demographers David B. Barrett and Todd Johnson place the total number of Christian martyrs at 70 million or nearly 1 percent (0.8 percent or 1 out of every 120 Christians in the past) with that figure holding quite steady throughout the ages, although, to be sure, episodical periods have alternated with quieter periods. The 70 million Christians compare with the 203 million total religious martyrs that include 80 million Muslims (an inflated figure due to the broader Muslim method of counting martyrs), 20 million Hindus, 10 million Buddhists, 9 million Jews, 2 million Sikhs, and 1 million Bahá'ís. Thus religious persecution and martyrdom has been a continuous human problem, not merely a temporary Christian one.[12]

Of the 70 million Christian martyrs, every major confessional group has participated. Christians in Russia and the East, where there have been more powerful political rivals to the Christian faith, have suffered more than have the Western churches. The ten largest martyrdom situations have occurred in the second Christian millennium, over half of the deaths have been twentieth-century casualties, over half have claimed Eastern Orthodox believers including 20 million in Soviet camps, and, embarrassingly, over 5 million have involved Christians (usually Roman Catholics) killing Christians, including during the sixteenth- and seventeenth-century Reformation Era. Major recent martyrdoms have occurred in Africa (e.g., Rwanda, Sudan, and the Democratic Republic of Congo). Major twentieth-century non-Christian massacres have included the Jewish holocaust in Europe, the Muslim–Hindu wars involving post-colonial geopolitics, and Confucianists in Communist China.[13]

So how does this historic record of Christian courage—and the lack thereof—relate to the situation of academic freedom in modern higher education? Here are some thoughts that may be relevant for the current scene.

1. There continues to be much evil in the world, including the tendency to force other people to believe as I/we believe with severe penalties for those who do not comply.
2. The best administrators of the truth-seeking business in the present will seek to understand how those with political, religious, and educational power in the past used that power for good or for ill.

The best educators will seek with intensity to find the best ideas about which to exercise courage in promoting, the best ways to promote them, and the best ways to allow others to promote their ideas.

CHAPTER 6

Prudence

Courage, the subject of the previous chapter, and prudence are best employed in concert. A readiness to act by itself is not necessarily a virtue. Many of the infamous oppressors of history displayed an abundance of impulsive actions. Caution by itself may involve excessive timidity and even fear. But together courage and prudence provide the energy to pursue a wise course of action. Prudence is the capacity to think carefully before acting ("let every man be swift to hear, slow to speak, slow to wrath").[1]

So much of success or failure in life is determined by how well one establishes well-thought-out values, goals, habits, and disciplines from early in life. These include learning from the mistakes of others, making choices on the basis of inner direction rather than peer pressure, developing the ability to see the long-term consequences of abusing one's body and mind, pursuing maximum educational opportunities early in life, establishing early and life-long habits of saving and investing, and living life as preparation for eternity.

Young people do well to regularly talk on a deep level with mature adults, including those who were not mature earlier in life. As an adolescent experiment in a combination of curiosity, witness, and entertainment, I queried adult smokers—in a period when smoking was more socially acceptable than it is now—as to whether they would advise a young person to start smoking. Only one response was even neutral ("Make up your own mind"); the rest advised against beginning the habit. Few things are more important for parents to seek to give their children than a sense of self-worth that makes it easier to resist the counterproductive behaviors that result from the intense peer pressure influences of the teenage years. In achieving this dignity there is no substitute for seeing how much one is loved by God both directly and also through one's own parents. Seeing life as a gracious gift, not only to receive but also to share, is a prime incentive to prepare for a life of service and the early acquisition of the training necessary for fulfilling one's calling.

An inadequate sense of self-worth often leads to efforts to feel fulfilled and approved by following the behavioral patterns of sometimes carelessly chosen social groups with the result often being personally destructive behaviors. Lack of self-worth is closely associated with lack of hope for the future. It is difficult to practice delayed gratification or to avoid long-range painful consequences when one has no vision beyond the pleasure of the evening. Many of our institutions of popular culture—especially cinema and television—contribute to this sense of behavioral myopia by portraying the short-term pleasures but not the long-term pains of undisciplined sexual practice, alcohol use, and narcotic use. Society has recently become increasingly honest about the pleasure/pain relationship of tobacco use.

Sometimes a person chooses to engage in self-destructive behavior in an effort to alleviate a sense of guilt. The guilt may be real or false, and the effort at self-punishment may be conscious or subconscious. I once worked with a brilliant colleague who, after behaving counterproductively to a degree that he failed to receive a contract renewal offer, proceeded to relax and make some very valuable contributions to the institution. Unfortunately, sensitive youth can sometimes receive an exaggerated sense of guilt from religious institutions that do not adequately balance their emphasis upon the fear of God with what should be the ultimate recognition of and focus on the grace and love of God. The pioneer American psychiatrist, Karl Menninger, wrote a classic study, *Man Against Himself*, describing the variety of ways—ranging from nail-biting to suicide—that people practice self-destructive behavior.

One of the major factors distinguishing the affluent from the impoverished in society is that the former have the ability and the discipline to save and invest wisely part of their income. Often, the affluent had the opportunity and discipline early in life to acquire enough education to enter a career that provided a level of income that made it not difficult to save. Saving is stewardship. One's attitude toward wealth and what one does with that wealth are prime tests of character. Wise spending, especially that which includes enlightened giving, is often more difficult than wise saving.

The ultimate way of practicing long-range thinking is to view life not as an end in itself but as preparation for eternity. Eternity, in the larger sense, of course exists now as does its ultimate purpose—never-ending, loving joyous fellowship with one's Maker. This relationship is the *Pearl of Great Price*. Valuing it above all else is both the best long-range thinking and the best short-range thinking.

It is one thing to be prudent in finding the best for oneself. But if a Christian seeks to love his neighbor as himself, then one will seek to contribute to the other person finding the best for herself. This does not necessarily mean telling the other person what you believe to be the prudent course for her; often that would be an imprudent action. But one always wants the best for the other, and one may then seek to follow the old Quaker counsel, "Act toward the other in the way most likely to lead to a response of goodness." Such concern for the other is most evident when involving parents dealing with children. Prudence is also very important when engaged in controversy with others.

How do you love your neighbor as yourself in the midst of controversy, even deeply felt controversy, and all the more so when it involves religious doctrine? Although controversy exists in part because we are flawed and finite, much controversy is natural and the inevitable consequence of the fact that God has created humans with the capacity of independent thinking, moral valuing, and intense caring. Problems develop when, in exercising these processes, we grant less freedom to one another than God has granted to each of us.

Here are some general principles to consider when engaged in controversy with others:

1. Value truth more than your pride. Desire to know the truth more than you do the ability, in retrospect, to perceive yourself as having been altogether right coming into the debate.
2. Always be open to new light. Even while holding firm to the base that gives stability to your life, actively embrace new truth and incorporate it into your belief system as God reveals it to you.
3. Humbly realize that God distributes His wisdom widely rather than having given it all to you.
4. Hope and pray that the other person or persons in the discussion want to hear God, and that they hear you only to the extent that your voice contributes to that greater recognition.
5. On controversial issues in general, compromise all that you can on secondary considerations, do not compromise at all on genuinely primary ones, and exercise great effort in seeking to understand the difference between the two.
6. Always exercise kindness in the midst of intense debate. Kindness does not preclude a clear recognition of differences; in fact it can contribute to it. A corollary to the classic saying, "Act toward the other in a way most likely to lead to a response of goodness" might be "Reason with the other in a way most likely to lead to receptivity of truth by all concerned." The process (charity) is no less important than the product (truth).
7. Recognize that the providence of God may allow for differing human perspectives on even significant issues.

8. Accept the idea that the reconciliation of human viewpoints is not altogether possible nor necessarily desirable.
9. Learn how to live in an environment of differing perspectives.
10. Celebrate differences as much as possible.

The wise participant in an intense discussion will recognize that often the passion of a given individual stems less from the specific issue at hand than from a longer-standing and more primary and more personal issue or issues. The latter may involve one or more of the following:

1. Fear that a group decision will displease God (or a God-like figure)
2. Fear that one or one's group will lose power or economic advantage
3. Fear or dislike of change
4. Insufficient respect for and/or understanding of traditions
5. Insufficient respect for the liberties of others
6. A need to overthrow, defeat, or defy a power figure
7. Fear that one's guilt will be revealed to oneself and/or others
8. Fear of discovering a truth which would conflict with one's desired belief system and/or lifestyle
9. An inordinate desire to win in all things, including debate
10. Anxiety because the issue at hand reminds one of a major, early-in-life, unresolved and often unrecognized issue, frequently involving one's family, church, or school

The compassionate participant in an intense discussion will seek to give the other person or persons what they most need, whether (1) comprehensive information or insight to clarify thinking on the issue at hand; (2) limited direct advice, gently probing questions, and time to process both; or (3) merely a supportive, listening ear. In each case the purpose is to assist the other(s) toward the resolution of long-standing, underlying issues.

There are several biblical models for dealing with controversy which are especially useful because of the universal principles that they suggest. Matthew, chapter 18, records Jesus affirming the dignity of all people and emphasizing the importance of gracious actions toward others, especially the young, the lost, the poor, and the offensive. More specifically, in this context Jesus, in verses 15–17, provides a process for dealing with people who have sinned against you, namely engaging in direct, immediate dialogue between the two of you, and if this does not achieve reconciliation, then bringing one or more wise friends into the effort of healing. If this procedure is appropriate for you to initiate when the other person has done the sinning, how much more so when (1) you have done the sinning, (2) the fault is shared or not clear, or (3) for whatever reason the relationship is threatened.

Acts 15 provides a classic example for dealing with church-wide controversy on doctrine and policy. Christianity, of course, grew out of Judaism. Early in the spread of Christianity the question surfaced, "Do Gentile converts need to observe the Old Testament Jewish law?" or "Can Gentiles become Christians without becoming Jews?" The issue emerged at Antioch, the early center of Gentile Christianity, and the Antioch church referred the issue to the apostles and elders at Jerusalem for resolution. The resultant Jerusalem Council determined that the Gospel is universal: reconciliation to God through Christ is available to all people in the context of their immediate culture. The universality of the Gospel is a logical development from the earlier Jewish insistence upon monotheism in contrast to belief in tribal religions.

As important as is the specific issue of the universality of the Gospel, the primary focus in this chapter is upon the general process of decision-making. In this respect, then, the important factors for the Jerusalem leaders can serve as a model for their heirs in the Christian tradition now; they include the following:

1. The church leaders earnestly sought the mind of the Holy Spirit.
2. They engaged in debate and discussion in an effort to reach consensus on their best understanding of the Divine mind.
3. They showed sensitivity to the minority group, compromising where they could on secondary issues and wanting not to cause needless offense because of their value upon unity as well as principle.
4. After their formal deliberations and decision-making, they considered their work incomplete until in a careful, personal, and sensitive manner, they reported to and provided measures for the implementation of the decision with the originating group.[2]

The last part of Acts 15 shows that even among people with the same primary purpose, some controversial issues are not totally resolvable, as the missionary team of Paul and Barnabas agreed to work separately because of their differences over having Mark become a third member of their working group.[3] Nevertheless, even when people agree to disagree on a specific issue, they still can agree to (1) desire the mind of God and truth, (2) wish the very best for the other party, and (3) talk and act graciously, loving the other as themselves.

A major problem in the American public arena in the twenty-first century has been a shortage of civil discourse. As stated by James Davis of Middlebury College, a scholar of and advocate for civility, especially when based upon the best Christian traditions, "our political environment has become noticeably more vitriolic and demeaning, from both ends of the ideological spectrum."[4] Recently 25 major religious leaders of various persuasions met in Washington D.C. three blocks from the capitol, to seek ways of increasing the decorum and dignity of public conversations. Among their ideas was the creation of a national day of civil discourse when preachers nationwide will ask their parishioners to give renewed emphasis to respectful conversation in their lives.[5]

Prudence, in summary, is wisdom in action. Paul, the peripatetic theologian of early Christianity, in his letters to the churches associated wisdom and graceful conversation ("Be wise in the way you act toward outsiders . . . Let your conversation be always full of grace, seasoned with salt . . . .")[6] with self-control and overcoming rage, bitterness, and anger, all because of being filled with the Spirit of God.[7] Here is a worthy model for the modern Christian scholar, to not only seek and speak truth but to do so with grace, humility, love, and respect.

CHAPTER 7

Love

The most important Christian idea is that God is love. God loves the world He created, especially each of us humans. We are made in the image of God and are designed to receive and reflect the love of God. Jesus, the Incarnation of God, declared as the greatest commandment to love God, with the second commandment derivative from the first, namely to love one's neighbor as oneself.[1] The Incarnation—the Christmas event—is the ultimate act of love as told in what most Christians identify as the central verse of the biblical record, John 3:16.

Jesus defines love less as feeling than as action. We show our love for God ultimately by our obedience.[2] Genuine love for one another involves inner affection, desire for the wellbeing of the other, and external actions of service.

Paul in perhaps his most eloquent statement extols the supremacy of love: "Though I speak with the tongues of men and of angels but have not love, I have become as sounding brass or a clanging cymbal . . . And now abide faith, hope, and love, but the greatest of these is love."[3]

John, the disciple closest to Jesus, is the theologian of love. His writings repeatedly emphasize people loving one another.[4] Love means little if not applied. There is a lovely apocryphal story that the other disciples criticized the Apostle John, complaining in this manner: "Can't you talk about anything besides the love of God?" to which John replied, "There isn't anything else to talk about." The story is powerful not because it is historical truth (it may not have happened) nor because it is logical truth (it is not literally true), but because it is heart truth (it resonates to the core of one's being), and the recipient responds with exuberance: "That's it! I have found the ultimate truth, and it is good!" In other words, for the seeking soul, to receive the love of God personally, experientially in the soul, so completely surpasses all other realities that it is as if they do not exist. John has been called the beloved disciple almost certainly not because Christ loved him more than the other apostles nor because God loved him more than any other human, but rather because he somehow was able to receive and appreciate the love of God more than have most people.

God loves it as we increasingly remove the barriers that prevent us from receiving more and more of His love. How many of the problems of the world would be solved if people would realize how much God loves them and then receive that love! The most significant way to remove the barriers to receiving the love of God is to discard the blinders that keep us from seeing His love. We have perceptual problems because we succumb to the distortions of Satan whose primary role in the world is that of the great deceiver of humans. For non-Christians, the primary barrier to receiving this love is a willfulness that says: "I want what I want rather than what God has to give me." For Christians the primary barriers are the related beliefs that (1) I have to earn God's love (works) and (2) I have to fear God's judgment more than trust His love.

I never cease to be amazed at the degree to which Christians and non-Christians alike believe in a works-based salvation. During the decade that I served as a minister, I found it common among unchurched people to respond to an invitation to visit or attend the fellowship by proclaiming: "I am as good a person as many of the church members." Of course, in many cases, their observation was correct, but it missed the central point. Oh that Christians might better reflect the image of redeemed sinners rather than that of good people, of one group of beggars telling another group of beggars where to find bread, of joyous participants in the ultimate church supper who wish to share our bountiful table with all who are hungry!

Yet Christians who understand the theory of grace often practice a works–salvation lifestyle more than they realize. People labor at a feverish rather than a relaxed pace, exhausting themselves in effort in their careers, communities, and churches. Why? They must really believe that they are not yet good enough for God. How refreshing it is then to be reminded, in the words of Brennan Manning, that

> God's love is based on nothing, and the fact that it is based on nothing makes us secure. Were it based on anything we do, and that "anything" were to collapse, then God's love would crumble as well. But with the God of Jesus no such thing can possibly happen. People who realize this can love freely and to the full. Remember Atlas, who carries the whole world? We have Christians Atlases, who mistakenly carry the burden of trying to deserve God's love. Even the mere watching of this lifestyle is depressing. I'd love to say to Atlas: "Put that globe down and dance on it. That's the way God made it." And to these weary Christian Atlases: "Lay down your load and build your life on God's love." We don't have to earn this love; neither do we have to support it. It is a free

gift. Jesus calls out: "Come to Me all you Atlases who are weary and find life burdensome, and I will refresh you."[5]

As with works, so also with fear: both the non-Christian and Christian allow it to keep them from the love of God. The nearly universal fear of death is essentially a fear of God. We pursue a myriad variety of diversions to keep from thinking about both. This is understandable for the non-Christian who believes that God is primarily a malicious even sadistic power who enjoys threatening and damning His creatures (Note the observation of Franz Kafka that "Our world is only a practical joke of God . . . "[6]). But God's love is more basic to His nature than is God's power. Understanding the power of God attracts our attention; understanding the love of God compels our affection. Power begets fear; love begets love. The fear of the Lord is the beginning of wisdom;[7] receiving, returning, and reflecting the love of God are the culmination of wisdom and the ultimate purpose of existence. God is not HALF love and HALF judgment. He is ALL love. His judgment, like all of His other characteristics, derives from His love. His judgment is designed to draw us to Himself. If I were going as a missionary to a superstitious, pagan society, the first concept of God that I would want to introduce is that God is good—"It is okay, you can calm down, the good God is for you; in other words, God is love."

So why do Christians who have received the redeeming love of God through Christ still remain inordinately fearful, "stuck in the fear gear," unable to fully experience the joy of their salvation? One reason is that even though the great deceiver has lost them to God, he delights in keeping them in doubt of that fact. Another reason is that the major commitment of the Christian churches toward mass evangelism necessarily places much emphasis upon fear to bring non-Christians to Christian conversion even while often failing to give equal attention to assuring the already converted. Guilt is a necessary way-station, but it is an awful place for a permanent residence. Third, in reaction to their perception that liberal Protestantism places too little emphasis upon the judgment of God, conservative Protestantism often places too much emphasis there—especially for the Christian community, thereby unwittingly contributing to the emotional duress of its most sensitive members.

Christians continue to experience both excessive guilt and a need to prove themselves through works in large part because both guilt and a strong work ethic are in themselves very good things. What a terrible place this fallen world would be if there was no sense of guilt. But guilt, like strong medication, is usually best prescribed and distributed on an individual basis as needed, rather than through indiscriminately applied mass inoculation.

A serious commitment to work is an important part of our Christian calling as faithful stewards of the kingdom. We enter the Kingdom gates freely and then delight in the work that is given to us to pursue within and for the Kingdom.

The Christian idea of the Incarnation focuses largely upon the teaching and redemptive nature of Christ, but also very important and often overlooked is the fact that Jesus also came to this world to improve our understanding of what God is like. "He who has seen me has seen the Father," Jesus proclaimed.[8] "I and the Father are one."[9] Still, countless people, including professing Christians, see God primarily as an angry Old Testament God of destruction and punishment or, in less harsh terms, as the high and mighty whistle-blower who keeps us from having fun.[10]

Oh that Christians might increasingly understand in theory and appropriate in fact the overwhelming love which the Holy Trinity individually and collectively have as their primary posture toward us humans! Such is the basis of all reality and all sanity.

When Jesus was asked to identify the greatest commandment, He included in His response what Christians have subsequently recognized as the central principle for interpersonal relationships, namely, "You shall love your neighbor as yourself." When He offered His disciples a model prayer,[11] its continuous use of the plural pronoun form (e.g., "Our Father," "Give us," "forgive us," "do not lead us," and "deliver us") suggests that the mind-set of the praying Christian should be much more than merely that of a person engaged in a private relationship with God. The Christian faith is social no less than it is personal, and any effort to move toward Christian maturity that does not fully recognize this idea is severely deficient. While concern for one's "personal relationship with Christ" is critical, it is also, in and of itself, incomplete.

A person who increasingly seeks to "love one's neighbor" does well to recognize how much the world does not operate this way. More typical than the "you and me together" philosophy is the "me versus you" pattern which Thomas Merton describes in bald form:

> I have what you have not. I am what you are not. I have taken what you have failed to take and I have seized what you could never get. Therefore you suffer and I am happy, you are despised and I am praised, you die and I live; you are nothing and I am something because you are nothing. And thus I spend my life admiring the distance between you and me; at times this even helps me to forget the other men who have what I have not and who have taken what I was too slow to take and who have seized what was beyond my reach, who are praised as I cannot be praised and who live on my death . . . .[12]

While most Christians will not see the preceding paragraph as describing themselves, if they are honest, they may find unsettling the following demanding test suggested—in different form—by C.S. Lewis: Imagine that you hear that your enemy did something evil, had something bad happen to him, or simply failed at something. Then a little later you hear that the first report was not true. What is your reaction to the second, or corrective account? Is it: "Thank goodness, the misfortune really did not happen!" or is it a sense of disappointment that you can no longer believe the initial report with its confirmation of your assessment of the person's evil character or just reward?[13] The ultimate question to ask in determining whether you love a person (or the extent to which you love him or her) is this: "Do I (or how much do I) want the best for this person?"

The easiest, most natural, and perhaps only way to increase your love for others is to increase your love for yourself. The only genuine way to increasingly love yourself is to increasingly realize how much God loves you and then to increasingly allow that love to come through to you. If you hesitate to do this for yourself, do it for the sake of others, for there exists a close correlation between your ability to see yourself loved, to love yourself, and to love others. Indeed one might say that the statement, "Love thy neighbor as thyself" suggests description as well as prescription: People tend to love others in proportion to their self-respect. Those who do not feel loved are likely to concentrate their attention on themselves to fill the aching void in their souls; people who genuinely feel loved are more easily able to concentrate their energies on loving others.

A second basic way to increase one's love for one's neighbors is to clearly distinguish between liking them and loving them. To like is to feel whereas to love is to do. If one does not possess affection toward a person, but acts in loving ways toward him or her, the positive feeling likely will follow. Love is a choice. Love actively seeks the best for the other.

If the other is very unlikable, start with the conviction that no situation is irredeemable. Difficult circumstances often provide the greatest opportunities for growth. The Christian must always be willing to initiate the healing process. A student once came to me seeking to identify debating points against the "Christian cult" to which her father belonged. Her father, who was a leader in a congregation of the movement, had deserted their family and she was understandably angry. I advised her that we could discuss theology together and then she could do the same thing with her father, but what she most needed to do was to show love and forgiveness to him. Otherwise she never would be communicating what—for her own soul at least—was the primary issue. Love is always the best apologia.

Our primary social mandate then is to love in deed those closest to us,[14] but this love is not unrelated to a spiritual love for all peoples in all places. Modern Americans have greater opportunity to express a truly universal love than have most peoples in other places or times. Ours is a worldwide immigrant nation like perhaps no country in history. Most of us can identify with another fatherland from where our ancestors emigrated, and most of us have many friends whose families came from many other countries. Since the early twentieth century, America, succeeding England, has been the primary missionary-sending and missionary-funding country in the world, and many of us grew up regularly hearing mission field adventure stories in church. Our current senior generation served on multiple continents in international wars, our middle generation increasingly works in multi-national corporations, and our current young people travel, study, and serve abroad like never before— and when they return, they run to their computers to surf the World Wide Web.

Of course, increased familiarity with the peoples of the world can breed contempt rather than compassion. But it also can allow one's empathy to be more focused and intense. Either way it produces greater responsibility to exercise greater love in spirit and deed for the growing number of the world's peoples with whom we can personally relate.

A scholar in her creative efforts works in imitation of the Creator. A scholar in his creative work is diminished if he doesn't love the part of the creation that he studies. Most scholars, especially at the post-secondary level, do indeed love the subject of their work. Many even sincerely love the students with whom they share their knowledge; it is unfortunate when they do not. The spirit of Frederick Buechner's challenge to ministers also applies to academic teachers: " . . . to preach the Gospel is not just to tell the truth but to tell the truth in love . . . with concern not only for the truth . . . but . . . also for the people . . . " to whom it is being told.[15] More difficult is the challenge to love professional colleagues who are competing for recognition and even prestige, and who are sometimes misunderstanding and even unfairly critical in their assessments of one's work.

Love, as C.S. Lewis reminds us, is an act of the will. One doesn't feel good about professional misunderstanding and discourtesy, but one can choose to be forgiving, and one can choose to act in love toward the other. Jesus' call to love your enemies is a hard commandment, but then He offers divine aid to His followers to do the difficult thing.[16]

To love perfectly is to want the best for the other and to act accordingly. No human achieves this, although some seem to nearly do so. Robert Fowler and Scott Peck in their typologies of spiritual maturity describe those few people who reach the highest level of spiritual development as distinguished from the rest of us by their ability to come close to fully "loving their neighbor as themselves." They courageously, fearlessly, and selflessly pursue their goals of universal dignity, justice, and brotherhood with little thought to personal safety and security. They are seekers who have become mystics who regularly, even constantly, commune with God and who have to a large degree come to share His vision of the dignity, beauty, and interrelatedness of all of creation.[17]

CHAPTER 8

Meaning

O ne of the definitions of the word "meaning" is "what is meant or what is intended." This definition, in turn, has multiple meanings, one being the essence of that which a speaker or writer wishes to communicate while a second is more philosophical as in the meaning of life or of a given life. The latter is the focus of this chapter. Christians believe that all of life has a purpose (e.g., the first question in the Westminster Shorter Catechism is "What is the chief end of man?" with the given answer being "to glorify God and to enjoy Him forever.")[1] and every individual life has a specific purpose for which the Creator brought it into existence. Christians talk regularly about seeking the will of God for their lives, and they sing with feeling such songs as

> May the mind of Christ my Savior
> Live in me from day to day,
> By his love and power controlling
> All I do and say.[2]

But not all people agree that life has inherent meaning. The twentieth century with its world wars, devastating new weapons, and brutal dictatorships brought an increase in pessimistic philosophies. One of the more significant of these was existentialism—sometimes called the philosophy of the Nuclear Age—which distrusted institutions including organized religion and even lost faith in science and reason. So existentialism represented a search for new sources of meaning. It was an umbrella philosophy with its adherents differing widely in some important respects (e.g., some—like Søren Kierkegaard, the "father" of existentialism—were Christian, while others—like Friedrich Nietzsche and John Paul Sartre—were atheist), yet they were bound together by a primary interest in the subject of human existence and its meaning or lack thereof. They concentrated on such difficult issues as death and the shadow it casts on life, the alienation of individuals from society and other individuals, and the inescapable presence of anxiety. Kierkegaard thought that the Lutheran Church of his day had lost its soul while Nietzsche argued that the entire idea of God was no longer relevant and the whole culture associated with Christianity should be discarded. Sarte, like Nietzsche before him, embodied the meaninglessness and despair associated with an atheism fully faced.[3]

While the Christian thinkers gasped at the expressions of the radical existentialist atheists, they admired their brutal honesty in contrast to the larger number of people who ignored God by focusing on a broad variety of escape mechanisms (or "diversions" as Blaise Pascal had earlier called them in his classic, *La Pensée*).[4] Many Christians and other theists agreed with the existential atheists that the logical alternative to religious faith was despair. As noted by Alfred North Whitehead, "The fact of the religious vision, and its history of persistent expansion, is our one ground for optimism. Apart from it human life is a flash of occasional enjoyments lighting up a mass of pain and misery, a bagatelle of transient experience."[5] If meaninglessness produces despondency and despair, the Christian vision, whether provable or not, results from hope.

Hope is the wish and even expectation that what one wants to happen will happen. The concept of Christian hope usually refers to the idea that life continues beyond death and in a better form. Hope contrasts with faith in that it is more general and more elementary. Essentially, hope is foundational for faith; if neediness is the parent of hope, hope is the parent of faith.

Lack of hope is nearly the worst thing a human can experience. Job did not lose all hope despite his lament, "My days are swifter than a weaver's shuttle and are spent without hope." Later he proclaimed in one of the most powerful Old Testament statements of ultimate trust, "I know that my Redeemer lives, and He shall stand at last on the earth; and after my skin is destroyed, this I know, that in my flesh I shall see God." By contrast, Judas, the betraying disciple, so despaired that he hanged himself.[6]

While Job temporarily may have lost hope for this life, he did not lose ultimate hope. Judas, whether with realistic perception or not, appeared to lose all hope. Judas's situation illustrates one form of hopelessness, namely the conviction that one has so completely failed the personal God that he or she cannot or should not find redemption.

While the Christian believers by definition do not experience the ultimate despair reflected by Judas and expressed by the existential atheists, they do fully experience the existential anxiety which is endemic in the human race. "All anxiety," psychologist Paul Tournier reminds us, "is reduced to anxiety about death." Is anxiety about death sinful? Not necessarily. Christ Himself experienced it. Lack of anxiety regarding death is more Epicurean and

Stoic than Christian; it usually involves repressed feeling more than courage. We do well to face fully the fact that death—and life-long knowledge of our mortality—is extremely traumatic for nearly all of us; it is our "last enemy."[7]

For Christians, our hope for our future throughout this life, at death, and for the next life becomes so intensely related to our relationship with Jesus that it becomes faith as well as hope. We say with Paul, "I know whom I have believed and am persuaded that He is able to keep what I have committed to Him until that day;" and with the writer to the Hebrews, "This hope we have as an anchor of the soul, both sure and steadfast . . . "[8]

When applied to everyday life, the concept of meaning correlates closely with the Christian sense of vocation. On a mundane level, vocation is simply work to earn a living, while on a more lofty level it is a divine calling to walk with God in all of life and serve humanity through one's daily work. It is first an attitude and second an action.

The idea of working hard and well is fundamental in the Bible and has remained so throughout most of the Christian tradition. It is a prime way of living our lives in the image of God as creators and contributors to the welfare of the world. All work is holy if it helps people and is pursued in a spirit of service to God. Note that in the creation narrative, Adam receives a vocation (gardener) immediately after his creation. The general curse that followed the entrance of sin into the world did result in labor becoming much more difficult but that does not preclude the idea that work, per se, is an existential blessing rather than a curse.

Unfortunately, in this sinful world many positions of work have involved more abuse than blessing. Invariably such situations involve a violation by those in power of the command to love your neighbor as yourself. Perhaps the most severe example of this is slave bondage in which people are denied the freedom of their person to serve the economic self-interest of others.

In modern capitalistic countries, due to their regulatory legislation, the likelihood of overt, gross misuse of the workers is much less than what existed during the earlier stages of the Industrial Revolution. Still our Western economic systems, driven largely by the profit motive, emphasize efficiency which leads to tightly controlled production processes, which, in turn, results in inadequate opportunities for workers to employ their creative abilities. Likely, this lack of creative participation is what was influencing the shift worker who, upon leaving a Detroit assembly plant, casually remarked to me as a young tourist, "Don't ever get a job in a place like this!" Not only professional workers and supervisors, but all workers are created in the image of God and function best when they are empowered to contribute creatively in their work environment rather than expected to exclusively perform mindless and even mind-dulling routines. The goal of economic planners and individual enterprises should be effectiveness (i.e., human development) rather than efficiency (getting the most "out of" the workers); ironically, the extent to which this happens, production no less than human happiness tends to increase. In addition to creating a constructive environment for employees, enterprise should be concerned with producing constructive products for consumers. Some products, of course, are inherently abusive.

The Bible identifies some correlation between hard work and financial and spiritual prosperity. Solomon, in his proverbs, Paul in his epistles, and Jesus in the parable of the talents emphasize the rewards of employing all of one's God-given resources in faithful stewardship.[9]

Of course, hard work is not always a good thing. Workaholics typically use it to escape facing a problem in another area of their lives and/or to pursue career and financial development even at the expense of neglecting other important things. While workaholics need protection from themselves, all workers need protection from the excessive demands of their work environments. This is the reason for humanitarian, work-related, protective legislation including wages and hour laws, worker health and safety legislation, child labor laws, and what was perhaps the earliest worker protection law of them all—the fourth commandment.[10] Actually, the idea of a day of rest is built into nature. The practice of freedom from regular labor on one day in seven compares to the yearly rotation of seasons and the daily rotation of day and night. Societies (e.g., France during its Revolution) and individual industries that work their population without a regular day free from the normal labor routine soon discover adverse effects in health and efficiency. There is a golden balance between work, recreation, rest, and spending time with family and friends. Problems result when one spends too much or too little time in any of these.

John Wesley noted another problem with working hard, namely that it often becomes a factor in loss of spirituality. Religious conversion, he observed, tended to make people work harder, which made them more prosperous, which in turn, made them more likely to trust in their affluence more and in God less. The solution he proposed was not to work less but to give more: "Make all you can, save all you can, and give all you can."[11] Humorous lore has Wesley describing in this manner the philosophy of those whom he saw as corrupted by their hard-earned wealth: "Get all you can, save all you can, and sit on the can."

Despite the risks of working hard and in spite of the difficulties in labor introduced by the fall, it continues to be true that work, in itself, is a blessing of God that gives meaning to our lives in a way that nothing else can. Life "is unbearable," Elton Trueblood reminds us, "unless it has meaning, and the chief way in which it can have meaning is for our little effort to contribute to some larger whole."[12]

So what then does this inquiry on the meaning of meaning have to do with the academic task in general and the subject of academic freedom in particular? The answer is everything—that is everything if one believes that the academy and its academicians should be free to train its students and inform its larger constituency in the task of reflection on ultimate values and the Ultimate Person rather than merely the mastery of data.

CHAPTER 9

Harmony and Balance

The previous chapter discussed the Christian ideal that meaning of life is found in union with God in fellowship and design. Such union is harmony; this leads to balance. It is inner-directedness rather than outer-directedness. Other-directedness, by contrast, means seeking to fill the God-shaped vacuum in the human soul by means of union with God-substitutes. Among the most common of these—varying in their appeal with one's disposition, age, and circumstances—are money, sex, entertainment, power, position, popularity, and acclaim. Often the attraction of these substitute gods lies less in what they inherently provide than in the status they bestow. We look to these human forms of acceptance to assure us that we are okay, that we are respected, that we are members of what C.S. Lewis, in his insightful essay of the same name, calls "the inner ring."[1]

A variant response to this universal need for relatedness is to deny its existence. For example, the secular form of humanism and the secular form of existentialism are both varieties—one positive and one negative—of self-reliance apart from God. Both are excellent half-truths or negative critiques. Both are good as far as they go in seeking to free people from the tyranny of being a fearful slave of the ideas and opinions of others. There is all the difference in the world, however, whether or not one exercises this independence of the opinions of others in order to whole-heartedly seek the mind of God. The secular humanist is headed for grave disappointment, and the secular existentialist acknowledgedly wallows in meaninglessness.

The struggle for the development of inner-directedness is not only an issue of the individual versus the world; at times it can also be an issue of the individual versus the church. Sometimes a person has to say no to the church in order to say yes to God. Some churches encourage or even demand an unhealthy dependency, but even in generally mature churches the individual must determine to listen intently to the leading of the Holy Spirit for specific guidance.

We must so desire to know the mind of God and carry out His will that it is as if we do not care what humans think of us. However, this does not mean to desert humanity entirely. Jesuit leader Anthony de Mello noted that "To walk away from the world of human beings as the prophets and the mystics did is not to walk away from their company but from their formulas."[2] Because the best of us do not perfectly understand the will of God, let alone perform it, we do, in fact, need to solicit and receive the thoughts of others about how we are living. These thoughts, especially from wise and godly confidants and those closest to us, are indeed an important source of information for self-evaluation. But they must only be sought as means to the end of discovering the good of the Divine for us.

With our central focus on the Incarnate God and our victory in Him, we can increasingly live with a settled confidence that keeps us calmly and steadily on the course of our calling without the excesses that stem from a neurotic quest for a self-defined fulfillment. In other words, proper being precedes proper doing. Harmony comes from being plugged into the power source of love, wisdom, truth, and purpose; only then can we naturally act. In the conflict between being and doing, the Christian ideal emphasizes primacy of being—being in Christ. Doing, then, follows being—it stems from it; it doesn't create it. To start with doing in the hope of it leading to being is to accept the burden of an impossible-to-please slave driver. You can never do enough. The irony is that many—perhaps most—Christians, who should know better, in part do this. Also, many Christian organizations encourage this. God's "burden," by contrast, "is light."[3] He simply calls us to faithfulness—not to specific results, not to human recognition. He calls us to strive toward holiness (e.g., wholeness); He does not ask us to save the whole world by ourselves. St. Dominic expressed well the desired balance between and order of being and doing: "Contemplate, and then . . . pass to others the things contemplated."[4]

With the aforementioned philosophy of being and doing in place, we can increasingly move toward harmony with our mental and physical universe as we increasingly rest in our Creator and Redeemer. More and more are we freed from the compulsion toward unbalanced thinking and living. Peace and harmony stem from obedience and fellowship as we receive and return His love and continuously seek His truth and wisdom. These elements, then, are the basis for a harmonious philosophy of life; they provide a harmonizing center that judiciously arbitrates among the competing attractions and claims of life.

Adjudicating among these claims is a lifelong process. It involves (1) seeking to avoid the bad; (2) finding among the good those things that, while not necessary for all, become a specific calling for you; (3) creating balance among those things that are essential for you—both those that are a part of your specific calling and those that are part of the calling for all; and (4) seeking to avoid an overall "busyness" state of mind whereby in a given time period you try to do more than what God is asking or wanting you to do.

Catholic mystic Thomas Merton and others have emphasized the importance of doing few—rather than many—things, but doing them well.

> Our being is not to be enriched merely by activity or experience as such. Everything depends on the quality of our acts and our experiences . . . If we strive to be happy by filling all the silences of life with sound, productive by turning all life's leisure into work and real by turning all our being into doing, we will only succeed in producing a hell on earth.[5]

Few people establish a life plan that includes a balancing of good and evil—we do not want to plan for evil at all! In practice, however, such a struggle is a reality, notes the Apostle Paul,[6] as we seek to reduce the degree of evil in our thoughts and actions. Our harmony with God, of course, is the key factor in achieving victory here. Not the least of the reasons for not doing bad things is that it steals time and energy resources from the effort to do good things.

There are so many good things that one could do in life. A large part of being a wise person is to find from the many good options those which are your specific calling. This is not always easy but it is always possible for those who are in fellowship with the One who said, "seek and you will find."[7]

Such a large part of being a balanced person is to devote neither excessive nor insufficient time and energy to each of the necessary and complementary elements of your calling. Some of these elements are unique to you (e.g., serving in a specific position during a specific period), but still need to be balanced with the many other valid demands that are common to most humans (e.g., responsibilities related to marriage, family, community, and recreation). Another model for viewing the call for balance is one that emphasizes the seemingly endless number of life situations, values, and tendencies whereby one good factor competes with a contrasting good factor, and in which victory is to be won not by triumph of one or the other force but in the optimum blending of the two. Note the following examples:

> Work and play
> Activity and rest
> Mental activity and physical activity
> Beauty and practicality
> Creation and re-creation
> Thought and action

Seeking to learn all that one can and accepting the fact that in this life,
     at least, one cannot perfectly understand
Fellowship and solitude
Giving and receiving
For those married, concern for the self and concern for the partner
For those with children, loving discipline and disciplined love
For all of us, receiving God's loving discipline and
     receiving His encouragement
The nearness of God and the remoteness of God
Heart religion and head religion
Critical inquiry and positive attachment
Doubt and belief
The development of breadth and the development of depth
Giving to those close to you and giving to those far from you
Satisfaction and continued pursuit
Freedom and security
Freedom and accountability
Loving your neighbor and loving yourself
Geographic base and universal citizen
"No man is an island" thinking, and "God and you make a majority" thinking
Living in the present moment and long-range thinking
Enjoying/using and nurturing/protecting the natural resources of God's earth
Self-confidence and humility
Purity and unity in the Christian fellowship
Process and product in decision-making
The best ideas in support of one position and the most compelling ideas
     favoring the contrasting view
The family and the community
Professional ministry and family ministry
The individual and the country
You and me
We and them
"There is no one any more important in God's sight than me" thinking, and
     "there is no one any less important in God's sight than me" thinking

The problem of busyness overlaps with but is different from—and often
more serious than—the problem of disbalance. Busyness manifests itself as
a time problem, but at its essence it reflects a misperception of what is
good. Some people spend undue time in one area of life to receive recognition for their hard work and/or excellence in an effort to correct a wrongly
perceived sense of inferiority. They need to understand that no one is inherently inferior and that to believe so is to accept a lie imposed by society or
the evil one himself. The ultimate solution is to receive the sense of self-
worth that comes with a realization of how completely their Maker accepts

them, and invites them—like all others—to pursue only His specific calling which is always doable and based upon faithfulness rather than comparative results.

Others overinvest time and energy in one area that is pleasant to avoid dealing with another area that is not. If the neglected area is a necessary one, then not facing it contributes to personal disharmony and sometimes disaster. Not the least of reasons for not being too busy is that usually such hyperactivity causes our listening to God to suffer. Of course, sometimes such communion is exactly that from which the busy person is seeking to escape; a person in such a state will never be at peace.

Some forms of busyness stem from the best of intentions. Many serious-minded people continue as a habit throughout adulthood a busyness mentality learned in their formative years (perhaps from idealistic and hard-working parents or teachers). When inspired by a call to complete commitment to Christ, the goal of excellence in one's profession, or simply for a high sense of stewardship, one needs to carefully monitor the fruits of one's work patterns. Do they produce internal disharmony or strained interpersonal relations? Do they allow one to work joyously and in a serving manner in each task without a preoccupied awareness of all the other things that one must rush on to do?

Finally, we need to continually remind ourselves that the effort to achieve joy, peace, harmony, and balance is no less a part of our calling than is hard work. Harmony and vocation need to be balanced. Maybe we could even say that harmony itself is our vocation.

The inspiring third verse of John Greenleaf Whittier's prayer poem "Dear Lord and Father of Mankind" is a good picture of this mentality:

> Drop thy still dews of quietness
> Till all our strivings cease;
> Take from our souls the strain and stress
> And let our ordered lives confess
> The beauty of thy peace[8]

The scholar must be freed up to be whole and not of divided loyalties. She must not be unduly influenced by any human institution including college, church, academia, profession, media, and governmental and economic systems. To accept the lordship of one's Creator is to refuse the lordship of any other. More specifically, one should seek to find a position where the conditions of one's employment and the ways that one chooses to implement those conditions (much disbalance in life is self-chosen) are not in conflict with either one's ultimate loyalty or one's other life responsibilities.

Some colleges may encourage such an emphasis upon faculty research that the students suffer. Others may encourage such an emphasis on spending time with the students that the faculty families suffer from neglect. Professors don't just teach subject matter; they also teach by personal example. A balanced and harmonious lifestyle is no less important than a balanced way of thinking.

CHAPTER 10

Community

The Christian ideal is that love, not power, is the basis of community. As Scott Peck observed:

> In genuine community there are no sides . . . the members . . . have learned how to listen to each other and how not to reject each other . . . they respect each [other's] gifts and accept each [other's] limitations, . . . they celebrate their differences and bind each . . . [other's] wounds, [and] . . . they are committed to a struggling together rather than against each other.[1]

Of course, in this respect as in others, Christians have lived up to their ideal imperfectly, sometimes very poorly. Community-building is the acting out organizationally of the second greatest commandment, the call to "love your neighbor as yourself." Community-building is partly about structures and systems but mostly about spirit and empowering people. On the assumption that individuals naturally give attention to themselves, the community ethos encourages the individual members to concentrate upon the development of the other members. Of course, this process automatically means that each member will receive aid as well as give it. Consistent with this emphasis upon giving help, the overall organization never demands primary loyalty or the suppression of personality, but rather serves the purpose of encouraging its individual members to understand and realize the call of God upon their lives.

The spirit of community identified above works most naturally in religious groups and most easily in small groups like the family and departmental work units, but many of its principles can work well in large and secular organizations such as corporations or even states and nations. The principles that contribute to the building of a genuine spirit of community in organizations include the following:

1. An effective sense of community is dependent upon a widespread and deeply held commitment to common values and interests by its

members. Whatever the specific nature and purpose of the organization, it must always hold as an underlying correlative cause the ennobling of the lives of its members. This mutual commitment of its members to their organization can be greatly enhanced if the organization has a rich tradition with which to identify. Each family, organization, movement and nation needs to have a story. For example, Christianity, the most historically-based of the major world religions, cites the creation of the world and the coming of God into human history as major parts of its tradition.

2. A community provides acceptance, safety, and a sense of belonging for its members, and wishes these for all peoples even if, because of natural limitations, they cannot accommodate all in their organization.

3. Membership in a specific organization is as inclusive as possible, given its nature and function. The constituency of a family is limited by who marries, is born, or adopted into it. Membership in a state is limited by geography. Membership in a religion, by contrast, can be worldwide with no limits for anyone who identifies with its articles of faith.

4. In one sense, the leadership of an organization should be as broad as the membership; in another sense leadership as executive leadership must be determined in a very careful manner. In genuine community everyone's ideas are significant, and therefore, in a real way, everyone is a leader; this ideal works best in smaller groups but is still possible, at least partially, in larger settings. In large groups and in special-focus, smaller organizations, the leaders for specific tasks must be carefully selected based upon expertise, character, temperament, and ability to encourage and inspire. Such leaders must care greatly for the organization and its individual members. They must consciously and constantly look for ways to give sacrificially of themselves and their resources for the welfare of the group and its cause. They must studiously be committed to fairness, to an awareness of their own limitations, and the establishment of group morale.

Transition into and out of leadership positions should be easy and natural. The organization and its cause should be larger than its most visible leaders, and the best leaders will work to make this happen. Then at the right time they can smoothly resume a less demanding role in the organization.

5. All members of the community think of how they can best contribute to the cause of the organization rather than of how to exert power over others. He or she thinks not "what position can I occupy" nor "what authority can I possess" but "what am I most effectively equipped to share of those things which are most needed?" There is general

recognition of the legitimate dynamic of giving; as Father Stephen Kumalo heard from his confidant, Msimangu, in one of the most moving novels of the twentieth century, Alan Paton's *Cry, the Beloved Country*: " . . . there is only one thing that has power completely, and that is love. Because when a man loves, he seeks no power, and therefore he has power."[2]

6. All members think of providing tangible assistance to others rather than acquiring prestige for themselves. Organizational watchwords are "cooperation," "disinterested benevolence," and "mutual burden-bearing." Also central is mutual counsel to assist individual members to best understand, exercise, and share their talents, and to best hear the personal instruction of the voice of God within.

7. The members of the group must be open and honest with one another. The more group members love one another, the easier this can happen. Such love allows one to trust her motives in initiating discussion on sensitive, interpersonal issues, and it compels the effort to communicate in a manner that promotes development and healing. Merely listening with empathy to others as they bare the troubles of their souls is almost invariably therapeutic. A general environment of openness between individuals does much in the group in general to reduce the human tendency toward pretense.

8. A richly meaningful and mature community is possible only when the group encourages and actively solicits broad-based participation in the ever-ongoing process of community-building (and maintenance). In a fully developed community, the views of all members and groups are inherently important. Essentially this is a description of a community-based as opposed to a hierarchical-based system of decision-making. Of course, except in very small groups, implementation decisions are best made in a hierarchical manner. By contrast, policy and personnel issues of major long-range and broad-based significance are best determined in a community mode, preferably in a Quaker-like consensus-building discussion manner. Thomas Jefferson's observation about effective government is broadly relevant to groups of all sizes: "That government is the strongest of which every man feels himself a part."[3]

9. The group works hard to develop and implement natural conflict-resolution procedures. It instructs the new members that even as they are deeply committed to the good of the organization, it is perfectly acceptable and normal for them to think differently from one another and to freely express their differences as appropriate. When differences in ideas or actions lead to strained relationships or when conflicts

in interpersonal relations occur, the community expects the members involved to immediately talk about their problems in calm voice, goodwill, and expectation of harmonious resolution. When necessary, they seek and receive the aid of one or more other community members. All of the above are formally defined as regular group processes.[4]

When a community is large and involves civic and economic responsibility for all people who live within a defined geographic region (e.g., parish, county, state, and nation), special considerations apply. A major test of the humaneness—or Christian-like nature—of a political entity lies in how it deals with the problems of poverty and delinquency internally and of how it views and relates to peoples in other political societies. In a perfectly humane society, everyone would work. The idea is less that everyone must work than that everyone would have the right to work, thereby not only earning their own keep but also acquiring the important satisfaction of contributing to society. (Appropriate provisions, of course, would be made for the very young, the aged, and the infirmed; students and the primary parental caregivers of young children would also not be expected to be otherwise employed.) This would not necessarily involve a collectivist economy, for under a primarily privatized system, the government could serve as the employer of last resort.

As children grew up in such a system, it would not only keep them meaningfully occupied during the potentially troublesome years of late adolescence; it would also greatly help to provide them with a sense of self-worth, the lack of which often contributes to delinquency. When the youth or their elders violate the criminal codes of the society, they would be treated with a "tough love" designed to correct rather than to punish for its own sake, on the understanding that as this is the way God treats us erring creatures, so also it is the way we should treat one another. Of course those who are a serious threat to the well-being of the others would need to be restrained.

A nation that operates from a spirit of community-building will not only seek the best for all its members; it will wish the best for all peoples in all nations. A morally sound community will consider the effects that their programs and policies have on other locales and seek the benefit of all involved. Therefore it takes great care to avoid practicing ethnocentric isolationism, narrow nationalism, or aggressive imperialism. In other words, the community-building nation, in seeking to "love its neighbors as itself," operates as did Jesus with a broad definition of the word "neighbor."

Anthony Diekema, in his classic work, *Academic Freedom and Christian Scholarship*, places major emphasis upon how "a sound sense of community is foundational to academic freedom."[5] Diekema, who is not only a long-time successful Christian college president but also a sociologist by training, has been heavily influenced by the pioneer French sociologist, Emile Durkheim—arguably the father of the discipline. Drawing from Durkheim, Diekema argues that "All communities establish moral orders with boundaries beyond which they do not allow their members to go without some reaction and repercussion." Developing the important Durkheimian idea that "deviance is normal," he states that "tension is both inherent and good in a healthy community," including academic communities, religious and secular. It is a constructive practice, then, for a Christian college community to both establish boundaries and to constantly test those boundaries. "Deviance is intended to maximize progress while deferring regress. For this to be done sensitively, yet vigorously, the academy must constructively nurture an ethos of freedom . . . in the constant search for and proclamation of truth." So much does Diekema believe this that he supports the idea of each college having an academic freedom council (with faculty comprising the majority of its members) to serve as the campus watchdog to see that neither professors nor administrative zealots violate the canons of free discourse. Taken altogether this is a remarkable statement for a Christian college leader.[6]

Most Christian colleges pride themselves on the degree to which a sense of community pervades their campus. They talk frequently about the common worldview, the common chapel experience, the common extracurricular involvement, and the faculty interest in and accessibility to the students outside of the classroom. Unfortunately they talk less often about a sense of community in the classroom. The colleges emphasize how they promote the integration of faith and learning in the classroom and how this distinguishes them from Sunday school, church, church camp, and the secular college. Yet this integration focus is primarily on what the faculty are doing. Perhaps if what the faculty are doing focused less completely upon monologue and more on dialogue or—better yet—monologue to set up dialogue, then the degree to which the Christian colleges operated with a sense of group participation in what is its most central element (faith and learning integration) would enhance the degree to which it operated as a fully-orbed Christian community.[7]

Now we transition from Section I to Section II of the book, from the part which discussed some of the major Christian virtues that have a bearing on the larger subject of academic freedom to the part which discusses how Christians—and others—in the past have sought to apply these principles and others to the practice of what in the twentieth century came to be known as academic freedom. In other words, we move from theological background to historic record.

SECTION II

The Development of Academic Freedom in America:
A Christian College Interpretation

This section is a history of the idea and practice of academic freedom in higher education in America—including its European antecedents— as told from the perspective of modern Christian higher education. It uses a broad definition of academic freedom to consider how not only professors but also students and institutions have sought to be free in the pursuit of truth as they understand it. It also explores how the economic limitations on access to the expensive Christian college model of higher education restrict the options of many students in their choice of how they wish to pursue their academic quest. Finally it considers how the traditional major divide within Christian higher education, namely that between Catholics and Protestants, has significantly narrowed in recent decades.

CHAPTER 11

The British Model: Anglican Dominance

In the history of higher education in the West, a dominant worldview has existed in almost any given place and time. Typically the balance between religious believers and seekers on one hand and doubters and skeptics on the other hand is more consistent among the general populace than in the college and university faculties. For example, in the United States the early college faculties were more religious than was society in general while in the modern period just the opposite is true. Colleges tend to institutionalize what at any given time is the majority view of their power brokers. On the eve of the founding of the American colonies and through the colonial era, the prevailing intellectual milieu in British higher education was provided by the official religion of the realm, the Anglican Confession.

The seventeenth-century Anglican colleges, Oxford and Cambridge, had their origin in the earliest era of European college founding in the late twelfth and early thirteenth centuries. The first universities included Bologna (1158, probably earlier in informal organization), Paris (1150), and Oxford (1167). Cambridge (1209) and perhaps 20 other institutions joined them after 1200 in what Richard Hofstadter calls "the first great century of university development." Bologna emphasized civil and canon law, while Paris stressed theology and the arts, including philosophy. Oxford and most of the later Northern European institutions followed the Paris example.[1]

The early universities emerged from the monastic and cathedral schools and were highly clerical in vocational preparation. The students wore the tonsure indicative of their priestly preparation. Although generally the medieval period is not known for its intellectual openness, the first institutions with their emphases on the scholastic method of debate and disputation were remarkable for encouraging the students to understand multiple positions on the major issues. Also, the instructors received a large measure of respect and thus recognition from both the clerical and political authorities. The fact that the latter powers were jealously guarding their prerogatives vis-à-vis one another was to the benefit of the intellectual freedom of the scholars. For example, in the earliest known written reference to academic freedom, Pope Honorius III in 1220 encouraged the University of Bologna to defend its "scholastic freedom" against the efforts of the local civilian authorities to demand a pledge of allegiance by its students to the city. Also, the first university founded by a pope, the University of Toulouse (1229), promoted itself to students with claims of scholastic liberty. William Hoye argues that in the period before the rise of the national university, patriotism was considered to be inconsistent with the idea of scholarly freedom.[2]

In general, the church and state allowed much liberty to the universities as long as their discussions remained "academic." When, however, the promotion of novel ideas threatened to lead to popular uprisings against the vested ideas and powers of the church and/or state, then the general tolerance could be quickly withdrawn. One can count 50 or so cases of judicial proceedings involving charges of heterodoxy against academic masters in the 1200–1400 period.[3]

Among the most celebrated of the late medieval cases were those of Marsilius of Padua (1275–1342), rector of the University of Paris; William of Ockham (c. 1280–1349), Franciscan teacher of theology at Oxford; John Wycliffe (1329–1384), lecturer at Oxford; John Hus (1373–1415), member of the arts and theological faculties at the University of Prague; and Martin Luther (1483–1546), Bible professor at the University of Wittenberg. As characteristic for the times, all five involved religious disputation.

These bold scholars called for a more spiritual religion and sided with the state over the papacy in the struggle between the two for temporal power. Most left their teaching positions but found the physical protection of a political ruler. Hus, of course, was burned at the stake.[4]

In general, as academic freedom specialist Richard Hofstadter concludes, "the medieval period was neither the nightmare of dogmatism, cruelty, and suppression that it was held to be by the rationalist scholars of the nineteenth century nor the magnificently open ground for free expression that some modern medievalists at times seem to be portraying."[5]

The English Reformation, as it worked through its several stages, brought a significant reduction in freedom of expression in the universities as well as in society as a whole. Henry VIII demanded pledges of loyalty through the legislation ratifying the transformation of the church from Roman Catholic status with the pope as the head to an English Catholic Church with the monarch as its head. Unlike the Lutheran and Calvinist branches of the Reformation, the driving force for the English Reformation was less theology than personal and political—Henry wanted a church structure that would approve his divorce and remarriage to enhance his chances of producing a male heir. To ease his conscience and secure his new authority, he demanded conformity without dissent to his sweeping actions. The university masters no less than the common populace were forced to consent.

The official religion of the realm changed sharply, back and forth, during the reigns of Henry's children, and the public was expected to modify their formal religious loyalty with each alteration under the Tudor monarchs. The tale went like this: from Roman Catholicism under Henry VII, to English Catholicism under Henry VIII, to Protestantism under Edward, to Catholicism under Mary, to a Conservative Protestantism under Elizabeth. During the reign of Mary, in which she executed 300 Protestants, clergy fled to Calvin's Geneva where they imbibed Calvin's more completely Reformed ideas. When it was safe to return after 1570 under Elizabeth, these Puritans sought to convert England to a more radical Protestantism. They established a significant base at Cambridge, especially in Emmanuel College, which was founded in 1584 by Puritan Walter Mildmay, Chancellor of the Exchequer under Elizabeth for over two decades. The Cambridge Puritans had as an able leader Thomas Cartwright, whose debates with Trinity College master John Whitgift and repeated calls for a Presbyterian polity placed him in constant trouble. He was forced out of his Cambridge professorship (repeatedly), placed in jail, and exiled.[6]

James I (1566–1625), the monarch associated with the King James Version of the Bible, was no friend of the Puritans. He imposed a loyalty test (to the Episcopacy) on all candidates for university degrees, thus effectively excluding from Oxford and Cambridge religious nonconformists. This ban was to continue until 1871. It gave impetus to the English Puritans to organize their own institutions of higher education (dissenting academics) and it contributed to the growing desire of many of them to migrate to America wherein they founded Massachusetts Bay as a colony like they wished England to be and Harvard as a college like they wished Cambridge and Oxford to be. More specifically, they wanted Harvard to be like Emmanuel College, Cambridge, where 35 of the university men in early New England and the majority of the Harvard founders had attended.

The two English universities in the early seventeenth century possessed physically attractive buildings and each enrolled approximately 3,000 students in total in their many colleges (18 at Oxford and 16 at Cambridge). The students matriculated as early as age 16, and studied the Latin and Greek classics, the church fathers, philosophy, rhetoric, and logic. The colleges were primarily teaching institutions with little research, and they placed a major emphasis on character development, personal refinement, and preparation for public service, especially to church and state. While the noble and gentry classes were well represented among the student population, they were surpassed in numbers by the common classes, especially those from clergy and prosperous business families. The teaching fellows were usually clergymen.[7]

The practice of dissent is an important component in the history of academic freedom. Of the two English universities, Oxford was more nearly the university of the establishment while Cambridge had a larger tradition of dissent. Notable and daring Cambridge students or professors included theologian John Duns Scotus; Bible translators Desiderius Erasmus and William Tyndale; Archbishop of Canterbury Thomas Cranmer, who like Tyndale suffered martyrdom; M.P. from Cambridge and Lord Protector of England Oliver Cromwell; blind poet John Milton; and Harvard namesake John Harvard. As with churches so also with colleges, dissenters had greater influence in the founding of America than they did in the home country. Those who "had it made" at home tended to stay at home while those who sought something better were more likely to leave. Of the nine colonial colleges, dissenting groups founded four (Harvard, Yale, Dartmouth, and Brown), Anglicans began two (William and Mary, and Colombia), establishment groups from other countries began two (Princeton and Rutgers), and Benjamin Franklin opened Pennsylvania as an independent institution.[8]

If the dissenting tradition at Cambridge was one major influence in the thinking of the founders of the early American colleges, the dissenting academies were another. Of the two, the latter were more creative and innovative, especially in the curriculum and pedagogy, promoting modern studies in science, history, language, and literature and encouraging free discussion in the classroom. Surely the liberating effect of the academies represented an early form of academic freedom. Among the more noteworthy of these institutions were Charles Morton's Newington Green north of London; Philip Doddridge's Northampton Academy in the Midlands; Warrington Academy in the North; and Bristol Academy in the Southwest.

Newington Green founder Morton later became a fellow and vice-president of Harvard; the academy's students included writer Daniel Defoe and Samuel Wesley, father of Methodist founders John and Charles Wesley. Doddridge not only taught at Northampton, but he also wrote profusely in hymns and letters, produced the classic, *The Rise and Regress of Religion in the Soul*, which he dedicated to academy alumnus and fellow hymn writer, Isaac Watts, and carried on a meaningful correspondence with Princeton President Aaron Burr. Joseph Priestly taught at Warrington. Bristol alumnus Morgan Edwards was a founding father of Brown, the Baptist college in Rhode Island. Other well-known alumni of the academies included Prime Minister Benjamin Disraeli, Bible commentary author Matthew Arnold, philosopher John Locke, philosopher and apologist (*Analogy of Religion*) Joseph Butler, and physician (Bright's disease) Richard Bright.[9]

Social historian Lawrence Stone describes an educational revolution as occurring in England between 1560 and 1640. These dates correlate closely with the rise of the Puritan movement. The number of students and their percentage in the population rose sharply during this period so that 2.5 percent of the 17-year-old male population was enrolling in college, a percentage not reached again until after World War I. "It may well be," Stone notes, "that early seventeenth-century England was at all levels the most literate society the world had ever known."[10]

Then came a period of decline in the English universities during the late seventeenth and eighteenth centuries, a period that coincided with the era of the founding of all the American colonial colleges save Harvard. In this period, the dissenting academics in England and Scotland and the universities in Scotland (St. Andrews, f. 1413; Glasgow, f. 1451; Aberdeen, f. 1495; and Edinburgh, f. 1582) provided more successful models for the early American colleges. The influence of the Scottish universities in particular was very large, especially at William and Mary, Princeton, Pennsylvania, and Columbia.[11]

Beginning in the late eighteenth century and continuing through the late nineteenth century, the Scottish common sense philosophy spread throughout American higher education and America in general. The presidents taught it to the students in the senior level capstone course, moral philosophy, and the populace absorbed it while scarcely understanding it. It became the de facto or working philosophy of many who didn't think in terms of having a philosophy at all.

Theistic common sense, as Mark Noll calls the radical new mode of thought from Scotland, emphasized the ability of each individual to understand, intuitively and by careful observation of human nature, the purpose of God for His morally endowed human creation. Developed by Scottish scholars Frances Hutcheson, Thomas Reid, and others, it became arguably the most popular philosophy in Great Britain and the United States during the century following the American Revolution. In concert with Republicanism and Evangelical Protestantism, it became the American worldview in this period.

The popularity in America of Scottish Common Sense philosophy stemmed from its ability to provide a new basis for social order following the overthrow of traditional sources of authority (English monarchy, social hierarchy, and state-church system). External control could be replaced by individuals following their best sense of the light within. After all the Bible had always taught that "God was the true light which gives light to every man . . . "[12]

In concert with the spirit of free will individualism which emanated from the Second Great Awakening (1800–1835) and swept through the colleges and the new nation in general, the spirit of common sense philosophy both articulated and represented a new force of liberty for the new nation. Whether or not one calls these new currents in the college by the label of "academic freedom," they certainly reflect the latter's spirit in seeking to incorporate individually and socially the best new ideas. In summary, the forces that influenced the origin and early development of higher education in America included the organic model of Oxford and Cambridge, the independent spirit of Cambridge and the dissenting academies, the innovative philosophy of the Scottish universities, and the general Enlightenment thought.

CHAPTER 12

The German Model: Secular Dominance

Although the small American Christian college with its emphasis on student learning, Christian ideas and piety, and residential living has always more closely resembled the traditional British colleges at Oxford and Cambridge, the large American university that emerged in the late nineteenth century, with its emphasis upon faculty scholarship and faculty academic freedom, and a de-emphasis upon religion, stems directly from the nineteenth-century German state universities. Whereas the English, in the words of Abraham Flexner, "believe in religion, in manners, in politics" (and thus operate with universities to prepare gentlemen for service to the church, the political establishment, and society),[1] the Germans, after the founding of the University of Berlin, believed foremost in independent scholarship while eschewing concern for character development.

The emergence of the new University of Berlin was revolutionary. "Never before or since," Flexner noted, "have ancient institutions been so completely remodeled to accord with an idea."[2] That idea was complete academic freedom for both professors and students. Lehrfreiheit, or teacher freedom, meant no prescribed curriculum to follow, no course exams to grade, no institutional committees on which to serve, and no institutional officers not of their own choosing. Although a professor usually offered four to eight hours of lectures each week and sometimes a seminar, he was essentially free to conduct his research as he willed. Similarly, each student was free of most restraints (lehrnfreiheit). He had to register and pay his fees. No one monitored his class attendance nor required a course exam. Of course he did have to prepare to pass a comprehensive test at the end of his course of study to graduate.

Although the founding of Berlin in 1810 was the impetus for the spread of the ideals of research and freedom throughout Germany and Europe and to America, there were earlier German university centers of innovative thinking and practice that influenced Berlin. These included the University of Göttingen (which was founded on liberal principles in 1734 by the elector of Hanover, who was also George II of England), the University of Halle (the onetime center for Pietism which then came to precede Göttingen and Berlin in emphasizing rationalism over Christian orthodoxy); the University of Königsberg (where Immanuel Kant taught); and the University of Jena (long one of the most politically radical universities in Germany, which was later renamed for the writer Friedrich Schiller who taught at the institution during the turn of the nineteenth-century era when its renowned faculty also included Gottlieb Fichte, G. W. F. Hegel, and Friedrich Schelling).[3]

German professors and students alike often moved from one institution to another, and when Wilhelm Von Humboldt, Prussian minister of education and brother of the scientific explorer Alexander Von Humboldt, founded Berlin, he recruited to its faculty the aforementioned Fichte (who became rector), Schelling, and Hegel plus theologian Friedrich Schleiermacher. Although science was later to become the premier discipline at Berlin, philosophy, including theology, played that role in the early decades of the institution.

Employing their new freedoms and the new rational critical methodology to the study of the Bible and the life of Christ, German scholars such as Schleiermacher at Berlin followed by Ferdinand Christian Baur and David Friedrich Strauss (*Life of Jesus*, 1846) of Tübingen University, and Ludwig Feuerbach (*The Essence of Christianity*, 1854) of the University of Heidelberg and others were associated with a new method (higher biblical criticism) and a resultant interpretive mode (liberal Christianity). Philosophical and methodological rationalism when combined with the vague religiosity of the Romantic poets such as Schiller "tended to erode the doctrinal content of the historic faith" and "dissipate the Christian context of university life."[4]

Young American college graduates enticed by the opportunity for postgraduate study and by a more questioning environment began to travel to Germany, especially to the most avant-garde universities like Berlin and Göttingen, during the century from 1815 to 1914. The first two education emigrants studied at Göttingen. They were Dartmouth graduate George Ticknor, who later taught Spanish literature at Harvard; and Harvard graduate Edward Everett, who later became a congressman, governor of Massachusetts, President of Harvard, Secretary of State, and ambassador to England. Famous as an orator, Everett preceded Lincoln in giving the longer and less remembered address at the 1863 dedication of the Gettysburg battlefield.[5] Ticknor was impressed with the freedom and industry of the German scholars:

there is an unwearied and universal diligence among their scholars—a general habit of labouring from fourteen to sixteen hours a day—which will finally give their country an extent and amount of learning of which the world has before had no example.

The first results of this enthusiasm and learning, which immediately broke through all the barriers that opposed it, were an unusual tolerance in all matters of opinion. No matter what a man thinks, he may teach it and print it, not only without molestation from public opinion which is so often more oppressive than the aim of authority. I know not anything like it exists in any other country.[6]

A second report by an American expatriate student in Germany describes the German university environment a half-century later with the same glowing tone as that supplied by Ticknor. James Morgan Hart, a Princeton graduate, spent four years studying in Berlin and Göttingen as well as the University of Geneva. His 1874 book-length narrative compares higher education in Germany and the United States. He spent his university teaching career at Cincinnati and Cornell. Reflecting the German emphasis upon theory rather than application, he noted "the evident tendency of their method [is] to produce theologians rather than pastors, jurists rather than lawyers, theorizers in medicine rather than practitioners, investigators, scholars, speculative thinkers rather than technologists and school teachers." Such instruction "does not attempt to train successful practical men, unless it be indirectly.... Its chief task, that to which all its energies are directed, is the development of great thinkers, men who will extend the boundaries of knowledge."[7]

Although 9,000 Americans were to study in German universities during the nineteenth century, most of them went overseas during the later decades, reaching a peak in the 1890s, after which the United States youth increasingly pursued their studies in the developing graduate schools at home.[8]

In the twentieth century, America and the world began to reassess just how good the nineteenth-century German innovation had been. If the German intellectuals were so advanced in their thinking and the German elite so well trained, how can one explain the rise of a society that would embrace militarism[9] and tolerate the Nazi genocide? Surely there must have been flaws in the celebrated educational system. And indeed there were. For one thing, the practice of academic freedom, while quite free in certain ways, was noticeably absent in others. The universities were state institutions in undemocratic governmental systems, and the professors were not free to criticize the government. Meanwhile the government and the nation celebrated itself and its army and its professors. The latter paid for their deference and acclaim by agreeing to limit their freedom to their internal government, classroom, and research lab where they pursued specialized science and abstract philosophy while avoiding comment on public policy. Walter Metzger noted that "... on most questions of national honor and interest (witness the performance of the German professors during the First World War), the academic corps had docilely taken its place in the chauvinistic chorus."[10] No society is truly free without welcoming and accommodating the best insights of its public intellectuals.

The undue deference to and celebration of the university professors in their limited role helped to make the scholars prone to an egotism that worked against the intellectual humility so necessary to the acquisition of deep wisdom and a prophetic expression. A realization of the latter could have been a powerful check against the excesses of the German state. American students, even in the midst of their positive assessments, noticed these unfortunate tendencies. "The professor has but one aim in life: scholarly renown," noted James Morgan Hart, while George Ticknor added "The professors are more envious and jealous of each other than can be well imagined."[11]

The climax of the German intellectual, academic, political, and moral decline, of course, came during the Nazi era. Students and Nazi storm troopers alike participated in the famous and widespread book-burning night of May 10, 1933. The largest of these bonfires took place in Berlin where 20,000 books deemed "un-German" (typical authors were Einstein, Freud, and Remarque) were taken from the University of Berlin library and set to the torch. A century earlier the German-Jewish poet, Heinrich Heine, had stated, "When they burn books, they will, in the end, burn human beings too."[12] Six million Jewish men, women, and children from many countries—especially Poland and Russia—perished in the systematic German slaughter, mostly during World War II. Earlier in the Hitler regime, Jewish scholars throughout Germany lost their university positions or fled the country. Noteworthy in this respect was the "Great Purge" of 1933 at Göttingen with its crackdown on "Jewish physics." Altogether some 1,500 Jewish scholar refugees fled Germany, including American immigrants Albert Einstein and Edward Teller from Göttingen who helped launch their new country into the Atomic Age. Emigrants of all types from Nazi Germany to America numbered perhaps as many as 200,000.[13]

Today, academic freedom is widely recognized throughout Europe. Approximately 750 universities have signed the Magna Charta Universitatum (drafted in 1988) which declares forthrightly, "Freedom in research and training is the fundamental principle of university life." Also the 2000 Charter of Fundamental Rights of the European Union states that "the arts and scientific research shall be free of constraint. Academic freedom shall be respected."

Nevertheless, England has a reputation within the European Union for its less enthusiastic support of the majority practices. English higher education scholar Terance Karran believes that "in terms of academic freedom" his country "is clearly the sick man of Europe," with no constitutional guarantee of free speech or academic freedom and minimum faculty input in institutional governance.[14]

When the idea and practice of academic freedom migrated from Germany to the United States in the early twentieth century, it developed into a distinctly American form. It was for professors much more than students, it did not restrict the professors from critiquing the government, and it found greater reception in the universities than in the liberal arts colleges.[15]

CHAPTER 13

The Early American Model: Protestant Dominance

During the colonial period and for the first century of the national period, with very few exceptions, to be a college in America was to be a Protestant college. Such was true of public no less than private institutions as the phenomenon of college founding spread from frontier New England to the east coast in general and inland to and across the Appalachian Mountains as those regions opened to settlement. Typically mission-minded zealots of the various denominational persuasions combined with town fathers to open colleges associated with the church organization of the former. In characteristic missionary spirit, they sought to enroll more students than could afford to pay the full cost; thus, colleges were partly charity institutions—offering charity to students and soliciting charity from sympathetic donors. Because of the constant financial need, the colleges followed the Yale model of governance by lay boards of trustees who, sometimes affluent themselves, could assist in the financial solicitations.

Most—perhaps ninety percent—of the presidents were ministers. By modern standards the professors possessed inadequate training for their role, having completed little more than the undergraduate curriculum that they were teaching. This explains much about why they relied upon the rote method of teaching rather than the lecture method which became more common in the late nineteenth century when the developing college instructors increasingly pursued graduate study.

Surprisingly, given the pervasiveness of the Christian religion in the often twice-daily (before breakfast and before the evening meal) chapel and elsewhere, there was almost no study of biblical literature in the formal curriculum. Rather the early American course of study relied heavily upon the classical curriculum inherited from Europe with its emphasis upon Latin and Greek language and literature, mathematics, a little science, and the famous senior-level course—usually taught by the president to the seniors—in moral philosophy (typically a combination of the social sciences, philosophy, and theology).

The earliest calls for a larger degree of academic freedom came not in the area of theology or politics but in the prescribed curriculum. Following independence from England came a growing sense of nationalism, a need for developing the economy, and a rising spirit of democracy and individualism. By the 1820s, educational reformers were calling for a broadened curriculum that would meet the needs of the rising youth in the new nation. The leading voices of reform included Eliphalet Nott at Union (NY), James Marsh at Vermont, Philip Lindsley at Nashville, George Ticknor at Harvard, Jacob Abbott at Amherst, and later Francis Wayland at Brown. Typical of the complaints were those of Wayland: "The wisdom of the ages might well be contained in the writings of ancient Greek and Roman authors, but it was successfully concealed from the student by coming to him through the medium of a foreign language and a dead one at that"; and Andrew Dickson White who, recalling his student days at mid-century Yale, lamented that the classical studies "made everything of gerund-grinding and nothing of literature."[1]

The reformers sought a parallel curriculum that would offer an alternative to the traditional classical study. It would feature modern language, modern and applied science, and even American studies. But such changes came very slowly and incrementally before the radical innovation of Charles Eliot's elective system at Harvard in 1869 on the eve of the rise of the American university. Helping to delay reform were the strong conservative sentiments proclaimed at influential Yale and Princeton (e.g., the Yale Report of 1828). Before 1869, the most significant widespread change was the introduction of the Bachelor of Science program at mid-century.

In many ways, the early literary societies were the most liberating feature of college life. The students were active participants. They could decide which society to join. They could debate opposite positions on a broad variety of theoretical, historical, and especially contemporary political and social issues. They took pride in collecting and housing their own libraries. They enjoyed how the societies fulfilled their social needs. In sum the literary societies provided the leading social and probably the leading intellectual activity in the period before football, fraternities, and a more practical curriculum. The key was student initiative, student choice, and student involvement.

The colleges did not often talk about academic freedom as such, but a major concern was to avoid the label of "sectarian." The state universities, which typically were Protestant institutions in practice, sometimes called the church colleges sectarian. The denominational schools frequently advertised

Table 13.1 Early American colleges

College	Date	Affiliation
1. Harvard (MA)	1636	Puritan/Congregationalist
2. William and Mary (VA)	1693	Anglican
3. Yale (CT)	1701	Congregationalist
4. Princeton (NJ)	1746	New Light Presbyterian
5. Colombia (NY)	1754	Essentially Anglican
6. Pennsylvania (PA)	1755	Primarily secular
7. Brown (RI)	1765	Baptist
8. Rutgers (NJ)	1766	Dutch Reformed
9. Dartmouth (NH)	1769	New Light Congregationalist
10. Washington (MD)	1782	Episcopal
11. Washington and Lee (VA)	1782	Presbyterian
12. Hampden-Sydney (VA)	1783	Presbyterian
13. Transylvania (KY)	1783	Presbyterian
14. Dickinson (PA)	1783	Presbyterian
15. St. John's (MD)	1784	Episcopal
16. Georgia	1785	State
17. Charleston (SC)	1785	Episcopal/municipal
18. Franklin (and Marshall) (PA)	1787	German Reformed
19. North Carolina	1789	State
20. Vermont	1791	State
21. Williams (MA)	1793	Congregational
22. Bowdoin (MA/ME)	1794	Congregational
23. Tusculum (TN)	1794	Presbyterian
24. Tennessee	1794	State
25. Union (NY)	1795	Protestant

Source: George P. Schmidt, *The Liberal Arts College* (New Brunswick, NJ: Rutgers University Press, 1957), 60–61.

themselves as nonsectarian, which usually meant that they admitted students irrespective of religious affiliation. Faculty hiring, of course, was a different matter. Many of the colleges that opened in the nineteenth century were community colleges as much as church colleges, a fact that led them to minimize denominational particularism. So the primary intellectual battle before the Civil War was not between Christian and secular nor Protestant and Catholic nor even public and private, but between sectarian Protestant and ecumenically broad, orthodox/evangelical Protestantism with the latter usually winning.[2]

So where did this situation leave the student who would prefer a non-Protestant-oriented education? Those preferring a Catholic education had a handful of colleges from which to choose, especially after 1830. These included Georgetown (DC), St. Louis (MO), Xavier (OH), Notre Dame

(IN), Fordham (NY), St. Joseph (PA), and Seton Hall (NJ). A Unitarian student might find intellectual encouragement at Harvard after 1805, at Antioch under Horace Mann, at Transylvania under Horace Holley, and at Washington of St. Louis; while a young transcendentalist probably could have been comfortable at Vermont under James Marsh. Jewish collegiate education did not exist until after 1860.[3]

The more secular-oriented schools were few in number before 1860; they included Benjamin Franklin's Pennsylvania and Thomas Jefferson's Virginia. By the late decades of the century, however, with the coming of the intellectual revolution, the fortunes of secular higher education improved markedly. Was the aforementioned antebellum student who preferred a non-Protestant-oriented education deprived of full academic freedom? The answer, of course, is yes he[4] was, in a similar—but opposite—way that the most recent college student who prefers a religiously informed education is often denied full academic freedom today.

The rest of this chapter will identify and discuss six major events or developments, which inform the academic freedom debate during this period of Protestant dominance.

Harvard President Converts

The first colonist to be called a college president was also the center of the first major academic freedom controversy in American higher education. Henry Dunster, possessor of two degrees from Magdalene College, Cambridge, and an instructor there, migrated to Massachusetts in 1640, where New England officials immediately elected him as president of the fledgling Harvard College. A Hebrew language specialist, he taught the entire curriculum himself for awhile and later served as the interim minister of First Church Cambridge. Widely respected as a leader, he served Harvard well, guiding the institution through its difficult early years.

But then the Puritan cleric studied and thought about infant baptism and concluded that this Puritan practice was not biblically tenable. The climax of the issue (1653) came when he refused to have his newborn son baptized in the Cambridge church, thus in effect publically announcing his conversion to the Baptist faith. Just as his conversion had been gradual so also the college's response to encourage him to resign was also gradual. Eighteenth-century Puritan historian Cotton Mather praised both Dunster, whom he called "learned," "worthy," and "able," and the Harvard overseers who "did as quietly as they could procure his removal . . . ." The separation was friendly, whether warranted or not.[5]

The Yale Governance System

Connecticut Puritans who objected to the departures from traditional Calvinism at Harvard opened Yale in 1701. In addition to seeking to maintain orthodoxy, the Yale founders established a system of government different from that which operated at the two older colleges, Harvard and William and Mary. Harvard had a bicameral system with insiders (the president and fellows) and outsiders (a board of overseers) sharing control, whereas William and Mary followed the medieval system of self-governance by the teaching masters. By contrast, the Connecticut General Assembly, in its original charter for Yale, placed total control of the new college in the hands of an outside board of mature congregational ministers who could found, own, and "make such rules as they wished." The Yale model was to set the pattern for higher education governance thereafter; even Harvard and William and Mary came to adopt it.[6]

So how has the Yale System of governance by an outside lay board worked historically for higher education in general? In the decision to accept outside lay governance, the collegiate educators surrendered the right to control their own profession. But they gained as much as they lost, for money has always been critical in higher education—especially in private schools. The trustees helped to promote the colleges to the outside public, thus helping to secure both students and funds, freeing up the professors to concentrate more completely on the more pleasant intellectual tasks. Did the less academically informed trustees restrict the academic freedom of the professors? Sometimes they did, although generally they deferred to the president and other internal administrators on personnel decisions. The alumni were also a major source of funds and students and an unofficial source of control. In short, colleges and their professors have been like Renaissance artists—they needed patrons of the arts to help subsidize them. The price is that they have had less autonomy than say the legal and medical professions, although more than the clergy.

The Dartmouth College Case

Dartmouth College v. Woodward (1819) was simultaneously (1) one of the most important decisions of the precedent-setting John Marshall era of the Supreme Court (1801–1835)—and of all American judicial history; (2) a landmark case in protecting contract rights and the rights of private property—and thus encouraging the developing of the American free enterprise system; and (3) a major development in distinguishing public and

Table 13.2 American colleges founded before the Civil War

By affiliation

	Denominational and other association	*Permanent colleges*
1	Presbyterian	49
2	Methodist	34
3	Baptist	25
4	Congregational	21
5	Catholic	14
6	Episcopal	11
7	Lutheran	6
8	Disciples	5
9	German Reformed	4
10	Universalist	4
11	Friends	2
12	Unitarian	2
13	Christian	1
14	Dutch Reformed	1
15	United Brethren	1
16	Semi-state	3
17	Municipal	21
18	State	21
Total colleges listed		**207**

By decade

	Periods before the Civil War	*Permanent colleges*
	Colonial era	9
	1780–1789	10
	1790–1799	6
	1800–1809	5
	1810–1819	7
	1820–1829	12
	1830–1839	35
	1840–1849	32
	1850–1859	66
	Total	**182**[1]

By state

	State	*Colleges*
1	Ohio	17
2	Pennsylvania	16
3	New York	15
4	Illinois	12

5	Indiana	9
6	Virginia	9
7	Missouri	8
8	Tennessee	8
9	South Carolina	7
10	Georgia	6
11	Iowa	6
12	Kentucky	6
13	Michigan	6
14	North Carolina	6
15	Wisconsin	6
16	Maryland	5
17	Alabama	4
18	California	4
19	Massachusetts	4
20	Connecticut	3
21	Louisiana	3
22	New Jersey	3
23	Vermont	3
24	Maine	2
25	Minnesota	2
26	Mississippi	2
27	Oregon	2
28	Texas	2
29	Delaware	1
30	Kansas	1
31	New Hampshire	1
32	Rhode Island	1
33	Arkansas	0
34	Florida	0
	District of Columbia	2
Total		182

Note: [1] Donald G. Tewksbury, *The Founding of the American Colleges and Universities Before the Civil War* (New York: Columbia University, 1932), 16, 31, 90; reprinted by Martino Publishing in 2011.

private colleges and in protecting the latter from the encroachments of the state. It is the third and latter feature that most concerns this narrative.

In the late colonial era, King George III had granted Dartmouth a charter as a private college with such charter to last forever. In 1817 the New Hampshire state legislature, encouraged by college president John Wheelock (son of the founder Eleazar Wheelock), voted to bring the college under considerable state control. The state Superior Court supported the action of the legislature but when the trustees appealed to the Supreme Court of the United States, the latter reversed the state court decision. This action supported the private and independent nature of the college and its academic freedom from undue federal government control.[7]

The Supreme Court trial featured the emotional and compelling defense of the fledgling young attorney, Daniel Webster, who in time was to become arguably the most eloquent American senator. Webster pleaded in this fashion:

> This, Sir, is my case! It is the case not merely of that humble institution, it is the case of every college in our Land! It is more! It is the case of every eleemosynary institution throughout our country—of all those great charities founded by the piety of our ancestors to alleviate human misery, and scatter blessings along the pathway of life! It is more! It is, in some sense, the case of every man among us who has property of which he may be stripped, for the question is simply this, "Shall our State Legislatures be allowed to take that which is not their own, to turn it from its original use, and apply it to such ends and purposes as they in their discretion shall see fit!"
>
> Sir, you may destroy this little institution; it is weak, it is in your hands! I know it is one of the lesser lights in the literary horizon of our county. You may put it out! But if you do so, you must carry through your work! You must extinguish, one after another, all those great lights of science which for more than a century have thrown their radiance over our land! It is, Sir, as I have said, a small college. And yet there are those who love it![8]

Modern Christian college advocates, concerned about maintaining institutional freedom from the federal government in issues to be discussed in Section III of this work, will do well to embrace Webster and his Dartmouth case as a part of their heritage.

The Pennsylvania and Virginia Contributions

The Christian college at its best, when committed to a sense of fairness, must be pleased when young people with secular preferences are not forced to enroll in an overtly Christian college merely because that is the only way they can achieve an education. In early America, Franklin's Pennsylvania and Jefferson's Virginia provided the best known of the very few alternatives to a traditional Protestant college experience. Pennsylvania, the sixth of nine colonial colleges offered both the traditional classical curriculum and a practical curriculum to train youth for business and public service. It was less concerned than were the older colleges with ministerial preparation, but it was moderately religious in nature. Franklin identified among his goals for the college that it should offer instruction in English literature and history with the latter providing "frequent opportunities of showing the necessity of public religion . . . and the excellency of the Christian religion above all others ancient and modern." The first president, Anglican minister William Smith, promoted Anglicanism as much as he dared. Still religion dominated less here than at most colleges.[9]

Jefferson's personal religion was a blend of Unitarianism and Christianity (e.g., he revered Jesus and his teachings but thought him to be only human), but he was an early and vigorous proponent of religious freedom. He strongly opposed the established churches—Anglicanism in the South and Congregationalism in New England. He asserted greater influence in defeating the former, viewing the Virginia Religious Freedom Bill of 1786 to be his greatest public accomplishment. He rejoiced when in 1818 Connecticut finally became the last state to surrender its church establishment.[10] His feelings were strong. He called the established church of Virginia "religious slavery," while of the Calvinism of New England he wrote that it "has introduced into the Christian religion more new absurdities than its leader had purged it of old ones."

When Jefferson founded the University of Virginia in 1819, he did not seek to keep out religion but rather to give no place to a privileged religion. To Jefferson, each student should freely choose his religion and his courses both.[11] The Jeffersonian model of higher education, more radical than that at Pennsylvania, was not widely imitated before the end of the century by which time the threat to academic freedom was starting to become less that of privileging religion than of discriminating against it. But in their early years, Pennsylvania and Virginia provided a valuable service in contributing to the freedom of choice for students when selecting their college.

The Rise of the State University as a Protestant College

An early president of Methodist Fort Wayne Female College (which was to become Taylor University), Cyrus Nutt, later served a lengthy (1860–1875) tenure as president of Indiana University. The religious nature of the two schools was not significantly different for both operated under Protestant influences. Such is not surprising as of the approximately 30 major state universities operating by the Civil War, most were functionally Protestant institutions.[12]

Like the early church colleges, the early state universities typically had a preacher for president, held required chapel services and religion courses, encouraged student participation in religious organizations, and sought to control student behavior in a manner similar to that found in the church colleges. The public and private colleges competed for students and public support and in doing so sometimes exaggerated their differences. The denominations, especially the Presbyterians, sought to control the state universities, and when they could not do this, they might express public criticisms. For example, in 1857, Michigan Methodist leaders stated "We are compelled to fear that [the university] is so defective in moral and religious restraints . . . that it cannot be patronized by our citizens without imminent peril to . . . those youths who may be sent there." In response to such concerns, President Erastus Haven of the University of Michigan observed that "it is not a Godless education that they fear, but a Christian education not communicated through the forms and channels over which they preside."[13]

The state universities could also be partisan. In several states, they were able to persuade their legislatures to disadvantage the church colleges if not eliminate them altogether. In the mid-nineteenth century when it was not yet clear whether the public or private colleges would be the dominant form of higher education for the future, the competition could be intense and not always fair. Such was unfortunate for

> The key to sound higher education in the antebellum period—as well as in later periods—was free competition between rival institutions and dialogue between prominent points of view. American higher education soon came to accept the former but only rarely has realized the latter. The public university, in particular, has an obligation to serve as a sounding board for all prominent points of view. On such controversial issues as religion, unfortunately, the free exchange of views has not regularly occurred. During the antebellum period, when orthodox Christian belief was prominent, most state institutions would not have tolerated an honest hearing for unorthodox views—those of agnostics or even of Unitarians, for example. Today the problem is reversed for as Andrew Ten Brook, a University of Michigan professor, realized as early as the 1870s, the likelihood that the university would fall under the control of some parochial religious group was much smaller than the likelihood that evangelical Christianity would be forced out of the university.[14]

The Second Great Awakening and the Democratization of Higher Education

Before the nineteenth century higher education was for the elite. The Second Great Awakening (1800–1830) set in motion forces that broadened access to higher education, and the democratization momentum continues to the present.

The Second Great Awakening provided America's national conversion to Arminian theology. It found formal expression in the "Yale Theology" of

Nathaniel Taylor and others, and popular expression in the meetings and writings of Charles G. Finney, the most prominent revival preacher of the awakening. No longer was the talk about election, but rather about "whosoever will may come" to God. The religious idea that anyone may come to God coincided with the growing political idea that more people ought to be able to participate in the political process. Jeffersonian and Jacksonian democracy enhanced the importance of the common people, and it was the lower-class religions, especially the Methodists and the Baptists, that profited most from the Second Great Awakening.

During the generation of the Second Great Awakening and the generation that followed it leading to the Civil War, the Methodists and Baptists zoomed from the status of minority religions behind the eighteenth-century leaders Congregationalism, Anglicanism, and Presbyterianism to become the two largest denominations in the country. Their growth came from frontier revivalism led by the Methodist circuit-riding preachers and the Baptist farmer-preachers. As they moved into the new states, they founded new colleges at a rate faster than all other denominations save the Presbyterians who had a head start upon them in both college-founding and deep commitment to education.

Later the growing Protestant zeal for popular education expanded to include colleges for women and blacks, beginning with Charles Finney's Oberlin College. Later during the "Third Great Awakening" under Dwight L. Moody, the continuing zeal of nineteenth-century revivalism led to the beginning of the Bible college movement to train common class youth in undergraduate theological preparation for evangelizing the lower classes in this country and abroad.[15]

During the Civil War, the federal and state governments followed the churches in the movement toward popular higher education by establishing the land grant college system to train youth in the practical fields of agriculture and engineering as the nation prepared to enter its Second Industrial Revolution that would sweep the country from perhaps the fourth industrial power in the world in 1865 to the world leader by 1900.[16] Increasing access to higher education, whether at the initiative of church colleges or public universities, has been one of the best expressions of academic freedom writ large.

The transition from the era of the Protestant liberal arts college to the period when higher education was primarily secular and public was a long one, beginning in the later nineteenth century and reaching its peak in the mid-to-late twentieth century. Major landmarks in this process included the Morrill Land Grant Act of 1862 which established state agricultural and engineering colleges, the founding of highly endowed colleges by the nouveau wealthy (e.g., Chicago, Stanford, Johns Hopkins, Vassar, Duke, Vanderbilt, and Emory), the maturing of Midwestern state universities (e.g., Michigan, Wisconsin, and Minnesota), the establishment of the American Association of University Professors (AAUP), and the gradual secularization of many of the best developed denominational colleges.

CHAPTER 14

The Later American Model: Secular Hegemony

I f Protestantism provided the overwhelmingly dominant model of Christian higher education for the first 250 years of American history, it has been the secular approach to learning which has dominated since then. The latter has never been as completely influential as was the former, with secularism reaching its peak in the mid-twentieth century. Since the late twentieth century, the Christian colleges have gotten stronger, the internal and external critiques of the secular model have increased, and consideration of the religious dimension has gained a larger voice in the secular institutions. Nevertheless, the secular model is still in control in the academy today, just less so than formerly.

In the late nineteenth century, the first generation of the movement toward secularization was led by moderate-to-liberal Christians who were still embracing Christian views and morality even while adopting secular methodology. The key elements of change were the growth of graduate programs, the emergence of professional disciplines and specialization in teaching and research within those disciplines, a new and broadened curriculum, and the movement of religious study to the mostly self-standing seminaries. These developments in themselves did not cause secularization, although they helped to facilitate it.[1]

Typical of the religious emphasis of the late-nineteenth-century leaders of the new university system was that of Daniel Coit Gilman, the founder, president, and, in many ways, the program designer of the new Johns Hopkins University (MD), arguably the first American graduate school. Gilman stated in 1886 that

the American university should be a place for the maintenance of religion, not . . . by forcing assent to formulas, or by exacting conformity to appointed rites, but by recognizing everywhere the religious nature of man, considered individually, and the religious basis of the society into which Americans are born . . . . American universities should be more than theistic; they may and should be avowedly Christian—not in the narrow sectarian sense—but in the broad, open, and inspiring sense of the Gospels.

In the last years of his life (1903–1908), Gilman was president of the American Bible Society. Similarly, James B. Angell, long-time president of Michigan, openly promoted Christianity on his campus, both because of personal conviction and also because he believed that the Northwest Ordinance ("Religion, morality, and knowledge being necessary to good government and the happiness of mankind, schools and the means of education shall forever be encouraged") urged such an emphasis.[2]

Simultaneous with the new structures of higher education came a new philosophy of education, and it was the latter that was at the heart of the movement toward secularization. The long-awaited and much needed curriculum reform, so long delayed through much of the nineteenth century came quickly and radically after President Charles Eliot of Harvard introduced his elective system. The integrated curriculum of the old-time college with its senior-level moral philosophy course, providing the capstone tying together the universe of knowledge under a Christian worldview, gave way to a decentralized, even disintegrated curriculum in which the emphasis in teaching and research was on specialized study of isolated parts of human knowledge. In science the detailed, careful scientific method too often moved from finding physical truth to a belief ("scientism") that this was the only viable method of finding any kind of truth. In the humanities, the methodology of "philosophical historicism," a new name for the relativistic idea that all truth is contextual to time and place, replaced moral philosophy and its search for universal principles and "eternal verities."[3]

By World War I, this new educational philosophy was largely in place in the major universities. The two major secular developments during and after the war were (1) the gradual movement of the second line public and many of the private colleges (including denominational colleges) in the direction of secularization and (2) the rise of the AAUP to give formal definition to the meaning of academic freedom. The primary founding document of the AAUP (the 1915 Declaration of Principles on Academic Freedom and Academic Tenure) states that historically the primary threat to academic freedom came from ecclesiastical sources and involved instructors in philosophy and science, but that by the early twentieth century the major dangers came from the business community and the state legislatures and involved social scientists.

The late-nineteenth-century Industrial Revolution witnessed the accumulation of vast sums of wealth by the "captains of industry," some of whom used major sums to found or endow a major university. The Progressive Era (1900–1915) was in part a response to the excesses of business. Big government was needed as a countervailing force to regulate big business. Many of the professors involved in the formation of the AAUP were economists, sociologists, or political scientists who identified with the Progressive Era reforms and the interests of the consumer and the laboring classes. Meanwhile, even colleges not founded by a business tycoon were increasingly sensitive to adding businessmen to their trustee boards. Charles and Mary Beard, progressive historians, noted that "at the end of the century the roster of American trustees of higher learning read like a corporation directory." Whether college trustees or not, the business community who supported colleges did not lightly receive the challenge by professors to the bases by which they had accumulated their wealth. Wealthy donors protested, professors cried interference with academic freedom, and presidents were caught in the middle. Among the classic turn-of-the-century cases involving political and economic expression were those of Henry Carter Adams at Cornell, J. Allen Smith at Marietta (OH), Richard Ely at Wisconsin, John R. Commons at Indiana, Edward Bemis at Chicago, and Edward Ross at Stanford.[4]

The case most directly leading to the organization of the AAUP was not one involving politics or economics, but rather theology. In 1913 Lafayette President Ethelbert Warfield, brother of the famous Princeton Seminary theologian, Benjamin Warfield, dismissed moral philosophy professor John Mecklin from the Presbyterian college faculty when the latter's views gradually changed from the traditional Presbyterian orthodoxy during his eight-year tenure. Mecklin publically protested, and the still quite new American Psychological Association and American Philosophical Association launched inquiries. Their investigation did not save Mecklin, but it did contribute to the subsequent formation of the AAUP with education reformer John Dewey of Columbia serving as the first president.

The Mecklin case at Lafayette showed the need for colleges to develop more explicit due process procedures and specific community educational philosophy statements including faith statements when relevant. The founders and subsequent leaders of the AAUP were secular educators who combined a modified version of German academic freedom practices with a conviction that colleges operating from a philosophical base in Christian theism were thereby, at best, second-rate educational institutions.[5]

The Christian college community can identify with much of the AAUP goals and history. It led in forming and formalizing better personnel practices in a new age and in arguing for the maximum possible amount of freedom in the intellectual enterprise. It specialized in protecting academic freedom for professors. While acknowledging academic freedom for institutions, however, it, intentionally or otherwise, often worked against the idea of academic freedom for institutions. Somehow it didn't recognize that higher education could involve the intentional coming together of scholars with shared worldviews as well as scholars acting as individual intellectual entrepreneurs within an umbrella-like academic setting.

Most telling are the clauses in the AAUP documents describing the surviving Christian colleges as inherently inferior. These especially include the statements of 1915, and 1970, and, to a lesser degree, those of 1940 and 1998. At best these clauses are naïve, and at worst they are arrogant. Either way they are condescending. One of the more authoritative critiques of the narrowness of the AAUP posture is that by University of Chicago constitutional lawyer Michael W. McConnell, who wrote that "the insistence on a single model of truth-seeking is inconsistent with the antidogmatic principles on which the case for academic freedom rests."[6]

In the early twenty-first century as the AAUP celebrates its 100th anniversary, it is concerned about both its decline as an organization and the decline in respect for its mission. Its membership dropped from 90,000 in 1971 to 43,600 in 2007. The decision to enter collective bargaining hurt as did competition from a rival more conservative organization, Foundation for Individual Rights in Education (FIRE), and increasing doubts about its ability to stop the decline in the degree to which university administrators respect the sacredness of academic freedom. The subtitle of the recent book by AAUP President Cary Nelson is telling; in *No University Is an Island: Saving Academic Freedom*, he outlines no less than 16 threats to academic freedom.[7]

Concurrent with this recent decline in influence of the AAUP has been a growing inclination of the secular universities to embrace the objective study of religion in religious study courses, majors, and institutes. In other words, the secular institutions are less secular now than they were a generation ago. Scholars like C. John Sommerville, John Schmalzbauer, Kathleen Mahoney, and Douglas and Rhonda Jacobsen have documented this major development in detail.

The American Academy of Religion in 2009 reported that the religious study major is "now establishing a widespread presence at state universities." Among the most academically respected programs are those at Duke, Princeton, Chicago, North Carolina, Boston, Emory, New York, Missouri, Pennsylvania, Penn State, Virginia, and University of Southern California. Although Iowa was something of a pioneer in beginning its program in 1927, religious study programs in state universities mostly date from the late 1950s and early 1960s, encouraged by Justice Thomas Clark's Supreme Court majority opinion in the landmark 1963 *Abington v. Schempp* and *Murray v. Curlett* cases on devotional Bible reading in the public schools. While these cases, taken in concert with the *Engle v. Vitale* case of the previous year, disallowed teacher-led devotional prayer and Bible reading in the public schools, Clark in his majority opinion stated that: "one's education is not complete without a study of comparative religion or the history of religion and its relationship to the advancement of civilization . . . . The Bible is worthy of study for its literary and historic qualities. Nothing we have said has indicated that such study of the Bible or of religion, when presented objectively as part of a secular program of education, may not be effected consistently with the First Amendment."

"We might conclude," notes religious studies scholar, Russell T. McCutcheon, "that the study of religion is among the few fields of study mandated by a Supreme Court decision!" Of course the type of religious study called for by the Court and to be practiced in the public universities is objective, not subjective, study.[8]

Beyond the religious study major, some are calling for the introduction of a religion course in the general education core for all college students. Such is the proposal of Warren Nord in *Does God Make a Difference?: Taking Religion Seriously in Our Schools and Universities* (2010) and Stephen Prothero in *Religious Literacy: What Every American Needs to Know—And Doesn't* (2008). Because of the historic leadership of Harvard in curriculum reform, it was significant that in 2010 it gave serious consideration to adding a required course in Reason and Faith. Louis Menard, a Pulitzer Prize-winning literary critic, led the curriculum review committee, which in the end withdrew the proposal because of objections led by evolutionary psychologist Steven Pinker, who argued that requiring a course in faith and reason could imply that those two components were equally worthy of consideration. It would be like requiring them to take a course in astronomy and astrology, he said.[9]

So where does all of this movement leave higher education today? The institutions are less dismissive of religious study than they were a generation ago. The faculty individually are less skeptical of the religious domain than their reputation would suggest (the research of Neil Gross and Solon Simmons published in 2007 found that 23.4 percent were atheists or agnostics, 19.6 percent believed in some type of a higher power, 16.9 percent acknowledged that while they have some doubts, they did believe in God, and 35.7 percent said that they have no doubts about the existence of God).[10] The students are more interested in studying religion than the faculty are in teaching it. The younger faculty are more open to religion than are the older faculty. The general momentum is toward greater recognition of the need to engage religion in the college experience.

Among the boldest prophets of a new order in higher education are C. John Sommerville and Page Smith. Although Sommerville thinks that the phasing down of secularization will happen slowly even as its phasing up came gradually over a century ago, the title of his 2006 work is explicit in announcing "the decline of the secular university." "The secularism that looked vital and self-sufficient in 1900 has exhausted itself," he declared. "... scholars have begun to recognize that secular rationalism itself is not a neutral, absolute system, rising above all faith commitments. Secularism is seeming more and more like a stage within history, rather than its final goal. We can see it as one way of thinking among others...." Page Smith lamented "the tendency of secularism to act in illiberal ways"—"academic fundamentalism" he called it. Already in 1990 Smith hoped and called for the day when "a new consciousness representing a synthesis of the two prior consciousnesses, the Classical Christian (thesis) and the Secular Democratic (antithesis)," would blend to "include the endearing elements of both traditions, powerfully reanimated and enthusiastically reconstructed." Perhaps an early sign that Smith's vision may be starting to come true is the issuance in 2005 of an ecumenical "statement on academic rights and responsibilities" initiated by the American Council on Education and signed by 26 higher education organizations including, most notably, the AARP and the evangelical Council for Christian Colleges and Universities. Drafted as a response to the more valid criticisms of right-wing critic David Horowitz and his Freedom Center, it recognized with dignity the right of many interested parties—professors of conservative and liberal persuasion, private and public institutions, and students. The statement, while not without aspects of controversy, is nevertheless the most inclusive such document ever produced, certainly more accommodating than the previous major AAUP statements. It is reproduced here in its entirety.[11]

American Council on Education

Statement on Academic Rights and Responsibilities

Intellectual pluralism and academic freedom are central principles of American higher education. Recently, these issues have captured the attention of the media, political leaders and those in the academy. This is not the first time in the nation's history that these issues have become public controversies, but the current interest in intellectual discourse on campus suggests that the meaning of these terms, and the rights and responsibilities of individual members of the campus community, should be reiterated.

Without question, academic freedom and intellectual pluralism are complex topics with multiple dimensions that affect both students and faculty. Moreover, America's colleges and universities vary enormously, making it impossible to create a single definition or set of standards that will work equally well for all fields of academic study and all institutions in all circumstances. Individual campuses must give meaning and definition to these concepts within the context of disciplinary standards and institutional mission.

Despite the difficulty of prescribing a universal definition, we believe that there are some central, overarching principles that are widely shared within the academic community and deserve to be stated affirmatively as a basis for discussion of these issues on campuses and elsewhere.

- American higher education is characterized by a great diversity of institutions, each with its own mission and purpose. This diversity is a central feature and strength of our colleges and universities and must be valued and protected. The particular purpose of each school, as defined by the institution itself, should set the tone for the academic activities undertaken on campus.

- Colleges and universities should welcome intellectual pluralism and the free exchange of ideas. Such a commitment will inevitably encourage debate over complex and difficult issues about which individuals will disagree. Such discussions should be held in an environment characterized by openness, tolerance, and civility.

- Academic decisions including grades should be based solely on considerations that are intellectually relevant to the subject matter under consideration. Neither students nor faculty should be disadvantaged or evaluated on the basis of their political opinions. Any member of the campus community who believes he or she has been treated unfairly on academic matters must have access to a clear institutional process by which his or her grievance can be addressed.

- The validity of academic ideas, theories, arguments, and views should be measured against the intellectual standards of relevant academic and professional disciplines. Application of these intellectual standards does not mean that all ideas have equal merit. The responsibility to judge the merits of competing academic ideas rests with colleges and universities and is determined by reference to the standards of the academic profession as established by the community of scholars at each institution.

- Government's recognition and respect for the independence of colleges and universities is essential for academic and intellectual excellence. Because colleges and universities have great discretion and autonomy over academic affairs, they have a particular obligation to ensure that academic freedom is protected for all members of the campus community and that academic decisions are based on intellectual standards consistent with the mission of each institution.

In summary, the secular universities and colleges in the early twenty-first century have become somewhat less dismissive of religion as a legitimate area of academic inquiry. In that respect, the academy possesses more academic freedom than it did a generation ago.

CHAPTER 15

The Modern Christian College

The focus of this chapter is upon some of the recent efforts within the Christian college community to study, understand, and implement the practice of academic freedom. An emphasis upon academic freedom most often comes with the intellectual and financial maturing of an institution. In early stages of development, the focus is more on elementary concerns like survival and establishment. The secular revolution in higher education dealt a blow to the Christian college movement, taking away many of their better developed institutions and placing in shock and survival mode many of the continuing Christian colleges. Thus the half-century from the 1920s to the 1970s was like a war and post-war reconstruction era for Christian higher education. As the Christian colleges recovered economically and grew in size during the most recent half century, they have increasingly focused upon moving toward maturity.

Perhaps no Christian college studies, articulates, and practices in a studied manner academic freedom more than does Calvin College, an institution of the Christian Reformed Church (CRC). Calvin is simultaneously one of the narrowest and one of the broadest colleges in the country. It is narrow within its theological niche and broad in terms of its worldview. Following the lead of former Dutch prime minister Abraham Kuyper, it believes that Christ's followers should seek to extend the Kingdom of God to all spheres of creation and society instead of restricting their focus to, say, evangelism. It is also broad in its theory of academic freedom where it seeks to cultivate "maximum academic freedom and due process within the bounds of . . . [its] covenantal commitment."

In September 2009, Calvin hosted a forum on academic freedom featuring three of its Calvin and Christian Reformed intellectual leaders who were highly qualified to address this subject. Sociologist Anthony Diekema has written the most fully developed statement on the theory and recent practice of academic freedom and Christian scholarship in the Christian college (see Chapter 10). Historian George Marsden, who spent the last part of his career at Duke and Notre Dame, has published as his best known book (*The Soul of the American University: From Protestant Establishment to Established Nonbelief*) what in large part is a study of academic freedom—or the lack thereof—in the secular universities. Of the three speakers, philosopher Nicholas Wolterstorff has studied academic freedom the least and he largely focused his remarks on his experience as a faculty member (1959–1989) at Calvin before relocating to Yale. Collectively their comments at the forum are among the most insightful short statements about academic freedom in Christian higher education and elsewhere. Diekema is a judicious practitioner, Marsden an authoritative and courageous interpreter of the past, and Wolterstorff, one of the best recognized contemporary Christian philosophers, is perceptive on almost anything to which he gives focus.

All three scholars concurred independently that every college, religious or secular, operates with self-definitions and thus boundaries within which they work. There is no school where "anything goes." Wolterstorff provided specific examples:

> No American college or university today would keep a Holocaust-denier on its staff; nor, so I guess, would an American college or university keep on its staff someone who insisted that the abolition of slavery was a great mistake. Other limits are peculiar to a given institution, or type of institution. St. John's was founded for the purpose of placing the so-called Great Books at the center of its curriculum. St. John's would not hire someone who vocally insisted that a Great Books education was a lot of nonsense; Calvin College and Yale University, by contrast, would have no problem with that. I do not know what St. John's would do with someone who, when he was hired, was a Great Books devotee, but who then, over the years, changed his mind and became a Great Books denier.

Diekema and Marsden distinguished between the "defender of the faith" Christian college and "the covenantal academic model." In the former, Marsden explains,

> The college is a direct extension of the church and its intellectual function is dominated by a defender of the faith ethos. Since church and school are not clearly differentiated, higher education is like advanced Sunday school. So it has a relatively high degree of indoctrination and a relatively low degree of intellectual exploration. A large part of the spirit of the place is to define and defend what "we" believe in contrast to what the outside world believes. Wheaton used to be such a fundamentalist defender of the faith school, but it no longer is. Liberty University would be a better example today.

The second model distinguishes more sharply between the functions of the church and those of the college. The church and college covenant together under the same overall creed and worldview but within that context the church recognizes and even encourages the distinct role of the university to probe deeply and widely in service to the church and in the common cause of best understanding the mind of God.

Wolterstorff testifies to the large degree of freedom which he had as a Calvin professor in expressing his views even when they were very controversial.

> When I was teaching here, the outcome of these factors for a person like me who identifies with the Reformed tradition was a quite astonishing freedom. It meant total freedom for me in what I did within my own field of philosophy. It also meant total freedom for me in what I said publicly about society and politics. I was a vocal critic of the Vietnam War. Although I received angry anonymous calls at my home in the middle of the night, nobody in the administration or on the board of Calvin ever so much as suggested to me that I should tone it down. I was and remain a vocal supporter of the cause of the Palestinians. Nobody in the administration or on the board ever suggested that I should tone it down. And so it goes for every other social or political cause on which I spoke out. I'm sure the president and members of the board often wished that I would tone it down; their life would have been easier. But none of them ever said that to me.
>
> It also meant freedom for me in what I said about the CRC. I was a vocal critic of the refusal of the CRC to ordain women—a policy that has now been changed. No one in the administration or on the board ever suggested that I should tone it down. I did on various occasions have some rather loud disagreements with one or another official of the denomination; but not even they suggested that I did not have a right to say what I said.[1]

Diekema's book offers advice to the several groups holding an interest in the role of academic freedom in the Christian college. Let me summarize in paraphrased form his major counsel.

Each faculty member should work hard and honestly to assure her initial and continuing fit with the college. He should exercise forthrightness, humility, and prudence in explaining his position on critical issues. Presidents and provosts should know the meaning of academic freedom for their institution and promote it openly. They should work to prevent the negative effect which such cases can have on faculty creativity and confidence. The trustees should consider it one of their most important duties to protect academic freedom from internal and external threats. They should insist upon a comprehensive academic freedom statement that is framed in the context of institutional mission, and be certain academic freedom cases follow established deliberate and orderly due process procedures. Students should view academic freedom cases as opportunities to learn about both important intellectual issues and also judicious decision-making procedures. Church officials should understand and be able to articulate the special role which Christian colleges play in the Christian community and the role which academic freedom plays in Christian higher education. All groups should understand both the differences between and the complementary roles of the Christian college and the Christian church.[2]

In 2000 Wolterstorff and Calvin economist George Monsma, who was instrumental in the development of Calvin's due process procedures in personnel decision-making, presented major papers at Baylor's Academic Freedom Conference. This conference was the first such gathering on a Christian college campus where the AAUP was a major participant. Other sponsors were the American Academy of Religion and the Society of Biblical Literature. The Wolterstorff and Monsma papers were published in the subsequent issue of the AAUP journal, *Academe*. Appearing in a later issue of *Academe* was another article by a Calvin professor, "The Value of Limitations" by philosopher Lee Hardy, which discusses the not very well-understood idea that for almost all Christian college professors, the limits of their institution are not constraints for them.[3]

If Calvin is the Christian college most known for its efforts in addressing and promoting academic freedom, Wheaton College is a Christian college known for real and perceived violations of academic freedom. So why has Wheaton received so much attention?

Colleges that seek to be both a defender of the faith institution and a seriously academic institution are prime candidates for conflict. If only one of these ingredients is present, controversy is less likely. At least since the presidency of James Oliver Buswell II in the 1920s, Wheaton has sought to be both of these things, and in addition its location in a major metropolitan area and its identification as the "Harvard of Fundamentalism" have made it a high-profile target. Most of the critiques of its academic freedom shortcomings have come from outside journalists, but the best developed such analysis came from an evangelical historian, Michael Hamilton of Seattle Pacific University, in the form of his 1994 Notre Dame doctoral dissertation under Wheaton alumnus, Nathan Hatch, now president of Wake Forest (NC).

Hamilton describes Buswell as being "a strong believer in academic freedom" and later philosopher Arthur Holmes as a champion of intellectual openness. By contrast, he presents the conservative board of trustees as a retarding force in the quest for free inquiry.[4]

Holmes's major contribution to the academic freedom discussion is a chapter in his widely read book, *The Idea of a Christian College*. The title of Holmes's book reflects the title of the nineteenth-century classic by the English cardinal John Henry Newman, *The Idea of a University*, in which the latter calls for religion to be an integral part of higher learning. Newman proclaimed,

> whereas it is the very profession of a University to teach all sciences, on this account it cannot exclude Theology without being untrue to its profession . . . supposing Theology be not taught, its province will not simply be neglected, but will be usurped by other sciences, which will teach without warrant, conclusions of their own . . . .

Holmes's chapter on academic freedom, while shorter, is as broad in perspective as Diekema's book. Holmes, who championed the cause of the integration of faith and learning, also called for the union of loyalty (to the institutional mission) and liberty: "Liberty without loyalty is not Christian, but loyalty without liberty to think for oneself is not education . . . . It is also true that education is impossible without loyalty to truth and intellectual honesty."[5]

Mark Noll is the most widely known and prolific Wheaton scholar of the past generation—and probably ever. Now at Notre Dame, his wide-ranging work in American religious history indirectly addresses the subject of academic freedom and Christian higher education. For example, in his book *Between Faith and Criticism: Evangelicals, Scholarship, and the Bible in America*, he notes a correlation between the prominence of evangelicals' involvement in biblical scholarship and the prominence of their involvement in higher education in general. Through most of the nineteenth century when theological seminaries were nearly the only form of graduate education, evangelicals were dominant. They still were the major players in the closing decades of the century but this situation changed by the turn of the century, and for a generation evangelical biblical scholarship was in retreat. From 1935 to 1975 it was in a recovery mode and since 1975 it has been a major player again. One characteristic of the most recent period is that even evangelical scholars outside of the areas of religious studies have given disproportionate attention to the religious dimensions of their disciplines.[6]

Wheaton provides a twenty-first-century example of how when a college places emphasis upon tight theological control even while training their students to think independently, the mix can sometimes be volatile. Many students don't like it when beloved professors are released over secondary issues of theology or when they find the intellectual environment in general to be inhibiting. Perhaps Wheaton's most awkward recent example of this involved both the content of an article and the history of the journey of the article itself from pen to print. Wheaton graduate, Andrew Chignell, now a philosopher at Cornell (NY), wrote an essay called "Whither Wheaton," describing the college's handling of such controversies as a professor converting to Catholicism, perspectives on homosexuality and origins, and theological nuance issues in general. When the article was ready for publication in *Books and Culture*, *Christianity Today*'s literary journal, it was mysteriously withdrawn at the last minute only to be published in *Soma: A Review of Religion and Culture*.[7]

In Christian higher education, Messiah College serves as a nice complement to Calvin and Wheaton. For one thing, it comes from an eclectic blend of Anabaptist, Pietist, and even Arminian traditions. For another, it represents a gentler, less theological, less polemic approach toward secular higher education. Its model in this respect is alumnus Ernest Boyer, who rose to become President of the Carnegie Commission for the Advancement of Teaching, and eventually the United States Commissioner of Education under Jimmy Carter. One sees this ecumenical spirit manifested toward other Christian colleges in the work of religious historian Richard Hughes (see, e.g., his *How Christian Faith Can Sustain the Life of the Mind*, Chapter 4), while Douglas and Rhonda Jacobsen demonstrate this posture in their "soft-evangelism" work with secular institutions that are open to becoming less secular and thus more completely embracing of the full spirit of academic freedom.[8]

With a Lilly Endowment grant, the Jacobsens visited over 50 colleges of various types to interact with key personnel on how they were engaging religion. As the title of their subsequent book (*No Longer Invisible: Religion in University Education*) suggests, they found a surprising amount of religious discussion in place, and in both their campus interactions and the book, they both seek to describe what they have witnessed and to encourage still more of the same. Their approach was something like this: "Here is what we see happening on your campus, here is what you are already doing, here are some models that we have found elsewhere, what do you think can work best here?" The Jacobsens encourage their discussants to practice academic responsibility as well as academic freedom. For example, they emphasize how the best professors not only deconstruct but also help their students to reconstruct, thus finding a better "place to stand" intellectually because of their reflection on issues of ultimate concern.[9]

The era of secular dominance described in the previous chapter and the period of decline in evangelical production in Bible scholarship discussed earlier in this chapter coincide with the era of evangelical anti-intellectualism described by the new Gordon president, Michael Lindsay in his *Chronicle of Higher Education* essay, "Evangelicalism Rebounds in Academe." Lindsay, formerly a sociologist at Rice University, views the defensive and somewhat barren era of the early and middle parts of the twentieth century as "an anomaly" in the long history of Christian scholarship. Lindsay's book *Faith in the Halls of Power: How Evangelicals Joined the American Elite* complements the earlier work by John Schmalzbauer, *People of Faith: Religious Conviction in American Journalism and Higher Education*, in illustrating the partial restoration to prominence of evangelicalism and evangelical scholars. The traditional secular community is increasingly cognizant of this development.

More directly addressing the issue of academic freedom is an essay by Gordon scholar and administrator Dan Russ. "Fear Not: Security, Risk and Academic Freedom" encourages the faculty in Christian colleges to be bold in their freedom in Christ, as encouraged by Paul in Galatians 5:1:

> Christian colleges and universities easily become either sanctified versions of secular institutions or oppressive and contentious organizations that drive honest questions and discussion underground and produce a scheming and polarized faculty and administration. Speaking the truth in love is the only way I know to live in the tension that we call freedom. If we believe that truth sets us free and that perfect love casts out fear, then we need to risk living, studying, teaching, and writing as truthfully and lovingly as we know how. It is risky. That is the nature of freedom whether political or academic. If our ultimate goal is to secure our job or to secure our institution financially, academic freedom is not possible . . . if we will not risk, we are not free.[10]

Christian college researcher and former chancellor of UNC Asheville Samuel Schuman found a similar spirit of boldness in a Westmont (CA) Admissions Office recruitment brochure which listed academic freedom as the first reason for choosing a Christian college.

> Professors and administrators at the world's top colleges and universities hold one concept dear beyond almost any other: the idea of academic freedom. In order to understand the truth and to allow the best ideas to have dominance in society, they say, we must have the freedom to discuss all ideas. To let them rise and fall on their merits. But just try adding a Christian perspective to the discussion in classrooms on secular campuses around the world, and you may find out where the limits to academic freedom lie. Most public institutions in this country are less than warmly receptive to faith-based perspectives and contributions in the classroom. Why limit yourself? . . . Westmont's commitment to academic freedom is obvious, not only in courses that demand your best critical thinking but also through a wide range of opportunities and organizations that explore the world of ideas.[11]

At Taylor (IN), the campus intellectual leader during the post-World War II period was dean and president Milo Rediger. He did not so much address academic freedom directly as create a spirit of openness and find ways of presenting alternative ways of thinking. For example he talked about "head first Christianity" and how a Christian college is not a church but an educational institution. One of his principles of learning was to "reject all ideas about God which if seen in a good man would be viewed as being morally inadequate."

A later Taylor president, lawyer Eugene Habecker, addressed the issue of institutional freedom by saying that "institutional mission" is a better phrase than institutional freedom for it is more inclusive of faculty and students. While some Christian colleges have a reputation for emphasizing institutional freedom above and even against individual freedom, this is not desirable. Rather all three parties, institution, faculty, and students, are to be respected as they unite to work together under an overarching institutional purpose. "The institution is legally charged with meeting the obligations of its charter," Habecker notes. "It is charged by the various accrediting associations with fulfilling its mission . . . . Mission must be paramount . . . Academic freedom must be subordinate to the overarching mission of the organization."

Habecker also emphasizes the importance of the "no surprise rule," in personal policy. "It is incumbent upon institutions of Christian higher education to identify in advance those substantive positions which may negatively impact a faculty member's employment."[12]

At Eastern Mennonite (VA), Ted Grimsrud, theologian and peace studies professor, embraced academic freedom less as an individual right than as a way for trained scholars to freely share their giftedness and informed insights with the believing community of which they are a part. "I am not fully comfortable," Grimsrud notes,

> with Enlightenment-centered rationales for individual rights and freedoms . . . . I find it more helpful to place the issues of appropriate expression . . . in the context of spiritual gifts . . . that [scholars] are hired to exercise . . . . However in practice open expression in a Mennonite College and 'academic freedom' in a state university might not look noticeably different.[13]

In some respects the Bible colleges are ahead of the Christian liberal arts colleges in encouraging the practice of academic freedom. The Association for Biblical Higher Education (ABHE, formerly the Accrediting Association of Bible Colleges) requires for institutional membership "a published statement of academic freedom and adherence to its principles within the context of institutional mission," and to publish the statement widely. They also require member schools to have grievance procedures for faculty and students. The number of accredited or affiliated institutions is approximately 200, and these tend to experience fewer formal academic freedom cases than do the liberal arts colleges. Long-time ABHE official Randy Bell advises that about one case per year, usually involving lifestyle or theological issues, comes to the organization which then seeks to achieve resolution at the staff level. If this fails, then there can be a full formal hearing.[14]

As Christian liberal arts colleges increasingly focus on enhancing their academic freedom practices, they may want to consider following the example of the Bible colleges and create their own academic freedom encouragement and monitoring organization rather than being dependent upon the less understanding AAUP for their services. Perhaps this function could be subsumed in the activities of an existing organization like the Council for Christian Colleges and Universities (CCCU). One model for such self-regulation might be the Evangelical Council for Financial Accountability which began in 1979 at the encouragement of Senator Mark Hatfield of Oregon.

CHAPTER 16

Institutional Academic Freedom

The most common use of the phrase "academic freedom" is to refer to academic freedom for professors. For many, academic freedom and professorial academic freedom are synonymous. But there are other types of academic freedom, of course—at least two other types, namely, institutional academic freedom (the subject of this chapter) and student academic freedom (the subject of the next one).

The AAUP acknowledges institutional academic freedom but emphasizes individual or professorial freedom. The Christian college community focus is just the opposite: it recognizes professorial freedom but emphasizes institutional academic freedom. The Christian college posture is thus a defensive one. In the modern era with the secular institution the dominant model and the AAUP, reflecting that philosophy, claiming to speak for all professors of higher education, the Christian colleges, as a minority group seeking to protect its uniqueness, naturally place greater emphasis on the rights of individual colleges to define the terms of their educational philosophy.

The best Christian colleges do not so much claim the priority of institutional over individual rights; that could degenerate into a power struggle between administration and faculty members. The ideal rather is the concept expressed by Eugene Habecker in the previous chapter, whereby cooperative-based institutional mission is the driving force of decision-making on personnel and all else. Surely we all do our best work when serving a cause larger than ourselves whether we are a student, faculty, administrator, or trustee. That said, it is still true that "institutional academic freedom" is the phrase most commonly used to describe the primary Christian college approach to the subject of academic freedom. It is the phrase used by Michael McConnell, the foremost scholarly and legal defender of the religious colleges in the academic freedom debate.[1]

McConnell, a First Amendment specialist, was a Professor of Law at the University of Chicago Law School when he wrote "Academic Freedom in

Religious Colleges and Universities." Later he became a federal judge on the Tenth Circuit Court of Appeals and a 2005 short-list candidate for the nomination to be Chief Justice of the Supreme Court. "I believe," he wrote, "that institutional academic freedom should be the dominant conception within religious institutions."[2]

McConnell views as appropriate the classic 1940 AAUP statement with its provision that "Limitations of academic freedom because of religious or other aims of the institutions should be clearly stated in writing at the time of the appointment." He then comments,

> If truth in advertising were the purpose of Committee A's activities, there would be no reason to object to its standards. Religious colleges and universities should not be shy to admit that their understanding of academic freedom differs from that of the AAUP, and a clear declaration to that effect should serve to prevent misunderstanding.

But McConnell registers strong criticism of the parochial bias that he finds in other AAUP documents both before and after 1940. Especially offensive were (1) the original 1915 statement which he found saying that even theological seminaries should give priority to the AAUP definition of academic freedom over religious considerations; (2) the 1970 statement which announced that the AAUP no longer endorsed the limitations clause of the 1940 statement; and (3) the 1988 subcommittee statement which said that religious colleges still wishing to invoke the limitations clause "forfeit the moral right to proclaim themselves as authentic seats of higher learning."[3]

McConnell concludes his article by noting:

> It would be far better for the secular academic world to return to the letter of the 1940 Statement, which allowed religious institutions to determine for themselves what "limitations" on secular academic freedom are necessary to maintain their own sense of mission, subject only to the requirement that these be stated clearly in advance. If it did so, secular and religious higher education would again be able to coexist in fruitful exchange, without intrusion or interference.[4]

Of course, the AAUP today is somewhat closer to the position McConnell is proposing than it was when he wrote the essay.

If the worldview battle between the Christian colleges and secular colleges (Christianity vs. secularism) forces the modern minority part to assume the defensive position of claiming institutional academic freedom, there have been times and situations when the secular colleges themselves were in a minority position (usually but not always regarding the federal government) and thus also sought the minority rights position of institutional academic freedom. This has happened most commonly during times of international crisis, such as World War I v. Germany, the Cold War v. Russian Communism, and the Post 9/11 War on Terrorism; and during the crusade for civil liberties of minority groups.

The AAUP was born during World War I, and after American entry in 1917, the government placed severe restrictions on freedom of speech through the Espionage Act of 1917 and the Sedition Act of 1918, with the latter being one of the harshest laws of its type in American history. Although the federal government did little to directly intervene with campus academic freedom during the war, it set the tone whereby a number of university administrators cracked down on dismissed professors judged to be unpatriotic.

A. Lawrence Lowell, legal scholar and Harvard president, gave the classic statement on academic freedom in wartime. He argued,

> Professors speaking in the classrooms or in scholarly writing in their area of expertise should have complete academic freedom in wartime as well as peacetime. In their extramural speech, their rights and limitations are like all other citizens—no less and no more. Their institutions cannot be responsible for censuring what they say extramurally on public policy issues, for if they were responsible for what they could not say, they would also be responsible for what they did say, and no institutions should have to assume that burden.[5]

No less significant were the repressions during the Cold War. These included congressional legislation—the Smith Act (1940), the Taft-Hartley Act (1947), the McCarran Internal Security Act (1950), and the Communist Control Act (1954); presidential executive orders—Truman's federal loyalty program (1947) and Eisenhower's security risk program (1953); and Supreme Court decisions—*American Communication Association vs. Douds* (1950), *Dennis v. United States* (1951), and *Sweezy vs. New Hampshire* (1957).

The Sweezy case was especially important for the evolving academic freedom debate. In 1951 during the middle of the anti-communist Red Scare, the New Hampshire state legislature adopted a Subversive Activities Act and subsequently required the state attorney general to find and prosecute violations of the law. Paul Sweezy, a self-proclaimed moderate socialist, member of the Progressive Party, promoter of peaceful political change, and an opponent of what he called American imperialism, had been a guest lecturer three times in a University of New Hampshire humanities class. Investigated by Attorney General Louis Wyman at a state trial, he answered some but not all of the questions asked of him. The court held him in contempt, and the state supreme court upheld the contempt charge. When Sweezy appealed to the federal Supreme Court, the latter reversed the earlier judgment, thus exonerating Sweezy.

The significance of *Sweezy v. New Hampshire* is that (1) it was the first case to make academic freedom a First Amendment issue and (2) through Justice Felix Frankfurter's famous citing of a South African case in his concurring opinion, it presented the classic definition of institutional academic freedom, namely that "the four essential freedoms" of a university are "to determine for itself on academic grounds who may teach, what may be taught, how it shall be taught, and who may be admitted for study."

Chief Justice Earl Warren in his plurality opinion spoke more broadly about how the Court interpreted academic freedom to be a First Amendment right:

> The essentiality of freedom in the community of American universities is almost self-evident . . . . Scholarship cannot flourish in an atmosphere of suspicion and distrust. Teachers and students must always remain free to inquire, to study, and to evaluate, to gain new maturity and understanding; otherwise our civilization will stagnate and die. [6]

Reinforcing the Sweezy case a decade later was *Keyishian v. Board of Regents* (1967), which ruled that the first amendment rights of faculty members were violated by a requirement that they sign a loyalty oath affirming that they were not and never had been a member of the Communist Party. In both Sweezy and Keyishian, the Supreme Court was asserting authority to review institutional policies and practice of academic freedom.[7]

Having established the precedent of intervention, the Supreme Court in a case involving the civil liberties of minority groups, *Regents of the University of California v. Bakke* (1978), stated that such intervention should be both rare and also an option, especially when involving broad national policy on issues of special concern such as equal opportunities for racial and sexual minorities. Allan Bakke, a white male, had twice been denied admission to the medical school at the University of California Davis. He brought suit against the university on the basis that his grades and test scores surpassed those of many minority students that were admitted. The court ruled that affirmative action in general was valid but the use of strict quotas in determining who was admitted, as in the 16 percent of places at California Davis for minority students, was not constitutional. Bakke then was admitted and affirmative action policies continued in many universities. *Grutter v. Bollinger* (2003) helped to clarify the court thinking on affirmative action by defining a specific plan that was more acceptable than was the California Davis formula. It ruled as constitutional the University of Michigan Law School admissions policy that while favoring underrepresented minority students took other factors into consideration as well.[8]

In the twenty-first century, the post-9/11 academic freedom crisis over America and the Near East effected the secular universities much more than the Christian colleges. While the Christian institutions were very interested in the Near Eastern conflict (see Chapter 27), they had very few Muslim and Jewish students and faculty, and their faculty members were less prone to utter inflammatory statements.

War and academic freedom do not work well together. While the Patriot Act (2001) passed by Congress early in the War on Terror reminded some of earlier restrictive legislation, the greatest threat to academic freedom in the public institutions came less from the government than from private special interest groups with significant funding and communication capabilities. Operating in a twenty-first-century environment of "culture wars," "identity politics," and cyberspace debates, such interest groups were often aggressive in demanding the dismissal of controversial professors.[9]

Among the more widely publicized academic freedom cases that followed in the wake of 9/11 were Ward Churchill of the University of Colorado Boulder (2001), Richard Berthold of the University of New Mexico (2001), Kevin Barrett of the University of Wisconsin (2006), and Steven Salaita of the University of Illinois (2014). Each involved professorial freedom of expression in wartime, and each involved a complicating issue. The secondary concerns included questions of (1) professional ethics (Churchill), (2) professional competence (Salaita), (3) professional judgment (Barrett), and (4) institutional response to a grievous, public, emotional outburst (Berthold).

Ward Churchill began employment at Colorado Boulder as a staff member in 1978, and, despite holding only a master's degree in communications theory, gained appointment as a tenured professor of ethnic studies in 1991. He held a special interest in the Native Americans. Shortly after 9/11, he wrote an essay (later expanded into a book), "On the Justice of Roosting Chickens." His thesis was that the airplane attacks of September 11, 2001, were a natural response to decades of Western imperialistic intervention in the Near East.

The article and book caused no great outcry until a 2005 invitation to speak at Hamilton (NY) led to professorial protests at the New York institution, which in turn led to an investigation by the Colorado Boulder regents, administration, and faculty committees. The institutional inquiry found that Churchill's specific comments about the 9/11 attacks were free speech protected by the First Amendment; however, the general investigation of Churchill's writings found unrelated multiple incidents of research misconduct. President Hank Brown said that the evidence against Churchill was overwhelming—"it was the depth of the falsification that ultimately led to the outcome," namely a 8–1 vote to dismiss. Churchill appealed all the way to the Colorado state Supreme Court which supported the university.[10]

Compared to the Churchill case, the Berthold incident involved an even more immediate and more impulsive response to the 9/11 attacks and one that involved ready remorse. On the morning of 9/11, Richard Berthold, veteran classical history scholar at New Mexico, was preparing to teach the Western civilization class that he had led for 30 years. Suddenly,

> I watched in amazement as two airplanes flew into buildings in New York City. A bit later in front of perhaps one hundred students, I uttered the remark that brought me my fifteen minutes of fame—or . . . infamy: 'Anyone who would blow up the Pentagon would have my vote.'

Berthold was neither a revolutionary nor an ideologue, but rather a self-admitted gadfly. He was as fluent and engaging as he was careless in his use of words. His students loved him, but the faculty and especially the administration were less admiring. Immediately after delivering his 11-word, half-serious declaration, he knew he had overstepped acceptable boundaries. He explained and then apologized:

> I have long been suspicious and more recently very disappointed in the military and civilian leadership of my country, and the remark, which referred to the Pentagon and said nothing about the World Trade Center, was clearly a reflection of my disagreement with much of our foreign policy. Over thirty years of teaching I have on many occasions made such comments about the government, inevitably to the amusement of students, and in fact three current and former Pentagon workers subsequently informed me that they made cracks like that all the time. But in an embarrassing moment of insensitivity and stupidity I made this observation when more than a hundred people had just died at the Pentagon, making those words an exercise in incredible callousness and setting myself up as a lightning rod for all the anger and frustration sweeping the nation.

The New Mexico administration chose to censor Berthold, relieve him from teaching his introductory course, and closely monitor his subsequent behavior. The latter he interpreted as harassment. Although the FIRE encouraged him to accept no punishment but rather launch a lawsuit, he declined to do so. In December 2002, weary of the continued administrative oversight, he chose to resign to escape the ongoing stress.[11]

Meanwhile five years after 9/11, an adjunct professor at Wisconsin came under fire for advancing a "conspiracy theory" interpretation of the 2001 attacks. Kevin Barrett had been a teaching assistant or lecturer of the Madison campus for a decade when his June 2006 appearance on a talk show deeply disturbed many members of the Wisconsin state legislature. On the program he explained his belief that the United States government planned the 9/11 air attacks and planted explosives in the World Trade Center. At the time he held a one-semester, one-course contract to teach, as an adjunct instructor, a course on Islam. Following the talk show, Wisconsin provost Patrick Farrell conducted a review to assess Barrett's fitness to teach the class. The provost concluded that despite Barrett's personal views, he was able to teach a balanced course. Subsequently in July over 60 Wisconsin legislators signed a letter demanding that Barrett not be allowed to teach his fall course. In response, Wisconsin political scientist and academic freedom specialist Donald Downs defended the provost's decision and reminded the legislators that the university's academic freedom processes defended conservatives as well as liberals including those on the right in the 1990s who "expressed ideas that conflicted with the agendas of political correctness" (e.g., the university's faculty speech code). While Downs described Barrett's ideas on 9/11 as "bizarre" and "outlandish," he was concerned that "firing Barrett from this one-course contract . . . in the face of political pressure would set a bad precedent." It would involve the university surrendering its claim to institutional academic freedom from state government interference. In the end, Barrett taught his course, but he was not hired again by the university.[12]

A fourth and very recent "War on Terror" period academic freedom case involved the appointment of Steven Salaita to teach at Illinois. Salaita had been an English professor at Virginia Tech when the American Indian studies program at the Champaign Urbana campus offered him a tenured faculty position to begin Fall 2014. He accepted in October 2013 and informed Virginia Tech that he would not be returning for the 2014–2015 year.

Then in August, 2014, Illinois chancellor Phyllis Wise, acting for the university, wrote to Salaita to withdraw the job offer after monitoring his July 2014 Twitter posts on Israeli military actions against the Palestinians. Suddenly Salaita was without a position at either Virginia Tech or Illinois.

Salaita's personal background led to his scholarly interests. Of Palestinian and Jordanian ancestry, his early professional work focused on anti-Arab racism in the United States, and Palestinian and American Indian comparative studies. As his work moved from academic presentation in print and relatively objective presentation in the classroom to more unrestrained, confrontational, and vulgar—his description is "passionate and unfiltered"— utterances on the Internet, he became a growing source of controversy.

Of the many academic freedom issues involved in the Salaita case, perhaps the most broadly important consideration for this present study is the extent to which one's right to academic freedom is constrained by one's concomitant obligation to civil discourse?[13]

Chancellor Wise stated, "What we cannot and will not tolerate at the University of Illinois are personal and disrespectful words or actions that demean and abuse either viewpoints themselves or those who express them." A trustee statement added, "speech that promotes malice is not an acceptable form of civil argument." The AAUP leaders offered a contrasting emphasis: "the AAUP has long objected to using criteria of civility and collegiality in faculty evaluation because we view this as a threat to academic freedom."[14]

Meanwhile the Salaita case continues with appeals and suits, while the public universities, as well as the Christian colleges, continue with their concern to maintain the institutional freedom to decide how best to balance professorial academic freedom with the other important components of the learning process. Thus, institutional academic freedom, while always normal for the Christian college, is sometimes necessary for the secular institutions also as both seek to assure that government legislation, regulation, and judicial review are as constructive as possible and not employed unnecessarily.

Institutional academic freedom is partial even as professorial academic freedom is partial. The one seeks to protect the integrity of administrative oversight while the other focuses on assuring the unfettered search for truth in the instructional and research processes. Both are critical but not complete in themselves, for there are other vital partners in assuring the welfare of the academic endeavor. These other partners include external constituencies that supply student customers and financial benevolences, and of course the internal clients, namely the students themselves. It is the latter that is the subject of the next chapter. Of all the approaches to academic freedom the one that is the most holistic is the one that in cooperative fashion recognizes the dignity, rights, and input of each valid component in the large community that comprises a college or university. The overarching umbrella that provides the basis for this community is the institutional mission, with all forms of academic freedom deriving from that. Such an organizational approach can be functional in the secular university no less than the Christian college.

CHAPTER 17

Student Academic Freedom

An emphasis upon student rights is both a very old and a relatively recent phenomenon. The medieval University of Bologna (Italy)—arguably the oldest university in the West—was a student-centered institution. Each year the students elected the faculty rather than the faculty selecting the students. The faculty promised obedience to the rector who was a student; with his fellow students, the rector supervised the behavior of the faculty who paid fines for violations including the offense of "[trying] to avoid a difficult question by postponing its treatment." There were rent controls for students' room payments. It was a striking system indeed, but it had little impact on the later history of higher education in northern Europe and North America; for the latter the professor-centered University of Paris was the early model.[1]

In the new world and beginning with Harvard, the colleges existed for the training of students until the intellectual revolution of the late nineteenth century added to the original purpose of transmitting knowledge a second purpose of discovering knowledge. Gradually research became more important than the teaching of students until the major student protest movement of the 1960s and 1970s, with the result being a somewhat increased formal recognition of student rights.

The balance of this chapter is a discussion of ways that institutions have restricted or can restrict the academic freedom of their students.

A Heavily Prescribed Curriculum

Students had little or no choice in the courses they studied through the first two centuries of American higher education. Beginning in the eighteenth century, however, the debating clubs or literary societies, as they came to be known, broadened the intellectual experience; their origin and operation were by student initiative. They helped to compensate "for the neglect of science,

English literature, history, music, and art" in the heavily classical curriculum. One of the most radical critics of the lack of student choice in the courses was Ralph Waldo Emerson who lamented that

> In college we thwart the natural love of learning by leaving the natural method of teaching what each wishes to learn, and insisting that you shall learn what you have no taste or capacity for. The college, which should be a place of delightful labour, is made odious and unhealthy, and the young men are tempted to frivolous amusements to rally their jaded spirits. I would have the studies elective. Scholarship is to be created not by compulsion, but by awakening a pure interest in knowledge. The wise instructor accomplishes this by opening to his pupils precisely the attractions the study has for himself.[2]

Even today when the prescribed curriculum (i.e., general education) comprises 30–40 percent of the four-year course of study, colleges do well to offer students multiple course options for meeting a requirement and professors do well to provide some choice within a required course for completing it. Students like other adults are most fulfilled when they can exercise a meaningful degree of control over the most important parts of their lives.

An Inadequate Emphasis upon Student Learning

After 1890 as the professors devoted more time to research, they placed less focus upon the students. A second factor contributing to the growing impersonalization of the faculty/student relationship was the sharp increase in enrollments which resulted in larger-sized classes and increased faculty/student ratios. No wonder that the students' discontentment and sense of alienation finally exploded into the sometimes violent Student Protest Movement of the 1960s and 1970s.

Beginning with the Berkeley (University of California) Free Speech Movement in 1964, the turmoil quickly spread to other campuses and involved complaints about many aspects of the educational process. The classes were too large; the faculty were too inaccessible; the courses were too irrelevant to problems of the modern world; the rules were too archaic for young adults; the giving of student grades to draft boards to decide draft deferments was intolerable; the military recruitment on campus and employee recruitment for defense-based industries were too cozy of a university relationship with the Vietnam War effort; and the university decision-making processes were too lacking in participatory democracy.

When the federal government finally investigated the causes of student unrest, the resultant Scranton Report gave primary blame to the long-lasting Vietnam War even while acknowledging that factors within the universities themselves needed reforming. "One of the most valid criticisms of many universities," the report noted, "is that their faculties have become so involved in outside research that their commitment to teaching seems compromised. We urge universities and faculty members to reduce their outside service commitments." Furthermore, "University governance systems should be reformed to increase participation of students and faculty in the formulation of university policies that effect them."[3]

The response in the universities was a partial change in policy. For example, in the discipline of history, the American Historical Association organized a teaching division with the goal of giving "the teaching function . . . a status and recognition previously reserved for research." Broader in potential application was the 1967 formal joint statement of the AAUP, the Association of American Colleges, the National Student Association, and others. The statement declared that students (1) "should be free to take reasoned exception to the data or views offered in any course"; (2) "should have protection through orderly procedures against prejudiced or capricious academic evaluation"; (3) should have "protection against improper disclosure" of their views, beliefs, and associations; (4) should in their organizations "be allowed to invite and hear any person of their own choosing"; (5) should be able to freely "express their views on institutional policy and on matters of general interest to the student body"; and (6) should, in their student newspapers, "be free of censorship and advance approval of copy."[4]

A Lack of Balance in Classroom Presentation of Worldviews and Interpretations

While the Christian colleges have long complained about the lack of balanced treatment of religious and secular perspectives in higher education, David Horowitz and his Students for Academic Freedom (SAF) have in recent decades charged that politically left-wing perspectives dominate in the political discourse in the universities. The SAF slogan is "you can't get a good education if they're only telling you half the truth." Although Horowitz's rhetoric is often harsh, his "Academic Bill of Rights" (2002) is a carefully worded document. He has persuaded several state legislatures to consider intervention in their state universities, and another measure of his effectiveness is that his more compelling arguments have forced the major higher education organizations to release increasingly judicious statements on academic freedom.

For example, the 2006 AACU Statement on Academic Freedom and Educational Responsibility acknowledges that "Academic freedom is necessary not just so faculty members can conduct their individual research and teach their own courses, but so they can enable students . . . to acquire the learning that they need to contribute to society." Furthermore, argues the AACU statement, the Horowitz emphasis to "teach all sides of the debate" is insufficient, for the faculty must also help the students "to engage differences of opinion, evaluate evidence, and form their own grounded judgments about the relative value of competing perspectives."

One recent noteworthy study by sociologist Kyle Dodson suggests that the academic experience tends not to convert students politically from conservative to liberal but from wherever they are toward a more nuanced centrist position.[5]

So how do the Christian colleges deal with conflicting political and economic ideas and claims? The best of them, while privileging the Christian faith, give no comparable priority to any human system of thought in the social sciences or elsewhere. In nearly every college, secular or religious, the faculty tend to be more liberal politically than do the students. At most Christian colleges, the students (and their families) are more Republican than Democratic, more conservative than liberal. The faculty in general, according to Ronald Mahurin, political scientist and former director of development and research for the CCCU, tend to be quite evenly divided between Republican, Democratic, and Independent, although the social scientists tend to be more liberal than do their colleagues in general. Among the more politically conservative Christian colleges are Grove City (PA), Harding (AR), Liberty (VA), Patrick Henry (VA), Regent (VA), Wisconsin Lutheran, Colorado Christian, and College of the Ozarks (MO).[6]

An Emphasis upon Indoctrination over Education

The difference between indoctrination and education can be a subtle one, but it is a difference between forcing and leading in the learning process. Often, it is measured by degree rather than in absolute terms, for virtually all institutions, Christian and secular, and most professors have elements of both indoctrination and education in the totality of their impact on students. The ideal way for a professor to avoid indoctrination is not to avoid presenting one's best conclusions on a topic, but rather to humbly share them rather than forcefully impose them. Usually it is less a matter of what the professor says than how he says it. By his total demeanor he must communicate the idea that it is not only each student's right but also her obligation to carefully process the ideas under consideration and reach her own best conclusions.

By contrast if a professor or university or an even larger educational system has as its driving spirit an emotional reaction against something that may well have needed correction, sometimes the effect can be to overreact, thus creating a new excess, albeit in a different direction. Billy Graham experienced this phenomenon at the Bob Jones University of the 1930s, where, as he described it,

> Teaching in every subject was dogmatic, and there was little chance to raise questions. Dr. Bob's interpretation of doctrine, ethics, and academics was the only one allowed. [But] we also loved Dr. Bob.... Sometimes as intimidating as a bull, he could also be as tender as a child. We could not help but sense that he had our best interests at heart in the policies he imposed.... I surely knew I was not fitting in where I was. I asked for an interview with Dr. Bob in his office and told him about my discontent and my thoughts of leaving. His voice booming, he pronounced me a failure and predicted more failure ahead. I left his office disillusioned and dejected.

When Graham transferred to Florida Bible Institute, he was much happier. "One thing that thrilled me was the diversity of viewpoints we were exposed to in the classroom, a wondrous blend of ecumenical and evangelical thought.... In their teaching, they were not afraid to let us know about other philosophies and even about views critical of Christianity."[7]

Historian of American religion Richard Hughes of Messiah emphasizes another way in which a college can restrict the learning process, namely in its policy and practice for selecting outside speakers to come to campus for major addresses. If such speakers tend to be of one persuasion, such as the right-wing political lecturers that typically visited Pepperdine where Hughes formerly taught, the effect can be more nearly indoctrination than learning. More subtle, but still limiting, is the practice in many Christian colleges that advertise how the integration of faith and learning characterizes the entirety of the learning process yet schedule mostly theologians to address the regular all-school chapel assemblies.[8]

Discouragement of Open Discussion

Some professors are skillful in lecture. This can be natural in a factual-oriented discipline like history and can work well especially when they are willing to receive a reasonable amount of questions and discussion. Even in the factual disciplines, discussion can be valuable when interpreting the facts. Some professors are skillful in leading discussion. This can be natural in the process-oriented disciplines like communications, and can work well when the professor first provides sufficient context for a meaningful discussion. Whatever the discipline and whoever the professor, the latter must never refuse to consider an honest inquiry whether in the classroom or in private counsel. The temptation in the Christian college is to refuse to examine ideas that challenge the institutional orthodoxy, while the temptation in the secular institution is to refuse to examine ideas that seriously consider religious interpretations of the human condition.[9] In either case, to succumb to the temptation is to deny the academic freedom of the students.

Lack of Fairness in Evaluation

A cardinal sin in the teaching profession is to be unfair in the assigning of grades. It is worse even than being boring or disinterested in presentation. The instructor must not only be fair but must appear to be fair. She should explain clearly her criteria for evaluation. She should explain clearly that students are welcome to disagree with the professor in thought, in classroom expression, and in written essays, and that evaluation of subjective matter is not on expressing the right conclusions but on the quality of the thinking and writing in reaching those conclusions.

There is a relationship between how the professor presents the class material and how much the students trust the professor to be even-handed in evaluating the students' expression of that material. The more a professor is seen as one-sided, the more the students will be fearful that for them to speak or write otherwise will place their grade at risk. Such a dynamic has a chilling effect upon the process of open and honest communication.

When a student believes that a professor has given her an unfair grade and a discussion with the professor achieves no resolution, may she appeal to the administrative hierarchy? Nearly all institutions have a grievance procedure. What if a hearing board rules in favor of the student? Has the professor's academic freedom been violated? The AAUP believes that the First Amendment protects the right of professors to assign grades.

On the issue of whether or when administrative officials or courts may overrule professors, the court decisions are mixed. In *Board of Curators of the University of Missouri v. Horowitz* (1978), Justice Lewis Powell expressed in his concurring opinion that professors should hold "the widest range of discretion" in judging the academic performance of their students. Similarly in *Regents of the University of Michigan v. Ewing* (1985), the high court ruled that court override should be rare, only occurring when there is "such a substantial departure from accepted academic norms as to demonstrate that the person or committee responsible did not actually exercise professional judgment." In the 1989 appellate court case of *Parate v. Isibor*, the court ruled that university officials could not compel a professor to change a grade as such would violate the professor's constitutionally protected speech rights. By contrast in *Stronach v. Virginia State University* (2008), a federal district court ruled in favor of the university over a professor with Judge Henry Hudson stating that while academic freedom protects the right of professors to assign grades, it even more completely protects the right of academic administration to change grades over the professor's objection.[10]

Insufficient Editorial Autonomy in Student Newspapers

Traditionally public colleges by definition as governmental entities provide First Amendment editorial freedom to the staff members of their student newspapers.[11] Private colleges are not similarly limited; however, if they choose to have a newspaper at all to train future journalists for the profession, they should provide at the least a functionally meaningful degree of editorial freedom. The Student Press Law Center argues that religious institutions that so highly value the religious freedom provisions of the First Amendment should be very careful about limiting their student editors in exercising their freedom of speech provisions of that same amendment.[12]

The coming of the Internet age has added greater complexity to the freedom of the student press issue. Online reporting "makes administrators nervous, especially at colleges which don't have strong journalism programs" notes Terry Mattingly, director of the CCCU Washington Journalism Center. "The minute you put...[a story] online, you're dealing with trustees, parents, donors, and potential students." *Christianity Today* reporter Sarah Eekhoff Zylstra adds that Christian colleges have been "slow and cautious" in deciding whether to publish on the Web, for they "worry about libel, unflattering articles, or unpredictable issues." For example, Taylor University that does not practice prior review for its campus paper, finally decided to publish an online edition in 2013 but only after each issue is reviewed by the University director of media relations.[13]

Another controversial issue is the existence of underground newspapers.[14] Sometimes these appear when the campus environment in general is deficient in intellectual openness or when the regular newspaper is excessively restricted. They can emerge, however, in the best of circumstances. Then the question is how to deal—or not deal—with them. Sometimes administrative heavy-handedness can cause more negative publicity than do irresponsible student articles.

In general Christian colleges offer a larger degree of freedom of belief to the students than they do to the faculty. Many Christian colleges do not require their students to be confessing Christians, a fact dramatically illustrated in 2013 when the student body president at Northwest Christian (OR) "came out" as an atheist. Widely respected on campus, he continued his leadership position.[15]

The next chapter continues the examination of student academic freedom by focusing upon one of the most basic academic liberties, namely the freedom to choose the type of academic environment in which to study.

CHAPTER 18

Economic Limits as Academic Limits: The Problem of Accessibility

M any Christian youth who would prefer to attend a Christian college cannot afford to pay—or aren't willing to pay—the increasingly high costs of doing so. The Christian colleges that have grown in popularity, prosperity, number, size, and quality during the past generation may have reached a peak in their enrollment capabilities with the traditional delivery model. The 2012 Bain and Company study, "The Financially Sustainable University," found much of higher education inefficient, overextended, and badly in need of reform. "Approximately one-third of colleges are spending more than they can afford. . . . Change is needed, and it's needed now." The colleges that the Bain brief sees as being at risk include many Christian colleges. Perhaps even more alarming is the assessment of Robert Andringa, former president of the CCCU. Andringa has identified approximately 900 currently or historically faith-related colleges among the 1,600 private institutions of higher education, and of the 900 he finds only 100 "whose financial foundations should make them competitive for decades to come." While "there remains a steady, dependable student market for distinctly Christian institutions," there currently exists an oversupply of institutions to serve this need. Affordability has become a major agenda item on the meetings of Christian college trustees.[1]

Is it possible that the most economically threatened colleges could respond to the "will to survive" by developing radically new and cheaper delivery systems that will attract the growing number of Christian young people who would prefer to have the "academic freedom" to enroll in a Christian college that would cost them no more than say the expenses of a four-year public university? More colleges would survive and more students would be served. How might this happen? The last and major part of this chapter explains some of the possible ways of achieving this reform.

Before discussing the issue of economic reform in Christian higher education, it is important to note the concurrent financial crisis in public higher education. If the problem in independent higher education is escalating tuition charges, the problem in the public universities is declining appropriations from the state legislatures. The Great Recession, a growing philosophy of fiscal restraint, and increased pressure from other areas of obligation (e.g., health care and the prison system) led to a 2000–2010 decade-long decline in state and local apportionments of 24 percent to research universities, 24 percent to master's universities, 20 percent to bachelor's colleges, and 20 percent to community colleges. Per pupil funding declined by 21 percent from $8,257 to $6,532 (adjusted for inflation based upon 2011 dollars). The public universities in turn responded by correspondingly raising tuition charges which by 2013 averaged $8,900 per year for four-year colleges and $3,300 for junior colleges. Paul Lingenfelter, president of the State Higher Education Executive officers organization, described the decreases in state appropriations and the increases in tuition as "unprecedented over my 40-year career in higher education." Educators talk about a "new normal" with little expectation that the funding patterns will recover in the foreseeable future.[2]

A "chain reaction" pattern has emerged: funding cuts led to tuition increases which led to higher student debt which led to higher student default rates which led to a mounting federal government concern which led to increased federal government action and intervention. When the federal student loan indebtedness passed the trillion-dollar mark (involving 40 million debtors) in 2013, it made headlines. The two-year default rate (percentage of students defaulting on their loans within two years of starting payment) rose to 10 percent in 2013 (the highest rate in two decades) and the three-year rate increased to 14.7 percent. States began to follow the federal government in seeking to moderate the effects of large debts on the younger adults.

The educational provisions of the federal Health Care and Education Reconciliation Act of 2010 consolidated major federal and private loan programs under the federal government and eased the terms of repayment. In 2014, Michigan became the most aggressive of 20 states considering a "pay it forward" tuition plan or "pay as you earn" (PAYE) repayment plan, whereby students would pay for college retroactively. Presumably this strategy would allow for more students to both attend college and then pay for it in reasonable proportions of their post-college earnings. The plan under debate in Michigan would have public-junior college graduates pay 2 percent and public university graduates pay 4 percent of their earnings for a five-year period for each year of college (i.e., four-year graduates would pay 4 percent of salary for 20 years).[3]

While there is little evidence to date that fewer students are enrolling in college because of the increasing cost, there is evidence that they are looking for less expensive ways of obtaining a degree. The high school graduation rate reached 80 percent for the first time in 2012, and the percentage of those graduates going directly to college rose from 54.3 percent in 1992 to 62.5 percent in 2010. A major portion of this latter increase came from economically disadvantaged, minority students enrolling in the more easily accessible private for-profit segment of higher education. These students to a disproportionate degree relied upon federal grants and loans and to a disproportionate degree defaulted upon the loans after graduation. To the credit of the private for-profit segment, it was a population that was largely bypassed by the public and private nonprofit institutions. With the dramatic growth of the private for-profit segment from 2 percent of college enrollees in 1990 to 11 percent in 2009, the junior colleges—the other major competitor for low income students—grew a modest 1 percent from 25 to 26 percent while the increasingly expensive sectors declined in market share (private nonprofit down from 22 to 19 percent, and public four-year down sharply from 51 to 44 percent) during the same period.[4]

Now this narrative returns to the major concern of the chapter, namely how can Christian higher education reconstruct itself so that more Christian youth are able to experience the freedom to access its type of learning? Let me suggest several ways that this might be done, dividing these reforms into three categories: (1) those that largely retain the traditional structures while reorganizing them to be less experience; (2) those that form new structures based upon new philosophies and that are organized in ways to incorporate new economies; and (3) those that work with the public universities to develop complementary programs on—or on the edge of—the public campuses. Others will design additional models or variations of these models to best serve their purposes. Many colleges are sufficiently satisfied with the nature, enrollment patterns, and financial stability of their existing structure so as to desire little or no change. Others desire or need to desire to reinvent themselves. The goal is not for all colleges to reform but for Christian higher education in general to offer its public more models in more price ranges for achieving a Christian higher education.

Traditional Structures Repackaged at Greater Economy

A college wishing to reform would do well to start its planning by asking the question, "how much do we wish our product to cost?" and then devising a system to achieve that goal.

The most discussed cost-saving reform of the twenty-first century is the Massive Open Online Course (MOOC), a large-scale, low-cost Internet design that can feature either a skilled lecturer or extensive learner interaction. Its efficiency lies in its economy of scale: one professor or learning system can serve an indefinite number of learners. Still in its infancy, the MOOC system attracted great attention when Harvard joined MIT's MOOC plan called "edX." Other pioneering MOOC systems have included "Coursera" led by Stanford, Princeton, Pennsylvania, and Michigan; "Udacity," which specializes in computer science; and "Khan Academy," funded by Bill and Melinda Gates and which focuses on secondary students. Many educational leaders would likely agree with former president Bill Clinton that (1) the student debt problem is unacceptable; (2) "the only sustainable answer is to find a less expensive delivery system"; and (3) finding a way to use MOOCs is the next step in the effort to drive down costs.[5]

To date the small liberal arts colleges have shown less enthusiasm for the MOOC concept than have the other segments of academe. The Christian colleges in particular will want to personalize the ways in which they offer their values-based education. But with cost reduction also one of their major goals, they will do well to consider combing the economies of the MOOC approach with a support system that both personalizes the learning process and incorporates their own values into it. For example, there is no reason that Christian colleges individually or in concert could not develop their own MOOC systems with their own skilled lecturers and teams of able tutors to assist.[6]

If MOOCs are good, or at least necessary, why would it not be even better in a given college to have the more skilled lecturers do the large-scale teaching in person? Increasing the faculty–student ratio for a larger number of classes and thus reducing the institutional payroll for the college as a whole is one of the more obvious ways to reduce tuition.

Most Christian college students are used to having a mix of large-scale and small-scale learning situations in their home church where the minister may address several hundred listeners in the worship service before the congregation disperses to the more intimate Sunday school classes, youth groups, and "small groups." Some students will prefer to have all small classes and have the ability and willingness to pay for it; it is good that they would have such colleges from which to choose. But it is also good to have colleges which seek a blend of personalization and economy for the larger number of students that would prefer that combination.

Still another economy model is the junior college with its focus on primarily large enrollment general education courses. A number of Christian colleges began as junior colleges (e.g., Messiah in Pennsylvania, Abilene Christian in

Texas, Spring Arbor in Michigan, and Concordia in Wisconsin) or as similarly inexpensive Bible colleges (e.g., Nyack in New York, Westmont in California, Gordon in Massachusetts, and Malone in Ohio). Some could convert to junior colleges if they saw that as the best way of continuing to provide service and stewardship for their constituency.

New Structures with New Philosophies and New Economies

L. Richard Meeth, a higher education financial analyst of the previous generation argued that small colleges erred when they too closely sought to imitate the structures and philosophies of the large universities. Rather they should be bold and creative in developing systems that best serve their situations and financial capabilities. In his *Quality Education for Less Money*, Meeth declared that "private higher education needs . . . managers who can challenge assumptions of higher education," and then he issued his own challenges. For example, he stated that "A growing body of research suggests that peer teaching can be more effective than teaching by traditionally prepared faculty, particularly at the beginning level of study," and "there is very little research evidence to support [the] conclusion [that] small classes produce better learning."[7]

There are a number of systems that one could develop from Meeth's thinking; let me suggest one possibility in some detail. This scenario develops from two assumptions, namely that (1) there is a clear need for less expensive models in private higher education and (2) peer learning is a valid, even important, mode of learning that long has been underutilized in formal higher education situations. This system could use a blend of MOOCs, large-sized classes with in-person lecturers, and small-sized tutor groups led by students who were more advanced than those whom they were leading. The professor would present the formal lectures or interpret the presentation of the MOOC lecturer and guide the tutors. Junior tutors could work with the freshmen and senior tutors with the sophomores. The juniors and seniors would receive academic credit for their tutoring as the assumption would be that one's own learning is greatly enhanced when one prepares to teach others.

A college could expand this tutorial concept by having M.A. students work with the professor/master teacher by tutoring the juniors and seniors. The graduate tutors would receive a stipend and/or credit toward an M.A. in education, a M.A.T. (Master of Arts in Teaching) or a discipline-specific degree as appropriate. If a college wished to depart less completely from the traditional pattern, it could have the regular faculty provide the instruction by themselves for the juniors and seniors.

The educational philosophy underlying this system would be learning-centered rather than teaching-centered. It would require fewer expensive lecturers but a larger number of informed coaches or resource people at various levels. It would require the students to do more reading but allow them to have more choice in what they read. It would train everyone in acquiring the discipline of life-long learning. Learning would be a cooperative effort in this community of learners.

The tuition rates in this system could be progressive as each succeeding level requires the efforts of more professors and more advanced tutors. The first and second years could be structured so as to be no more expensive than the area four-year public colleges. Some of the less affluent underclassmen will enjoy their first two years sufficiently well to seek to find a way to continue. Those who are not able to do this will at least have had the advantage of a learning experience in a Christian environment for part of their college career.

One recent major study found that noninstructional student services represented the "fastest growing salary expense in many types of institutions between 2002 and 2012." The colleges defend such expenditures by arguing that the students and their families called for such services. Apparently many of them are no longer interested in paying for them. Some colleges, therefore, may wish to reduce spending sharply in this area.[8]

Work within the Public Revenue System

Christian higher education is expensive because it mostly operates outside of the public revenue flow. But does it need to do so? If the First Amendment forbids aid to religious institutions, it does not forbid aid to individual citizens who could then exercise their academic freedom to choose the type of institution in which they study. So goes the argument for a "voucher system" as advanced by economists Richard Vedder and Milton Friedman. There is precedent for a broad-based voucher plan in the GI Bill and the Pell Grants on the federal level and the Colorado system on the state level. Additionally many states already have scholarship programs which their youth may use in any college—private as well as public—in the state.[9]

Christian college lawyer-administrators John E. Brown III and Eugene Habecker with philosopher William Hasker believe that if the courts could define religion broadly enough to see that no college or university is religiously neutral, it would even more completely create the occasion for government aid to be student-centered rather than institution-centered. This, of course, would greatly reduce the out-of-pocket costs for students to attend a Christian college.[10]

A very different way for Christian higher education to access the public revenue sources would be for the Christian college to move to the state university. Financially struggling Christian colleges, rather than closing, could consider this option as a survival strategy while the more affluent colleges could complement their main campus program with a lower cost model "satellite campus" at a nearly public university. The easiest such programs to implement would be those which would add limited academic programs (say in religion and faith and learning courses) to an existing Christian student center. A more fully developed model would include a residence center with student development services and selected courses perhaps taught by professors from the home campus. The students, of course, would be enrolled in the public university for most of their course work. Models of such satellite institutions presently exist. Note, for example, the half-century-old Conrad Grebel University at the University of Waterloo (Ontario), one of the largest and most prestigious universities in Canada; and the much newer network, the Consortium of Christian Study Centers (CCSC) led especially by Presbyterian Church in America scholars and located on a dozen or so major campuses.[11]

One of the most comprehensive and creative lists of alternate ways of financing Christian higher education appears in the Robert Andringa essay previously referenced in this chapter. He includes some of the ideas already discussed in this chapter plus others. The latter include partnering with a nearby community college, changing from nonprofit to for-profit status either by oneself or in partnership with another enterprise, and engaging in an entrepreneurial business venture or ventures (e.g., assisted living retirement centers) some of which could employ the students. Examples of colleges presently employing such alternative methods include Indiana Wesleyan, LeTourneau (TX), College of the Ozarks (MO), and Pensacola Christian (FL). In the nineteenth century many Christian colleges operated secondary academies to help support their collegiate program.[12]

In the long history of education in America, one of the most common themes is the movement toward enabling larger percentages of the population to access larger degrees of learning. Parallel with this development in education has been the movement toward a free will theology—especially during the Second Great Awakening—and a participatory democracy, including a broadened franchise in politics during the century after 1820. Landmarks in the movement toward popular education have included the emergence of the common (elementary) school in the 1840s, the Land Grant College Act of the 1860s, the beginning of the Bible college movement in the 1880s, the public secondary school after 1900, and federal student aid beginning in the 1930s. More recently, in 2015, President Obama issued a call for free community college education. In similar spirit hopefully the Christian colleges of the twenty-first century will find ways to follow in this long tradition by increasing popular access to their highly desirable product.

CHAPTER 19

Evangelicals and Catholics: Narrowing the Gap

Since Pope John XXIII and the 1960s Vatican II Council, there has occurred what historian Mark Noll (Wheaton and Notre Dame) calls a minor revolution. Never since the Reformation of the 1500s has the distance between the Catholics and Protestants been so small with most of the movement coming from the Catholics. The specific Catholic changes included: (1) greater respect for Protestants, (2) greater use of the vernacular language (which meant English in most US churches) and the sermon in the performance of the Mass, (3) more emphasis upon Bible reading and Bible studies, (4) more lay singing of Protestant songs and more reading of evangelical books, (5) more adoption of evangelical theology, (6) less severe clothing styles for nuns and priests, (7) greater demand for a married clergy, (8) reduced deference to the authority of the bishops in particular and the hierarchy in general and greater respect for the influence of the laity, (9) greater disregard of the church's prohibition of artificial means of birth control, and (10) significant participation in the ecumenical Charismatic movement.[1]

Meanwhile its reduced denominational loyalty made the Protestants less prone to rigid distancing from and even discrimination of Catholics. The mainline denominational churches have been losing members while independent Protestant churches have been growing. Many churches that still are affiliated with a denomination deemphasize the denominational label in the church signage.

In addition to the Charismatic movements' ability to bring together conservative and liberal Protestants, Roman Catholics, and Eastern Orthodox believers, another highlight of the growing late-twentieth-century ecumenical dialogue was the 1994 signing of the Evangelicals and Catholics Together (ECT) Statement with 40 signatories including conference organizers Charles Colson (Prison Fellowship) and Richard John Neuhaus

(*First Things* magazine), evangelical college academicians Kent Hill (Eastern Nazarene), John White (Geneva), Mark Noll (Wheaton), James I. Packer (Regent College), Pat Robertson (Regent University), and Catholic university academicians Avery Dulles (Fordham), Robert Destro (Catholic University), Joseph P. Fitzpatrick (Fordham), Nathan Hatch (Notre Dame), James Hitchcock (St. Louis), Peter Kreeft (Boston), and Matthew Lamb (Boston). The immediate impetus for the conference and statement was the desire to work less competitively and more cooperatively, especially in Latin America and Eastern Europe. The Statement is an impressive document that focuses upon the many things that the two groups have in common.[2]

An early harbinger of the improved Evangelical/Catholic relationship was the personal relationship between Billy Graham and Cardinal Richard Cushing stemming from Graham's 1950 Crusade in Boston. Cushing wrote an editorial for the diocesan paper entitled "Bravo, Billy!" encouraging Catholics to attend the Graham meetings, and Graham invited priests to serve as counselors in the revival campaign. Later during the 1964 campaign in Boston, Cushing, in the ecumenical spirit of the fresh Vatican II Council, announced after a meeting between the two, "I am 100 percent for the evangelist," and then noted, as Graham recalled, "that if he had half a dozen Billy Grahams, he would not worry about the future of his church."[3]

The growing ecumenical spirit carried over to many of the evangelical and Catholic colleges. Sometimes the cooperation developed from personal friendship and similar goals at the presidential level. Father Michael Scanlan of Franciscan University of Steubenville (OH) and Charles MacKenzie of Presbyterian Grove City (PA) encouraged and advised each other in their mutual efforts to strengthen the spiritual orientation of their institutions during their long-overlapping tenures in the 1970s and 1980s. Franciscan became the first Catholic college to join the Council for Christian Colleges and Universities (CCCU). Grove City graduate and Catholic convert Scott Hahn is a Franciscan theologian who travels widely to preach evangelistically to a broad variety of Christian groups.[4]

A different set of presidents working together to achieve a different common purpose—that of religious freedom in a specific application—were Philip Ryken of Wheaton and John Garvey of Catholic University. In July 2012, Wheaton joined Catholic in filing a lawsuit managed by the Becket Fund for Religious Liberty against the federal Department of Health and Human Services and its mandate to provide their employees with health insurance that offers access to such abortion-causing drugs as "morning-after" and "week-after" medications. In the "first-ever partnership between Catholic and evangelical institutions to oppose the same regulation in the same court," Garvey noted, "I am happy to express solidarity with our evangelical brothers and sisters from Wheaton College as they challenge the HHS mandate." By 2014, the number of cases filed over the mandate had reached 100 and involved many Catholic dioceses and evangelical colleges (see Chapter 28).[5]

One of the more significant evangelical/Catholic dialogues on the professorial level took place at Gordon College in 2006 when Thomas A. (Tal) Howard organized a forum involving Mark Noll of Wheaton and Notre Dame and James Turner of Notre Dame. Howard compared the two participants to two irenic and erudite scholars from the Reformation era, Lutheran Philip Melanchthon and Catholic Desiderius Erasmus. The discussion resulted in the book, *The Future of Christian Learning: An Evangelical and Catholic Dialogue*.[6]

Noll emphasized that the Evangelicals and Catholics "have a special need for what each offers the other.... American Catholics enjoy the legacy of Christendom, but that legacy is now confused.... American evangelicals are heirs to a strong revival tradition, but more and more evangelicals perceive that tradition as incomplete and distorted." Among the strengths of Catholicism which Noll believed could inform an improved Evangelicalism are "a positive, God-honoring place for matter... and for reason, a parish ideal of community (all classes, races, dispositions in one common institution), and a positive acceptance of history and tradition as gifts from God," while he cited evangelical strengths to which he believed Catholics would do well to more fully incorporate: "a sharp awareness of how religious formalism and mindless tradition can anesthetize thought, a well-practiced demonstration of the virtue of voluntary organization..., an insistence on personal engagement, in faith and in learning..., and above all, the inestimable value... of the priesthood of all believers."[7]

Turner's list of Catholic strengths included a deep intellectual tradition and a richly worshipful appreciation of liturgy. While he gave the Catholic Church high marks for its work in the spiritual formation of priests, he sees it doing less well in this regard with its laity including the students. "Insofar as they aspire to faith formation,..." Turner commented, "Catholic colleges have something to learn from the practices of other Christian traditions, including notably evangelicalism."[8]

Still another Notre Dame scholar who has thought deeply about how Catholic higher education might improve its product is theologian Kenneth Garcia. The central recommendation of his award-winning 2012 book, *Academic Freedom and the Telos of the Catholic University*, is that the Catholic university should be academically free to seek to incorporate theological insights into the various academic disciplines as opposed to a two-sphere approach that separates theology and the liberal arts. Such an emphasis sounds remarkably similar to the central emphasis of many of the evangelical

CCCU colleges, namely the integration of faith and learning. Drawing upon the ideas of John Courtney Murray, American Catholicism's leading theologian during Vatican II, Garcia declared that

> the mission of the Catholic university is to ensure that the entire continuum of reality is explored in both its full, finite extension and its full spiritual depth. Knowledge of the finite world should be viewed in relation to knowledge of the infinite, and there should be as clear an articulation between them as possible—moving from conceptually separate domains within the continuum of reality to the divine ground of the entire continuum. Not all scholars must follow this directionality, but Catholic universities should insure that there are *some* faculty members in each academic department who not only want to pursue knowledge beyond their disciplines, but to actually explore its relation to Christian philosophy and theology, even while respecting their distinctive methods and subject matters.[9]

Catholic higher education like Protestant higher education experienced a secularization movement; however, for the Catholic schools the movement came later and has been less complete. Some of the urban universities, primarily Jesuit ones, secularized the most, while, in response, some newer conservative institutions have begun. The majority of the Catholic schools, while becoming less Catholic in faculty and student composition and in subservience to the Papal Curia, still have retained a religious identity—perhaps comparable to the "critical mass" Protestant colleges. During the last two decades, many of these majority colleges have been seeking ways to enhance their spiritual influence in the lives of their students. Boston College legal scholar Gregory Kalscheur believes that they have achieved some success with their students in the development of spiritual formation commitment to social service projects, and in focus upon the spiritual dimension of vocational calling. He thinks that they have done less well in reawakening an appreciation for the Catholic intellectual tradition.[10]

Many of the Catholic colleges would welcome an even-handed partnership with the evangelical colleges, even to the point of learning what the latter may be able to teach them about faith formation and faith and learning integration. Could the evangelical colleges see this invitation to openness as a Macedonian call-like opportunity without being presumptively paternalistic in the process? And can they enter into such a partnership without an undue fear of having some of their students and faculty convert to Catholicism? After all they can cite some of the "best and brightest" of evangelical college graduates or faculty who have made such a change (e.g., Thomas Howard,[11] Peter Kreeft, Scott Hahn, Christian Smith, and Francis Beckwith).[12]

So how can the evangelical colleges best deal with both the promise and the threat of working more closely with the Catholic colleges? Some of the most compelling advice that I have heard on this subject comes from veteran Missionary Church theologian and missionary, David E. Bjork, who has spent 30 years in France working with and, informally, through the Roman Catholic Church. His graduate work includes degrees from two seminaries, Fuller and Trinity, and Ph.D.'s from two French universities, Paris and Strasbourg. He advises evangelical colleges that have not previously worked with Catholic scholars or institutions to begin slowly, building confidence and creating a format for nonconfrontational and ever-respectful dialogue to see what each can learn from the other. Do all of this deliberately in a step-at-a-time process before considering whether or not to employ a professor of the other tradition. Bjork emphasizes strongly how the dominant goal of both evangelicals and Catholics should be to make mature disciples of Christ, not to win converts to a specific church tradition. With such discipleship as the common mission, the two traditions have a common base on which to work together in a variety of specific ways. Bjork presented his experience and conclusions in a 2013 address as the Ray Fitzgerald Lecture at Taylor (IN). The lectureship series is designed to explore ways in which Protestants and Roman Catholics might best cooperate in the advancement of the cause of the Gospel.[13]

In these cooperative efforts, college leaders can find encouragement from the recent statements of their leaders. Note, for example, the 1975 encyclical *Evangelii Nuntiandi* of Paul VI, and the 1995 encyclical *Ut Unum Sint* of John Paul II. The viewpoint of the Catholic Church toward non-Catholic Christians has changed from "heretics" after the Council of Trent to "separated brethren" after Vatican II to "other Christians" or even "fellow Christians" since the mid-1990s.

A similar collaborative spirit appears in the documents of such major world conferences of Evangelicals as the Lausanne Covenant of 1974, the Thailand Statement of 1980, and the Manila Manifesto of 1989.[14]

Heretofore, the evangelical colleges have moved more deliberately in their ecumenical overtures than have the Catholic colleges. The separatist fundamentalist heritage of the early twentieth century still creates a wariness. Yet there is progress. In this mixed record, Wheaton College is perhaps representative of evangelical higher education. The same Wheaton which produced the progressive Billy Graham and Mark Noll, and which, since literary scholar Clyde Kilby, has celebrated both Catholic and Anglican literary scholars in its renowned Wade Center, is also the Wheaton that dismissed young medieval philosopher, Joshua Hochschild after he converted from Episcopalianism to Catholicism in 2004. By contrast, some evangelical colleges are more open to the selective hiring of Catholic scholars; for example, Messiah (PA) employs a dozen Catholics among its 170 faculty and, as mentioned earlier, the large majority of the CCCU faculty would not automatically disfavor hiring a compatible Catholic scholar.

What makes the Hochschild dismissal so problematic is that if an evangelical college was to have a Catholic faculty member at all, Hochschild is a good fit both in terms of personality and scholarship with his knowledge of the best thought in the pre-1500 Christian era. Furthermore, President Duane Litfin, the point person in the dismissal, is broader in instinct and preference than in action, for he has declared that he would enjoy teaching in an evangelically ecumenical college with all Christian groups represented.

Even if Wheaton continued its policy of not hiring evangelical Catholics or evangelical Orthodox believers, it would have given a strong witness in support of Christian community had it chosen to retain one of its own disciples of Christ. The spirit of the 1993 Religious Freedom Restoration Act which Wheaton and others have invoked in their contemporary debate with the federal Department of Health and Human Services calls for the government to allow the religious groups widest possible latitude in their exercise of religious freedom. Should not a Christian college adopt a similarly broad posture with its internal personal practices? An exemplary spirit of Christian community is no less important than a faithful commitment to Christian orthodoxy.[15]

What is needed on the issue of ecumenical relationships is what is also needed in the additional contemporary issues to be considered in Section III of this book, namely continuing reflection and dialogue to learn how best to balance purity and unity in the Christian fellowship, balance process and product in decision-making, and give primary focus to the central mission as opposed to secondary concerns.

SECTION III

Testing the Limits: Recent Case Studies in Christian Higher Education

O f the three sections of this book, this third and last one is the most specific, the most controversial, and the most contemporary. It discusses how the Christian colleges have sought to apply their ideas about academic freedom and the Christian worldview to some of the most significant of their recent intellectual debates. Some of these case studies involve subjects that long have been sources of intense controversy in higher education (e.g., evolution and theological precision). Others focus on subjects of more recent intensity (e.g., sexual and gender identity and government restrictions). The section and the book end with a consideration of one of the most important factors in academic discourse, namely that of fairness and generosity of spirit.

CHAPTER 20

The Origins Debate (I)

If Section I of this book focused on philosophy and Section II emphasized history, this section examines current events. More specifically, this
section examines recent case studies in some of the more controversial
areas where academic freedom of one party, usually a faculty member, conflicts with the vested interests of another party, most often a college, a church,
or the government.

One of the oldest and most continuous controversies in the history
of Christian higher education in America is that of Darwinian biological
thought. When I examine the long history of the various theories of origins
and the passions exerted by many of their various holders in higher education
and society in general, I wonder whether the conclusion that a given person
reaches is as important as the process that one uses to reach that conclusion.
Surely the greatest qualities to be employed in the search for truth in this
area include humility, honesty, openness, freedom to dissent from one's peers,
extending that same freedom to others, and holding a spirit of tentativeness
toward one's best understanding to date. Those who search from a base in
most or all of these qualities still reach a broad range of conclusions. By contrast, narrowness in the search appears in various forms including (1) the
evolutionist who combines a worldview of naturalism or scientism with the
pure scientific method to reach a conclusion that he still calls pure science and
(2) the Christian who is too certain that she knows exactly how God created
the world and is intolerant of those who reach other conclusions.

During the first generation following the publication of Darwin's *Origin
of Species* (1859) and *The Descent of Man* (1871) the reaction among the
college scientists and other scholars was mixed. Swiss-born Harvard zoolo-
gist Louis Agassiz, arguably the most renowned scientist in America at that
time, rejected Darwinism ("common character by no means proves common descent") even while his botanist Harvard colleague Asa Gray, the

first American Darwinist, argued that the new theory was compatible with Christianity. By 1880 when a New York journalist asked the presidents of Yale, Rochester, Princeton, Lafayette, Amherst, Union, Williams, Brown, and Hamilton whether they allowed the teaching of the descent of man from the animals, they each said that they did not. Within a decade, however, President James McCosh of Princeton was seeking to reconcile his evangelical Protestantism with Darwinism by declaring that "we are to look on evolution simply as the method by which God works....I am not prepared to prove that evolution is the best way that God could have proceeded....All that I propose to do is to show that the method is not unworthy of God."[1]

In this nineteenth-century period, American higher education was still largely Christian in orientation and the scientists were still mostly evangelical in faith. So looming large for the scientists was the question of how much of Darwinism is reconcilable with biblical faith. Arnold Henry Guyot of Princeton and Canadian John William Dawson of McGill (QC) were cautious and skeptical, while Princeton theologian Charles Hodge was more clearly in opposition. Prominent geologists James Dana of Yale and George Wright of Oberlin worked together with Gray to design a Christian form of Darwinism. Congregationalist Wright, Methodist Alexander Winchell (Michigan and Vanderbilt geologist), and Presbyterian George Macloskie (Princeton biologist) sought to help their respective denominations understand how evolution could blend with traditional biblical understanding.[2]

Modern evangelicals will find it surprising, even startling, to note that early fundamentalists James Orr and B. B. Warfield embraced a form of evolution. Orr, a widely known Scottish apologist, favored a Christian—not a Darwinian—version of evolution. " 'Evolution,' in short," he argued, "is coming to be recognized as but a new name for 'creation,' only that the creative power now works from *within*, instead of as in the old conception, in an *external*, plastic fashion." For Orr, as for all evangelical evolutionists, divine design and oversight was an essential part of their explanation. Then there was Warfield, the last of the major Calvinist defenders at Princeton. Historians David N. Livingstone and Mark A. Noll note that "one of the best-kept secrets in American intellectual, history," is that "B. B. Warfield, the ablest defender of the theologically conservative doctrine of the inerrancy of the Bible, was also an evolutionist." Orr, Warfield, and the aforementioned George Wright all contributed essays to *The Fundamentals*, 1910–1915, which publication is generally recognized as the beginning of the early twentieth-century Fundamentalist Movement.[3]

The evolution debate coincided with other forces in what might be called the Intellectual Revolution of the late nineteenth and early twentieth centuries. These other forces included higher criticism in biblical interpretation, a de-emphasis upon the supernatural elements in theology, a growing naturalism in the humanities and social sciences, and scientism in the sciences. The resultant growing secularism produced, by World War I, an academic environment that increasingly embraced an evolutionary thought system that divorced itself from questions of design. As historian of science Edward Davis noted, "most Protestant scientists and clergy who accepted evolution at that time coupled their high view of science with a low view of orthodox Christian theology, rejecting the Incarnation, the virgin birth, the bodily Resurrection of Jesus, and even in some cases, the idea of a transcendent God." Plus the evangelicals were starting to lose control of the mainline denominations and their major colleges and universities. They were frustrated, angry, and ready to join a movement that could give voice to their frustration and anger. This was the occasion for the launching by long-time reformer William Jennings Bryan of what became his last cause, the crusade against evolution.[4]

Bryan was known as the Great Commoner because of his long career as a popular reformer in liberal causes for farmers, laborers, and women. A journalist, congressman, secretary of state, and three-time presidential nominee of the Democratic Party, he was especially known for his dramatic speaking skills ("the silver-tongued orator") which he employed before countless audiences. So how did his identification with economic and social justice for the common classes relate to his opposition to Darwinian biology? The Darwinian emphasis on the survival of the fittest and its application to society—"social Darwinism"—seemed to him another attack on the rights and dignity of common folk. Together with Nietzschean superman philosophy, it seemed to justify the militaristic spirit in Germany and elsewhere which led to World War I. If Nietzsche was Bryan's anti-hero, Russian novelist Leo Tolstoy, with his emphasis upon the common people, peace, and Christian hope, was his hero.

Bryan's grand entry into the anti-evolution crusade was his 1921 delivery of the James Sprout Lectures at Union Theological Seminary in Richmond, Virginia. The printed version of these lectures sold over 100,000 copies. Here he expressed his concern that "students . . . learned that humans were nothing but animals and that animals that survived only through violence and hatred had little reason to care for the 'weak and helpless' among them." Bryan was concerned about the growth of macroevolution in the churches as well as the colleges, and he decided to run for the top position in his denomination to counter this effect. A long-time Presbyterian elder, he now challenged Wooster (OH) President Charles Wishart, an aggressive promoter of the teaching of evolution, in the race for moderator of the General Assembly of the Presbyterian Church in the United States. Bryan lost by a vote of 451–427. He also lost in an effort to stop denominational funds from going to Presbyterian colleges which taught Darwinism.

Ideologically, Bryan was a moderate in his anti-Darwinism. He accepted the geological record, an old earth, and the possibility of evolution in the animal domain (micro-evolution). But he strongly opposed the materialism implicit in the Darwinian scheme and the idea of the descent of man. In his fight against evolution, Bryan is best known for his effort to support state laws against the teaching of evolution in the public schools (e.g., the Scopes Trial). For one who had crusaded for Populist Movement legislation to protect farmers and Progressive Era Reforms to promote democracy, it was natural to seek the protection of legislation in his latest reform effort.[5]

The mid-twentieth century witnessed the emergence of two lines of thought in the evolution discussions in the Christian colleges. The dominant line among scientists was associated with the founding (1941) and development of the American Scientific Affiliation (ASA), the first of many faith and learning organizations of orthodox Christians who identified with a specific academic discipline. The smaller and more narrowly focused line associated with a theory of origins that emphasized a young human race, flood geology, and sometimes a young earth. The ASA reflected an evangelical ecumenism that in science and other respects wished to break with what it saw as the unnecessarily withdrawn posture of Fundamentalism.

The Flood Geology Movement dates to Seventh Day Adventist (SDA) teacher George McCready Price who in *The New Geology* (1923) and other writings argued for a seven 24-hour days interpretation of the creation story[6] and a worldwide Noahic flood that caused the upheavals in the geological record. The Price cosmological history received little attention outside SDA circles until it was repackaged at midcentury by disaffected ASA member, Henry Morris, a Virginia Polytechnic Institute engineer, and theologian John C. Whitcomb Jr. of Grace Theological Seminary (IN). They combined efforts to revise Whitcomb's doctoral dissertation as *The Genesis Flood* (1961), which became the Bible of the flood geology movement. The success of the book and the resultant Institute for Creation Research and related organizations is not measured in how many Christian college scientists they converted (the number was small) but in how much influence they had in conservative Protestant churches. Key in this success has been their public relations coup in co-opting the term "creationism" as a synonym for the young human race, flood geology version of creationism. Many equate creationism with Whitcomb–Morris thought like many equate evolution with Darwinian thought. Lack of precision in definitions and understanding continues to be a major barrier in the evolution discussion.

The ASA today is an umbrella organization, more cerebral than visceral, that seeks to unite the various strains of Christian scholars in the science-related disciplines into a forum for informed discussion on issues of common concern. One of these major concerns, of course, is the issue of origins. The ASA website identifies

> two things which unite the members: 1) belief in orthodox Christianity as defined by the Apostle's and Nicene creeds, and 2) a commitment to mainstream science, that is, any subject on which there is clear scientific consensus....The ASA is not an advocacy organization. Where there is honest disagreement on an aspect of science and Christian faith, or the relationship between the two, the ASA strives to create a safe environment in which dialogue can flourish, and diverse, even contrasting, ideas can be discussed with courtesy and respect.

In many respects the ASA, and similar faith and learning organizations in other disciplines, practice the spirit of academic freedom better than do the Christian colleges with their desire to not offend donors, denominations, and families of current and prospective students.[7]

The modern Christian college scientists hold a range of views on the evolution issue ranging from theistic evolution (TE) to young-earth flood geology. Perhaps 10 percent would hold to a young earth creation (YEC) position. The others divide between old earth creationism (OEC) and TE— also known as evolutionary creationism (EC)—with historically more on the OEC side but the momentum moving toward TE. Young earth creationism is the strongest in the colleges which more or less identify with the Fundamentalism Movement or the SDA church. These include Liberty (VA), Bob Jones (SC), Pensacola (FL), Cedarville (OH), Grace (IN), San Diego Christian, Master's (CA), Bryan (TN), Andrews (MI), La Sierra (CA), and Patrick Henry (VA). OEC is more common in the CCCU colleges. On most academic issues in most colleges the students are more conservative than are the faculty; this generalization applies specifically to the origins issue in the CCCU schools. A 2012 CCCU survey by Abilene Christian (TX) scholars Samuel Joeckel and Thomas Chesnes, although employing general terminology, still pointed to a clear faculty/student divide. On the statement "The theory of evolution is compatible with Christianity," the faculty showed 54 percent support and 35 percent disagreement while the students by contrast disagreed with the statement by a margin of 67 to 23.[8]

Amidst the range of creationist views, there exists one strongly held common position, namely a dissent from any form of evolution that denies the possibility that a divine hand could have controlled the coming into existence of the cosmos and all that it contains including especially human life.

For example, legal scholar Philip E. Johnson (California Berkeley) in his hard-hitting book, *Darwin on Trial*, declares:

> The philosophically important part of the Darwinian theory—its mechanism for creating complex things that did not exist before—is therefore not really part of empirical science at all, but rather a deduction from naturalistic philosophy. In brief, what makes me a "critic of evolution" is that I distinguish between naturalistic philosophy and empirical science, and oppose the former when it comes cloaked in the authority of the latter.

Less aggressive but no less incisive is the critique of philosopher Alvin Plantinga in his work with a telling title, *Where the Conflict Really Lies: Science, Religion, and Naturalism*. In his introduction to the book, Plantinga explains his theories:

> My overall claim in this book: *there is superficial conflict but deep concord between science and theistic religion, but superficial concord and deep conflict between science and naturalism.*
>
> Naturalism is what we could call a worldview, a sort of total way of looking at ourselves and our world. It isn't clearly a religion: the term "religion" is vague, and naturalism falls into the vague area of its application. Still, naturalism plays many of the same roles as a religion. In particular, it gives answers to the great human questions: Is there such a person as God? How should we live? Can we look forward to life after death? What is our place in the universe? How are we related to other creatures? Naturalism gives answers here: there is no God, and it makes no sense to hope for life after death. As to our place in the grand scheme of things, we human beings are just another animal with a peculiar way of making a living. Naturalism isn't clearly a religion; but since it plays some of the same roles as a religion we could properly call it a *quasi*-religion.
>
> If my thesis is right, therefore—if there is deep concord between science and Christian or theistic belief, but deep conflict between science and naturalism— then there is a science/religion (or science/quasi-religion) conflict, all right, but it isn't between science and theistic religion: it's between science and *naturalism.*[9]

At some point in this general narrative, we must pause to examine the specific record of origins study at Wheaton College because of the school's long history of having a geology curriculum and because the institution emerged in the 1920s as a pacesetter among the Christian colleges that survived the secular revolution in higher education with their earlier religious mission essentially intact.

The first president of Wheaton, Jonathan Blanchard, had enjoyed his study of science as an undergraduate at Middlebury (VT) and determined to develop a notable science curriculum at Wheaton. He traveled to the East to consult with such leading scientists as Louis Agassiz of Harvard, Benjamin Silliman of Yale, and Edward Hitchcock of Amherst. They recommended that Blanchard hire George F. Barker, a recent graduate of the Yale Scientific School and an employee of Harvard Medical School. So Barker became a professor of geology and natural science at Wheaton.

An early student in Wheaton's predecessor institution, Illinois Institute, was John Wesley Powell who contributed to Wheaton's geological collection some of the specimens that he gathered from the West. Powell, who lost an arm in the Civil War, later gained fame as leader of the first known passage through the Grand Canyon, second director of the U.S. Geological Survey, and director of the Bureau of Ethnology at the Smithsonian Institution.

Science at Wheaton over the years has accepted the standard old earth dating of the geological discipline, thus placing it at odds with Price, Whitcomb, Morris, and the other young earth advocates. The second Wheaton president, Charles Blanchard, was an active crusader against macroevolution, and after the Scopes Trial and the death of anti-evolution crusader, William Jennings Bryan, Blanchard wanted to raise $25 million to create a comprehensive university named for Bryan. But Blanchard soon died, and others opened Bryan College in the Tennessee town of the Scopes Trial.

At mid-century, Wheaton biologists Russell L. Mixter and J. Frank Cassel helped to lead the ASA away from an anti-evolution posture and more toward an open acceptance of parts of the biological evolutionary hypothesis. These mid-century developments in science coincided with a parallel movement in theology where, led by Wheaton graduates Carl F. H. Henry and Billy Graham, the more progressive elements in the Fundamentalism movement were moving toward a new identity as evangelicals or neo-evangelicals to reestablish a connection with the nineteenth-century evangelicals who, with their more open attitude toward science, had been the majority faith in the country.

The most significant recent development in the origins debate at Wheaton has involved neither science nor evolution directly but biblical interpretation and ancient history. In 2009, theologian John H. Walton published his then revolutionary and compelling work *The Lost World of Genesis One: Ancient Cosmology and the Origins Debate*. Walton's thesis was that Genesis, chapter 1, needs to be interpreted not as modern science but as ancient literature. For him, a "literal interpretation" of early Genesis means finding what it meant to its original audience. He explains that the recent "decipherment of ancient languages and the recovery of their texts . . . opened . . . an understanding of an ancient worldview that provides the backdrop of the biblical world." *Genesis One*, therefore, is not an account of material origins but of functional origins—the creation of the cosmos as a temple where God abides amidst his creation. Consequently "there is no reason to believe that biological evolution teaches something contradictory to the Bible (though some evolutionists are proponents of metaphysical conclusions that contradict the Bible)." It will be very interesting to observe the degree to which the evangelical scholarly and popular worlds accept the Walton interpretation.[10]

Over the years, the origins debates have caused significant internal conflict at Wheaton. In the late 1930s, chemist/geologist L. Allen Higley, a gap theory (a gap of time existed between two distant creations in a period after Genesis 1:1 and before Genesis 1:2) proponent accused President and theologian J. Oliver Buswell, a day-age (the "days" of creation each represent long eons of time) proponent, of advocating "the very foundation of evolution and modernism," and of seeking to "make a Modernistic College of Wheaton." Higley left the college in disgrace the next year and Buswell was gone the following year. In the late 1950s Mixter and Buswell's son, anthropologist James Oliver Buswell III, accepted enough of the Darwin system (thus approaching EC) to place their jobs in jeopardy.

Then there was the recent case of the tenure track anthropologist Alex Bolyanatz who thought it would be a helpful proactive move to invite new provost Stanton Jones to visit his class to observe his efforts to integrate origins views and science. Months after the six visits and despite previous favorable reviews and the support of his department and the college Faculty Personnel Committee, Jones issued the general statement to Bolyanatz that "during your term at Wheaton College, you have failed to develop the necessary basic competence in the integration of faith and learning, particularly in the classroom setting." A *Chicago Tribune* reporter noted that "Although he suspects that his lectures about evolution in his anthropology class may have played a role in his dismissal, Bolyanatz says he never received a straight answer from Wheaton officials as to why he was fired." Perhaps the Bolyanatz decision was influenced by the general orientation of the trustees who hired as president seven years earlier the conservative Duane Litfin who, in one of his first acts as president, announced that Wheaton's Statement of Faith was too imprecise and that he was going to ask the scientists to sign a statement assuring that they "reject the idea that Adam and Eve were created from pre-existing human-like creatures or hominids." The current Wheaton statement reads, "We believe that God directly created Adam and Eve, the historical parents of the entire human race."[11]

The next chapter will continue the discussion of the origins issue by returning from the Wheaton case study to examine the major new controversies of the late twentieth and early twenty-first centuries.

CHAPTER 21

The Origins Debate (II)

The two major recent origins issues have been (1) the emergence of a controversial movement known as Intelligent Design (ID) and (2) the completion of the historic Human Genome Project directed by Francis Collins and his subsequent founding of the influential BioLogos organization.

ID is largely an aggressive form of old earth creationism that is more calmly and forthrightly advanced by such organizations as Hugh Ross's Reasons to Believe. The approach of ID is more "attack dog" than "come let us reason together." Its strength is its ability to expose the subjectivity of those secular-oriented Darwinists (e.g., Richard Dawkins) who mix science and the worldview of materialism indiscriminately and proclaim that the result is pure science. ID founder and lawyer Philip E. Johnson (introduced in the previous chapter), in prosecuting attorney-like fashion, is especially skilled at this tactic. The result is that some of the secularists, sensing their vulnerability, strike back in anger, and in the process they often expose some of the vulnerabilities of the ID movement.

The ID movement also strongly criticizes some of its fellow creationists, including young earth groups like the Institute for Creation Research and Answers in Genesis on the right and theistic evolutionist/evolutionary creationist groups on the left. The latter it considers "accommodationalist." In turn, young earth groups view ID as not sufficiently Christian in proclamation, nonbelieving Darwinists see it as too religious, and many critics, religious and nonreligious, are suspicious of its claims that the evidence for an intelligence behind creation is scientific evidence as well as religious evidence. Among the latter doubters was Judge John E. Jones who in the classic *Kitzmiller v. Dover* case (2005) ruled that the ID movement was a form of creationism and thus religion rather than science. The scientists in the Christian colleges are mixed in their assessment of ID.[1]

A major question in the ID debates is this: can, and if so how, may science and faith be related? Many of the Christian colleges emphasize the importance of seeking to integrate faith and learning. Does this apply to science where there is a strong emphasis upon the separation of scientific discovery and religious inquiry? Perhaps the best resolution lies in a Kierkegaardian process of seeking first to get the facts as accurate as possible and then, because few find that sufficiently satisfactory by itself, look to the metaphysical realm to try to find an explanation for the hard data. Kierkegaard calls this an intelligent as possible leap into the dark.

ID is more of an academic freedom issue for the secular institutions than for the Christian colleges; however, a major controversy over ID did develop at Baylor at the turn of the century. Baylor President Robert Sloan, largely on his own, established the Michael Polanyi Center with ID scholar William Dembski as director in 1999. It was the first ID study center in a research university. But it was to be short-lived. Apart from the controversies surrounding ID itself, the Baylor scientists were offended by their lack of involvement in the decision to establish the center. Under pressure Sloan removed Dembski as director in 2000 and downgraded the center to a program under the Baylor Institute for Faith and Learning. Granted the vulnerabilities of ID, nevertheless, one is amazed at the degree of passion and overreaction displayed by not an insignificant number of scientists, both Christian and secular, against ID.

Sloan thought the objecting Baylor scientists were more concerned about political correctness than about academic freedom. Then when eight Baylor scientists sent a long letter to Congressman Mark Souder (IN), an Education Committee member who had been a co-sponsor of a 2000 Baylor ID Conference, advising him how he had been duped by ID proponents, he responded by making a presentation to the House of Representatives, reading and then giving his interpretation of the letter:

> One senses here not a defense of science but rather an effort to protect, by political means, a privileged philosophical viewpoint against a serious challenge....As the Congress, it might be wise for us to question whether the legitimate authority of science over scientific matters is being misused by persons who wish to identify science with a philosophy they prefer.[2]

The most significant recent development in the evolution debate is the chain of events beginning with the release of the findings of the Human Genome Project, the desire of its Christian director, Francis Collins, to found the BioLogos Foundation, and the impact of these two developments on the Christian colleges and others.

When the preliminary results of the Human Genome Project were released in 2000, President Bill Clinton, with Francis Collins by his side, announced

"Without a doubt, this is the most important, most wondrous map ever produced by humankind.... Today we are learning the language in which God created life." Collins' description of the implication of the project's findings for the origins debate included the statement that "the study of genomes leads inexorably to the conclusion that we humans share a common ancestor with other living things." Then he added:

> At this point, godless materialists might be cheering. If humans evolved strictly by mutation and natural selection, who needs God to explain us? To this, I reply: I do. The comparison of chimp and human sequences, interesting as it is, does not tell us what it means to be human. In my view, DNA sequence alone, even if accompanied by a vast trove of data on biological function, will never explain certain special human attributes, such as the knowledge of the Moral Law and the universal search for God.

This human discovery, Collins concluded, "merely shows us something of how [God] operates." The final Human Genome report came in 2003, Collins's classic book *The Language of God* appeared in 2006, Collins founded the BioLogos Foundation in 2007, and in 2009 President Barak Obama appointed Collins as director of the National Institutes of Health, the country's medical research agency.

BioLogos is an advocacy organization for the compatibility of science with faith in general and evolutionary creationism in particular. Among Christian college scientists, the latter is a growing position. The recent leaders of BioLogos have included Deborah Haarsma, astrophysicist formerly of Calvin; Jeff Schloss, ecologist of Westmont; Edward B. Davis, historian of science, Messiah; Darrel Falk, biologist emeritus at Point Loma Nazarene; and R. Judson Carlberg, president emeritus at Gordon. Among the Advisory Council members are John Walton of Wheaton; Amos Young of Regent (VA); Randy Isaac, director of the American Scientific Affiliation; Andy Crouch, executive editor of *Christianity Today*; and Denis Alexander, emeritus director of the Faraday Institute for Science and Religion at Cambridge.[3]

The response to the Genome Project findings, Collins's book, and his advocacy organization is marked, varied, and has led to much reassessment and even strong conflict and academic freedom battles. If one wishes to observe a larger context historically for Christian college scholars coming under fire for more or less articulating evolutionary positions, the list is long, including Alexander Winchell of Vanderbilt in the 1870s, William Poteat of Wake Forest in the 1920s, and Grove Samuel Dow of Baylor also in the 1920s.

In the current era following the release of the Human Genome findings, Calvin chemist Arie Leegwater, when editor of the ASA journal *Perspectives in Science and Christian Faith*, asked two Calvin theologians, Daniel C. Harlow and John R. Schneider, to contribute articles to the September 2010 issue of the journal which focused on the meaning of the genome findings. Harlow wrote that the human race could not be traced back to only a single pair, Adam and Eve, and that Genesis 1–3 is not a factual account but a symbolic literary one. Schneider added that recent genomic evidence strongly supports the theory of common ancestry. Coming in the wake of the 1980s Calvin controversy when Howard J. Van Till wrote his *The Fourth Day*, which attempted to harmonize scientific and biblical accounts, conservative elements in the sponsoring CRC protested vigorously. The result was that Schneider agreed to leave the college, an unhappy Harlow continued, and the science faculty in general was unnerved. The current Calvin Geology Department website states forthrightly: "We teach evolutionary theory as the best scientific explanation for the dynamic diversity of life on Earth....We believe that God brings forth the creation through evolutionary means."[4]

A different response to the genome findings and the position of Collins' BioLogos organization occurred at Bryan College in Dayton, Tennessee, where college namesake William Jennings Bryan had led the prosecution in the famous Scopes Evolution Trial of 1925. Bryan biologist Brian Eisenback and Bible scholar Ken Turner received a grant from BioLogos to create a curriculum "that explores a range of Christian positions on origins." In February 2014, the college invited the Colossian Forum, a science/religion dialogue organization, to present a public discussion between former BioLogos president Darrel Falk and young earth creationist Todd Wood.

At the end of the discussion, Bryan president Stephen Livesay said he wanted to make a statement about the college's position and how he disagreed with the BioLogos view. Negative reaction to the president's comments resulted, and the Bryan trustee board moved to offer a new working "clarification" of the traditional Bryan statement of faith provision on creation despite the fact that the Bryan charter declares that the Statement of Belief may not be changed. This new clarification/amendment reads: "We believe that all humanity is descended from Adam and Eve. They are historical persons created by God in a special formative act, and not from previously existing life forms." The result of the Livesay intervention and board action was widespread faculty and student protest. The faculty had to decide whether to sign their new contracts with the new statement of faith stipulation, and they responded by approving a 30–2 vote (6 abstentions) of no confidence against Livesay who nevertheless retained the support of the board.[5]

The Olivet (IL) case involving biologist Rick Colling is significant in part because the Nazarene college is a part of the Wesleyan Holiness tradition that emphasizes Christian experience more than theological precision. Colling supports the BioLogos interpretation of the Human Genome Project:

This letter-by-letter document reveals humanity's present and past genetic connections with all other life with levels of precision never before imagined. This is not your mother or father's gap-laden fossil record. Rather it is an exquisitely-defined map of our entire evolutionary history! So, in the midst of such a documented record of evolution, how do we Christian educators in the sciences help people recognize that their fear of evolution is unnecessary?

Colling and a fellow Nazarene educator Darrel Falk of Point Loma (CA) and BioLogos—like Paul Little of InterVarsity a half century ago—emphasized the central importance in the evolution debates on the personal faith and religious consequences for the students. For example note this moving story which Colling tells of his not isolated experience with one of his students:

> Michael (not his real name) looked across my office desk, discouraged and visibly shaken. As if I were his last spiritual lifeline, his eyes, filled with confusion, pleaded with me to reassure him that what he was learning in his biology classes about evolution was not really true.
>
> All of his life he was told that evolution was a "lie of Satan," starkly incompatible with Scripture and the Christian faith. The passionate anti-evolution teachers during Michael's formative years were the people he loved and trusted most: his parents and pastors.
>
> My heart ached as he related his story. Both his parents and pastors had recently informed him that if he accepted evolution, he could neither be a Christian nor a part of the church fellowship.
>
> Michael was an inquisitive and bright college student. He simply could not comprehend why acceptance within his faith community required him to check his God-given intellect at the door of the church.
>
> We talked for a long while that afternoon and several times during the semester. I prayed with him, each time encouraging him to hold fast to his faith—explaining that many Christians, including myself, saw no conflict with evolution and the Christian faith. Nevertheless, at the end of the term, Michael transferred to a nearby state university. The last I inquired, he had apparently abandoned the Christian faith altogether.

After teaching biology at Olivet for 28 years, Colling came under fire in 2004 when he published *Random Design* in which he argued that one could believe in both God and evolution. No choice was necessary. At first, the Olivet officials defended him from denominational critics, but then, under increasing pressure, they barred him from teaching the general biology course and anyone at Olivet from teaching from his book. The college dropped these limits after the AAUP ruled that Colling's rights were violated. In 2009 he resigned in an agreement with the college.[6]

The more conservative denominations and origins organizations generally have not altered their thinking since the genome report, although some of their college scientists have done so. The SDA church, where the current twentieth-century, young-earth, flood-geology movement began, notes in its current statement on creation that "we believe that the biblical events recorded in Genesis 1–11, including the special creation of human beings, are historical and recent, that the seven days of creation were literal 24-hour days forming a literal week, and that the Flood was global in nature." When SDA college La Sierra (CA) biologist Lee Greer and three trustees sought to reconcile the long-standing controversy over creation and evolution, which threatened the institution's regional accreditation, they were dismissed, presumably over a procedural issue. More positively, the SDA denomination for nearly half a century has sponsored the Geoscience Research Institute (GRI) at Loma Linda (CA) to seriously study the SDA differences with establishment science. Although "Progressive Adventism" is a significant voice in the denomination, the GRI has failed, so far, to find a position that is broadly acceptable to the majority of both Adventist church officials and Adventist scientists. GRI molecular biologist Tim Standish, an Australian, reports that the genome findings "have not been a game-changing thing alone" in the SDA. Similarly, Nathaniel Jeanson and Brian Thomas of the ICR team in their review of the "ENCODE" project phase of the study of the Genome Project observe that "genome science continues to clearly confirm creation."

Also Southern Baptist seminarian Kenneth Keathley at Southeastern, Wake Forest (NC), reports in a 2012 BioLogos interview that "most . . . Southern Baptists hold to young-earth creationism (YEC). Among the faculty of over six seminaries, one would find a mix of YEC proponents and OEC (old-earth creationism) adherents . . . I am not aware of any SBC seminary faculty who advocate theistic evolution or evolutionary creationism (EC)."[7]

So how might we best live together in harmony amidst our differences on the origins issue and other controversies? Certainly one way is to continually emphasize the limitations of even our best insights, realizing with the Apostle Paul that we all "see in a mirror dimly." Another way is to avoid too easily accepting the doctrine of scientific objectivity. In history, including the history of science, most contemporary scholars, while endorsing the goal of objective inquiry, reject the idea that it is fully realizable in practice.

The twentieth-century Hungarian polymath Michael Polanyi argued compellingly that all knowledge is personal; thus, he proclaimed that "I start by rejecting the ideal of scientific detachment." His interpreter, chemist Walter

Thorson of the University of Alberta, developed this idea as follows: "Scientific inquiry and scientific knowing are obviously concerned with what we should call 'an objective external reality,' or so at least our culture believes today; we [do well to] remind ourselves that such an assumption was not so obvious in earlier ages, and that it may not be so obvious in the future." In other words, the individual scholar seeking to be as objective as possible and enlisting the aid of the spirit of God in his inquiries may well reach better overall personal understanding than the scholar who unduly relies on what at any given time is the consensus of the scholarly community. Of course she will want to allow such independence of thought to other scholars as well.[8]

CHAPTER 22

Sexual and Gender Identity (I)

F ew social issues have so occupied the public consciousness in general in the twenty-first century as has the debate over same-sex marriage. Few social issues have so shaken the evangelical college community in particular in the second decade of the twenty-first century as the religious, economic, and political challenge of same-sex marriage.

The polling data of the Pew Forum on Religion and Public Life has carefully traced the change in public thinking on this issue. Whereas in 2001 Americans opposed same-sex marriage by 57 to 35 percent, only a decade later, in 2013, they supported the idea 50 to 43 percent. Even more significant was the fact that two-thirds of the young people—the wave of the future—favored same-sex marriage. Also of note is the finding that by religion categories the unaffiliated were most supportive (up from 61 to 74 percent over the decade) while the white evangelical Protestants showed the least approval (up from 13 to 23 percent). Still the increase of evangelical support by over 75 percent during the decade is remarkable and parallels the evolving conversation on the Christian college campuses.[1]

The 2011 comprehensive Baylor Religion Study, funded by the National Science Foundation and the John M. Templeton Foundation and using polling data supplied by the Gallup Organization, produced results showing somewhat more support for same-sex marriage than did the Pew Forum data. The Baylor/Gallup results identified 53 percent overall agreeing with same-sex marriage. The support among those unaffiliated with religion was 88 percent while all religious groups showed less than 50 percent support. The figure for evangelical Protestants was 37 percent. By comparison, the support for civil unions showed all major religious categories at about the 50 percent level (59 percent for evangelicals). A more nuanced analysis of the Baylor data on evangelicals showed 41 percent as "gay rights opponents," 35 percent as "cultural progressives" (correlating closely with the 37 percent above who support same-sex unions), and 24 percent in the "messy middle" who support civil unions but not gay marriage.[2]

The difference between the Pew and the Baylor/Gallup data in accessing evangelical support for same-sex marriage (37 and 23 percent) is significant. A recent 2013 study by Richard Powell, a University of Maine political scientist, claims that polls may understate by 5–7 percent the extent of opposition to same-sex marriage. He bases his conclusions on his research comparing pre-election polling data with Election Day results when same-sex marriage measures were on the ballot.[3]

Governmental action since 2000, like popular opinion, shows a marked movement toward greater support for same-sex marriage. In 2003 Massachusetts became the first state to legalize same-sex marriage; by 2014 thirty-six states had done so. In 2012 President Obama announced his support for gay marriage. On a single day in 2013, the Supreme Court issued two major decisions. In *United States v. Windsor* it declared unconstitutional the Defense of Marriage Act (1996) which had blocked federal benefits including Social Security survivor benefits to gay couples who had been legally married in their states. Second in *Hollingsworth v. Perry* it chose to leave intact a lower court ruling to allow gay marriage to proceed in California. The effect on lower courts of the Windsor case has been swift and dramatic. Within 13 months the same-sex marriage forces won over two-dozen victories with no losses in the lower courts. Lawrence Tribe, a constitutional law scholar at Harvard, noted, "I can't think of any Supreme Court decision in history that has ever created so rapid and so broad a lower-court groundswell in a single direction as Windsor's."[4]

Meanwhile the American churches were debating, sometimes intensely, the gay marriage issue. The America Baptist Convention (ABC) experienced the secession of its Pacific Southwest Division in dissent from the denomination's reluctance to discipline congregations that welcomed gay members. The Baptist tradition of congregational autonomy called for such a hands-off approach, the ABC leaders explained. Other major denominations also have allowed for local decision-making—the Episcopalians by bishops, the Evangelical Lutheran Church in America (ELCA) by congregations, and the Presbyterians by ministers. By contrast the United Church of Christ (UCC) endorsed gay marriage from the top (the General Synod) even while not mandating that position to local congregations. Few evangelical denominations or congregations provide for same-sex marriage.[5]

Lesbians, gay men, bisexuals, and transgender adults (LGBT) tend to be wary of the organized church, thinking it is usually not friendly toward them. The 2013 Pew poll found that nearly half (48 percent) claim no religious affiliation, a much higher percentage than the 20 percent of the general population. LGBT people reporting that they attend church weekly is only 13 percent compared to the 37 percent of the general public. The percentages of LGBT viewing specific religious groups as being unfriendly toward them were as follows: Muslims 84 percent, Mormons 83 percent, Catholics 79 percent, Evangelicals 73 percent, Jews 47 percent, and nonevangelical Protestant churches 44 percent. The major Protestant denomination with policies and practices most accepting of the same-sex community is the UCC; its "open and affirming" statement welcomes "the full participation of LGBT people in the UCC's life and ministry."[6]

Of course, the LGBT community now has its own denomination. It was founded by former Pentecostal minister Troy Perry in southern California in 1968. The Metropolitan Community Church (MCC), as its name implies, is mostly an urban-based ministry. LGBT people appear in all major groups and when they "come out" they usually relocate to the larger cities where they can find greater acceptance and fellowship among the like-minded. Currently there are MCC members in every state, and churches in 39 of them plus Washington, DC. The 240 congregations operate in 40 countries, mostly in the Western Hemisphere. MCC holds observer status in the World Council of Churches. Inclusion is one of the major MCC points of emphasis. "Love is our greatest core value and resisting exclusion is a primary focus of our ministry. We want to continue to be the conduits of a faith where everyone is included in the family of God and where all parts of our being are welcomed at God's table."[7]

In 2013 *Inside Higher Education* published an exchange of "open letters" between a "still-in-the-closet" gay faculty member at a Christian college and a leader of a prominent Christian college. The letters illustrated how (1) the issue of homosexuality has become an open and prominent one on Christian campuses; (2) while students have become increasingly willing to "come out"—and alumni even more so—faculty are much less willing to do so for fear of losing their jobs, or at least their community credibility; (3) repression of a major part of one's identity is unhealthy, limiting one's ability to be whole; (4) many Christian colleges would accept as a faculty member a person of homosexual orientation, but few would accept as a faculty member a person who engages in homosexual practices; and (5) Stanton Jones, Wheaton chancellor, has emerged as a major spokesperson for what is still the standard for human sexuality upheld by most Christian college official policies on the subject, namely "sexual chastity if one is not in a monogamous, traditional marriage."[8]

Jones is a psychologist with a research specialty in homosexuality. His major ideas on the subject, some of which have been expressed with fellow researcher Mark A. Yarhouse of the Institute for the Study of Sexual Identity at Regent (VA), include the following:

1. The secular scholars in the social science establishment (e.g., the American Psychological Association) who proclaim that homosexuality is "normal," "positive," and "legitimate" are basing their conclusions upon extra-scientific conclusions rather than pure scientific data. It is regrettable when many in the general public, even including some Christians, accept their claims to be presenting scientific fact.

2. The best of the most recent scientific studies demonstrate that the percentage of homosexuals is lower than previously claimed—certainly less than 3 percent and maybe less than 2 percent of the population.

3. The argument of many religious and social conservatives that all homosexual people could change their orientation if they tried hard enough, and the claim of many religious and social liberals that sexual orientation for all is fixed at birth are both wrong. The best scientific evidence favors an "interactionist hypothesis" in which both genetic and environmental factors, in varying degree, best explain the cause of same-sex orientation.

4. The primary concern of the church is not with sexual orientation but with sexual practice. Human beings are free moral agents who can and do make choices. "Homosexual behavior violates God's revealed will."

5. "There were persons in the New Testament fellowship who were once participants in homosexual practice but who identified with such practices no longer" (1 Corinthians 6:9–11).

6. While it is often difficult, some homosexuals do change their orientation. Research from the generation after 1950 found positive results in about 30 percent of cases, but better and more recent studies would be helpful.

7. For the homosexuals who cannot change, the Christian standard is celibacy. It is not as if they are the only people who need to practice celibacy, for all heterosexuals need to live in chastity for part of their lives and some heterosexuals need to do so for all of their lives. " . . . the church can no more guarantee healing to homosexuals than it can guarantee marriage to disconsolate single heterosexuals."

8. " . . . given the historic consistency of the church's sexual ethic, the burden of proof is on those who want to change the church's historic position . . . . Those who want to change the church's position have failed to date to produce a compelling case."[9]

Among those in Christian higher education who wish to "produce a compelling case" for an alternate way of viewing the same-sex issue are two scholars at Hope (MI), and the related Western Theological Seminary. Psychologist David G. Myers and theologian James Brownson have produced books within the last decade supporting same-sex marriage. Earlier Myers, with Malcolm Jeeves, had written the psychology volume in the Christian College Coalition series of faith and learning integration books; it was entitled *Psychology through the Eyes of Faith* (1987). With independent scholar Letha Scanzoni, Myers in 2005 wrote *What God Has Joined Together? A Christian Case for Gay Marriage.* The specific ideas expressed by Myers in the latter book and elsewhere include the following:

1. The Bible in general has very little to say about homosexuality. In particular the recorded words of Jesus say nothing on the subject.
2. While Jesus had nothing to say about homosexuality, he had much to say "about people who were hurting and regarded as outcasts."
3. Nothing in Scripture addresses "naturally disposed same-sex orientation" nor "loving, committed homosexual relationships."
4. The limited biblical texts that talk about "same-sex acts" must be read in their context which condemns "idolatry, lust, promiscuity, and exploitation."
5. The scientific data is "pretty conclusive," especially for males, that same-sex orientation cannot be wished away.
6. "The world would be a happier and healthier place for all people if love, sex, and marriage went together . . . . The threat to the institution of marriage in western civilization is not gay marriage but heterosexual non-marriage . . . if implemented as part of a pro-marriage initiative, inviting gay couples to say 'I do' may help reverse the growing tendency for straight couples to say 'we don't.' "
7. When reflecting on the same-sex issue, modern Christians would do well to consider the counsel of Messiah and Eastern Mennonite theologian Reta Halteman Finger to concentrate on Romans 14 and 15 no less than Romans 1. The latter is the most difficult passage for those supporting same-sex marriage, whereas the former discusses how to deal with serious differences of opinion in the Christian community.

Following publication of the Myers–Scanzoni book, Hope declared that Myers spoke for himself and not the college. Five years later the college, under pressure from some alumni same-sex advocates, reconfirmed its position of "chastity among the unmarried and the sanctity of marriage between a man and a woman." In 2014 Brownson published his pro same-sex book, *Bible, Gender, Sexuality: Reframing the Church's Debate on Same-Sex Relationships* following years of study spurred by the homosexuality orientation announcement of his son.[10]

Significantly Jones of Wheaton, Myers of Hope, and Hope College as an institution, all three, declare the need for humility in declaring one's best understanding on this issue. Hope's declaration was "well-intentioned Christians may disagree on scriptural interpretation." Perhaps the same-sex debate in Christian higher education can rise to a more noble level with greater realization that on this issue like so many others there may not need to be an institutional winner and an institutional loser, but that both sides can simply agree to disagree. Isn't the Christian college at its best an open forum on the seeking together of the mind of God?

Now this chapter will transition from reviewing the recent intellectual history of the debate to examining the recent political insurgency of the pro-gay or "affirming" lobby in its challenge to the traditional position in Christian higher education. Especially in the second decade of the current century, (1) the gay students are starting to become open in declaring their orientation; (2) the gay alumni are becoming assertive in their encouragement of one another and the current same-sex students, and in their calls for institutional change; (3) the gay constituency is debating among themselves the merits of position A (same-sex marriage) versus position B (celibacy); (4) the colleges are discussing how to handle on-campus cases of "bullying," requests for on-campus organization and/or discussion sites, and the lobbying efforts of alumni groups and others; (5) the colleges are debating whether they should establish—or modify—an institutional position on same-sex marriage; and (6) the colleges are discussing how they might respond to a future government or accrediting association declaration that they not discriminate against people in same-sex marriages in their hiring and personnel practices.

A significant gap exists between the degree to which Christian college students accept gay marriage and the thinking of their parents and grandparents on the subject. As more youth of same-sex orientation announce their status, the issue for their friends increasingly becomes a personal one. Do I identify more with my pastor or parents or college which say that this issue is about being faithful to the Bible, or do I support my friend who is hurting. Surely empathy for the despised is a Christian virtue also, their thinking goes. So the question becomes is or is not the apparent dichotomy a real one? Or are there more options?

Stanton Jones acknowledges that there is a "growing lack of consensus on this issue." So far the orthodox Christian colleges have largely held the line, the critical mass Christian colleges somewhat less so. In 2012 the annual meeting of CCCU presidents featured a panel discussion on the controversial issue. The *Inside Higher Education* writer covering the meeting reported, "the presenters made one thing clear: American culture may have changed, but their institutions' interpretation of the Bible—which presents homosexuality as immoral—will not." Thus the presidents focused primarily on how to deal with pressures from some students, alumni lobbying groups, and external regulatory forces.[11]

One external advocacy group that helped to increase the conversation level on the Christian college campus is Soulforce, which since 2006 has visited many colleges. The goal of Soulforce, which began in 1998, is to "end the religious and political oppression of LGBTQ people" by following the aggressive but nonviolent tactics of Martin Luther King in the Civil Rights movement. The Soulforce subgroup "Equality Ride" specifically targeted Christian colleges with bus traveling teams and, more recently, from regional "equality ride houses." The organization states that by 2014 it had visited 101 colleges, contributed to 17 school policy changes, and helped to organize over 30 student and alumni groups. Still another Soulforce-related organization operated under the name Safety Net. It has operated a computer-based system linking local Christian college organizations and individuals with one another and desired resources. The Soulforce founder was Mel White, graduate of Warner Pacific (OR) and Fuller Seminary, former Fuller professor, and former writer for evangelical leaders such as Billy Graham, Pat Robertson, and Jerry Falwell. After struggling for decades with his sexual identity, he declared openly in 1991, divorced his understanding wife, Lyla, and married his gay partner. His frank autobiography is *Stranger at the Gate: To Be Gay and Christian in America* (1994). More recently he has written a devastating critique of the "gay bashing" tactics of many of his former colleagues, *Holy Terror: Lies the Christian Right Tells Us to Deny Equality*.[12]

Another organization that has helped to bring together the Christian college gay community is the Gay Christian Network. Founded in 2001 by Wake Forest graduate Justin Lee, it claims a membership of 20,000. It emphasizes its comprehensiveness within the gay Christian community, serving both those who support same-sex marriage (side A) and those who advocate celibacy for same-sex Christians (side B). Lee personally advocates celibacy before marriage and faithfulness within marriage: "Sex is powerful and deserves to be treated with reverence . . . . [It] has the power to form a sacred bond between people. And it's a bond I want to form with the guy I'm going to spend the rest of my life with, not just some cute guy who danced with me in a club one night." Lee travels widely to speak but is best known through his Internet blog, podcasts, YouTube videos, and online chatrooms. His book is *Torn: Rescuing the Gospel from the Gays-vs.-Christians Debate* (2013).[13]

One of the most significant developments in the coming-out movement is the growth since 2011 of individual campus, computer-based alumni groups, including OneWheaton, OneGeorgeFox, Biola Queer Underground, and BJUnity. Open letters of encouragement from alumni gay and gay supporters to current same-sex students reportedly collected approximately 750 signatures at OneWheaton and 400 signatures at OneGeorgeFox.

By 2014 dozens of Christian colleges were providing facilities and/or official recognition for their students who had an interest in discussing sexual and gender identity issues. For example, Seattle Pacific hosts a club called "Haven" with faculty advisor sociologist Kevin Neuhouser, and "Choros" (Greek for "open space") operates as a Taylor discussion organization with philosopher Kevin Diller as sponsor. A similar organization at Wheaton is called "Refuge." Also, by 2014 there appeared to be a declining number of expulsions for gay students in Christian colleges. A number of colleges invited celibate gay leaders to speak in chapel; these include theologian and Wheaton graduate Wesley Hill and Moody professor Christopher Yuan.[14]

Homosexuality has thus become a widely discussed phenomenon, emerging more openly at all or nearly all of the Christian colleges. The individual colleges have been responding to the issue in diverse ways. The next chapter will discuss some of these individual college stories.

CHAPTER 23

Sexual and Gender Identity (II)

The previous chapter discussed the overall record of the emergence of homosexuality as a prominent issue in Christian higher education. This chapter examines how the general pattern has developed at specific colleges.

Augustana (IL) and Sewanee (TN)

Augustana president Steve Bahls opened the college chapel to same-sex weddings in 2012 when two male students asked permission to hold their ceremony there. The college is affiliated with the Evangelical Lutheran Church in America which allows individual congregations to decide whether or not to perform same-sex unions. The college is not a congregation but it previously had adopted a nondiscrimination policy based on sexual preference. Prior to June 2014, when same-sex unions became legal in Illinois, a gay couple wanting to marry on campus could combine the chapel wedding with a civil ceremony across the river in Iowa. Bahls reported that the responses he received to his decision were positive by a ratio of 12:1.

Another college affiliated with a strongly divided denomination was Sewanee (TN), also known as the University of the South, an Episcopal institution. The denomination defers to its bishops to decide the gay marriage issue within each of its dioceses. So where did that leave Sewanee which was owned by 28 dioceses, governed by 28 bishops, and located in a state in which same-sex marriages were not legally valid? The 2012 solution was this: "Gay and lesbian couples who meet the other requirements for a Sewanee wedding will be able to have their union blessed in the college chapel, as long as their bishops are supportive."[1]

Azusa Pacific (CA), California Baptist, George Fox (OR), and Spring Arbor (MI)

Transgender sexual identity became a widely publicized issue at three West Coast colleges in 2013 and 2014. In the fall of the former year, 15-year theologian Heather Ann Clements of Azusa Pacific returned to campus as Heath Adam Ackley, a transgendered man. Ackley said he "was living in compliance with the schools' position on human sexuality and living chastely outside of marriage." The college promptly asked him to resign from his teaching duties but invited him to stay on contract for the rest of the year. Ackley believed that the college was less concerned about any theological implications of his case than about public relations reactions. He also stated that "his insurance was denied when he sought hormone treatment and 'top surgery' for his chest area." He has given birth to two children.

In 2014, a George Fox student, who was originally female and had transitioned to male, asked to live in male student housing. His request was denied on the basis that the college-supporting denomination, the Society of Friends, believes that people are male or female from birth. The federal Department of Education (DOE) agency administering Title IX funds granted a religious exemption to the college in its desire to provide private housing for the student, known as Jayce, instead of the regular group facilities. Subsequently, George Fox stated that it would house transgender people if they have undergone "gender reassignment" surgery. Jayce's lawyer in his case was Paul Southwick, the widely known George Fox graduate and gay activist, who co-founded OneGeorgeFox, produced the video series *On God's Campus: Voices from the Queer Underground*, and serves on the board of SafetyNet.

Also in 2014, a California judge ruled that California Baptist was within its religious freedom rights in dismissing Domaine Javier, a male-to-female transgender nursing student in 2011. Javier is a biological male who identifies as a woman and had applied to California Baptist as a woman. The university stated that they dismissed her because of fraud. The judge did rule for Javier on one count of five, however, because the university excluded her from university-controlled businesses that are open to the public including dining facilities, libraries, and online classes. Once again, the lawyer for the defendant was Paul Southwick.

Earlier than these three recent cases, Spring Arbor reached a settlement with a male-to-female administrator. John/Julie Nemecek, who had been with the college for 16 years, agreed in 2007 to termination conditions after a mediation hearing before the U.S. Equal Employment Opportunity Commission. Nemecek had been living as a woman since 2004, but chose to continue a marriage of 35 years.[2]

Baylor (TX)

Baylor became the focus of women's collegiate basketball when Britney Griner, a 6'8" all-American center and two-time Naismith winner, led its team to the 2012 national championship. She again became a center of attention when, after her senior season, she declared her lesbian identity even while noting that her coach Kim Mulkey had encouraged team members not to be open about their sexual identity so as to avoid unnecessary controversy when recruiting. In her 2014 memoir, *In My Skin*, she stated:

> The more I think about it, the more I feel like the people who run the school want it both ways: they want to keep the policy, so they can keep selling themselves as a Christian university, but they are more than happy to benefit from the success of their gay athletes. That is as long as those gay athletes don't talk about being gay.

Baylor's statement on sexual misconduct items has included "homosexual acts" although the university does permit the Sexual Identity Forum to meet in the student center.[3]

Belmont (TN)

The Belmont women's soccer coach, Lisa Howe, resigned and/or was released in 2010 after announcing to her team that she and her same-sex partner Wendy Holleman, the team's former assistant coach who was carrying their child, were going to become mothers. Within weeks the university added "sexual orientation" to its nondiscrimination statement. The university only recently had separated from the Tennessee Baptist state convention.[4]

Calvin (MI)

Calvin's recent involvement with gay-related issues has included a controversial theatrical production, a controversial trustee action, and an embarrassing national listing. In 2007, Calvin theater professor Stephanie Sandberg produced a play entitled *Seven Passages: The Stories of Gay Christians*, the text of which included only Bible quotations and interviews with self-described gay Christians, many of whom were raised in the Christian Reformed Church, Calvin's supporting denomination. The seven actors were from a Western Michigan acting troupe, and the production had its initial 2007 run in the Grand Rapids Actors Theatre. A year later, the troupe performed the play in London before many of the 650 Anglican bishops attending the once-in-a-decade Lambeth Conference. Also in 2008 the play was made into a film. The response to the play by the Calvin trustee board was to issue a 2009 memo to the Calvin faculty that "advocacy by faculty and staff, both in and out of the classroom, for homosexual practice and same-sex marriage is unacceptable." The response of the faculty to the trustee memo was to object to its arbitrary process; the Faculty Senate voted 36–4 to request the board to rescind the memo. "The board of trustees' action does not work with the way we usually do things at Calvin," declared Karin Maag, the vice chair of the Faculty Senate. "They should be in consultation with the faculty and staff."

Calvin alumnus Joel Meredith led a group of alumni, faculty, and students, who were dismayed by the college's regular appearance on the *Princeton Review* list of colleges "most unfriendly to LGBT students." Most of the institutions on the 2013 list are religious institutions, including Grove City, College of the Ozarks, Wheaton, Notre Dame, Brigham Young, Wake Forest, Calvin, Baylor, Catholic University, and Pepperdine. In 2012 Meredith launched a petition via the neutral website, change.org, to Calvin president Michael LeRoy calling for greater efforts to find ways to make Calvin more exemplary in its welcoming of a despised minority. Calvin's then vice president for student life, Shirley Hoogstra, noted that Calvin has made progress in recent years but could do much more. "Hospitality is a core Christian virtue," she noted, "and being on that list undercuts a Christian virtue that is important to us."[5]

Those who wish to provide the maximum acceptance of gays as people without accepting gay marriage may wish to note the Christian Reformed Church position as a plausible model:

> Homosexuality is a condition of disordered sexuality that reflects the brokenness of our sinful world. Persons of same-sex attraction should not be denied community acceptance solely because of their sexual orientations and should be wholeheartedly received by the church and given loving support and encouragement. Christian homosexuals, like all Christians, are called to discipleship, holy obedience, and the use of their gifts in the cause of the kingdom. Opportunities to serve within the offices and the life of the congregation should be afforded to them as to heterosexual Christians.
>
> Homosexualism (i.e., explicit homosexual practice), however, is incompatible with obedience to the will of God as revealed in Scripture. The church affirms that it must exercise the same compassion for homosexuals in their sins as it exercises for all other sinners. The church should do everything in its power to help persons with homosexual orientation and give them support toward healing and wholeness.[6]

Christ Evangelical Bible Institute (IN)

Joseph Adam Pearson founded Christ Evangelical Bible Institute (CEBI) in Phoenix in 1991, and then relocated the school to Michigan City, Indiana, in 2007. It is a ministry training school "for Christians who have experienced discrimination and rejection," primarily for those of same-sex orientation. It offers a one-year worker's certificate and a three-year Bachelor of Ministry degree. The founder has written *Christianity and Homosexuality Reconciled: New Thinking for a New Millennium!* (2014).[7]

Eastern University

Eastern (PA) has long been the home base of sociologist Tony Campolo, the noted public speaker who in recent years has partnered with his wife Peggy, an Eastern graduate, to travel widely presenting a pro-and-con performance on the same-sex marriage debate. While both oppose promiscuous lifestyles and both support legal unions, they disagree on whether same-sex marriage should receive the blessing of the Christian church. Peggy affirms while Tony does not, calling rather for celibacy. In particular they disagree over how to interpret Romans 1, with Peggy arguing that Paul is condemning sexual orgies related to the worship of Aphrodite, the ancient goddess of love.

Peggy's experience illustrates how sensitive, empathetic Christians can often come to support same-sex marriage. The Campolos loved to vacation in the coastal resort of Provincetown, Massachusetts, but she lamented the sadness and loneliness she found there among the significant gay population. Then she became known as a sympathetic "listening ear" to the gay and lesbian students at Eastern who came to her to share their experiences:

> As I listened to their stories, a rage began to build in me. In all my life, nothing had ever seemed so unfair as the lives these young men and women had to live. Nobody understood. Most of their parents were unfair, if indeed they had even found the courage to risk telling their parents. The college wanted them to be silent, and their churches just never seemed to be there for them. Either these young people had heard such condemnation from the pulpit that they knew better than to approach their pastors, or their pastors had been so silent on the issue that they had no idea what might happen if they took their heartaches to him or to her. So they hurt, in silence and often all alone. I marveled at how "together" many of them were able to be, in spite of the forces marshaled against them.[8]

Eastern Mennonite (VA) and Goshen (IN)

Mennonites and other Anabaptists have a history of being more than normally sensitive to identifying with the deprivations of the poor, the needy, and even despised people in general. Note, for example, the relief work of the Mennonite Central Committee and the Mennonite Disaster Service, and the Goshen general education core study/service program whereby each student spends a semester overseas not for cultural appreciation in Europe but to live in an underdeveloped country. Among the CCCU colleges, Eastern Mennonite has been early in seriously examining how the Christian community might best relate to the gay population. In the fall of 2013, Eastern Mennonite began a formal review of "current hiring policies and practices with respect to individuals in same-sex relationships." Six months later, the college extended the period of evaluation so as to coordinate its actions with those of the parallel review in its related denomination, the Mennonite Church USA. On July 16, 2015, the Eastern Mennonite board voted to employ individuals in same-sex marriages. One day later, Goshen made the same decision. Thus these two institutions became the first CCCU colleges to adopt such a rule.[9]

Franciscan (OH)

Franciscan, formerly the College of Steubenville, has been part of the Charismatic renewal movement and is the only Catholic college in the CCCU. In 2012, the "Franciscan Gay Alumni and Allies" issued a press release objecting to the university's course description for Social Work 314, "Deviant Behavior." The description read: "The behaviors that are primarily examined are murder, rape, robbery, prostitution, homosexuality, mental illness, and drug use." The alumni group, of course, objected to the inclusion of homosexuality on the list of deviant topics. The result was that the social work program faced an inquiry from its professional accreditation agency, the Council on Social Work Education. The university's explanation was that it used the word "deviant" in the clinical sense of "different from the norm" rather than in making a moral judgment.[10]

Geneva (PA)

Geneva played a prominent role in one of the most widely known homosexual-to-heterosexual conversion stories of recent years. Many in the Christian college community rejoiced to learn the story of a practicing lesbian scholar who transformed her lifestyle and Unitarian-Universalist faith to become a Reformed Presbyterian preacher's wife. Rosaria Champagne Butterfield had been an associate professor in English and women's studies with a specialty in Queer Theory, at Syracuse University when her research on the religious right and the hermeneutics of homophobic hatred led to her interactions with a local senior evangelical pastor who was courteous and thoughtful. The minister's son was also a Syracuse professor who served as board chair at Geneva, a Reformed Presbyterian institution. Her research and her new Christian faith led to a one-year visiting professor appointment at Geneva, and then a romance with and marriage to Kent Butterfield, a graduating seminary student at Reformed Presbyterian Seminary in nearby Pittsburg.

Some readers of the Butterfield story will note its exceptionality, and that the transformation from homosexuality, while always difficult, is more possible when the attraction, as is this case, appears to be more psychologically and emotionally based than physically and cognitively based.[11]

Gordon (MA)

When President Obama, in July 2014, issued an LGBT Non-Discrimination Executive Order forbidding any federal contractor from discriminating on the basis of sexual orientation or gender identity, Gordon, led by its president D. Michael Lindsay, joined a group of other religious organizations in sending a letter to the president requesting an exemption so as to continue its practice of not hiring people who practice homosexuality. The issue, of course, was one of religious liberty versus civil rights. The most important immediate consequence of the Gordon request was a decision of the college's regional accreditation organization. The New England Association of Schools and Colleges asked Gordon to submit a report within a year explaining how its policies are not discriminatory. For further details on the Gordon case, see Chapter 28. The college's 2014 public statement on homosexuality is as follows:

> In our statement of faith and conduct we affirm God's creation of marriage, first described in Genesis, as the lifelong one-flesh union of one man and one woman, designed both for companionship and for a stable environment for the procreation and rearing of children. Along with this positive affirmation of marriage as male-female union, there are clear prohibitions against same-gender sexual relations in the Scriptures. It is important to note that the Gordon statement of faith and conduct does not reference same-sex *orientation*—that is, the state of being a person who experiences same-sex attraction—but rather, specifically, homosexual acts. The Gordon community is expected to refrain from any sexual intercourse—heterosexual

or homosexual; premarital or extramarital—outside of the marriage covenant. There is currently much debate among believing Christians about the nature and causes of homosexuality, and about a faithful Christian response to same-sex attractions, but we acknowledge that we are all sinners in need of grace, all called to redeemed humanity in Christ. We recognize that students at Gordon who struggle with their sexual orientation have often felt marginalized and alone, and recognize the pressing need for a safe campus environment for all students.[12]

Grace (NE)

Grace University, formerly Grace Bible Institute, expelled Danielle Powell in 2011, during her last semester before graduation, for falling in love with another woman. The school then asked her to reimburse them for $6,000 in federal loans and grants that were due because she did not finish the semester. Grace readmitted her in 2012 and then abruptly reversed that decision. Nearly a year later, Powell married another woman, Michelle Rogers, who initiated a petition on change.org asking Grace to forgive the tuition bill. Also involved in the case was Lambda Legal, a national organization to protect the civil rights of LGBT people. Lambda Legal lawyer Ken Upton reported that it was unusual in such cases for the college to demand repayment.[13]

Notre Dame (IN)

For 15 years or so, the Notre Dame administration had rejected student and faculty requests for official approval of a gay-straight alliance club and the inclusion of sexual orientation on its list of legally protected categories. Finally after a five-month review, President Father John Jenkins decided in 2013 to "make a virtue of necessity" not simply giving the desired recognition but embracing the campus gay community as an area of comprehensive pastoral concern. There was to be a formal club, to be sure, but one that operated within the context of a larger Catholic support and guidance system. The name given to the new initiative, which is administered by the Office of Student Affairs, is "Beloved Friends and Allies: A Pastoral Plan for the Support and Development of GLBTQ and Heterosexual Students." Critics of the plan feared that it would lead to a de facto recognition of an active gay lifestyle. Others were more positive. The local Fort Wayne-South Bend Bishop Kevin Rhodes noted, "This pastoral care should help the students not to feel unwelcome or alienated in the community, but also help them to lead chaste and holy lives ... people, especially youth who feel isolated or alienated, can be more susceptible to destructive unchaste behavior ... " He also emphasized that ministry to the gay community was an essential reflection of the Christian belief in the inherent dignity of all people.[14]

A year after the introduction of the "Beloved Friends and Allies" plan, the Notre Dame athletic department launched a new campaign to emphasize the full acceptance of open, gay-oriented athletes. A featured video included testimonies from athletes on every Notre Dame team.

Assisting in the project was a 2006 Notre Dame graduate, Patrick Burke, co-founder of "You Can Play," an activist organization devoted to the full acceptance and respect of gay athletes. "The church is supposed to be a place where people come together, where people are united in an idea of love and caring for each other," Burke stated. "When you start being exclusion-ary, that is not what Jesus taught. From day one, nothing we have . . . done has . . . contradicted Catholic teaching . . . ."

Both the student affairs program and the athletic department initiative provide test cases for how well an institution can achieve the dual goals of an embracing environment for gay students and acceptance of celibacy by the gay students.[15]

Nyack (NY)

Nyack appeared on the AAUP censure list from 1994 to 2006 because of the 1992–1993 case involving English professor June S. Hagen. A small "support gay rights" button attached to her briefcase led to complaints that reached the administrators and trustees. In an investigation, she told the president that the button reflected her concern about violence against homosexuals, and that she fully supported the Nyack statements of faith and lifestyle expecta-tions including the provision about homosexuality. The president cleared her and recommended her for reappointment. The trustees, however, both over-ruled the president's recommendation and removed him from office. A new administrator advised her of her nonappointment, denied to provide a rea-son for the negative decision, and stated that there could be no grievance hearing. The AAUP investigating committee found the college in violation of Hagen's academic freedom both in their decision on the button issue and in the process—or lack thereof—whereby they reached the decision. Twelve years later, the AAUP removed the censure when the college agreed to free speech and due process policy changes.[16]

Pepperdine (CA)

For years Pepperdine had rejected the request of its Gay-Straight Alliance, Reach Out, for official recognition, and many had associated the university with the widely publicized efforts of two of its law school professors (Kenneth

Starr and Richard Peterson) in opposition to the California referendum (Proposition 8) on gay marriage. Therefore it came as a surprise when Pepperdine announced in 2013 that it was offering the Vinci-Ellsworth need-based scholarship for a student who has contributed to the physical or mental health of the LGBT community.[17]

Point Loma (CA)

The same-sex debate at Point Loma featured the 2011 "coming out" of student-elected, student chaplain Todd Clayton, the son of two Nazarene pastors. Clayton not only declared his orientation but did so in a candid, articulate, and even crusading manner. He found it deeply healing to no longer hide a basic part of his nature, and felt a calling to help others to be similarly liberated. Following his Point Loma years, he continued his quest for both self-understanding and bringing healing to other gays and the evangelical church, by writing widely and studying at Union Theological Seminary (NY) where, upon graduation in 2014, he became the executive assistant to the president.[18]

Shorter (GA)

While many Christian colleges were debating whether they wished to be more accommodating of same-sex students and faculty, Shorter moved in the opposite direction. As discussed in greater detail in Chapter 24, the conservative resurgence in the Southern Baptist Convention (SBC) and its state conventions resulted in greater conservative control of the SBC seminaries and some of the SBC colleges. When Shorter sought to escape from this trend in 2005 by separating from the control of the Georgia Baptist Convention, it failed. Then, with growing conservative control on the Shorter trustee board, the latter introduced a newly revised faith and lifestyle statement that, among other changes, required faculty and staff opposition to homosexuality. Subsequently 37 percent of its faculty and nearly 50 of its staff members resigned.[19]

Southern Wesleyan (SC)

Beth Stuart, a 10-year faculty member at Southern Wesleyan, lost her position in 2013 when she refused to give up her support, as sponsor, for SWUnity, the campus LGBT organization. Normally a person who wants to fit in rather than challenge an organization, she said "I never wanted to rock a boat except for this one." For her, this cause was very personal, for her daughter wanted to be a boy at age 5, emerged as a lesbian in high school, and transitioned to a male in 2010.[20]

Westmont (CA)

Administrators and student leaders at Westmont had been "quietly talking for some time about how to make the college less isolating for gay students" when suddenly there appeared in 2010 an "op-ed" article in the college's student newspaper, *The Horizon*. The short essay, which was to have a dramatic effect, was not written by a Westmont student but rather by a 1976 graduate of another Christian college (Asbury of Kentucky), Artie Van Why. The result was that over 100 students and alumni signed a letter telling the college of the "doubt, loneliness, and fear" that LGBT students experienced during their undergraduate days. When this second letter appeared in the paper, over half of the faculty submitted a third letter asking "forgiveness for ways we might have added to your pain." The original Van Why letter, presumably submitted to multiple student newspapers of Christian colleges, was objective and practical.[21] It read as follows:

Dear Editor:

The recent suicides of gay teens has moved me to think of students currently on Christian campuses who are gay. This letter is to them.

I know what it is like to be gay and to be at a Christian School. In 1972 I was a freshman at a Christian college. I was a fairly new Christian. And I was gay. My four years there I lived with that secret and a fear that I was going to hell, pleading with God to change me, afraid to tell anyone.

We are assuring our gay youth that "it gets better." And it does. I also want you to know you have choices. You didn't choose to be gay (just as no one "chooses" to be heterosexual), but you can choose how to live with your sexuality.

You can believe homosexuality is a sin and try to change on your own, by praying or by entering into an "ex-gay" ministry. I tried all three, and speaking from my personal experience and years of meeting other gay Christians who tried doing the same, I don't think one can become "ex-gay" any more than one can become an "ex-heterosexual."

You can believe that it is not a sin to be gay, except when acted upon. I know gay Christians who accept their orientation and choose to live a life of celibacy.

You can marry someone of the opposite sex, concealing your same sex attractions, determined you have it under control. I know gay men and women who have done just that.

In each and every case, after what might have been years of suppression, they eventually ended up acting upon their impulses, some leading a double life. Inevitably the lies and secrecy caught up with each of them, revealed either by their own confession or an inappropriate situation they put themselves in.

Of all these people I know, each of their marriages, except for one, ended in divorce—the unsuspecting spouse's life was shattered, as well as the children's.

You can decide to be honest with your future spouse, trusting he or she will be willing to partner in your decision to live heterosexually. I know couples who are doing just that. Publicly, they present themselves as a typical heterosexual couple. I don't know how they conduct themselves in private.

You can choose to reexamine the scriptures that are used against homosexuals and decide if they are speaking out against same-sex attraction as we know it today. You can choose to believe God honors a same-sex monogamous committed relationship. You can choose to believe you can be both gay and a Christian.

I, personally, lived through years of struggle and anguish after college, trying everything I could to change. The end result was clinical depression and my own thoughts of suicide.

As the years have passed, I've come to trust that God does love and accept me as an openly gay man. I do look at those scriptures in a different light. I believe God sanctions any relationship (gay or straight) that is loving, committed and monogamous.

I belong to a church in one of the most conservative counties in Pennsylvania, the only openly gay man there. I was welcomed warmly by the pastor and the majority of the congregation. My presence there has generated an open dialogue within the church about homosexuality and the Bible.

People have told me that their views on homosexuality have changed because of knowing me, some acknowledging I'm the first gay person, they're aware of, that they've known.

Our church now has an outreach ministry to let the gay community know our doors are open to them. That we not only welcome them, we also affirm them, their committed relationships and the families they are creating.

Know that there are churches, and Christians, who will accept you as you are.

If we are to be judged, it will be by God.

Maybe at that time it won't be a matter of who was right and who was wrong. Maybe God will look at each of us and ask if we lived our lives being true to who we were. Maybe God will assure us that He's always loved us even during those times we were told He didn't.

It does get better. And you do have choices. The decisions you come to are between you and God.

Know that, whatever you decide, there is a place for you at the table.

Whitworth (WA)

Whitworth is a leader among the CCCU colleges in providing enhanced recognition for the LGBT community on campus and beyond. The Whitworth Gay Straight Alliance is a fully recognized club of the Associated Students of Whitworth University, the university's student government.

Whitworth constitutional law scholar and lawyer Julia Stronks has special interests in religion, gender, poverty, and discrimination. On the conflict between religious freedom and civil rights, she has written that there are limits to religious freedom "because some religious beliefs harm others. When courts have tried to balance religious freedom against possible harm caused to others, they have used the compelling interest test. They find for religious freedom unless limiting this freedom is the least restrictive alternative to protect others."

Moving from theory to a specific application, Stronks, with another lawyer/Ph.D. in the political science department, Kathy Lee, wrote a brief/petition to World Vision in support of the latter's first of two 2014 statements on same-sex married employees. The first of the World Vision statements announced that it would be open to hiring such couples. Then after 10,000 child sponsorships were lost in protest, the Christian relief and development organization promptly reversed its decision.

The Stronks–Lee open letter/petition received nearly 1,000 signatures within a month. It stated in part:

> Sincere Christians believing in Scripture as God's Word can disagree about the meaning of different Scriptural passages. There are committed Christians who believe, honestly, that a few passages in the Bible referencing sexual activities between people of the same gender have been historically misconstrued . . . we support the initial decision of World Vision. And we call on Christian institutions to employ LGBT brothers and sisters in Christ who help further the mission of their institutions.

Also in 2014 Whitworth awarded an honorary doctorate degree to alumnus Richard Cizik, a 20-year staff member of the National Association of Evangelicals (NAE) where he served as vice president of Government Affairs. Although Cizik lost his position at NAE because of his increasing focus on environmentalism, world poverty, and gay rights, nevertheless his position on the latter is more moderate than that advocated by Stronks. Cizik is a board member of Evangelicals for Marriage Equality which calls for Christian support for same-sex civil unions. His explanation for the latter is as follows:

> While I haven't come to a conclusion on gay marriages within the Church, . . . I am convinced that we cannot deny basic societal and constitutional rights—equal protection and due process under the law—to people based upon their sexual orientation or practice . . . we . . . must be more humble and recognize that our interpretations of what is sinful may be wrong. The sometimes-abusive language directed at LGBT citizens by our Evangelical Movement has led to a backlash against evangelicals and a diminution of our public witness. This can and must change.[22]

In conclusion, hopefully the Christian colleges and the federal government working separately and together might find policies that provide the optimum blend of openness, sensitivity, respect, religious liberty, and civil freedom. Here are some thoughts on how this might be achieved.

1. To the extent to which colleges are denying recognition of the existence and suffering of the LGBT members among them, they must no longer deny.
2. Colleges by definition are places for free exchange of ideas in the context of respect for those participating in the discussion; this principle should apply to the social and personal issue of same-sex orientation and marriage no less than any other issue.
3. The issue invokes both civil rights and religious freedom concerns, and public opinion on the issue is evolving. Christians need not and should not ask that all of their views on social issues be made public policy. The government needs to follow a very high standard in the protection of religious freedom. While public opinion is still changing, that changing consensus itself may be decisive in many cases; the government therefore can afford to be deliberate about making sweeping pronouncements.
4. The government could and should defuse much of the resistance by Christian colleges if it would alter its thinking to associate economic aid programs more with individual students and less with institutions. Individuals from a broad variety of religious traditions pay the taxes that provide the resources for the aid. The government has no independent source of wealth from which it distributes its largesse.
5. Governments, Christian colleges, and Christian churches all need to move beyond the thinking that in decision-making for one side to win, the other must lose. There are other resolutions that more nearly can achieve a win–win result.

6. The Christian colleges will present their best case for maximum institutional freedom from government control if they support with enthusiasm minority rights for gays for civil unions and provide freedom within their institutions for Christians to differ among themselves on this issue. In turn, the government will better command the respect of Christian colleges—and even Christian churches—if they allow the latter groups to continue their present pattern of becoming more progressive and thus develop new policies, if they so choose, on their own rather than by force against their will.

CHAPTER 24

Church and College: Complement and Conflict

This chapter has what some will consider a bold, perhaps even radical, thesis, namely that the churches and the Christian colleges both could provide much more academic freedom than they do, all within the bounds of historic orthodox Christianity. The church and its colleges have different but complementary roles. The church proclaims the truth that it has found, while the college assumes that there is more truth to be found and it seeks it. The primary function of the church is to catechize the youth, celebrate the good news with all believers, and evangelize. The function of the Christian college is to explore all of revelation and to seek the mind of the author of truth in all things. The church's role is primarily priestly; the college's role is primarily prophetic. The priests emphasize loving God with your heart; the prophets emphasize loving God with your mind. The priests and the prophets help each other; the priests and the prophets need each other. The students coming from home and church to the Christian college should embrace all that they can from their heritage and then seek to improve upon it.

Such is the theory. Things work out less ideally in practice because of the issue of freedom and control. Some central controls, even if only serving as operating principles or institutional mission statement, are necessary to provide institutional definition. But some controls are excessive and counterproductive. One might even ask why the church should govern the college any more than the converse? Or could there be a mutuality in the relationship with both together serving the lordship of a common cause? Churches that seek to be the most controlling of their colleges are also the ones that seek to be the most controlling of their parishioners. Much of this control involves secondary theological and cultural issues. Many lay people are accepting of—and even desirous of—other people defining truth for them, whereas academicians tend to expect, promote, and even demand a greater amount of personal discretion. Did the idea of control in the early church come from the one who said, "I am the way, the truth, and the life," and "the truth shall make you free," or did it come from Caesar?

After Anthony Diekema wrote his book on academic freedom, he told me he received inquiries from ministers who wondered if they, like professors, might qualify for academic freedom. Perhaps the question should extend to the laity as well. Perhaps church membership should call for unity on only the central Christian idea that God has come to us in Christ to redeem us to Himself (the Christmas story). Then the church could intensely study all kinds of secondary issues (even denominational distinctives) while very carefully distinguishing in its written statements between the primary issue and any secondary issues to which it wished to give some degree of emphasis. The result might well be a more thoughtful laity and an enhanced appreciation for the central idea of life. A wise person believes fewer things but believes them more deeply. If primary and secondary things are blurred together, the effect is to depreciate the former.[1]

If churches gave greater theological discretion to their laity, then it should be easier for them to give greater academic freedom to their intellectual colleagues, the Christian college professors. If the employment contracts for Christian college faculty called for concurrence on no secondary issues, the result would be greater collegiality, fewer academic freedom cases, and an improved learning environment.

The most significant recent example of a denomination seeking to exercise control over its colleges in a controversial manner is that of the Southern Baptist Convention (SBC) in conjunction with its state conventions. The SBC is the largest Baptist denomination in the world, the largest Protestant denomination in the United States, and the denomination with the largest number of more-or-less evangelical or continuing Christian colleges in the United States. In the midst of the Southern Baptist Controversy of 1970–2000, the denomination lost control of a dozen or so of its colleges, including Richmond (VA), Wake Forest (NC), Baylor (TX), Mercer (GA), Furman (SC), Stetson (FL), Belmont (TN), Grand Canyon (AZ), Houston Baptist (TX), Ouachita (AR), Samford (AL), Mississippi, Meredith (NC), and Georgetown (KY). Meanwhile the Southern Baptists have added relationships with conservative Baptist colleges Liberty (VA) and Cedarville (OH).[2]

The secession of the colleges is part of the larger controversy which changed the nature of the denomination and its six traditional seminaries: Southern (KY), Southwestern (TX), New Orleans (LA), Golden Gate (CA), Southeastern (NC), and Midwestern (MO). Preceding the controversy during the last third of the twentieth century was the seminary purging of the

1950s and the 1960s when at least 18 professors lost their positions for being too liberal. These included Ralph Elliot of Midwestern whose *Message of Genesis* (1961) interpreted the early Genesis account as parable rather than historic or scientific fact, and the so-called Dirty Dozen progressives at Southern who wished to openly challenge the denominational conservatives. Southern President Duke McCall, also a progressive, preferred to avoid such a confrontation. The McCall strategy was a microcosm of the traditional denominational strategy for dealing with its factions. Most of the denominational membership was conservative while most of the seminary professors were moderate to progressive. To keep the peace, the "Grand Compromise" was to select moderates to the leading denominational positions, for their moderation was in temperament as well as theology. The concern for moderation was not just peace for its own sake, but a desire to present a united front to the outside world in promoting the important causes of evangelism and world mission.

But this compromise began to fail in the 1970s. The conservatives, worried about the direction of the seminaries, influenced by the conservative element of northern evangelicalism led by Harold Lindsell, and sensitized to their latent political power, began to devise strategies to take over control of the denomination and, through the appointment power of the denominational presidency, to determine the seminary trustee board membership. This, in turn, would allow them to control the professorial retention and hiring processes. Houston Judge Paul Pressler, a long-time critic of the seminaries and knowledgeable in political strategy, teamed with young professor Paige Patterson and—to a lesser extent—popular Memphis preacher Adrian Rogers to gradually design a strategy that resulted in the conservatives replacing the moderates as the annual winners of the presidential elections. Beginning with Rogers' victory in 1979, the conservatives won every election. The SBC elections were heavily contested in the 1980s, while the political battles moved to the state conventions in the 1990s. By the end of the late 1990s the moderates had accepted their indefinite replacement in the SBC power positions. Some of them, however, chose to reorganize as the Cooperative Baptist Fellowship, a quasi-denomination with some 1,900 churches (the SBC retains 45,000 churches) and 15 seminaries, including Truett at Baylor and McAfee at Mercer.

When the Southern Baptist colleges saw the conservatives using their new power to alter what was theologically and socially acceptable in the seminaries, a number of them moved quickly to seek legal independence of their state conventions. Perhaps a dozen obtained separation, and the remainder adapted with varying degrees of willingness in the process. Probably no college experienced a more difficult transition than Louisiana, but as this complex case involved due process issues even more than theological ones, I will discuss it in the last chapter. The conservatives focused upon an inerrant mode of biblical interpretation as the benchmark of what was sufficiently conservative theologically. An important secondary consideration was conformity on the issue of a male-only ministry. The conservatives encoded both of these issues into a new version (2000) of what had become a near-creedal statement for the denomination, the Baptist Faith and Message.[3]

With the Southern Baptist Controversy impacting so many colleges in so many states, perhaps a focused look at the experience of six SBC colleges in two states, namely Georgia and Tennessee, might illustrate in some depth the overall pattern of this phenomenon. These six colleges include three in Georgia: Mercer, a successful leader in the resistance movement; Shorter, which sought intensely to resist but failed; and Truett-McConnell, which gladly complied; and three in Tennessee: Belmont, which went independent only by paying the Tennessee Baptist Convention (TBC) $11 million; Carson-Newman, which sought to separate from the TBC to avoid a fundamentalist takeover while settling for declaring an evangelical orientation; and Union which remained remarkably free from controversy even while deeply connected with both the Southern Baptists and nationwide evangelical traditions.

Mercer is the largest, oldest, and best known of the Baptist colleges in Georgia. In 1997 the Georgia Baptist Convention (GBC) defeated a fundamentalist/conservative effort to gain control of Mercer, and by 2005, voted to break formal ties with the university. Long-time Mercer president, R. Kirby Godsey (1979–2006), has been an eloquent spokesperson for the moderate cause. A summary of his views follows:

> Accountability to our church constituency has increasingly been translated to mean the exercise of some form of denominational control.... More often than not, the assurance of accountability through control by a church constituency is usually only a thinly veiled effort to impose ideological and doctrinal boundaries on the institution. We need to build together more constructive and enduring processes that preserve the principles of accountability without restraining genuine freedom of inquiry.

> ... The special mission of a Baptist college or university, in contrast to a so-called secular university, relates to our historical foundations, our responsibility for moral education, our focus on the relationship between faith and learning, and our commitment to intellectual and religious freedom.

> ... Finally we are accountable ultimately to the truth we pursue. Our calling as Baptist educators is not to package the truth, promote the truth, or even defend the truth. Our calling is to pursue the truth. Searching for truth is

the bedrock of any institution that claims to be a college or university. In the language of faith, our accountability to truth may also be viewed as our ultimate accountability to God. The search for truth may be seen, indeed, through the eyes of faith, as a searching for the face of God.[4]

Like Mercer, Shorter sought to escape from the GBC, but unlike Mercer it failed in the process. The result was that it changed from a critical mass Christian college to a conservative variety of orthodox Christian college. During the first decade of the century, the GBC had increasingly appointed conservative college trustees without consulting the college president. When the Southern accrediting association expressed concern, the college trustees voted to sever ties with the convention, and the resultant legal fight went all the way to the state supreme court where in 2005 the court by a single vote determined that the college could not separate from the convention. Then in 2011, the trustees required all faculty to sign a newly revised statement with provisions embracing biblical inerrancy and forbidding homosexual practice. Eighty-three Shorter faculty and staff resigned including over one-third of its faculty.[5]

Meanwhile, the relatively young Truett-McConnell (founded in 1946, graduated to senior college status in 2002) voted to adopt the 2000 Baptist Faith and Message statement as its college creedal statement. Baptists historically have been wary of embracing creeds, preferring to say that believing in the Bible itself is sufficient. In a sense this action illustrates how the conservative insurgence in the SBC marks a movement away from the historic Baptist faith and toward early twentieth-century American fundamentalism. President Emir Caner proudly proclaimed, "We will be the first Southern Baptist college to require a signature to affirm the Baptist Faith and Message...." Caner, a convert from Islam, positioned his college with the new SBC and in contrast to colleges like Mercer: "The 20th century saw the degradation of sound biblical theology. But thankfully on a national level our seminaries, mission agencies, the Ethics and Religious Liberty Commission, and our other agencies are faithful to the Word of God, but we can't say the same about all our state Baptist colleges."[6]

In Tennessee, the urban Belmont had been enrolling a majority of non-Southern Baptist students and in recognition of this the trustees wanted to have Southern Baptists comprise no more than 60 percent of the governing board. The TBC rejected this idea. In a subsequent 2006 lawsuit, the TBC asked for between $50 million and $60 million as a "divorce" settlement allowing them to recover their previous payments to the college over the years. The final separation agreement involved the college paying the state convention $11 million.[7]

After years of continuing criticism and threats of a takeover from the Tennessee fundamentalists/conservatives, the TBC Subcommittee on College and University Accountability in 2012 exonerated Carson-Newman, especially the Religion and Biology departments, of any current erroneous teachings but did encourage the college to take proactive measures (like faith and learning integration statements) to reassure the Tennessee Baptist laity. The current Carson-Newman statement of faith is strongly evangelical and the trustees felt the need in 2007 to issue a brief "trustees' statement" of belief about the Bible. It states: "we . . . affirm Holy Scripture as being given by God through people, to people. The complete and final Word of God is revealed in Jesus Christ." In other words, the statement emphasizes the authority of the Bible, but avoids the word "inerrancy" and emphasizes the ultimate Word of God as Jesus the Logos as opposed to the written text describing Jesus.[8]

Union seems to have largely escaped unscathed from the Southern Baptist wars primarily because of the long-term (1996–2014) steady leadership of President David Dockery. During his tenure, enrollment grew from under 2,000 to over 4,000, and the *Chronicle of Higher Education* cited the college as one of 30 colleges with the best working environments. Dockery had a strong working relationship with both Southern Baptists and Northern evangelicals. His college was a model for Southern Baptists on how to avoid moving toward sectarian fundamentalism on the right or drifting toward an anchorless secularism on the left. Union is one of the 12 colleges, including Baylor and Samford, of the Southern Baptist tradition that now are members of the CCCU.[9]

Dockery's summary assessment of the overall effect of the Southern Baptist conflict is as follows:

> The past thirty years have been characterized by a very public controversy. In so many ways, there have been many good things develop . . . including the recovery of the gospel and a renewed commitment to the fullness of Scripture. But the programmatic uniformity and cultural homogeneity that held us together for so many years has almost entirely evaporated. The controversy over first-order doctrinal issues has seemingly degenerated into ongoing infighting over secondary and tertiary matters resulting in a fragmented and even balkanized convention.[10]

Three other denominations are similar to the Southern Baptists both in claiming a large membership and also in having experienced major divisions that have affected the way in which the church views its colleges. These include the Lutheran Church Missouri Synod (LCMS), 2 million members; the Christian Church/Churches of Christ (CC/CC), 1.1 million members;

and the SDA Church, 1.1 million members. Each of these three groups shares a tendency to isolate itself from other Christian groups.

The LCMS church began when C.F.W. Walther and other Saxon Germans objected to a growing rationalism and ecumenism in the state church, and migrated to America to more easily practice their preferred Lutheran confessionalism. A major twentieth-century controversy both with other Lutheran denominations and within the synod itself involved questions of how much openness to practice toward other Christians. Compounding these tensions was the appearance of higher Biblical criticism in the synod's major seminary in St. Louis. The climax came when conservative president Jacob Preus with the LCMS launched an investigation of the St. Louis seminary with the result that he called for the dismissal of seminary president John Tietjen for harboring the teaching of "false doctrine." Consequently in 1973 the large majority of the faculty and students exited the campus to form a separate seminary—Seminex (seminary in exile) which survived for a decade.

In a parallel move 270 churches left the LCMS to form the more progressive Association of Evangelical Lutheran Churches (AELC) which, during its 11-year history, had as its most notable contribution providing leadership for the 1988 merger of the American Lutheran Church and the Lutheran Church in America into the largest American Lutheran body, the now 4.3 million member ELCA. The exodus of the LCMS progressives meant that the synod became even more conservative with a determination to watch over the purity of its ten denominational colleges, all named Concordia from the 1580 Book of Concord which codified the ten recognized creedal documents of Lutheran confessionalism, including the Augsburg Confession of 1530.

The AAUP entered Lutheran politics when in 1975 it cited the LCMS St. Louis Seminary with lack of due process in the dismissal of theologian Arlis J. Ehlen. This continues to be one of the oldest unresolved cases on the AAUP Censure List. Once again in the 1980s the AAUP censured an LCMS Seminary, this time Concordia Fort Wayne headed by Robert Preus (brother of Jacob Preus, a principal in the 1975 controversy) primarily for dismissing a tenured full professor for advocating for the ordination of women.

Many MSLC insiders expressed embarrassment and many outsiders conveyed shock when denominational authorities reprimanded ministers for participating in interfaith prayer services following national tragedies. For example, Valparaiso dean of the chapel Joseph Cunningham hosted an interfaith memorial involving Muslim, Jewish, and Christian clergy on the first anniversary of the 9/11 New York City terrorist attacks. Valparaiso is not under the control of the LCMS but Cunningham held ministerial credentials with the synod. A decade later an LCMS minister was forced to apologize for participating in a public interfaith vigil with President Obama two days after a gunman killed 26 children and adults at the Sandy Hook, Connecticut, elementary school.[11] Perhaps the strongest advocates of LCMS separatism is an organization called "Brothers of John the Steadfast," one of whose leaders, Timothy Rossow, remarked in response to a question about whether he thought the actions of the participating clergymen was worse than those of the school gunman: "Yes, I do. The gunman killed the body which lasts for 70 or 80 years.... False teaching and practice kills the soul which lives for eternity in heaven or hell."[12]

The CC/CC is one of three divisions of the Stone–Campbell Restorationist Movement of the nineteenth century. Like the LCMS it has struggled with how much it can work with other evangelical churches. The membership of seven of its colleges in the CCCU shows its progressive tendency, while the claim that it is not like "the denominations" because of the purity of its name illustrates its exclusivist tendency. The liberal/conservative split already developing in the late nineteenth century resulted in a formal division in 1906 into the more strict, largely southern Churches of Christ and the more progressive Christian Church (Disciples of Christ). A further division from the Disciples in 1927 produced the CC/CC which is held together loosely by the North American Christian Convention based in Cincinnati. When divisions fix themselves in the collective memory and receive continued reinforcement, it can produce an overemphasis upon distinctive issues of secondary importance and an inclination of the churches to vigilantly monitor the colleges. In any given Protestant group, including the evangelical ones, the churches tend to be more conservative than do the colleges.[13]

Two recent academic freedom cases of note involve CC/CC institutions Lincoln Christian (IL) and Emmanuel Christian Seminary, which is becoming affiliated with Milligan (TN). New Testament scholar Anthony Le Donne faced intense criticism from the constituency of Lincoln Christian following the publication of his *Historical Jesus* (Eerdmans, 2011). The result was his dismissal which he described as follows:

> After over a year of pressure from Lincoln Christian University donors, concerned Christians, and certain employees, the president of the university has decided to terminate my employment. I have been told that this decision is a direct response to the publication of my popular-level book, *Historical Jesus* (Eerdmans 2011). I have no doubt that the LCU administration made a stout effort on my behalf, but eventually needed to assuage the fears of (what I am told) is a largely anti-intellectual constituency.[14]

Near Eastern scholar Christopher Rollston of Emmanuel Christian also faced strong criticism in response to a publication, namely an essay on "The Marginalization of Women: A Biblical Value We Don't Like to Talk

About," which appeared on the progressive news and commentary website *The Huffington Post.* Perhaps his most vocal critic was an Emmanuel colleague, church historian Paul Blowers. Rollston resolved the tension by resigning to accept a position at George Washington University.[15]

The SDA denomination grew out of the millennial teachings of New York Baptist preacher William Miller (1782–1849) who, in the early nineteenth century, began proclaiming his belief that, based upon the Book of Daniel, Christ's second advent would occur sometime in 1843 or 1844. By the early 1840s, he had accumulated up to 500,000 followers nationwide. When his prophecy failed, he apologized and withdrew from the movement as did most of his followers. But a remnant remained including Hiram Edson who, the day after the "Great Disappointment," announced that he had received a vision that something really did happen on the day of expectation, namely that Jesus did move into a heavenly sanctuary (parallel to the Old Testament temple Holy of Holies) to complete the work of Atonement for believers. Edson's story inspired others including Joseph Bates who added a Sabbatarian emphasis, Ellen White who became the writer-prophetess for the movement, husband James White who published the movement's early journal, and J. N. Andrews who in 1874 became the first SDA missionary. The denomination formally began in 1861 in Michigan, and early developed a pattern of promoting education, health care, and overseas missions. Today the SDA counts nearly 18 million members worldwide and nearly 8,000 educational institutions including over 100 colleges.

The SDA operates 13 colleges in North America including four that have been involved in recent academic freedom cases: Loma Linda (CA), Southern (TN), Pacific Union (CA), and La Sierra (CA); and one that has joined the CCCU, namely Walla Walla (WA). The major academic freedom issues have involved (1) due process, (2) degree of freedom to differ from the ideas in general of co-founder and prophetess Ellen White, (3) degree of freedom to differ from the unique Edson idea of investigative judgment or the heavenly sanctuary, (4) the degree of freedom to differ from the Price idea of deluge geology (see Chapters 20 and 21), and (5) the degree of freedom to differ from the Bates thinking about Sabbath worship. The Progressive Adventists are the ones most likely to challenge one or more of these doctrines.

In the 1970s Loma Linda, a major medical university, dismissed historian of science Ronald Numbers in the wake of his biography of Ellen White, and in the 1990s the institution gained citation on the AAUP academic freedom censure list for dismissing three faculty members without employing due process procedures (see Chapter 29).

The late 1970s/early 1980s cases focused on the sanctuary doctrine, an issue central to the integrity of the SDA. After Christ did not return by

October 22, 1844, the Millerite movement was demoralized and largely dis-banded, but the discovery of the sanctuary idea as a fulfillment of the original prophecy, when embraced by Ellen G. White and others, became the basis for reviving the nearly dead organization. But was this idea a credible revelation? Mid-twentieth-century evangelical leader Donald Grey Barnhouse thought it was not despite the fact that he, with Walter Martin, had led in the transfor-mation, in evangelical eyes, of the SDA from cult to fringe evangelical status. Barnhouse, radio preacher and founder of the now defunct *Eternity* mag-azine, described the sanctuary doctrine as "the most colossal psychological face-saving phenomenon in religious history."[16]

Thus the church would not take lightly the doubts on the sanctuary idea expressed by authority figures such as college professors Jerry Gladden, Old Testament scholar of Southern Adventist, and Desmond Ford, Australian three-year visiting New Testament specialist at Pacific Union. Gladden came under heavy pressure from Southern Adventist administrators and resigned for what he believed rather than for what he taught. Following Ford's similar controversy at Pacific Union College (PUC), he lost his credentials as an SDA minister and professor.

In 1987 the SDA adopted "A Statement on Theological and Academic Freedom and Accountability" for pastors and workers (including professors in SDA colleges). A professor may not teach as truth anything not in compliance with "The 28 Fundamental Beliefs" of the church. The statement, however, does call for the denominational colleges to have in place explicit grievance procedures to follow in academic freedom cases, including, by implication, situations where a professor believes that the denomination could improve its doctrinal statement.[17]

In terms of the worldview center to Christian higher education—the "uni" in university—the question a century ago was whether the center could hold by resisting the temptation to move toward secularization. Today the issue is less whether the center will hold than whether it will become diluted by peripheral issues permeating into the central core. This concern of the present chapter will continue into the next chapter where the focus will be on how individual Christian colleges sometimes fight ideological civil wars.

CHAPTER 25

Theological Nuance

There are church battles and then there are church college battles. Both are intramural struggles—Christian v. Christian. When I wrote *The Christian College: A History of Protestant Higher Education in America (1984, 2006)*, the chapter which most interested readers was the one on "The Movement toward Secularization." That, by contrast, was a process that transmigrated away from and beyond the Christian church, the Christian college, and the Christian faith. It still frightens the continuing Christian college community, as well it should. Many today in the evangelical church and the Christian college community worry about a person or an institution "becoming liberal" or "growing liberal" while using such terms in an ambiguous or "catch all" manner. But to "move liberal" (or "move conservative") *within* the Christian faith is a second (or less)-order issue while to "move liberal" (or "move conservative") *beyond* the central Christian idea of the incarnation is a first-order issue. Much damage to people and the cause of academic freedom in Christian higher education stems from confusing or blurring the two orders.

Within the Christian college community in recent decades the two theological issues that have caused the greatest controversy are (1) biblical inerrancy and (2) the openness of God. The biblical inerrancy debates after World War II had their origins in the Princeton theology of Benjamin Warfield in the late nineteenth century and the Fundamentalism Movement of the early twentieth century.[1] It has been associated more with the Calvinist than with the Arminian branch of evangelicalism, and more with the former's scholastic and rational element than with those who emphasize experiential faith. The Evangelical Theological Society (ETS) began in 1949 with inerrancy as its defining doctrinal test for membership, although the older National Association of Evangelicals has been more open on the subject, as has the CCCU.[2]

The emotional volatility of the inerrancy debate increased with the publication of Harold Lindsell's controversial *Battle for the Bible* in 1976. Lindsell, who had fought on the losing side of the issue at Fuller Theological Seminary (CA), identified specific denominations, colleges, and seminaries that he believed had been lax in tolerating professors who did not accept his understanding of inerrancy. He especially focused on the institutions of two of the largest denominations that had mostly escaped the influences of Protestant modernism earlier in the century, the same Southern Baptists and Missouri Synod Lutherans featured in the previous chapter.

Two years after *The Battle for the Bible*, nearly 300 evangelicals gathered in Chicago for the International Council on Biblical Inerrancy where they signed the "Chicago Statement on Biblical Inerrancy." The statement declared that "Scripture in its entirety is inerrant" with the proviso that this claim "applies only to the autographic text of scripture." In other words inerrancy doesn't apply entirely to any Bible now in print.[3]

Evangelical critics of inerrancy argued that it (1) placed the emphasis in the wrong place; (2) was needlessly divisive; (3) was needlessly alarmist; (4) failed to openly acknowledge the problem areas in the biblical record; (5) was an extreme overreaction to the limited amount of recent departure from orthodoxy; and (6) was part of the agenda of Calvinist elitism within Evangelicalism. Christian college statesman Robert Sandin (Bethel, Northwestern, North Park, and Mercer) contended that the crisis over inerrancy "lies in the understanding of what is the essential content of the biblical message. It is at this level that the faithful church should take up its polemic. Contending for a certain doctrine *about* the Bible is of secondary importance at best; what is of primary importance is contending for the system of saving truth expressed *in* the Bible." The irenic ETS secretary Vernon Grounds (Denver Seminary), who was distressed about the agitation caused by the organization's doctrinal statement, distributed to the other officers a resignation letter of "one of our active leaders" which cited in support the idea that "the inerrancy . . . claimed for the Bible is really an inerrancy claimed for fundamentalist interpretations of it," and lamented the implication of many that only inerrantists are truly evangelical. Such assumptions, of course, exacerbated the internal divide in evangelicalism between the Calvinists and the Arminians/Wesleyans.[4]

One leading Arminian theologian, Roger Olson of Bethel and Baylor, told the following story to illustrate his observation that the distinction among evangelicals who are and who are not inerrantists in more is theory than in practice.

> Not too long ago I had a debate with [a] leading conservative evangelical inerrantist . . . . After much communication back and forth we realized that we

differ hardly at all about the Bible. Given his qualifications of inerrancy and my high view of Scripture (supernatural inspiration and highest authority for life and faith) our accounts of the Bible were nearly identical.

. . . a person (such as I) can affirm everything many leading inerrantists believe about the Bible and yet be rejected and even criticized. I fear they have elevated a word into an idol.

Another noteworthy critic of inerrancy is Notre Dame scholar Christian Smith, arguably the leading sociological interpreter of contemporary evangelicalism. Smith views inerrancy as one of the key components of what he calls "Biblicism," a theoretical approach to Scripture that he says is

not so much 'wrong' as . . . impossible . . . . It simply does not work as proposed and cannot function in a coherent way . . . . Biblicism . . . presumes that the Bible speaks with one, clear, discernible voice on matters of relevance and interest in doctrine, practice, and morality . . . . If it was correct, we would not have anything like the disagreement, conflict, and division that we in fact do have in Christianity today—especially among evangelical Biblicists.[5]

Many of the leaders in the inerrantist movement believe their position and cause to be necessary to avoid a projection in the churches and colleges along the "slippery slope" to secularism, in an understandable desire to avoid a repeat of the 1890–1960 period. Historian George Marsden who described the early phases of that secularization process in higher education in his oft-cited *The Soul of the American University* seeks to assuage such fears: "I do not think that the patterns that dominate the story in *The Soul of the American University* are applicable to the current state of the great majority of CCCU schools." In fact he sees the Christian colleges of recent decades as maturing, replacing some of their arbitrary behavior rules and enhancing an emphasis on faith and learning integration in the classroom.[6]

The leader of the inerrantist movement, through his books and his editorial positions at *Christianity Today*, was the aforementioned Harold Lindsell. Crusading and polemic by nature, he had his greatest success in encouraging the Southern Baptist conservative/fundamentalists in their takeover of the denomination, its seminaries, and many of its colleges where advocacy of inerrancy became a key mark of such institutions. If Lindsell was divisive within evangelicalism, he was also divisive within his own inerrancy camp. Carl Henry, concerned with respectability for evangelicalism, worried that just as the latter was starting to receive attention and even some measure of respect in the general media, it was also starting to look like "a cult squabbling over inerrancy" as opposed to a "dynamic life-growing force." J. I. Packer (Regent) was similarly critical: "Lindsell almost (not quite) implies that you don't believe in inerrancy unless you interpret all Scripture as he does . . . " Then Packer added . . .

> the questions of inerrancy and interpretation must be kept separate. Acknowledging that whatever biblical writers communicate on any given subject is God-given truth does not commit you to advance to any one method or school of interpretation, nor to any one way of relating Scripture to science, nor to any one set of proposed harmonizations of inconsistent-looking texts . . . medievalists allegorized, Reformers interpreted literally, but both maintained inerrancy. Covenant theologians and dispensationalists, Calvinists and evangelical Arminians have significantly different hermeneutics . . . but all may agree on inerrancy . . . .

Even Lindsell himself later regretted that in the heat of battle he had been emotionally excessive in his attacks.

Evangelicals who were uncomfortable with the term inerrancy often used words like "infallible" or "authoritative" or phrases like "without error in all that it teaches" or "authoritative in all matters pertaining to salvation." Christian college catalogs vary widely in the terms that they use—or do not use—in their institutional statements of faith clauses on the Bible. On the inerrancy issue the primary difference lay in whether an institution wished to defend a blanket inerrancy of the biblical authors' statements on facts—sometimes incidental in nature—of history and science as well as on spiritual and moral teachings. Those outside the evangelical tradition often found it difficult to understand why some conservative Protestants place such an importance on these distinctions. For example, Marcus Borg, Bible scholar and Jesus Seminar fellow, noted "Though some argue that inerrancy and infallibility are not identical, the differences at most are subtle."[7]

The differences may indeed be subtle, but they certainly are real at many Christian colleges. The previous chapter discussed the major role which the issue has played in two major conservative Protestant denominations (the SBC and LCMS) and their colleges. Few Christian colleges have been unaffected to one degree or another, with situations ranging from a state Supreme Court hearing (see Chapter 29) to major conflicts between trustee/administrators and faculty to controversial faculty dismissals. Not only have there been differences of opinion, but also differences on the importance of these differences. Differences as such are normal, even inevitable; the goal of academic freedom and Christian charity, however, is to reduce the importance given to narrowly nuanced distinctions.

Less widespread than biblical inerrancy as a recent significant theological controversy in Christian higher education is the "openness of God" debate. "Open Theism" as a modern movement has its origins in the 1980 publication of *The Openness of God: The Relationship of Divine Foreknowledge and Human Freewill* by Adventist theologian Richard Rice of Loma Linda; however, it became more widely known and discussed in 1994 when four other authors (Clark Pinnock, John Sanders, William Hasker, and David Basinger) joined Rice to produce the InterVarsity title, *The Openness of God*. Essentially, open theism is Arminianism plus a partially open view of the future. According to its adherents it is Western philosophy rather than the Bible that has influenced the conclusions of classical theology on the omniscience of God, particularly His foreknowledge. Appealing to the biblical narrative, they note that in his dealings with humans, God changes His mind (Exodus 32:14, Joel 2:13–14), regrets His actions (Genesis 6:5–6, I Samuel 15:11, 35), is surprised by developments (Isaiah 5:3–7, Jeremiah 7:31), and asks questions about the future (Genesis 22:12, Numbers 14:11). From this data the open theists conclude that God chooses to limit His foreknowledge so as to offer humans real freedom to choose for Him.[8]

If Harold Lindsell was the central figure in the inerrancy debate, Clark Pinnock played a similar role in the open theism controversy. Pinnock is best known for his dramatic transformation from young rational defender of evangelical Calvinism, inerrancy, and meticulous providence, to middle-age champion of freewill theism and, then, open theism. Evangelical scholars tended either to admire him or lament him. His understanding that God was open to and affected by his human creatures led to Pinnock being increasingly open to learning from Christians of other persuasions including Eastern Orthodox, Roman Catholic, and Pentecostal. His most thorough explanation of open theism was *Most Moved Mover* (2001) while perhaps his most compelling work was a study of the Holy Spirit, *Flame of Love* (1996). His biographer is Anderson theologian Barry Callen who wrote *Clark H. Pinnock: An Intellectual Biography* (2000).[9]

Open theism experienced noteworthy controversy in the Calvinist-leaning ETS and at the freewill-oriented Huntington (IN) and Bethel (MN). ETS founding member Roger Nicole (Gordon) sought expulsion from the society of Pinnock and Sanders in 2002. Nicole declared that "Open theism is a cancer on the Evangelical Theological Society." By contrast the then presiding ETS president, Darrell Bock of Dallas Seminary, supported the defendants, arguing that the organization should be an open forum without narrow boundaries. The membership voted overwhelmingly to sustain Pinnock and narrowly to retain Sanders.

Sanders did not fare as well in his own college, for in 2004 Huntington dismissed him from his teaching position. Huntington President Blair Dowden defended Sanders calling him a "brilliant scholar" and an "excellent teacher" but in the end could not resist the negative pressure from leaders of the supporting denomination, the United Brethren in Christ. Interestingly the college chose to retain other open theism believers among the faculty including well-known philosopher and former editor of the *Christian Scholars Review*, William Hasker. Sanders now teaches at Hendrix, a Methodist institution in Arkansas.[10]

The similar case of theologian Gregory Boyd at Bethel (MN) met with a slightly different result. The dynamic Boyd during his 16-year tenure at Bethel founded a Baptist church of the same denomination (Baptist General Conference, a freewill Baptist group) that sponsored the college. When the pressure on Boyd within both the college and denomination mounted, he simply resigned from the college to devote his time to writing and leading what had become a megachurch.

Boyd's most high-profile critic was John Piper, a fellow pastor of a twin city Baptist General Conference megachurch who also had an early-career teaching stint at Bethel. Piper was a pronounced Calvinist whose best known writing was *Desiring God: Mediations of a Christian Hedonist.*[11] As the controversy surrounding Boyd and his open theism grew within the denomination and especially in the twin cities, the university conducted a formal inquiry that exonerated both Boyd and the openness movement. The Bethel committee review of Boyd's view of God concluded:

> It appears that the details of the view of God defended by Boyd are an outworking of a certain form of an Arminian view of God. This view is the work of a professional theologian spelling out the specifics of his world view as part of a scholarly calling. This form of Arminianism is, in some ways, more straightforwardly biblical than certain evangelical alternatives. It does not use anthropomorphism to offset the literal sense of certain biblical statements. Rather it takes almost all the relevant biblical descriptions as literally true. Boyd accepts at face value those texts which indicate that God changes his mind in response to historical events, regrets certain things that happen, and uses conditional prophesies and statements. Boyd's view of God is a biblically-oriented contemporary form of Arminianism.[12]

In addition to the prominence of open theism debates in the ETC, Huntington, and Bethel, it is noteworthy that the SBC in 1999 passed a resolution in opposition to the new view. Accordingly, the 2000 version of the Baptist Faith and Message added a new sentence in its declaration about the Divine: "God is all powerful and all knowing, and His perfect knowledge extends to all things, past, present, and future, including the future decisions of His free creatures."[13]

Also on the list of institutions that have attracted attention recently for their intramural theological conflicts are Cedarville, Northwestern (MN),

Westminster Seminary (PA), and Erskine (SC). The first three of these had their beginnings in the Fundamentalist protest movement of the post-World War I era. The General Association of Regular Baptists (GARB) organized in 1932 as a breakaway movement from the mainstream Baptists in the North, the American Baptist Convention (ABC). It placed greater emphasis on separation than did a 1947 division from the ABC, the Conservative Baptists. Both splinter groups found unacceptable the degree to which liberal Protestant thought had entered the ABC and secularization had influenced many of its colleges. Since its beginning as Baptist Bible Institute in Cleveland in 1941 and its relocation downstate to the town of Cedarville in 1953, Cedarville has positioned itself somewhere on the border between fundamentalism and evangelicalism. Following the stable 25-year (1978–2003) presidency of Paul Dixon, during which the student enrollment grew threefold, the college experienced major internal turmoil over minor theological distinctions.

William Brown, president of Bryan College, succeeded Dixon in 2003, understanding that he had a mandate from the trustees to continue moving Cedarville more toward the Christian college mainstream. Meanwhile the GARB had remained more separatist-minded than had the college, and the college decided to loosen its connection with the church. The fundamentalist/evangelical tensions found focus in the Bible Department where under Brown some conservative professors lost their positions; these included David Hoffeditz who appealed his case to the AAUP which ruled in 2009 that the college failed to follow due process procedures in his dismissal (see Chapter 29).[14]

Although an overstatement, to outsiders it appeared that Cedarville has switched from dismissing Bible professors for being "too conservative" under the Brown administration to more recently releasing Bible professors and others for being "too liberal." The later included Michael Pahl who affirmed the college's statement of faith but not for the right reasons, according to the college. This fine distinction is reminiscent of the serious "truth and certainty" debates a few years earlier when the dispute was "whether Christians can have *certainty* that the bible is *true* (the position attributed to the so-called conservatives) or merely assurance or *confidence* that the bible is *accurate* . . . ." In 2012 and 2013, trustee, administrator, and faculty dismissals/resignations (including President Brown and the popular, relatively progressive dean of students Carl Ruby), often with little explanation, left students confused, alumni taking to the social media chat rooms, and the Christian and secular media giving broad publicity to the drama. For the present it appears that the more fundamentalist faction has won with Southern Baptist conservative leader Paige Patterson, now a Cedarville trustee, and one of Patterson's major administrators at Southwestern Seminary, Thomas White, now in the Cedarville presidency.[15]

In some respects the Northwestern story parallels the Cedarville one. Both institutions were fundamentalist in origin and had been moving modestly toward the evangelical mainstream, having joined the CCCU. Northwestern—where a young Billy Graham once served as president— began in 1902 as one of the first and most significant Bible colleges and as one of the first and most significant fundamentalist colleges. It added a four-year liberal arts program in 1944, and 12 years later closed the Bible school to concentrate fully on the liberal arts program.

By the administration of current president, Alan Cureton (2002–), the faculty included both veterans who had known the older fundamentalist focus of founder William Bell Riley (1861–1947) and others, and the newer, younger faculty whose orientation was more broadly evangelical. Dissonance resulted and enlarged when some of the alumni, led by 1997 graduate Dallas Jenkins, and some of the students, led by the student government organization, believed that Cureton was too aggressive in favoring the more progressive element. Jenkins, a filmmaker and son of Jerry Jenkins who, with Tim LaHaye, authored the popular and controversial *Left Behind* series of end-times novels, employed his media savvy to organize a website, "NWC Truth," and protest movement. Similarly, the student government called for the resignation or removal of Cureton. The charges against the president included major communications errors, for which Cureton apologized, and "theological drift."

The trustees took seriously the charges—and the negative publicity which they produced. They employed both a law firm and a task force with outside representation to investigate. The resultant reports confirmed the continuing orthodoxy of the college. Trustee Arnold Lindstrand noted "we live in an Internet Age—and sometimes small minorities can make lots of noise." The episode did confirm, however, a need for the college to establish a new identity with a redefined basis for institutional unity.[16]

Westminster Seminary was another institution whose origins in the early-twentieth-century fundamentalism controversies helped to make its recent leaders hypersensitive to slight deviations from a tightly defined base of theological orthodoxy. Westminster began when J. Gresham Machen—author of the compelling *Christianity and Liberalism*—and other scholars withdrew from Princeton Theological Seminary to form the new orthodox seminary in Philadelphia. After Old Testament scholar Peter Enns published his 2005 book, *Inspiration and Incarnation: Evangelicals and the Problem of the Old Testament* with Baker Academic, his own colleagues spent two years discussing it. Enns stated that just as Jesus possessed both a divine and a human nature, so also did the Bible. The purpose of his book was to show the human side of the Scriptures. Later Enns realized that he should have presented his findings on the human element in Scripture and Scripture writing in the context of what he also believed about its divine element and message.

When the faculty voted on the compatibility of the book with the institutional statement of belief, they supported him by a vote of 12–8. Subsequently the seminary trustees reversed that decision by an 18–9 vote to remove Enns, and he left Westminster in 2008. The minority trustees all resigned. Enns's post-dismissal public statements were forthright but remarkably evenhanded.

Like Anthony Diekema, Enns believes that it can be a good thing for Christian colleges and their professors to test their limits—or "approach . . . the perimeters of [their] theological parameters," as Enns expresses it. His great contribution may be his ability to save for the Christian faith those thoughtful and sensitive young scholars who have difficulty accepting traditional explanations of the more problematic biblical passages. Other recent Westminster dismissals for theological reasons have included long-time president Samuel Logan (from president to chancellor) in 2005, and 22-year veteran Old Testament scholar and theologian Douglas Green in 2013 (to take effect in 2015).[17]

Erskine is the only college of the small (250 churches) Associate Reformed Presbyterian Church (ARP), and, like some parents of an only child, the denomination has hovered closely over the college and its board at least since 2010 when it developed the conviction that it needed to micromanage the college because of "theological drift." In the spring of 2010, the ARP voted to fire most of the trustee board for being lax in enforcing inerrancy and anti-macroevolution standards and tolerating classroom discussion of controversial issues. In response, the college and its alumni association filed multiple suits against the denomination. The AAUP became involved and the Southern Association of Colleges and Schools placed the college on its "warning list" because of governance issues. The crisis eased somewhat when the church reversed the decision to fire many of the trustees and the college dropped its lawsuits.

But the crisis flared up again when the college fired veteran English professor William Crenshaw, who for years had been both the target of conservative ire and the recipient of student devotion. A favorite teaching technique of Crenshaw was the Socratic method of questioning assumptions (even religious ones). This technique extended beyond the classroom to overall educational and governance policies, including criticism of church conservatives who wanted science taught from the Bible rather than based upon the consensus of scientists. Crenshaw believed that "Science is the litmus test on the validity of the educational enterprise. If a school teaches bogus science, everything else is suspect . . . . I want a real college, not one that rejects facts, knowledge, and understanding because they conflict with a narrow religious belief. Any college that lets theology trump fact is not a college; it is an institution of indoctrination. It teaches lies. Colleges do not teach lies. Period." Crenshaw's nemesis was a website called ARP talk, which served as a rallying center for denominational conservatives. It called Crenshaw "an evangelist of infidelity."

A new young president, David Norman (2010–2013) thought he could bring the factions together. Seeking consensus, he announced, "I'm a big fan of diversity," but he expected the seminary to teach denominational beliefs. He announced, "I believe in a historical Adam and Eve" yet declared that Francis Collins is "one of the people I most greatly respect on this planet," for his ability to blend evangelical Christianity and evolutionary science. In 2008, the ARP adopted an inerrancy statement for the church and college. While Norman supported inerrancy, not all of his faculty did, including theologian Richard Burnett, tenured before 2008, who had written a 56-point rebuttal against it. Norman resigned in 2013, announcing, "I am exhausted."[18]

It is a difficult challenge for a Christian college both to maintain the continuing integrity of its central mission, and simultaneously to welcome diversity of thought beyond that. Yet it is possible.

Throughout church history, Christian groups have experienced inevitable tension between the desire to maintain correct belief and experience on one hand, and the desire to achieve unity of spirit and organization on the other hand. Most would agree with the general solution expressed eloquently by seventeenth-century Puritan minister and theologian Richard Baxter, who certainly experienced more than his share of religious controversy:

> In necessary things, unity;
> In doubtful things, liberty;
> In all things charity.

The difficulty has existed in applying this formula to specific situations. For example, few groups have agreed on the exact list of beliefs to be called "necessary." There has also been, as previously noted, disagreement over the importance of the disagreements. Perhaps the biggest failure has been the lack of sufficient charity in dealing with the differences; ironically, of all the aspects of theological debate, this is the one over which there should be the most control.

CHAPTER 26

Gender, Race, and Ethnicity

This chapter is about treating all people with dignity and charity, recognizing that "There is neither Jew nor Greek, there is neither slave nor free, there is neither male nor female; for you are all one in Christ Jesus."[1] Are there occasions when other concerns should override this spirit or when the best implementation of this spirit requires a departure from strict equality? Or are most failures in this domain simply explained by a lack of willingness to live up to professed ideals?

On the issue of gender, the largest organization of Christian liberal arts colleges, the CCCU, lists 60 percent of its students and 35 percent of its full-time faculty as women. During the 12-year period ending in 2010, the percentage of women in senior-level positions (vice president or above) increased from 8 to 17 percent. In 2009, of the 111 CCCU institutions there were six women presidents and 17 female chief academic officers. On the 2012 Joeckel and Chesnes survey asking the CCCU faculty whether women were treated equally to men in their colleges, 77 percent of the male instructors and 54 percent of the female instructors responded in the affirmative, while on the related question of whether women should have the right to become pastors, 66 percent of men and 80 percent of women said yes. In the same survey, by a margin of 57 percent to 30 percent, the CCCU students believed that women should have the right to become pastors. On the subject of marital roles, most evangelicals—the group from which most of the Christian college students come—embrace a theory of *both* husband headship and egalitarianism. In other words, the husband has primary responsibility for the economic, spiritual, and physical welfare of the family and when really necessary makes the final decision on critical matters, but the normal basis of decision-making is by consensus.[2]

Nineteenth-century evangelical revivalism had a close association with the women's rights movement of that period. Charles Finney, the most prominent revivalist of the Second Great Awakening, scandalized many people by encouraging women to testify publically in his meetings (critics thought this to be a sort of "spiritual undressing"). Also his Oberlin College was the first institution of higher education to admit women on an equal basis with men, thus beginning the practice of coeducation.

Evangelical women appear to have faced fewer restrictions professionally in higher education and the ministry during the early decades of the twentieth century than they did in the subsequent 1920s to 1960s period. Dwight L. Moody, the most prominent evangelist of the Third Great Awakening (c. 1875–1895) invited Frances Willard, founder and leader of the Women's Christian Temperance Union (WCTU), to speak in his revivals and, at the turn of the century, Moody Bible Institute scheduled women as evangelists, conferences speakers, and teachers of classes of men and women together, and women graduates freely served as pastors. Historian Rebecca Groothuis noted that a 1909 Moody publication stated that "A woman's highest call is Christian ministry, not the joys of motherhood." In the late 1920s, women were still graduating from the institute's pastor's program.[3]

Groothuis also found that both Wheaton founder Jonathan Blanchard—who was a friend of Charles Finney—and Gordon founder A. J. Gordon "championed the legal recognition of the rights of women." Gordon in "The Ministry of Women," and his wife, Maria, in "Women as Evangelists" argued for a public ministry for women. Maria herself taught at the college and served as the president of the Massachusetts WCTU. Another early-twentieth-century Christian college president's wife to serve as a state president of the WCTU was Culla Vayhinger of Taylor (IN) who probably held a larger reputation for public speaking than did her president husband, Monroe.[4]

Presbyterian minister A. B. Simpson founded Nyack (NY) and the Christian and Missionary Alliance as agencies for his worldwide missionary vision, and they solicited the aid of all hands—men and women—in the cause. Indeed, overseas missions became one of the earliest professions open to women on an equal basis with men. By the early 1900s, the over 40 denominational women's missionary societies helped to send abroad the women foreign workers who, by that time, outnumbered their male counterparts. Especially significant was the female role in leading pre-collegiate missionary schools. Historian Page Smith has noted the distinguished record of women educational missionaries:

> Mission schools, in many instances founded by women and with women making up the great majority of teachers up to the college level, were the most pedagogically advanced in the world. The women who established

girls' schools had been trained in excellent institutions themselves—Oberlin, Antioch, Frances Willard's Female Academy, and, later, Smith, Mt. Holyoke, and literally dozens of small denominational colleges with high educational standards. In India, or China or Africa they were free to introduce the most modern educational notions without battling conservative school boards, suspicious parents, or hidebound principals. We often find such subjects as psychology and sociology taught in mission schools decades before they made their way into American curriculums. It would then not be too much to argue that the best free elementary or secondary education in the world in, let us say, 1910, was probably to be found in a girls' school in Beirut, Bombay, or Foochow....[5]

On the home front, Simpson employed women on all levels of the college and denominational ministry, including Bible professors, ministers, evangelists, and administrators. His philosophy on the role of women as ministers is set in the context of his view of the outpouring of the Holy Spirit upon all people (see Joel 2:28–29; Acts 21:9):

> The heart of Christ is not only the heart of a man but has in it also the tenderness and gentleness of a woman. Jesus was not a man in the rigid sense of manhood as distinct from womanhood, but, as the Son of Man, the complete Head of Humanity, He combined in Himself the nature both of man and woman ... in the Old Testament we find God revealing Himself under the sweet figure of motherhood.... And this aspect of His blessed character finds its perfect manifestation in the Holy Ghost, our Mother God.[6]

Denominations and colleges that shared the Simpson emphasis upon the work of the Holy Spirit tended to be more open to a large public role for women than did those that did not. Thus the women's movement had significant influence in denominations of the Wesleyan and Holiness Movements (e.g., 20 percent of the early Nazarene and Church of God, Anderson ministers were women), inner city missions (e.g., the Salvation Army), overseas missions, Bible colleges, and the Temperance Movement.

While one might argue that there was sympathy for women's ministry in the early Fundamentalist Movement (e.g., at Moody and William B. Riley's Northwestern), by the 1920s things had hardened and a reactionary defensiveness swept aside much of the gains that women had achieved during the previous generation. Aiding the growing Fundamentalist Movement was a surging Dispensationalism that together led to the "Great Reversal" which the later evangelical women's movement began to challenge by the 1970s. Other leaders of the conservative view on the role of women in ministry included Southern Baptists, Missouri Synod Lutherans, and the CRC as influenced by the thinking of early leader Abraham Kuyper.[7]

When the largely secular women's movement of the 1960s had a general consciousness raising effect, a parallel form of equal rights crusading arose within the evangelical community. One of the earliest high-profile academic freedom cases was that of Patricia and Stanley Gundry at Moody in the 1970s. Stanley was a professor of theology at Moody from 1968 to 1979, and he also served as president of the ETS in 1978. When Patricia published her pro-egalitarian book, *Woman Be Free*, in 1977 and Stanley supported her work, Moody officials were sufficiently embarrassed by constituency complaints that they felt compelled to dismiss Stanley from his teaching position. Stanley gives an account of his transformation from a hierarchical to an egalitarian view of the relationship between men and women in "From *Bobbed Hair, Bossy Wives, and Women Preachers to Woman Be Free*: My Story."[8]

Just as the Gundry case at Moody was preceded by an institutional change from a progressive to a conservative position, so also the Sheri Klouda case at Southwestern Baptist Seminary occurred in the wake of a conservative insurgence in that theological school and its supporting denomination, the SBC. In 2000 the SBC, now with conservatives in political control, amended its Baptist Faith and Message document to include "While men and women are both gifted for service in the church, the office of pastor is limited to men as qualified by Scripture," and "A wife is to submit herself graciously to the servant leadership of her husband even as the church willingly submits to the headship of Christ." In 2002, Southwestern hired Klouda, more recently at Taylor University, as a tenure-track assistant professor of Hebrew. Klouda thought that if any woman instructor could survive at Southwestern, she could. Well known in the Dallas area, she had graduated from both Criswell College and Southwestern, and held a doctorate in Hebrew, a field in which it was not easy to find qualified candidates. Furthermore, she was not a controversial person; she simply wanted to teach. But the powerful conservative Paige Patterson became seminary president in 2003, and in 2004 through a subordinate administrator, she learned that "Patterson would not be recommending her for tenure because she is female."[9]

Brigham Young (UT) denied continued status to English professor Gail Turley Houston primarily for her feminist positions including, most particularly, her support for the practice of praying to "Heavenly Mother as well as Heavenly Father." Dean Russell Jones stated, "I find it a problem when someone openly advocates praying to a Mother in Heaven, especially when specific instructions have been given to us from the First Presidency not to." An AAUP investigating committee found that the Brigham Young administration violated Houston's academic freedom while James D. Gordon III, associate academic vice president, countered, "We take academic freedom very seriously" and thought that the negative AAUP report was due to its "goal to impose a secular model on religious universities."[10]

Calvin College, in conjunction with the closely related CRC, dealt with the role-of-women issue in a deliberate manner. After a generation of technically considering the issue, a CRC study committee voted in 1990 to recommend ratification by the denomination of the right of women to serve churches as elders and ministers. Final ratification came six years later. Meanwhile the Calvin Center for Christian Scholarship had devoted the 1989–1990 year to a major study of "Gender Roles: Stability and Change within the Context of a Christian Worldview." Psychologist and philosopher Mary Stewart Van Leeuwen led the effort which involved five full-time and three part-time scholars. The result was a constructive work that emphasized understanding and healing, namely *After Eden: Facing the Challenge of Gender Reconciliation*. During the first 15 years that women were eligible for ordination, 13 percent of the CRC-approved candidates had been women. By 2011 local churches still selected men for 97 percent of the senior or solo ministerial positions. The college now offers a gender studies minor.[11]

While the Calvin/CRC effort was progressing, Mary Todd, graduate of Valparaiso (IN) and former historian at *Concordia River Forest* (IL), failed in her effort (see her book, *Authority Vested: A Story of Identity and Change in the Lutheran Church—Missouri Synod*) to convince the LCMS to accept women as ministers. As of 2014, the denomination website declared: "The church which wishes to remain faithful to the Word of God cannot permit the ordination of women to the pastoral office."[12]

The evangelical women's movement coalesces around three major positions, each represented by a formal organization. The organizations are Evangelical and Ecumenical Women's Caucas (EEWC) on the left, Christians for Biblical Equality (CBE) in the center, and Council for Biblical Manhood and Womanhood (CBMW) on the right. The EEWC is the oldest of the three, having begun in 1973 as the Evangelical Women's Caucas (EWC) within the progressive Evangelicals for Social Action, which is associated with the document Chicago Declaration of Evangelical Social Concerns and has been led by theologian Ron Sider of Eastern (PA). An alternate name for EEWC since 2009 is Christian Feminism Today. The organization's current self-description includes "We value the gifts God has given every individual and have long advocated for the full equality of women and LGBTQ people in church and society" and "we expand metaphors for God to include biblical female imagery." The growing identification of the EWC with the LGBTQ community led part of the membership to withdraw and organize the CBE in 1988.

Long-time leaders of EEWC have included Letha Scanzoni (Moody and Indiana undergraduate), Nancy Hardesty (Wheaton undergraduate), and Virginia Mollenkott (Bob Jones undergraduate). Scanzoni wrote with Hardesty *All We're Meant to Be* (1975) and with Mollenkott *Is the Homosexual My Neighbor: A Positive Christian View* (1978), both early influential books. Hardesty and Mollenkott have taught in both Christian colleges and state universities while Scanzoni has been an independent scholar.

CBE is an egalitarian organization with the goal of "advancing a biblical foundation for gift-based rather than gender-based ministry and service." The founding group included Gilbert Bilezikian of Wheaton, W. Ward Gasque of Eastern (PA) and Regent (British Columbia), Stanley Gundry of Moody and Zondervan Publishing Company, Gretchen Gaebelein Hull (independent scholar), Catherine Clark Kroeger of Gordon Seminary, Jo Anne Lyon, now general superintendent of the Wesleyan Church, and Roger Nicole of Gordon Seminary. Kroeger, now deceased, was the first president of CBE. A classical scholar, she, like nineteenth-century medical missionary and reformer Katherine Bushnell, engaged in a careful study of the ancient Greek texts to best understand the original meaning of such difficult verses as I Timothy 2:12. The result was the book, *I Suffer Not a Woman* published with her Presbyterian minister husband, Richard. Kroeger's successor as CBE president, Mimi Haddad of Bethel (MN) identifies Bushnell as the pioneer interpreter of the egalitarian perspective. Her 1921 book, *God's Word to Women* was republished by CBE in 2003. Bushnell wrote it only after years of study in the original language of every biblical reference which might be interpreted to mean that women are inferior to men. She believed that the original equality of women was lost with the Fall but restored with the redemptive work of Christ, and that the Pauline epistles rightly interpreted and translated were not opposed to the leadership and preaching of women. Haddad also salutes Bushnell for her crusading efforts against prostitution in Wisconsin lumber camps and the British army in India, with corrective political action resulting in both cases. The CBE believes that accurate biblical interpretation reduces abusive actions against women.

The CBMW was organized in 1987 as a contrast to the more radical feminism of the EWC and the more moderate egalitarianism of the CBE. Emphasizing what it calls complementarianism, it calls for husband headship in marriage and male control of the top leadership positions in the church as being the most faithful way of interpreting the relevant Pauline passages. The original leaders of the CBMW were Wayne Grudem of Trinity Divinity School and John Piper, former professor at Bethel (MN). Its current president is Owen Strachan of Boyce (KY) and Southern Baptist Seminary (KY), and its nine board members are all men. The founding document is the Danvers Statement, and its defining book is John Piper and Wayne Grudem, eds., *Recovering Biblical Manhood and Womanhood: A Response to Evangelical Feminism* (1991), whose contributors include Paige Patterson and Elizabeth Eliot.

The CBMW believes that the EEWC and the CBE do not hold as high a view of the Bible as they do. By contrast, CBE-type people wonder how the CBMW would respond to a sensitive young woman who asks "why would God give some women the ability to do something and then forbid all women from doing it?" or an innocent young girl who engages in conversational prayer as follows:

> Dear God,
> Are boys better than girls?
> I know you are one,
> But try to be fair.

The EEWC complains that the CBMW, even more than the CBE, is unduly tolerant of the demeaning abuses—subtle as well as overt—committed by men against women. Among CCCU women faculty members, perhaps two-thirds would hold views more nearly consistent with the CBE while the number who would identify with the theology of the thinking of the CBMW might be no higher than 15 percent.[13]

Moving from gender to race, the most significant recent academic freedom issue involving race occurred at Bob Jones University (BJU), a southern college as well as a fundamentalist one. Evolving through many stages over a generation, the question of racial integration of the student body reached its climax in the Supreme Court case of *Bob Jones University v. the United States* (1983). Until 1970 the federal government allowed tax-exempt status to private schools irrespective of racial admissions policies. But in that year, given the civil rights legislation of the 1960s, the Internal Revenue Service (IRS) determined that it must update its policy. BJU partly adapted by changing its policy against enrolling blacks to accept married black students. After the federal courts became more explicit in prohibiting racial exclusion in private schools (see *Runyon v. McCrary*, 1975), the university agreed to admit unmarried blacks, but to still forbid interracial dating and marriage. Meanwhile in 1975, the IRS notified the university that it was revoking its tax-exempt status and doing so retroactively, thus charging the university $1/2 million in back taxes. The university appealed the case with hearings in multiple courts with differing results until it was heard before the Supreme Court in 1982. By an 8–1 vote (William Rehnquist dissenting), the court upheld the action of the

IRS against the university. In 2000, BJU president Bob Jones III removed the ban on interracial dating after the limitation became an issue in the presidential campaign of that year during the visit to campus by Republican nominee George W. Bush.

Later President Stephen Jones began a scholarship fund for African-American students and issued a formal apology of past practices:

> We failed to accurately represent the Lord and to fulfill the commandment to love others as ourselves. For these failures we are profoundly sorry. Though no known antagonism toward minorities or expressions of racism on a personal level have ever been tolerated on our campus, we allowed institutional policies to remain in place that were racially hurtful.[14]

More recently Calvin experienced an unfortunate incident involving an Afro-American professor of education. "Professor Denise Isom loves her work at Calvin College and her Grand Rapids, Mich. church, Messiah Missionary Baptist," reported the CRC *Banner*. "The problem: Isom must choose one or the other." The Calvin board has a requirement that regular faculty appointees must be members of a CRC church; the requirement, however, provides for a transition period for new professors and the option of applying for an exception. Isom sought such an exception noting that while she enjoyed working in the largely Dutch, overwhelmingly white culture during the week, "I need a place of worship that is already consistent with my culture and able to grapple with issues of race in ways which make it a respite, a re-charging and growing place for me, as opposed to another location where . . . I am 'other.' " The college denied her request for an exception in 2010 after seven years of service.[15]

More positively, the CCCU colleges in the new century have made a focused effort to recruit more African-American students. A 2008 study in *The Journal of Blacks in Higher Education* found that in the decade after 1997 there was a threefold increase in the number of CCCU institutions enrolling over 10 percent blacks and a 50 percent reduction in the number of CCCU schools with less than 2 percent such enrollment. Calvin was one of the nine CCCU colleges with less than 1 percent black students.[16]

While African-Americans comprise a meaningful and growing minority and women an actual majority of the students on the Christian college campuses, Jews and Palestinians have almost no presence at all. Nevertheless the increased public awareness of the details of the modern mid-eastern Arab/Israeli crisis has led to both major interest and major change of perspective on this subject on the CCCU campuses. The Christian college students as direct heirs of the Judeo-Christian tradition had long been aware of the difficulties of the modern Israelis in achieving a safe state; however, knowledge of the simultaneous plight of the Palestinians has been a newer revelation to them.

Marcy Jane Knopf-Newman in *The Politics of Teaching Palestine to Americans* describes how the liberty to present the Palestinian perspective has become a significant academic freedom concern on many campuses. Even though a Jew, Knopf-Newman believes that Zionism has been synonymous with the oppression of the Palestinians. Opinion polls over the decades since Israeli nationhood have consistently shown Americans, led by the evangelicals, as favoring Israel over Palestine by wide margins; but this margin has been diminishing recently, especially on the Christian college campuses where, except for a few pockets of continuing strong support (e.g., Jerry Falwell's Liberty in Virginia, Pat Robertson's Regent in Virginia, Tim LaHaye's San Diego Christian, and Dallas Theological Seminary), Christian Zionism is largely absent. The modern students are less interested in historical rivalries than in issues of contemporary justice, and with their heightened awareness of the Palestinian sufferings, that situation to them seems full of injustice.[17]

Harvard trained lawyer David Brog, executive director of Christians United for Israel (CUFI), laments the growing sympathy for Palestine at the evangelical colleges: "the effort to delegitimize Israel is . . . being waged on America's Christian campuses," citing Bible professor Gary Burge of Wheaton, Board chairman Mart Green of Oral Roberts (OK) and President and First Lady Jay and Lynn Barnes of Bethel (MN) as prime offenders. For example, Burge, according to Brog,

> travels the country and world accusing the Jewish state of the worst of crimes and engaging in a mockery of Judaism that borders on anti-Semitism. When CUFI announced plans to hold an event at Wheaton in January, 2009, Burge went on the offensive. CUFI's student members came under such intense pressure that they moved their event off campus: There would be no pro-Israel event at the evangelical Harvard.[18]

The growing consensus on Christian college campuses would probably be to identify less as pro-Israel or pro-Palestine than as both pro-Israel and pro-Palestine—and pro-justice for all.

The subjects of this chapter—gender, race, and ethnicity—are political issues as well as religious and academic freedom ones. On the subject of politics in general Christian colleges experience a reputation for being politically and economically conservative (see Chapter 17) but they are less likely to have political and economic academic freedom issues than are the secular institutions. In the recent CCCU faculty survey, 46 percent identified as Republican, 25 percent as Independent, and 22 percent as Democratic while the students divided 63 percent Republican, 12 percent Independent, and 12 percent Democratic.[19]

CHAPTER 27

Secular University Restrictions and Their Broader Implications

Most of the chapters of this book focus upon the practice of Christian higher education. This chapter, however, departs from that general pattern to consider some specific ways in which secular universities restrict the expression of religious—and other—ideas by their students and faculty. With the growing hand of government regulation in education, what happens in the secular universities influences the Christian colleges at least indirectly and sometimes very directly. For example, in the case of the sexual identity issue, the implications have been major.

Chapter 14 discussed how American higher education moved toward secularization after 1880. In a sense this chapter is a sequel to that one as it offers case studies of the limits on religious practice in modern, secular, primarily public universities.

Student Christian Organizations

The 2010 Supreme Court case of *Christian Legal Society v. Martinez* was a landmark decision. By a 5–4 vote, the High Court upheld the action of the University of California Hastings Law School to require the local chapter of the Christian Legal Society to allow homosexuals to hold leadership positions and, by implication, that all student groups must open all positions to all students. Similarly, in 2011 the Supreme Court chose not to hear an appeal of a decision by San Diego State to require its Christian organizations to be willing to accept as leaders students who did not share their beliefs. Then in 2014, the entire California state system of 23 campuses "de-recognized" its local chapters of InterVarsity Christian Fellowship for not accepting as student leaders non-Christians and gays.[1] The broader effects of the California decisions were less in the extent to which they led secular universities in other states to tightly regulate their Christian student groups than in the degree to which they spurred the cause of gay rights in general and threatened the Christian colleges that resisted the hiring of practicing homosexuals.

InterVarsity has been a leader among the campus ministry groups in opposing the efforts of some universities to restrict the access of such religious groups to official standing and use of institutional resources. By 2014, its biggest losses were in California. Elsewhere with a presence on over 600 campuses, it notes that by 2013 it had faced major challenges in over 40 of these. On many of these campuses (e.g., Michigan, Ohio State, Minnesota, Maryland, Harvard, and Rutgers), the negotiations resulted in solutions satisfactory to InterVarsity.[2]

Resistance was stronger, however, at Vanderbilt, Bowdoin, Rollins, and Grinnell, all private institutions that are less bound by the First Amendment free exercise provision. In 2012 Vanderbilt adopted the "all comers" philosophy of the Martinez case, determining that none of its 14 religious organizations could limit its leaders to adherents of their faith and still be eligible for the privileges that come with official institutional recognition. Unusual for a private university, Vanderbilt receives significant state appropriations and operates its own state-authorized police force. The Tennessee state legislature, in response to the university actions against its Christian organizations, passed legislation requiring Vanderbilt to provide greater religious liberty for its students; the governor, however, vetoed the legislative action.[3]

Grinnell, long recognized as a major Christian social gospel institution, saw its IVCF chapter divide in two in 2011 when several homosexual members sought to compete for leadership positions. The result was that the Student Government Association revoked its recognition of the InterVarsity chapter, the latter reorganized and renamed itself, and some of its former members formed a more progressive group, "Grinnellians Seeking Christ" (GSC), with membership and leadership open to LGBTQ students.[4]

At Grinnell and elsewhere, among the ways in which some LGBT Christian students explain their concerns to the traditionalists is

> I just want what you have, namely the right to live out my Christian faith in the supportive fellowship of Christian believers while expressing my sexuality in the way God has made me in a loving, faithful, life-long monogamous relationship with my chosen partner.

In addition to the InterVarsity battles, other contests—all victories for the cause of equal treatment for religious organizations and individuals—were won at the Universities of Virginia, Wisconsin, and Eastern Michigan.

In the 1995 Supreme Court case of *Rosenberger v. the University of Virginia*, constitutional law scholar Michael McConnell argued successfully that the university had to fund (from student fees) a Christian student publication in the same manner that it financed other registered student organizations. In 2011 the Supreme Court declined to hear an appeal from the Seventh U.S. Court decision of 2010 ruling for Badger Catholic, the Roman Catholic student foundation at the University of Wisconsin. This left standing the verdict that the university could not distinguish among the foundation's activities, funding only those programs that were deemed less promotional. The Sixth Federal Circuit Court in 2011 ruled that Eastern Michigan denied the religious freedom rights of Julia Ward when it dismissed her from the graduate counseling program when, for religious reasons, she asked to be excused from counseling a gay patient. Alliance Defending Freedom (begun in 1994 as the Alliance Defense Fund) led the successful defense in the last two cases. It now lists in its membership 300 organizations and 2,400 attorneys.

The Shifting Balance between Religious Freedom and Civil Liberties

As of the writing of this book, and even of this chapter, in 2014, there are intellectual, cultural, and political crosscurrents in operation in society in general and in both secular and Christian higher education. The same environment that is producing a greater interest in spirituality in general and religious discourse in the secular universities in particular (see Chapter 14) is also leading to a declining interest in protecting religious freedom in general and religious privilege in particular—especially for the historically dominant Christian faith. The single greatest driving force for this change in thinking and valuing is the growing concern to guarantee sexual identity equality as a civil right on par with gender and racial equality.

In the rapidly changing landscape of the twenty-first century, evangelicals and Catholics have become nearly the last groups to hold restrictions based on sexual conduct. For these groups who are used to viewing themselves as exemplary in human compassion, it is disconcerting to hear themselves increasingly described as discriminatory.[5]

Speech Codes

Beginning in the 1980s, the secular universities sharply increased their efforts to protect their vulnerable minorities (e.g., race, ethnicity, religion, and sexual preference) from verbal abuse by establishing sweeping rules against such expression. By 1995, over 350 colleges had adopted regulations of this type.

But in an attempt to solve one problem, they had created another. Freedom of speech now joined freedom of religion and even freedom of assembly, as First Amendment rights that the secular universities were willing to de-emphasize to achieve the goal of equality and respect for minority groups.

The public outcry against the speech codes was widespread. The AAUP, while sympathetic with the aims of the speech codes, was sharply critical of the means used to achieve them. Its formal statement on speech codes declared that

> while we can acknowledge both the weight of these concerns and the thoughtfulness of those persuaded of the need for regulation, rules which ban or punish speech based upon its content cannot be justified. An institution of higher learning fails to fulfill its mission if it asserts the power to proscribe ideas..., however repugnant... by proscribing any ideas, a university sets an example that profoundly disserves its academic mission.[6]

In a similar vein, the ACLU added, "Where racist, sexist, and homophobic speech is concerned...more speech—not less—is the best revenge. This is particularly true at universities whose mission is to facilitate learning through open debate and study, and to enlighten."[7]

The FIRE has been an intense observer of the speech code movement, especially effective at publishing the excesses of the latter. Led by Greg Lukianoff, its president, FIRE has cited such incidents as the student at Ohio University who was prevented from posting on her residence hall door a statement that neither major candidate for president in 2012 (Obama and Romney) was worthy of office, or the Yale students who could not wear to the Harvard game t-shirts which carried the F. Scott Fitzgerald quotation (from his 1920 novel *This Side of Paradise*), "I think of all Harvard men as sissies." FIRE founders Alan Kors (University of Pennsylvania historian) and Harvey Silverglate (Cambridge, Massachusetts civil rights lawyer) told of an incident at Sarah Lawrence (NY) in 1993 when a student, Marlin Lask, was convicted for laughing when another student called a third student a "faggot." Refusing his sentence, he transferred to another college for a year. Lukianoff cited a major 2010 study by the American Association of Colleges and Universities that only one-third of the students and one-fifth of the faculty agreed that it was "safe to hold unpopular opinions on campus."[8]

Since at least 2007, FIRE has been publishing regular reports on the impact of speech code restrictions on the freedom of expression in higher education. Its 2014 report surveyed the four-year public and the major private institutions and found that 59 percent of these universities imposed codes that "seriously infringe upon the free speech rights of students," a number down noticeably from the 75 percent figure of 2007.[9]

When the speech codes have faced court challenges, they usually have lost. Among the best known of these court cases are *Doe v. the University of Michigan* (1989) and *UWM Post v. Board of Regents of the University of Wisconsin* (1991). The ruling in the Doe case (United States District Court for the Eastern District of Michigan) read in part:

> It is an unfortunate fact of our constitutional system that the ideals of freedom and equality are often in conflict.... While the court is sympathetic to the University's obligation to ensure equal educational opportunities for all its students, such efforts must not be at the expense of free speech. Unfortunately, this was precisely what the University did.

In the Wisconsin case, the federal district court ruled as unconstitutional the university "Design for Diversity" plan, which prohibited addressing any individual with comments that demean, race, sex, religion, color, creed, disadvantage, sexual orientation, national origin, ancestry, or age.[10]

In 2013 the executive branch of the federal government joined the universities in mandating speech codes, in this case involving all colleges and universities in the area of sexual harassment speech. The broad joint decree from the Departments of Education and Justice defined "sexual harassment" as any unwelcome conduct of a sexual nature including "verbal conduct . . . if the listener takes offense to sexually related speech for any reason, no matter how irrationally or unreasonably, the speaker may be punished."[11]

The movement of the federal government into the speech code activity is an illustration of how, on many levels, it recently has claimed a larger role in the control of higher education. The next chapter will consider that development in greater detail.

CHAPTER 28

Government Restrictions and Accreditation Uncertainties

The degree to which the federal government has chosen to become involved in regulating private higher education increased sharply in the early twenty-first century. Several reasons explain this new assertiveness: (1) the desire of the Obama administration to obtain as much of a national health-care plan as possible, (2) the desire of parts of the federal government to achieve full civil rights for the LGBT community, (3) a concern about the disproportionate tuition increases for a college education, and (4) a concern about the poor loan repayment record by the former students of the for-profit colleges.

Historically, the federal government expressed much interest in higher education early in the Washington administration, introduced a new emphasis upon applied learning during the Lincoln era, entered the domain of student financial aid during the Franklin Roosevelt years, and reached its current, comprehensive, and sustained involvement beginning with the Great Society of Lyndon Johnson, who took pride in being known as "the education president."

The Constitutional Convention delegates discussed the idea of launching a national university. Washington mentioned it in his first annual message to Congress and in his last address to Congress; and the idea had the support of all of Washington's presidential successors through the Federalist Era. The Morrill Land-Grant College Act of 1862 authorized the federal government to give away what it held in abundance, namely land, to each of the states at a rate of 30,000 acres per senator and representative, with the proceeds from the sale of the lands going to finance the establishment of a state college for teaching agriculture and the mechanical arts.[1] The more recent idea of the federal government helping to fund the expenses of individual college students began with the National Youth Administration during the

Great Depression of the 1930s and continued with the widely known GI Bill plan introduced in 1944 to provide both reward and encouragement to the returning World War II and later veterans who were interested in acquiring post-secondary training. Already by 1946, the GIs comprised one-half of all college students. Cold War competition concerns inspired the National Defense Education Act of 1958, but it was the Higher Education Act of 1965 that marked the beginning of the federal government's broad-based, long-range commitment to aiding public and private colleges through grants and loans to their students.[2]

The Health Insurance Mandate Battle

Many of the twentieth-century American presidents favored Congressional passage of a universal health plan; none of them succeeded in achieving it, although Franklin Roosevelt introduced social security and Lyndon Johnson obtained Medicare and Medicaid. Thus the United States remains as nearly the only industrialized country without national health insurance; what we have after the 2010 Patient Protection and Affordable Care Act (popularly known as Obamacare) is a mixed public/private plan. The major advantage of the new program is that many more people gained coverage. A major disadvantage is that the new rules violated the religious conscience of many Christian individuals and organizations. One of the provisions of Obamacare is the establishment by the government of minimum standards for employer-provided plans. The primary offensive provision, as interpreted by the federal department of Health and Human Services (HHS), required employers to provide abortifacient medications and procedures in their plans.

The outcry by evangelical and Catholic organizations in general and their colleges in particular was loud and widespread. The Becket Fund for Religious Liberty became the primary advocate for the dissenting organizations. Following the 2010 Congressional Act, the Department of HHS in 2011 issued its mandate requiring religious institutions to include the abortion treatments in their plans. A year later, Wheaton and Catholic University, symbolically representing evangelical and Catholic higher education in general, filed suit in partnership seeking exemption from the offensive provision in the name of religious freedom.[3]

What Wheaton and Catholic represented for religious higher education, Hobby Lobby, the arts and crafts company with its chain of 500 stores, represented for businesses owned by devoted Christian families. The Hobby Lobby lawsuit of 2012 resulted in a 2014 Supreme Court case in which the high court heard that case together with a similar suit from Conestoga Wood Specialties, a Lancaster, Pennsylvania, company owned by a Mennonite family.

By a 5–4 combination decision, the Court ruled that the two closely held for-profit, family companies with sincerely held religious beliefs about life beginning at conception should not be required by the government to provide in their insurance plan contraceptives that end life.[4]

Shortly after the Hobby Lobby decision, the Supreme Court, in a 6–3 vote, granted a temporary injunction to Wheaton and others to prevent HHS from fining them while their cases are pending. Meanwhile, HHS continues to modify its rules (its eighth edition came in 2014) to try to satisfy the religious dissenters, while the latter evangelical and Catholic organizations appeared to want nothing less than the freedom of conscience which the government on this issue had granted to churches. The Becket Fund reports that as of 2014, over 300 plaintiffs have filed over 100 cases against the HHS mandate. These suits involved many evangelical and Catholic colleges.[5]

Traditional Marriage and Obama's Executive Order of 2013

Of the three major divisions of the federal government, the executive branch has been the most prominent in seeking to impose new restrictions on the Christian colleges. Just as the executive Department of HHS has pressured the evangelical and Catholic colleges and other Christian organizations to include coverage for certain abortion procedures in their health insurance policies, so also it is the executive department through a presidential executive order that has decreed that the Christian colleges and other faith-based organizations must be willing to hire same-sex practicing faculty and staff members.

By contrast, the Congress has been more protective of religious freedom in this area. When the Senate passed the Employment Non-Discrimination Act of 2013, updating the 1964 Civil Rights Acts to add sexual identity to the protected categories, it included an exemption for religious organizations: "This act shall not apply to a corporation, association, educational institution or institution of learning, or society that is exempt from the religious discrimination provision of title VII of the Civil Rights Act of 1964." As of mid-2015, the House of Representatives has not acted on this bill. Both sides in the same-sex marriage debate look forward to a definitive Supreme Court decision on this issue. The Christian colleges, in particular, will be eager to see how broad the religious exemption might be in such a decision.[6]

Although President Obama moved cautiously toward embracing same-sex marriage, once he accepted it he quickly became aggressive in his activism for it. His position had been undecided when running for Congress in 2000 and opposed when running for president in 2008. During his first term, with the gay lobby pressuring him, his wife, Michelle, encouraging him, and his vice president Joe Biden preempting him in support, he conceded that, as a personal ideal, he thought that same-sex couples should be allowed to marry. Then with his reelection secured, in his second inaugural address in 2013 he forcefully compared the LGBT cause to the Civil Rights Movement of the 1950s and 1960s. Eighteen months later and frustrated by the reluctance of Congress to adopt his agenda on this subject and others, he issued his controversial executive order barring the federal government and its contractors from discriminating against LGBT employees. "Federal contractors" included about one-fifth of the workforce and nearly all Christian colleges because of their administration of federal financial programs for their students. Significantly, unlike the act passed by the Senate, this provision recognized no exemptions for religious dissenters.[7]

In anticipation of the July 21, 2014, executive order, several weeks earlier—on June 25—140 evangelical leaders, including the heads of over 20 evangelical colleges, submitted a letter to the president requesting an exemption from this decree for faith-based organizations. "Our requests," the letter read,

> are grounded in the historical context of strong federal legal protections for religious organizations' hiring practices. Under the Civil Rights Act of 1964, as upheld by the Supreme Court, religious organizations are free to consider religion when deciding who is most qualified to join their respective staffs. They are free under Title VII to maintain a conduct standard that reflects their religions' sincerely held beliefs, which included deep convictions about human sexuality.[8]

Gordon President D. Michael Lindsay did not sign the June 25, 2014, letter, but he did join 13 other religious leaders who sent a second similar letter, dated July 1, 2014. Signatories with Lindsay were two former Obama associates, namely Joel C. Hunter and Michael Wear. Hunter has been a close spiritual advisor to Obama, while Wear served as the presidents' liaison to faith communities during the 2012 presidential campaign. Both Hunter and Wear were officials in Obama's White House Office of Faith-Based and Community Partnerships.

The July 1, 2014, letter attracted wide attention when shortly afterward the New England Association of Schools and Colleges (Gordon's regional accreditation organization) announced that it would review the Gordon position to see if it "is at odds in any way with our standards and policies." In September, the association and Gordon announced in a joint statement that the college will not need to alter its policies radically in order to satisfy the accreditation association. In a sense, the Gordon situation is a test case for the accrediting association to display how strongly it wishes to remain independent of pressures to act as a government enforcement agency.[9]

Rules and More Rules

Although in general the idea of an expanded role for the federal government in domestic affairs has been a characteristic of Democratic administrators more than Republican ones, it was the Republican George W. Bush who initiated the recent movement of Washington into the regulation of first elementary and secondary education and then higher education. Based upon a program in Texas, the No Child Left Behind Act of 2001, passed during the first year of the Bush presidency, required states to develop assessment programs of all students at selected pre-collegiate grade levels. Increasingly teaching focused upon test preparation and the maintenance of detailed progress reports. The law expired in 2007, and Obama and Congress could not agree on a satisfactory new version. Meanwhile, Obama promoted rigorous teacher evaluation systems.[10]

On the college level, Bush's Secretary of Education, Margaret Spellings, established a Commission on the Future of American Higher Education to address and deal with the problems of the higher learning system. It identified real problems including access and mounting cost, but it exaggerated when describing higher education as being in a state of deep crisis. Rather than offering functional solutions, the divided commission merely proposed, in the words of one of its members, "the federalization of the process by which colleges and universities are accredited and their students become eligible for federal student-aid programs."[11]

Subsequently in the College Cost Reduction Act of 2007 and the Higher Education Reauthorization Act of 2008, Congress offered continued encouraging financial aid and repayment support for college students but also continued the movement to federalize the control of higher education, adding extensive regulations and reporting requirements for the beneficiary colleges. Judith Eaton, president of the Council for Higher Education Accreditation, found in the 2008 act "110 new rules or reporting obligations for higher education and accreditation." Eaton's assessment in 2010 was that the previous decade had brought a "sea change" in the relationship between higher education and the federal government. The traditional "core academic values . . . —institutional autonomy, academic freedom, and peer and professional review—may no longer be able to flourish." In her own domain of accreditation, Eaton noted with lament: "more and more often, accreditors are forced to view their work through the lens of 'What does the federal government want?'—in contrast to the traditionally more productive question of 'How do we work with institutions and programs to enhance quality in the service of students?' "[12]

An example of how the DOE can engage in excessive control is its method of dealing in 2010 with a limited amount of financial aid irresponsibility and even fraud, especially in private for-profit institutions. Instead of simply dealing directly with the accused institutions, the DOE required each state to develop a "substantive" procedure for licensing all of its private colleges to determine their eligibility for financial aid, ignoring the fact that longstanding authorization procedures already existed. "My concern is that there appears to be no limit to what factors a state can consider when granting or withholding authorization, and no mechanisms for appeal or due process," noted Blair Dowden, Huntington president, in a hearing before a House of Representatives Committee. Shapri LoMaglio, government relations director for the CCCU, added that the DOE mandate is "a complete overreach into the institutional autonomy that private colleges need in order to function as the independent and unique institutions that they are."[13]

In the Reauthorized Higher Education Act of 2014 (or later) the Senate has passed a version that provides large federal oversight, while the slower House deliberations point to a more limited federal role. When in 2013, the House Education and the Workforce Committee asked the American Council on Education to submit its recommendations for the 2014 Act, the council on behalf of 39 higher education associations submitted a comprehensive list of suggestions including this one: "To encourage . . . experimentation and implementation of effective strategies to control costs, Congress should use FIPSE [Fund for Improvement of Post-secondary Education] to develop and disseminate scalable cost reduction approaches . . . through pilot programs or competitive . . . grants." More than by creating countless rules, the federal government could best contribute to achieving cost reductions in Christian higher education by providing financial incentive through FIPSE and in other ways for the development of less expensive models of higher education such as those suggested in Chapter 18.[14]

Concern in Canada

Canada is a more secular country than is the United States. Among Christians, the declining number of Protestants and Anglicans represented only 11 percent of the national population in 2010, down from 45 percent in 1950. Similarly, the Evangelicals have reduced from 25 to 8 percent during the same time period. In higher education, the nearly 400 colleges, universities, and technical institutions include 83 independent universities. Christian Higher Education Canada, the counterpart of the CCCU in the United States, counts 34 member campuses, including 11 universities, 16 colleges, and 17 seminaries and graduate schools located in seven of the ten provinces.[15]

The Canadian Association of University Teachers (CAUT), the national faculty labor union, is more sharply opposed to the Christian college movement than is its nearest United States counterpart, the AAUP. The CAUT website frankly declares that

> universities violate academic freedom when they require academic staff to commit to a particular ideology or statement of faith as a condition of employment.... CAUT will investigate all cases where universities are alleged to impose a faith or ideological test. If the allegations prove true and the university is unwilling to change its practice, it will be listed on this web page.

The cited "web page" is a censure list, and by 2014 it included five institutions: Canadian Mennonite (MB), Crandall (NB), Providence (MB), Redeemer (ON), and Trinity Western (BC).[16]

Trinity Western University (TWU) has been the major target of the crusading secularists. The college began in 1962 as an institution of the Evangelical Free Churches of Canada and America. When the British Columbia College of Teachers (BCCT) with its certification authority denied recognition to TWU's teacher education program because of the university position on homosexuality, TWU pursued the case to the Supreme Court of Canada where in 2001 the high court ruled that BCCT violated TWU's right to religious freedom. Later, TWU sought to open the first Christian faith-based law school in Canada; by 2014 six provincial legal societies had voted to accredit the school while three, including British Columbia, had voted against recognition. In 2005, Canada had become the fourth country in the world to legalize same-sex marriage.[17]

While Canada has no national system of higher education accreditation, and the general regulation of higher education is by individual province, in practice, institutional membership in the Association of Universities and Colleges of Canada (AUCC) in conjunction with approval to operate by the specific province serves as de facto accreditation for a university. "The danger for the Christian colleges," notes John Stackhouse, theologian at Regent (BC), "is that the continuous pressure from CAUT and other forces might cause AUCC to withdraw the membership of one or more of the Christian colleges." Meanwhile, the danger of these Canadian proceedings for the United States Christian colleges is that the greater secular spirit in Canada might give encouragement to the less tolerant tendencies of the secular educational and political forces below the border.[18]

While Christian churches retain a large amount of religious freedom to teach and practice their 2,000-year-old views on traditional marriage, the same is no longer true for Christian colleges, with their major dependency upon government student aid. By 2014 Christian lawyers specializing in higher education law or First Amendment rights were issuing stark warnings to the Christian colleges. "Start planning now," they say, "for the possibility, perhaps even likelihood, that within the near future you may have to choose between being willing to accept LGBT employees or facing the loss of aid for your students." "Even if a college is able to replace the government revenue flow," notes Shapri LoMaglio, "there is no guarantee that the accrediting agencies will continue to grant colleges wide latitude in defining their nature and mission, especially as the federal government, since the Spellings Commission Report of 2006, has been pressuring the accreditors to become more regulatory in nature."[19]

In summary, by mid-2015, the Christian colleges, especially the evangelical ones, saw the increasing demands of the federal government as intrusive, costly, and threatening to institutional mission—and perhaps even institutional survival. While the June 26, 2015, Supreme Court decision, *Obergefell v. Hodges*, decreed in a 5-4 vote that the states must provide for same-sex marriage, it is not yet clear what the impact of this action might be for religious colleges.[20]

CHAPTER 29

Due Process

Once an organization defines its nature and goals, its primary concern must be the welfare of its constituency. The primary business of a college is truth-seeking. The primary business of a Christian college is truth-seeking from the common base of the Christian faith. The primary base of the Christian faith is love and justice. The focus of this chapter is upon justice and how it should and how it does and does not operate in the Christian college community, especially as it relates to the welfare of its faculty in their vocation of truth-seeking.

As the cardinal sin of a teacher is not to be boring but to be unfair, so also the most serious violation of academic freedom in a Christian college is to be unjust in the conduct of its personnel procedures. The first principle in assuring institutional justice is a well-developed statement of academic freedom in the creation of which there was broad faculty participation. The second principle is an institutional commitment to faculty participation in decision-making on major issues. Although not always appreciated and not always accurate in its understandings, the AAUP, in general, has performed a valuable service to the Christian colleges by helping them operate with an integrity that is consistent with their high ideals.

Many of the cases reviewed in this book involved considerations of both content and process. In deciding which cases to discuss in this chapter, I have chosen to focus largely, but not exclusively, on those that the AAUP has identified—usually directly, sometimes indirectly—as involving questions of due process.

The basis for the idea and practice of due process in the Christian college in America includes the Old Testament idea of justice (e.g., Deuteronomy 19:15), the New Testament formula for resolving personal disputes within community (Matthew 18:15–17), the English Magna Carta of 1215, and the United States Constitution's judicial emphasis on due process and trial by a peer jury (Article III, Section 2 and the Fifth, Sixth, Seventh, and Fourteenth Amendments).

Just as Calvin has been the leader among Christian colleges in emphasizing the importance of academic freedom in general, so also individual Calvin-related scholars have led in articulating the primacy of due process structures within a fully developed system of academic freedom. George Marsden spent the early-to-middle part of his career at Calvin before transferring to Duke and then Notre Dame. He is widely known for his exposure of the limitations on academic freedom in the secular universities; however, in what is arguably the most important oral presentation of his career—his 1992 presidential address to the American Society of Church History—he focused on the lack of due process by the president of a then Christian college, Ethelbert Warfield of Lafayette (PA). In Warfield's battle with the leaders of the fledgling AAUP over Warfield's dismissal of religion professor John Mecklin in 1913, Marsden notes, "the AAUP founders clearly had the better argument. If institutions were to have operative boundaries, they should state them clearly in advance . . . . It is essential that due process be protected."[1]

Like Marsden, philosopher Nicholas Wolterstorff spent the first part of his career at Calvin before leaving, in his case, for Yale. He observes that while Christian colleges are in some ways more intellectually free than their secular counterparts, nevertheless too often they employ arbitrary administrative procedures that "violate the personhood" of some of their professors. "Over the years," he notes,

> I have acquired a rather broad acquaintance with the religiously-based colleges and universities of America; in the course of that experience, I have learned that the history of these colleges and universities is littered with stories of unjust—often grossly unjust—infringements on academic freedom. These stories constitute a shameful blotch on the reputation of those institutions . . . almost always it is in the procedure . . . that the injustice lies. Where there is no rule of law but only the command of persons, where secrecy and arbitrariness reign, where one never knows when and where the axe will fall, there justice weeps.[2]

Long-time Calvin President Anthony Diekema (1976–1995), in his path-breaking book on academic freedom policy development in the Christian college, counsels presidents and provosts to both fully understand and openly champion the cause of academic freedom in all of its aspects and procedures as it best fits their campus and then to educate, as needed, the college constituencies to "appreciate how academic freedom protects the very essence of the academic enterprise." Develop procedures if they are not already in place. Having done this well early and updated periodically, he notes, it will be much easier to deal equitably with specific cases when they arise. Diekema advises trustees to acknowledge that they have a "fiduciary obligation to protect the academic as well as the financial well-being of the institution," and therefore "must protect academic freedom from both internal and external threats" and must "insist on the existence of a comprehensive statement of mission...that includes or refers to a statement on academic freedom with clearly and precisely outlined...procedures for 'due process' in academic freedom cases..." For church officials in denominational colleges, Diekema repeats the specific recommendation to "Support and promote the deliberate use of due process in the adjudication of academic freedom cases."[3]

Now this chapter examines in some detail a series of Christian college due process cases. Most of these cases appeared in the *AAUP Journal*.

Bethune-Cookman (FL)

The 1921 merger of two historically black colleges in Florida, Cookman Institute of Jacksonville and the Daytona Educational and Industrial Training School for Negro Girls, produced the co-educational organization now known as Bethune-Cookman University (B-CU) in Daytona Beach. The name Cookman comes from a Methodist minister benefactor, while the name Bethune stems from the civil rights and women's rights leader Mary McLeod Bethune, who founded the Daytona school in 1904 and served as its president for 40 years. Bethune, who studied for two years at Dwight L. Moody's Bible Institute in Chicago, founded the National Council of Negro Women in 1935 and served as an advisor to multiple presidents, most notably Franklin Roosevelt.

In 2004, Trudie Kibbe Reed became the fifth president of B-CU after serving as president of Philander Smith (AR). When in 2009 her administration arbitrarily dismissed four professors on charges of sexual harassment against students and notified 34 other faculty and staff members that their employment was ended because of the loss of institutional income due to the financial crisis of 2008, several of the professors, including the first group of four, appealed to the AAUP. The AAUP investigating team found that (1) the administration in many ways did not follow its own institutional guidelines for faculty dismissals, (2) these institutional guidelines, even if followed, were severely deficient when measured against applicable AAUP-recommended standards, and (3) the administration "supports favorites and ignores or punishes those who fall out of favor or who question, contend, or appeal." In 2012, Edison O. Jackson succeeded Reed as the chief executive officer of B-CU.[4]

Cedarville (OH)

The Cedarville case involving New Testament scholar David Hoffeditz, while mentioned in Chapter 25, is discussed in greater detail here. As in the Bethune-Cookman case, the AAUP determined both that the university's due process procedures were deficient in themselves and also that the institution in certain ways failed to follow its own written procedures. Hoffeditz, a Cedarville alumnus with tenure as a New Testament scholar and whose wife was a Cedarville counselor, was dismissed by the president in 2007, supported in 2008 by a faculty grievance panel that determined that the administration had made "missteps" in the termination process, and then dismissed again later in 2008 by the board of trustees.

The Hoffeditz case developed from a dispute in the Bible department between conservative and progressive factions over an issue obtuse to most outsiders (see Chapter 24). Rather than encouraging the department members to learn to live with their fine distinctions, the administration of President William Brown appointed a committee headed by department chair Thomas Cragoe to find a consensus position that they and the rest of the university could accept and thus present a united front to their constituency as the institution launched a campaign to fund a new Bible department building. Meanwhile the trustees, apparently impatient with the rate of progress of the faculty committee, created their own solution and posted it on the campus website, thus creating new controversy by surpassing the faculty committee. The conservative element of the faculty was also offended by the moderate parts of the trustee report.

Meanwhile the administration was pressing dissenting members of the Bible department to resign or face dismissal, and requiring all faculty members to sign the new trustee statement. It was in the wake of these developments that in July 2007, three months after signing his 2007–2008 contract, Hoffeditz received a letter of dismissal effective one month later. President Brown said that the administration and trustees did not dismiss Hoffeditz for his dissenting theology but because of his violating university standards of decorum such as "how you treat each other, how you talk to each other."

The two-person AAUP investigating committee included Calvin philosopher David Hoekema. The AAUP committee found that

(1) The Cedarville administration violated AAUP standards for dismissal by not providing Hoffeditz a hearing of record before a duly constituted faculty body prior to a decision for dismissal.
(2) The Cedarville stated guidelines for contesting a dismissal denied Hoffeditz due process in multiple ways including placing the burden

of proof on him and denying him access to the evidence and witnesses against him.

(3) There exists among the Cedarville faculty a climate of "outright fear ... inside and outside the Bible department," a "lack of a meaningful role in governance and ignorance of individual faculty rights ...."

As of 2014, Cedarville still remained on the AAUP censure list of institutions with unresolved cases.[5]

Charleston Southern (SC)

The turn-of-the-century confrontation between the AAUP and Charleston Southern University (CSU) over the latter's dismissal of history professor Robert Crout (1999) and English professor David Aiken (1998) represents the clash of two philosophies of faculty personnel practice. The AAUP is faculty-centered and CSU largely institution-centered. The former favors maximum allowance for faculty individualism, while the latter is less tolerant of faculty who don't adapt easily to institutional and administrative "team-play" expectations. The university viewed both professors as able teachers and scholars but as possessing difficult personality traits. Crout was often brusque in his interpersonal communications including with administrators and the external public. Aiken had a more-than-normal tendency, especially early in his CSU career, to prefer to teach within a given course the topics of greatest personal interest rather than the full span of the curriculum as described in the course catalog.

The most publically embarrassing of Crout's actions was a 1999 funeral eulogy which he delivered for a faculty colleague. Crout used the occasion to describe how CSU had treated the deceased unfairly. By contrast, Aiken appeared to be increasingly cooperative during his six years at CSU. Crout held tenure; Aiken did not.

The 2001 AAUP report indicted the university for dismissing Crout without demonstrated cause before a hearing of record before a faculty committee and without an adequate time period of notice before dismissal. It also found a campus "atmosphere that inhibits the exercise of academic freedom." Furthermore the report criticized CSU for providing Aiken neither the reasons for not renewing his contract nor an opportunity for a faculty review of his belief that CSU violated his academic freedom.[6]

Two questions in conclusion: (1) Is the AAUP presumptive in expecting that all institutions should follow its sometimes labor-union-like standards for faculty due process? and (2) If individual Christian colleges don't like the idea of the AAUP sitting in moral judgment over them, then who should? Christians no less than non-Christians need systems of accountability.

Cumberlands (KY)

In 1980, James H. Taylor became the president and Robert Day enrolled as a student at the University of the Cumberlands (formerly Cumberland College), a Southern Baptist institution in Williamsburg, Kentucky. In 2000, Day returned as a social work professor. As a student, Day had been highly respected as a cofounder of the Mountain Outreach program which recruited student volunteers to construct homes and provide other services for impoverished families in the area's mountain communities. When, as a professor, the college faced a severe financial crisis in 2003, with looming faculty and staff cutbacks, Day employed his social worker problem-solving instincts to try to design plans to deal with the institutional deficiencies. But President Taylor was not used to having professors—especially young assertive ones like Day—telling him what to do. The result was a major clash.

The college lacked both an official and unofficial means for faculty to participate in institutional governance. So Day, with anonymous colleagues, created an organization and a website to accomplish this purpose. The organization, the Committee for Accountability and Reform in Education (CARE), created an off-campus website on which it proposed that the Cumberlands administration act upon ten initiatives, five dealing with financial "accountability" and five dealing with religious "reform" to halt the institution's perceived "drift toward secularization." The initial website included a list of 21 questions, some of which focused on the president personally. These included: (1) Could President Taylor get a vote of confidence from the faculty? (2) How did a man who had no experience in academia get to be president of the college? and (3) Why does the president of a Christian college belong to a secret society?

At some point during the website's first week of operation in October 2003, the president discovered its existence. One of his administrators commented, "I've never seen [President Taylor] this mad before." When Taylor summoned Day to his office, the latter technically agreed to resign, but then changed his mind by the next day when he sought to withdraw his oral resignation. The president refused the withdrawal, and within weeks, the professor sought the intervention of the AAUP.

When the AAUP advised President Taylor that it had appointed an investigating committee, he replied as follows:

Cumberland College[7] has no relationship with your association. Therefore, the college will not receive any committee the association may appoint . . . members of any such committee . . . should not understand themselves to be invited to the college's campus for this or any other purpose . . . your association's opinion, counsel, and advice on the subject of the college's employment policies and practices are totally gratuitous and irrelevant.

Because the AAUP committee was unwelcome on campus and because several of the Cumberlands faculty did not wish easily to be seen talking with the committee, for fear of reprisals, the interviews took place at a site 25 miles from campus.

The major conclusions of the AAUP committee include the following:

(1) It is "unconscionable" that the president allowed his initial confrontation with Day to move so quickly to discussions of Day's resignation that there was no meaningful discussion of Taylor's concerns with the website during the meeting that lasted less than five minutes. "This action was hardly consistent with the college's own policies that call for 'great and serious care' in such matters."

(2) The president who "reserves the right to modify, eliminate, and add to" the institutional personnel policies and practices has excessive power compared to that of the faculty. Thus, the Day case reflects a larger university problem.

(3) While academic freedom appears to exist within the classroom, it is largely absent outside of it where "the campus is permeated by a culture of fear that stifles questions about administrative decisions, policies, and practices."

(4) The demand which the administration placed upon Day's department chair, James Bailey, to participate in their orders against Day, and, with his refusal, subsequently to offer him an unusually inferior contract for the next year, violated Bailey's academic freedom.

(5) The Cumberlands grievance procedure that did not allow either Day or Bailey a faculty hearing of any kind is grossly deficient of common higher education standards of due process.

As of 2014, Cumberlands remained on the AAUP censure list and James Taylor remained, now in his 35th year, in the Cumberlands presidential office.[8]

Greenville (IL)

In 1998, President Robert Smith and his team invited Greenville alumnus Gerald W. Eichhoefer to return to his alma mater to "bring life into a failing [computer science] program." Instead, beginning in 2000, his coming brought six years of controversy to the entire Free Will Methodist college.

After two years on the faculty Eichhoefer determined that the college in general and the department of religion and philosophy in particular were insufficiently conservative in theology despite the fact that the college was a member of the CCCU and the smaller Christian College Consortium and required its faculty to subscribe to orthodox Christian confessions such as the Apostle's Creed. Apparently Eichhoefer wanted the college to give greater prominence to using the word "evangelical" in its promotional literature, and to be less intellectually open in the classroom.

More significant in causing offense than the content of Eichhoefer's criticism was the method of his critique. In electronic newsletters with such titles as the "Greenville Evangelical Voice," he broadcast his discontent to students and trustees as well as the faculty and administration. Vice president for Academic Affairs Karen Longman advised that it would have been preferable for him to express his concerns directly to those with whom he had the greatest concern and/or to have filed a formal grievance. After more meetings, forums, and conflict, the faculty in 2004 adopted a resolution of confidence in the Religion and Philosophy Department, with the vote being 44–4 in favor.

When in the fall of 2004 the college experienced a budgetary shortfall due to an enrollment decline—perhaps precipitated by the theological controversies—it decided to reduce some faculty and staff positions for the next year. On November 22, Vice President Longman met with Eichhoefer to advise him that because of his failure to achieve mutually agreed-upon goals for the computer science department and his poor student evaluations, his position was one of those to be cut. His choice was to resign with some incentive benefits or be dismissed. He chose not to resign so on March 30 President James Mannoia released him effective the end of the school year. Eichhoefer then obtained a lawyer and, in April 2005, sought the assistance of the AAUP. After a six-month period of negotiations with the college, the AAUP decided to send an investigating committee to campus, with the visitation taking place on October 30–31, 2005.

The AAUP committee determined, with the college's concurrence, that the dismissal was primarily for performance, and thus focused their attention on the procedure used in reaching the decision to dismiss. The committee concluded that (1) the Greenville faculty handbook provisions for terminating tenured appointments—save for those involving financial exigency and program elimination—were "severely deficient" compared to AAUP-recommended standards; (2) Eichhoefer's campaign to change the college's theological identity, "however obnoxious others may have found it, was in significant part, an exercise" in academic freedom; and (3) Greenville failed to provide evidence of Eichhoefer's unsatisfactory service in a hearing before an appropriate faculty group; it is likely that part of the basis for the professor's dismissal was his "dissentient activities, particularly his perceived lack of 'supportiveness' for the administration."

An important addendum to the final report described the "welcome news" of Greenville's prompt response to a preliminary draft copy of the report. It noted that the college dealt with the issue of Eichhoefer's due process rights by negotiating a settlement with him on March 15, 2006, and showed good faith intentions to develop a hearing process for faculty dismissal cases that is more in line with the AAUP guidelines. Greenville is no longer on the AAUP censure list.[9]

The Greenville case is a complicated and multifaceted one. One way of looking at it is to note how it could fit into the chapter on theological nuance. The primary AAUP concern—and an important one—is due process considerations for faculty. The primary institutional concern is that a given faculty member not severely disrupt the internal sense of campus community, the external goodwill and respect for the college, and the related economic viability of the college. This too is of major importance.

Grove City (PA)

Grove City may be the only college to have its name appear on both a Supreme Court case and the AAUP censure list. This is no coincidence as both situations reflect the college's strong commitment to institutional freedom—in the first case from the federal government and in the second from the standards of the AAUP. In *Grove City College v. Bell* (1984), the college lost by a 6–3 decision in its long-standing suit over the Title IX requirement of the Department of Health, Education, and Welfare that for its students to continue to receive federal aid, it must sign an assurance of compliance that it was not discriminating based on gender. The court ruled that the requirement did not violate Grove City's First Amendment rights and that it applied only to its financial aid office. The college did not practice gender discrimination but feared that this regulation would be the opening wedge in a growing federal effort to control higher education. When Congress three years later confirmed the fear of the college by passing the Civil Rights Restoration Act of 1988, which made the entire college subject to federal regulation, the college responded by deciding to no longer have its students receive federal aid and to seek to replace the lost aid by its own fundraising efforts.

Grove City's determined and independent spirit was led by its four-decade long board chairman, J. Howard Pew, the president of Sun Oil Company. Pew was actively involved in organizations that promoted free enterprise principles and conservative political practices.

The Grove City AAUP case involved history professor Larry Gara. A graduate of William Penn (IA) and the University of Wisconsin, Gara was a convinced pacifist and a member of the Society of Friends. He spent three years in prison for refusing to register for military service during World War II and served another stint in jail for counseling a Bluffton (OH) student to not register for the draft. He had been a young instructor at Bluffton during the Cold War.

During his fifth year of teaching at Grove City in 1962, President J. Stanley Harker and Dean William Sweezy advised Gara that they would not offer him a contract for the next year. The charge was "indifferent teaching and ruthless grading." Harker added that the dismissal had nothing to do with his pacifism and prison record. However, the AAUP visiting committee held unconfirmed doubts about the latter claim. A faculty member who served on the editorial board of the right-wing *American Opinion* magazine (published by the John Birch Society) recently had participated in a newspaper debate with Gara over Cold War politics, with the former accusing the latter of intellectual as well as ideological deficiencies, and of advocating a "rather red than dead," philosophy. Trustee board chair Pew was also connected with *American Opinion*, as an editorial advisory board member. Also, Gara stated that one month before his formal dismissal, two private investigators visited the campus for several days asking about and researching Gara's writings.

Two weeks before the inquiry visit by the AAUP committee, the trustees voted to disregard the results of the upcoming investigation. The administration then adopted what the investigating committee described as a "hostile attitude" toward the AAUP. Accordingly, the committee held its meetings in the local Penn Grove Hotel where it interviewed 31 members of the faculty. Ultimately, it found that the college had "no tenure policy, written or oral," had "no established procedures . . . for adjudicating dismissal actions," and held no hearing before a representative faculty or trustee group. The college, on its part, did not recognize the right of the AAUP to pass judgment on it. To this day the case remains as the longest unresolved dispute on the AAUP censure list.[10]

Loma Linda (CA)

Among Christian colleges, Loma Linda University (LLU) operates one of very few major medical training and research facilities. Save for religion, the major areas of study are all in the medical sciences. The large majority of the over 4,000 enrollees are graduate students, and they come from more than 80 countries. The 1,500 faculty are paid not by university salaries but by the income they earn from serving thousands of patients annually in the related LLU Medical Center.

The university is one of the major institutions of the SDA church, which is known for its emphasis upon missions, education, and health. Its influence is global, with operations in 216 of the 238 countries of the world, where it enrolls 18 million church members and operates 7,800 schools, 113 colleges, and 175 hospitals and sanitariums. One of the early church leaders, Ellen White, emphasized healthy lifestyle practices including a vegetarian diet and the avoidance of tobacco and alcohol. Compared to Californians in general, the Adventists in the state have longer lifespans—by 7.3 years for men and 4.4 years for women.

In the summer of 1991, LLU dismissed three veteran faculty members— George Grames and Stewart Shankel, both professors of internal medicine, and Lysle Williams, professor of emergency medicine. In late summer of 1991 Shankel, who was chair of the department of medicine, was at the center of a general faculty opposition to administrative decision-making with regard to academic reorganization, major expenditures, and treatment of faculty researchers. Grames and Williams were among the 20 faculty members, mostly in Shankel's department, who sent a letter of concern to the LLU board of trustees. After the three dismissals, each faculty member was offered a grievance process. President Lyn Behrens and the AAUP associate general secretary exchanged letters in which they expressed a marked difference on whether the LLU medical faculty qualified for consideration under the AAUP standards on faculty dismissals.

While the investigating AAUP committee found no restrictions on freedom to teach and research, it did identify a lack of freedom in general, the fact that faculty are subject to dismissal with or without cause on 60 days' notice, an "unacceptably small role of the faculty in academic governance" (which was a major factor in the Western Association of Schools and Colleges decision to place the institution on probation in 1989), the dismissal of the three professors in question without a prior faculty hearing, and a general campus and denominational environment that is unduly deferential toward authority figures.[11]

Louisiana

At the beginning of the research for this book, I asked a specialist on the modern Christian college to identify institutions that were struggling with academic freedom issues. He emphasized Louisiana. Because of its serious problems over many years, I include it in the group of ten featured in this chapter even though it did not receive an official investigation by the AAUP. Louisiana is an apt example of what can happen when "product" (achieving a specific goal) is emphasized unduly over process (the means of achieving the goal). It was one of a significant number of Southern Baptist colleges in which the conservative/fundamentalist forces sought to gain control of the state conventions and through them control of the college trustee boards.

By the early twenty-first century, the conservatives had become the majority force on the trustee board. One major early issue involved control over classroom textbooks. Leading conservative trustee Leon Hyatt in 2004 sent a letter to the majority of his fellow trustees calling for new board leadership that would dismiss any faculty or staff who adopted or approved inappropriate textbooks. The plan was that the vice president for academic affairs and the appropriate department chair would have to approve each professor's book list. Earlier that year, President William Lee had removed from the bookstore copies of Scott Peck's *The Road Less Traveled* and Ernest Gaines' *A Lesson Before Dying*.

In the spring of 2004, President Lee, vice president for academic affairs Benjamin Hawkins, and the trustee board chairman resigned. Then in early 2005, the college's newly called president, Malcolm Yarwell, suddenly withdrew his candidacy, because of "governance issues."

Quickly and amidst controversy, the trustees settled on a presidential candidate whose philosophy was more in line with their ideals. An education professor at Louisiana, Joe Aguillard, strongly identified with the Baptist Faith and Message 2000 document, the conservative theology of three-time SBC president, Adrian Rogers, opposition to Calvinism, and defense of biblical inerrancy, but he also possessed difficulty in understanding the value of tolerance in a liberal arts institution.

Shortly after taking office, Aguillard found himself in trouble with the faculty and the regional accreditation association for a combination of forced conformity and administrative mismanagement. During the 2004–14 decade, the string of disruption may be without parallel in Christian higher education. There were multiple faculty dismissals; a startling amount of faculty turnover (one veteran faculty member counted 49 of 71 faculty members leaving the college for a variety of reasons between 2004 and 2007); multiple accreditation probations; multiple lawsuits; multiple critical websites and efforts to block them; and reports of (1) misappropriated funds, (2) lies to donors, administrators, and trustees, (3) forged documents, and (4) payment of hush money. Perhaps the most amazing thing was that the trustees allowed the situation to continue as long as it did. Aguillard survived multiple close crisis-of-confidence votes until finally released in 2014 only to be praised by the trustees, named president emeritus, and placed in a tenured teaching position.[12]

Messiah (PA)

Former CCCU vice president for Professional Development and Research, Ron Mahurin, notes that Christian colleges have gotten better in recent decades in developing sensitive academic freedom statements and processes. The Messiah case of theater professor Earl Ross Genzel and its aftermath, although not involving the AAUP, illustrates this improvement.

Genzel tells how in 1993 his class was having a discussion on homosexuality. When a student asked if he would give his views, he responded that he "disagreed with people who use the Bible to condemn gay Christians living in a monogamous, loving relationship." Subsequently, the college dean, Dorothy Gish, announced that she would not renew his contract even though he insisted that he had not advocated homosexual behavior, which was a violation of the college code of behavior. Genzel was unhappy, the campus AAUP chapter was unhappy, and the new incoming president Ronald Sawatsky, declaring that he definitely would not "dismiss a person out of hand . . . for saying that homosexuality is not sinful," stated that there were other factors involved in the case.

Sawatsky hired a new dean and introduced a new process whereby any faculty member alleged to be in violation of the college faith statement would have a hearing before a faculty committee rather than being solely at the mercy of the judgment of one or two administrators. The president of the campus AAUP chapter, sociologist Steven Cobb, reports that the change has brought "an improvement of morale among the faculty."[13]

Patrick Henry (VA)

When a charismatic religious leader has founded a modern Christian college, the operational mode, especially in the early years, has tended to be more that of "follow the leader" than of "come, let us reason together." Such was the case at one of the newest of such institutions, Patrick Henry, begun by Michael Farris in 2000. A constitutional lawyer who has argued before the Supreme Court, Farris founded the Home School Legal Defense Association in 1983. His primary purpose in opening Patrick Henry was to train high-ability, Christian, home school graduates in a classical liberal arts education that would prepare them to serve the cause of the conservative political agenda in Washington, DC and elsewhere.

While well versed in law and government, Farris at the outset showed little understanding of or willingness to implement the academic collegiality, faculty intellectual empowerment, and shared governance necessary to run a respected institution of higher learning. By 2006, a major crisis developed when five of the then 13 faculty members departed from the college under protest of lack of freedom. One of the five, classics professor David Noe, stated "We were brought here on false pretenses. We are leaving due to a long train of abuses by Farris in violating academic freedom and due process." While Farris had described the college as "a place that encourages 'a free flow of ideas' beyond some core principles" such as "existence of God . . . and the infallibility of the Bible," in practice, when the faculty prepared formal papers or delivered classroom lectures, they could find themselves in difficulty if the president didn't personally agree with their ideas.

After the wave of faculty resignations Farris agreed to step down from the presidency, apparently realizing that he could best serve the college in another capacity. "If I'm the problem—well, I'm going to be gone," he stated. The outside media reporters were very hard on the new college, in many respects appropriately so. On the other hand, it usually takes a new institution a while to mature. The ultimate question, of course, is the degree to which it wishes to develop.[14]

In summary, as Christian colleges continue to work to refine their due process procedures, it is important for them to remember that their own best religious, political, and educational traditions call them to seek to be exemplary in their personnel practices, including those involving the process for determining whether a faculty member should be dismissed. The New Testament repeatedly cites the Old Testament admonition against convicting a person on the evidence of a single accuser. The political ideas of democracy, checks and balances, and trial by jury, while at times inefficient and even messy, hold as their genius the recognition that all humans are corrupted by sin and partial in understanding and therefore none can be entrusted with absolute power, thus the distrust of solo decision-making on the most important issues by political, religious, and educational leaders. This explains why, as seen repeatedly in this chapter, the AAUP directs its sharpest criticisms against Christian colleges when administrators dismiss faculty members arbitrarily without the benefit of a clear and comprehensive institutional academic freedom statement or before the benefit of the meaningful counsel of a duly elected faculty group after the latter has participated in a formal hearing with the accused faculty member.

Epilogue

Consistent with the arguments advanced earlier in this book that scholars do their work best when they seek to present data objectively and then offer their conclusions openly and humbly, let me here at the end present in summary form my major views on the subject of this book.

1. All colleges—public and private, secular and religious—do academic freedom imperfectly. Academic freedom is the ideal, but we are finite and even flawed in the purity with which we seek truth ourselves and allow freedom to others to do the same. Nevertheless, we must ever strive toward the noble vision.

2. Freedom is not an end in itself. Truth is. Freedom does not exist in a vacuum; it always exists in context. Absolute freedom, if it were to exist, would be absolute anarchy, even absolute tyranny. We are born with the freedom—and the need—to choose to connect with the Ultimate.

3. Do not fear truth. Fear bad theology or bad science or bad sociology. Do not fear truth; fear missing the truth. For where truth is, there is God. God is light, and God is truth.

4. A Christian college is a community. Community (people who have something in common) by definition involves mutual commitment to a common vision or purpose or experience.

5. Christian community by definition involves mutual commitment to the central idea that God has come to us in Christ to redeem us to himself.

6. A Christian college is a voluntary community of those who on their own have embraced the incarnational idea and who on their own choose to join like-minded believers in an ongoing, unfettered search for and understanding of the Creator and the Creation. As the members freely join the community, so also are they free to leave the community, intellectually and physically.

7. Some Christian colleges will choose to add to the central Christian idea a set of secondary convictions as a basis for membership. This is

not necessary to be a Christian college, and may be counterproductive to Christian unity, academic collegiality, and an unfettered search for truth.

8. If a college does identify secondary conditions for membership in its community, it must do so clearly and at the time of original employment.

9. The Christian college in the United States celebrates the value placed by the Constitutional framers in their very First Amendment, upon the freedom of private assembly and the freedom of openly expressing oral and written thought, especially in the religious domain.

10. Academic freedom is, in itself, central to the educational process and this should be viewed positively and embraced heartily by the Christian college community. The purpose of positional power—in academe or elsewhere—is not to dominate others but to empower others.

11. The Christian colleges should identify as much as possible with the major academic freedom statements of the general academy but confidently and graciously critique these statements when they are partial or incomplete.

12. The Christian colleges tend to focus primarily upon institutional academic freedom. The secular institutions tend to focus largely upon individual academic freedom for the professors. The best colleges and universities seek to integrate both and also show deep respect for the academic freedom and rights of students.

13. The secular academic community best acknowledges the concept of freedom when, among other things, it seeks to understand the mind of the Christian college scholarly community and how not all in academia view the concept of freedom in the same manner. The Christian college academic community best acknowledges the concept of freedom when it, together with its constituency, seeks to understand the difference between a college and a church and how their spheres can be complementary and cooperative rather than competitive.

14. In a Christian college, everything stems from institutional mission. An institution must identify its mission first and then liberally provide academic freedom within that context.

15. The subject of religion engenders fear in much of the academy. Some secular institutions directly or indirectly discourage its consideration. Some Christian colleges directly or indirectly discourage a fair hearing for religious or secular views other than their own. The result is a "chilling effect" upon many professors and students alike, in both types of institutions, who would prefer to rigorously examine all topics related to the human condition.

16. With respect to the status of religion, the ideal Christian college begins with an institutional commitment to a Christian worldview and then invites into its community of learning those scholars who, already of their own volition, have chosen this worldview as the framework through which they can best find truth. Then to assure that their students receive a fair understanding of the major worldviews, they employ charitable, fair-minded, no less than Christian, instructors, and regularly provide campus forums that present a variety of perspectives on primary issues. By contrast the ideal public university neither privileges nor disprivileges a specific worldview but presents each of the major ones, at least, clearly, respectfully, and fairly.

17. Multi-position books on issues over which Christians differ is one way in which Christian publishing houses contribute to academic freedom. Christian colleges do well to structure similarly open-ended learning experiences (e.g., multi-position forums, team-taught courses with philosophically differing instructors, and pro and con lectures by individual professors).

18. Of the major academic freedom issues of focus in Christian higher education, macroevolution is the one of longest standing, homosexuality is the greatest current controversy—in part because of how it may threaten continuing government aid and tax benefit policy, while the most important one is due process because of how it lies at the heart of the sense of Christian community ("By this all will know that you are my disciples if you have love for one another," John 13:35).

19. The current societal debate on homosexuality and the pressure that it may exert on public policy may well force some or many Christian colleges to modify current policies or to find different ways of operating to make them less dependent on the present favorable aid and tax policy. Whether of economic necessity or a desire to provide less expensive models of Christian higher education to serve the less affluent, the Christian colleges—or some of them—need to plan seriously and creatively for a broader variety of variously priced delivery systems (see Chapter 18).

20. The Christian church in general and the Christian college in particular have long sought to maintain a constructive balance between purity and unity—between giving vigilance to adhering faithfully to the central principles that define them and celebrating those principles with grace, tolerance, and oneness of spirit. During the early twentieth century, orthodox Protestantism was on the defensive and its colleges faced the challenges of the movement toward secularization. Much of the Fundamentalist response may have been necessary at the time, but

the extent to which it created a permanent mind-set of suspicion was unhealthy. As a norm, the Christian church and the Christian colleges should be known by what they are for rather than what they are against.

So then, we do well to hold fast to Christ at the center and let that be the basis for fellowship, liberty, unity, harmony, and community in the ongoing quest to know as we are known.

Notes

Preface

1. Lee Hardy, "The Value of Limitations: Is Religion an Academic Liability?" *Academe: Bulletin of the AAUP* 92, no. 1 (2006): 23-27; Todd C. Ream and Perry L. Ganzer, *Christian Faith and Scholarship: An Exploration of Contemporary Developments* (Hoboken: Wiley, 2007), 87, 94, 100; Douglas V. Henry, "Can Baptist Theology Sustain the Life of the Mind? The Quest for a Vital Baptist Academy," *Perspectives in Religious Studies* 33, no. 2 (Summer 2006): 203-226.

2. Melissa Steffan, "Crisis of Faith Statements," *Christianity Today* 56, no. 10 (Nov., 2012): 16; Kina Mallard and Michele Atkins, "Changing Academic Cultures and Expanding Expectations: Motivational Factors Influencing Scholarship at Small Christian Colleges and Universities," *Christian Higher Education* 3, no. 4 (2004): 373-389; Martin E. Marty, *Church Related Higher Education and the Common Good* (San Francisco: Jossey-Bass, 2000).

3. Ronald Mahurin in conversation with the author, Spring, 2013; "The CCCU Research Agenda," *The Council for Christian Colleges and Universities*, April, 2012, https://www.cccu.org/~/media/Files/Professional_Development/Research/CCCU-Research-Agenda-2012.pdf; Ralph Enlow, letter to author, October 31, 2013.

4. Kenneth Swan in conversation with the author, December 12, 2013.

5. Neil Gross and Solon Simmons, "How Religious Are America's College and University Professors?" *Social Science Research Council*, religion.ssrc.org/reform/Gross_Simmons.pdf; C. John Sommerville, *The Decline of the Secular University* (Oxford, New York: Oxford University Press, 2006), 85-86, 121; Douglas and Rhonda Jacobsen, *No Longer Invisible: Religion in University Education* (New York: Oxford University Press, 2012), 3-9, 104; Tyler O'Neil, "Secularism: A Dying Faith," *Hillsdale National Law Review* (blog), November 10, 2011, http://hillsdalenaturallawreview.com/2011/11/10/secularism-a-dying-faith/; Quentin Schulze, "The Two Faces of Fundamentalist Higher Education," in *Fundamentalism and Society* eds. Martin E. Marty, R. Scott Appleby, and Jose Casanova (Chicago: University of Chicago Press, 1993), 490-494; D. Michael Lindsay, "Evangelical Rebounds in Academe," *Chronicle of Higher Education* 54, no. 31 (May 9, 2008): B12-B14.

Chapter 1

1. Richard S. Emrich, *Earth Might Be Fair* (New York: Harper and Brothers, 1945), 78.
2. Mark 12:30–31.
3. John 14:15ff; I John 5:3.
4. See I Corinthians 6:12, 10:23.
5. "Love God and do whatever you please: for the soul trained in love to God will do nothing to offend the One who is Beloved." This quotation is one of many commonly and variously cited and paraphrased quotations from Augustine's "Love Sermon" based upon I John 4:4–12.
6. Jacques Ellul, *The Ethics of Freedom* (Grand Rapids: Eerdmans, 1976), 187–189, 191, 193.

Chapter 2

1. Psalm 42:1.
2. Augustine, *Confessions*, book 1, chapter 1, in *Great Books of the Western World*, ed. Robert Maynard Hutchins (Chicago: Encyclopedia Britannica, 1952), vol. 18, 1.
3. Jeremiah 29:13; Matthew 7:7.
4. I John 1:5; I John 4:8.
5. Raymond A. Moody Jr., *Life After Life* (New York: Bantam Books, 1976), 92–93.
6. David L. Jeffrey, "Biblical Literacy, Academic Freedom, and Christian Liberty" in *The Bible and the University*, ed. David L. Jeffrey and C. Stephen Evans (Grand Rapids: Zondervan, 2007), 299.
7. John 14:9b.
8. Peter Kreeft, *Heaven: The Heart's Deepest Longing* (San Francisco: Ignatius Press, 1989), 66–67.

Chapter 3

1. Matthew 13:3–9, 18–23.
2. William Shakespeare, *Hamlet*, Act 1, Scene 3.
3. Kreeft, *Heaven*, 164–165.
4. M. Scott Peck, *People of the Lie: The Hope for Healing Human Evil* (New York: Simon and Schuster, 1983), 71–78, 203–204.
5. I Corinthians 13:12a.
6. See Karl L. Popper, *The Logic of Scientific Discovery* (New York: Routledge, 2002).
7. See Søren Kierkegaard, *The Concept of Anxiety* (Princeton: Princeton University Press, 1981).
8. George Seldes, *The Great Thoughts* (New York: Ballantine Books, 1996), 140.
9. John Stuart Mill, *On Liberty* (New York: W. W. Norton and Company, 1975), 36.

10. Note Psalm 133:1: "Behold how good and pleasant it is for brethren to dwell together in unity!"

Chapter 4

1. Genesis 18:27.
2. Numbers 32:10.
3. Proverbs 3:34.
4. Micah 6:8.
5. Luke 1:46–48a.
6. Isaiah 61:1.
7. Matthew 5:3.
8. Frank S. Mead, ed., *12,000 Religious Quotations* (Grand Rapids: Baker Book House, 2000), 237.
9. C. S. Lewis, *Mere Christianity* (New York: Macmillan, 1952), 109.
10. Philippians 2:3b; I Timothy 1:15b.
11. Thomas á Kempis, *The Imitation of Christ* (New York: Hurst and Company, 1843), 84.
12. See Isaiah, chapters 40–66, and Philippians 2:5–11.
13. W. Jay Wood, "How Might Intellectual Humility Lead to Scientific Insight?" *Big Questions Online*, December 10, 2012, https://www.bigquestionsonline.com/content/how-might-intellectual-humility-lead-scientific-insight.
14. Robert C. Roberts, "What Is It to Be Intellectually Humble?" *Big Questions Online*, June 21, 2012, https://www.bigquestionsonline.com/content/what-it-be-intellectually-humble; also see Robert C. Roberts, "Humility as a Moral Project," *Spiritual Emotions: A Psychology of Christian Virtues* (Grand Rapids: Eerdmans, 2007), 78–95.
15. William Barclay, *And Jesus Said* (Philadelphia: The Westminster Press, 1970), 18–21.

Chapter 5

1. Exodus 3–15; Joshua 1–24; Matthew 26–27; Hebrews 2; Acts 6–7; Acts 13–24.
2. Deuteronomy 31:6.
3. Deuteronomy 31:3–6, 2:32–34.
4. First Maccabees.
5. Matthew 5:1–12, 6:38–48, 26:47–65; John 18:36; II Corinthians 10:4; Ephesians 6:10–20.
6. John 15:20b.
7. Acts 7:51, 60.
8. Acts 23:11; II Timothy 2:1–13.
9. Kenneth Scott Latourette, *A History of Christianity*, vol. 1 (New York: Harper and Row, 1975), 81–91; William H. C. Frend, "Persecution in the Early Church,"

Christian History IX, no. 3 (1990): 5–11; Robert L. Wilken, "The Piety of the Persecutors," *Christian History* IX, no. 3 (1990): 16–19.

10. William G. Bixler, "How the Early Church Viewed Martyrs," *Christian History* IX, no. 3 (1990): 28–30; John O. Gooch, "Cowards Among the Christians," *Christian History* IX, no. 3 (1990): 34–36.

11. William H. C. Frend, "When Christianity Triumphed," *Christian History* IX, no. 3 (1990): 11.

12. David B. Barrett and Todd M. Johnson, *World Christian Trends, A.D. 30–A.D. 2200* (Pasadena, California: William Carey Library, 2001), 228–234.

13. Ibid.

Chapter 6

1. James 1:19b.

2. Acts 15:1–35.

3. Acts 15:36–39.

4. James Calvin Davis, "Resisting Politics as Usual: Civility as Christian Witness," *Colombia Theological Seminary*, 2012, http://www.atthispoint.net/articles/resisting-politics-as-usual-civility-as-christian-witness/225/; also see James Calvin Davis, *In Defense of Civility: How Religion Can Unite America on Seven Moral Issues that Divide Us* (Louisville: Westminster John Knox Press, 2004); and Richard J. Mouw, *Uncommon Decency: Christian Civility in an Uncivil World* (Downers Grove, Illinois: InterVarsity Press, 1992).

5. Lauren Markoe, "Religious Leaders Seek to Overcome Polarization," *Religion News Service*, May 16, 2013, http://www.religionnews.com/2013/05/15/christian-leaders-seek-to-overcome-polarization/.

6. Colossians 4:5–6.

7. Ephesians 4:26, 30–32; Galatians 5:22–23.

Chapter 7

1. Mark 12:30–31; also see Leviticus 19:18b and Deuteronomy 30:6.

2. John 14:15; I John 5:3.

3. I Corinthians 13:1, 13.

4. I John 4:8, 10–12; John 15:12; Matthew 5:43–44.

5. Brennan Manning, *Lion and Lamb: The Relentless Tenderness of Jesus* (Grand Rapids: Baker Book House, 1993), 18.

6. Joseph L. Baron, *A Treasury of Jewish Quotations* (New York: Crown Publishers, 1956), 554.

7. Proverbs 9:10a.

8. John 14:9b.

9. John 10:30.

10. See J. B. Phillips, "Resident Policeman," *Your God is Too Small* (New York: Macmillan, 1961), part I, chapter 1.

11. Matthew 6:9–13.

12. Thomas Merton, *New Seeds of Contemplation* (New York: New Directions Publishing, 1961), 48.
13. C. S. Lewis, *Mere Christianity* (New York: Macmillan, 1979), 106.
14. John 10:25–27.
15. Frederick Buechner, *Telling the Truth: The Gospel as Tragedy, Comedy, and Fairy Tale* (New York: HarperCollins, 1977), 8.
16. Lewis, "Charity," *Mere Christianity*, book III, chapters 7 and 9.
17. James Fowler, *Stages of Faith: The Psychology of Human Development and the Quest for Meaning* (San Francisco: Harper and Row, 1981), chapter 21; M. Scott Peck, *The Different Drum: Community Making and Peace* (New York: Simon and Schuster, 1988), 192.

Chapter 8

1. "The Westminster Shorter Catechism," *The Orthodox Presbyterian Church*, http://www.opc.org/sc.html.
2. Kate B. Wilkinson, "May the Mind of Christ, My Savior," 1925, *NetHymnal*, http://cyberhymnal.org/htm/m/a/maytmind.htm.
3. William Barrett, *Irrational Man: A Study in Existential Philosophy* (Garden City, New York: Doubleday and Company, 1962), chapters 2, 7, 8, 10.
4. See Peter Kreeft, *Christianity for Modern Pagans: Pascal's Pensées* (San Francisco: Ignatius Press, 1993), chapters 5, 13.
5. Alfred North Whitehead, *Science and the Modern World* (New York: Macmillan, 1950), 275.
6. Job 15:25–26 and 5:25–26; Matthew 27:3–5.
7. Paul Tournier, *Learn to Grow Old* (New York: Harper and Row, 1971), 216–24.
8. II Timothy 1:12b; Hebrews 6:19a.
9. Proverbs 19:15, 20:4, 24:30–34, 26:13–16, and 31:10–31; Romans 12:11; II Thessalonians 3:10; Matthew 25:14–30.
10. Exodus 20:8–11.
11. Will Willimon, *A Peculiar Prophet* (blog), willimon.blogspot.com.
12. Elton Trueblood, *The Common Ventures of Life: Marriage, Birth, Work, and Death* (New York: Harper and Brothers, 1949), 100.

Chapter 9

1. C. S. Lewis, "The Inner Ring," *The Weight of Glory* (New York: Simon and Schuster, 1980).
2. Anthony de Mello, *The Way to Love* (New York: Doubleday, 1995), 97.
3. Matthew 11:29–30.
4. John A. Hardon, "History of Religious Life: St. Dominic and the Apostolate of Teaching the Word of God," *The Real Presence Association*, http://www.therealpresence.org/archives/Religious_Life/Religious_Life_020.htm.

5. Thomas Merton, *No Man Is an Island* (San Diego: Harcourt Brace, 1983), 123–127.
6. Romans 7:22–23.
7. Matthew 7:7.
8. John Greenleaf Whittier, "Dear Lord and Father of Mankind," *NetHymnal*, http://www.cyberhymnal.org/htm/d/e/dearlord.htm.

Chapter 10

1. Peck, *The Different Drum*, 71.
2. Alan Paton, *Cry, the Beloved Country* (New York: Macmillan, 1987), 39.
3. Thomas Jefferson, letter to H. D. Tiffin, 1807 in "Government Founders Speak Out," *Free Republic*, http://www.freerepublic.com/focus/news/670189/posts.
4. See Matthew 18:15–17.
5. Anthony Diekema, *Academic Freedom and Christian Scholarship* (Grand Rapids: Eerdmans, 2000), 39.
6. Ibid., 39–42.
7. See Arch Keen Wong, Rod Remin, Rick Love, Ray Aldred, Peter Ralph, and Charles Cook, "Building Pedagogical Community in the Classroom," *Christian Higher Education* 12, no. 4 (2013): 282–295.

Chapter 11

1. Richard Hofstadter, *The Development of Academic Freedom in the Age of the College* (New York: Colombia University Press, 1961), 3–6; D. W. Bebbington, "Christian Higher Education in Europe: A Historical Analysis," *Christian Higher Education* 10, no. 1 (2011): 10–24.
2. William J. Hoye, "The Religious Roots of Academic Freedom," *Theological Studies* 58, no. 3 (1997): 409, 414–415, 417–418.
3. Ibid.; William J. Courtenay, "Inquiry and Inquisition: Academic Freedom in Medieval Universities," *Church History* 58, no. 2 (June, 1989): 169–173, 180–181.
4. Ibid., 168–169, 180–181; Hofstadter, *Development of Academic Freedom*, 21.
5. Hofstadter, *Development of Academic Freedom*, 15–16.
6. Ibid., 72–77; David L. Edwards, *Christian England* (Grand Rapids: Eerdmans, 1984), 162–163.
7. Wallace Notestein, *The English People on the Eve of Colonization* (New York: Harper and Row, 1962), 130–145; Hofstadter, *Development of Academic Freedom*, 74.
8. Modern Cambridge scholar and governing board member Ross Anderson has argued that Cambridge more than Oxford has been the English university most open to new ideas. See his essay "Cambridge University—The Unauthorised History," *Cambridge University*, http://www.cl.cam.ac.uk/~rja14/unauthorised.html.

9. David C. Humphrey, "Colonial Colleges and English Dissenting Academics: A Study in Transatlantic Culture," *History of Education Quarterly* (Summer, 1972), 187–188, 192; Frederick Rudolph, *The American College and University: A History* (New York: Random House, 1965), 30.

10. Lawrence Stone, "The Educational Revolution in England, 1560–1640," *Past and Present* 28, no. 1 (July, 1964): 68–69,77.

11. Bebbington, "Christian Higher Education," 14–15; Humphrey, "Colonial Colleges," 187, 192.

12. Mark Noll, *America's God* (New York: Oxford University Press, 2002), chapter 6; Nicholas Wolterstorff, *Thomas Reid and the Story of Epistemology* (Cambridge, England: Cambridge University Press, 2001), ix; John 1:9.

Chapter 12

1. Abraham Flexner, *Universities: American, English, German* (New York: Oxford University Press, 1968), 222–224.

2. Ibid., 311.

3. Ibid., 311–321; Leo L. Rockwell, "Academic Freedom: German Origins and American Development," *Bulletin of the American Association of University Professors* 36, no. 2 (Summer, 1950): 227–228; Bebbington, "Christian Higher Education in Europe," 10–24; Walter P. Metzger, *Academic Freedom in the Age of the University* (New York: Columbia University Press, 1964), 95–99; Friedrich Paulsen, *The German Universities: Their Character and Historical Development* (New York: Macmillan, 1895), 198ff.

4. Laurence R. Veysey, *The Emergence of the American University* (Chicago: University of Chicago Press, 1965), 125–133; Flexner, *Universities*, 324; Bebbington, "Christian Higher Education in Europe," 17–18.

5. Rudolph, *The American College and University*, 116–121.

6. "Ticknor on Freedom and Advanced Scholarship in Germany, 1815–16" in *American Higher Education: A Documentary History*, ed. Richard Hofstadter and Wilson Smith, 2 vols. (Chicago: University of Chicago Press, 1961), I, 258.

7. James Morgan Hart, "The German University and the American College During the 1860s" in *American Higher Education*, ed. Hofstadter and Smith, II, 569, 573, 577.

8. Veysey, *Emergence of the American University*, 130–131; Daniel Falon, "German Influences on American Education" in *The German-American Encounter: Conflict and Cooperation Between Two Cultures, 1800–2000*, ed. Frank Trommler and Elliott Shore (New York: Berghahn Publishers, 2001), 83.

9. For an insightful commentary on German militarism, see Herbert Butterfield, *Christianity and History* (New York: Scribners, 1950), 48–53.

10. William Adrian, "Perils of the Life of the Mind: Lessons from the German University," *Christian Higher Education* 2, no. 2 (2003): 155–168, 155–161, 164–167; Metzger, *Academic Freedom in the Age of the University*, 109–110, 114.

11. Hart, "The German University," II, 577; "Ticknor on Freedom and Advanced Scholarship in Germany" in *American Higher Education*, ed. Hofstadter and Smith, I, 259.

12. George Seldes, ed. *The Great Thoughts* (New York: Ballantine Books, 1996), 199; "1933 Book Burnings," *United States Holocaust Memorial Museum*, www.ushmm. org.

13. Jean Madawar and David Pyke, *Hitler's Gift* (New York: Arcade Publishing, 2000), chapter 7; "1933 Book Burnings," "Immediate American Responses to the Book Burnings," and "German Jewish Refugees, 1933–1939," *United States Holocaust Memorial Museum*, www.ushmm.org.

14. Terence Karran, "Academic Freedom in Europe: A Preliminary Comparative Analysis," *Higher Education Policy* 34, no. 3 (September 1, 2009): 289–290, 309.

15. Rudolph, *The American College and University*, 412–413.

Chapter 13

1. George P. Schmidt, *The Liberal Arts College* (New Brunswick, New Jersey: Rutgers University Press, 1957), 60–61.

2. William C. Ringenberg, *The Christian College: A History of Protestant Higher Education in America* (Grand Rapids: Baker Academic, 2006), chapters 1–2.

3. Donald G. Tewksbury, *The Founding of the American Colleges and Universities Before the Civil War* (New York: Columbia University, 1932), 74–75, 129–30, 132; Frederick Rudolph, *Curriculum: A History of the American Undergraduate Course of Study* (San Francisco: Jossey-Bass, 1977), chapter 3.

4. The old-time college served primarily young men. Very few women enrolled.

5. "Cotton Mather on Harvard's First President, Henry Dunster," *Magnalia Christi Americana*, in *American Higher Education*, ed. Hofstadter and Smith, I, 20–21.

6. Schmidt, *Liberal Arts College*, 20–22; Brooks Mather Kelley, *Yale: A History* (New Haven: Yale University Press, 1974), 6–9; Richard Warch, *School of the Prophets: Yale College, 1701–1740* (New Haven: Yale University Press, 1973), 30.

7. Rudolph, *The American College and University*, 207–212.

8. Daniel Webster, "Peroration, The Dartmouth College Case," *Dartmouth College*, 2014, https://www.dartmouth.edu/~dwebster/speeches/dartmouth-peroration.html.

9. Benjamin Franklin, "Proposals Relating to the Education of Youth in Pennsylvania," *Penn University Records and Archives*, 1749, http://www.archives.upenn.edu/primdocs/1749proposals.html; "William Smith (1727–1803)," *Penn University Records and Archives*, www.archives.upenn.edu/people/1700s/smith_wm.html; Rudolph, *Curriculum*, 32.

10. Massachusetts retained a partial Congregational establishment until 1833.

11. Edward S. Gaustad, *Sworn on the Altar of God: A Religious Biography of Thomas Jefferson* (Grand Rapids: Eerdmans Press, 1996), 162–180; Edward S. Gaustad, "Thomas Jefferson" in *The Encyclopedia of Protestantism*, ed. Hans J. Hillerbrand (New York: Routledge, 2004), vol. 2, 975–977; Robert M. Healy, *Jefferson on Religion in Public Education* (New Haven: Yale University Press, 1962), 17–31,

102; Thomas Jefferson, *Writings*, ed. Merrill D. Peterson (New York: Library of America, 1984), 285.

12. William C. Ringenberg, *Taylor University: The First 150 Years* (Grand Rapids: Eerdmans, 1996), 23–24; Thomas Clark, *Indiana University* (Bloomington: Indiana University Press, 1970), 103–128.

13. Ringenberg, *The Christian College*, 79–82.

14. Ibid., 82–83.

15. Ibid., 57–59, 85–96, 155–169; Nathan Hatch, *The Democratization of American Christianity* (New Haven: Yale University Press, 1989), 3, 6, 213.

16. John Thelin, *A History of American Higher Education* (Baltimore: Johns Hopkins University Press, 2004), 74–81.

Chapter 14

1. Jon Roberts and James Turner, *The Sacred and the Secular University* (Princeton: University of Princeton Press, 2000), xi–9, 14, 16, 66–67; George Marsden, *The Soul of the American University: From Protestant Establishment to Established Nonbelief* (New York: Oxford University Press, 1994), 3; Ringenberg, *The Christian College*, chapter 4.

2. Marsden, *Soul of the American University*, chapters 9–10; Page Smith, *Killing the Spirit: Higher Education in America* (New York: Viking Penguin, 1990), 100–101; Laurence R. Veysey, *The Emergence of the American University* (Chicago: University of Chicago Press, 1965), 162.

3. Roberts and Turner, *Sacred and Secular University*, chapters 1, 4, 5; Rudolph, *Curriculum*, chapters 3–4; Ringenberg, *The Christian College*, 114–116.

4. Ringenberg, *The Christian College*, 125–138; Metzger, *Academic Freedom in the Age of the University*, 138–206; "AAUP 1915 Declaration of Principles on Academic Freedom and Academic Tenure," *American Association of University Professors*, 1915, http://www.aaup.org/NR/rdonlyres/A6520A9D-0A9A-47B3-B550-C006B5B224E7/0/1915Declaration.pdf; Marsden, *Soul of the American University*, 296–301.

5. Metzger, *Academic Freedom in the Age of the University*, 201–202; Marsden, *Soul of the American University*, 301–306.

6. Robert K. Poch, *Academic Freedom in American Higher Education: Rights, Responsibilities and Limitations* (Washington, DC: School of Education and Human Development, George Washington University, 1993), no. 4, 59–60; George Marsden, "Liberating Academic Freedom," *First Things* 88 (1998): 11–13, http://www.firstthings.com/article/1998/12/liberating-academic-freedom; "AAUP 1940 Statement of Principles on Academic Freedom and Tenure," *American Association of University Professors*, 1940, http://www.aaup.org/report/1940-statement-principles-academic-freedom-and-tenure; "AAUP, The Limitations Clause in the 1940 Statement of Principles on Academic Freedom and Tenure: Some Operating Guidelines," *American Association of University Professors*, 1940, http://www.aaup.org/report/1940-statement-principles-academic-freedom-and-tenure; Michael W. McConnell, "Academic Freedom in

Religious Colleges and Universities," *Law and Contemporary Problems* 53, no. 3 (1990): 312.

7. Robin Wilson, "The AAUP, 92 and Ailing," *Chronicle of Higher Education*, June 8, 2007, http://www.csun.edu/pubrels/clips/June07/06-05-07A.pdf; Cary Nelson, *No University Is an Island: Saving Academic Freedom* (New York: New York University Press, 2010), 53–59; also see Edward J. Carvalho and David B Downing, eds., *Academic Freedom in the Post-9/11 Era* (New York: Palgrave Macmillan, 2011).

8. C. John Sommerville, *The Decline of the Secular University* (New York: Oxford University Press, 2006); John Schmalzbauer and Kathleen Mahoney, "Religion and Knowledge in the Post-Secular Academy" in *The Post-Secular Question: Religion in Contemporary Society*, ed. John Torpey, David Kyoman, and Jonathan Van Antwerpen (New York: New York University Press, 2012), 216ff; Douglas and Rhonda Jacobsen, *No Longer Invisible: Religion in University Education* (New York: Oxford University Press, 2012); American Academy of Religion, "The Religious Study Major and Liberal Education," *Liberal Education* 95, no. 2 (2009): 48–55; National Research Council, "Doctoral Programs by the Numbers: Religion," *The Chronicle of Higher Education*, 2010, http://chronicle.com/article/nrc-religion/124664/; Russell T. McCutcheon, "What is the Academic Study of Religion?" University of Alabama, http://rel.as.ua.edu/pdf/rel100introhandout.pdf; "School District of Abington Township v. Schempp," Legal Information Institute, http://www.law.cornell.edu/supremecourt/text/374/203.

9. Warren Nord, *Does God Make a Difference? Taking God Seriously in Our Schools and Universities* (New York: Oxford University Press, 2010); Stephen Prothero, *Religious Literacy: What Every American Needs to Know—and Doesn't* (New York: HarperCollins, 2008); Lisa Miller, "Why Harvard Students Should Study More Religion," *Newsweek*, February 10, 2010, http://www.newsweek.com/why-harvard-students-should-study-more-religion-75231.

10. Neil Gross and Solon Simmons, "How Religious are America's College and University Professors?" *Social Science Research Council*, February 6, 2007, ssrc.org/reforum/Gross_Simmons.pdf.

11. Sommerville, *Decline of the Secular University*, 86, 121; Smith, *Killing the Spirit*, 304–305. "Statement on Academic Rights and Responsibilities," *American Council on Education*, http://www.chea.org/pdf/ACE__Statement_on_Academic_Rights_and_Responsibilities_(6_23_2005).pdf; Scott Jaschik, "Détente with David Horowitz," *Inside Higher Education*, June 23, 2005, https://www.insidehighered.com/news/2005/06/23/statement.

Chapter 15

1. "Seeking Truth: Three Views on the Calvin Approach to Academic Freedom," *The Calvin Spark*, Winter, 2009, http://www.calvin.edu/publications/spark/2009/winter/truth.htm.

2. Diekema, *Academic Freedom and Christian Scholarship*, 133–143.
3. Lori Scott Fogleman, "Baylor Hosts National Conference on Academic Freedom," *Baylor Media Communications*, April 6, 2000, http://www.baylor.edu/mediacommunications/news.php?action=story&story=3697; Nicholas Wolterstorff, "Ivory Tower or Holy Mountain?: Faith and Academic Freedom," *Academe* 87, no. 1 (2001): 17–22; George N. Monsma Jr., "Faith and Faculty Autonomy at Calvin College," *Academe* 87, no. 1 (2001): 43–47; Lee Hardy, "The Value of Limitations," *Academe* 92, no. 1 (2006): 23–27.
4. Michael S. Hamilton, "The Fundamentalist Harvard: Wheaton College and the Continuing Vitality of American Evangelicalism, 1919–1965," (doctoral dissertation, Notre Dame University, 1994), 142, 152–156, 166–170, 235–240.
5. John Henry Newman, *The Idea of a University* (Notre Dame: University of Notre Dame Press, 1982), 74; Arthur F. Holmes, *The Idea of a Christian College* (Grand Rapids: Eerdmans, 1975), 77.
6. Mark A. Noll, *Between Faith and Criticism: Evangelicals, Scholarship, and the Bible in America* (San Francisco: Harper and Row, 1986), 2–13.
7. Scott Jaschik, "Academic and Publishing Freedom," *Inside Higher Education*, January 20, 2010, www.insidehighed.com/news/2010/01/20/wheaton; Andrew Chignell, "Whither Wheaton," *Soma: A Review of Religion and Culture*, January 13, 2010, http://www.somareview.com/whitherwheaton.cfm.
8. Also significant for its explanation of how the Christian community at its best reflects grace and the other fruits of the Spirit in its witness to the secular world is Douglas Jacobsen's work with former Messiah president Rodney Sawatsky, *Gracious Christianity: Living the Love We Profess* (Grand Rapids: Baker Academic, 2006).
9. Douglas and Rhonda Jacobsen, *No Longer Invisible: Religion in University Education* (New York: Oxford University Press, 2012), xii–xiii, 3–5, 15–29, 125, 131.
10. Michael D. Lindsay, "Evangelicalism Rebounds in Academe," *Chronicle of Higher Education* 54, no. 35 (May, 2008): 12; Dan Russ, "Fear Not: Security, Risk, and Academic Freedom" in *The Christian College Phenomenon: Inside America's Fastest Growing Institutions*, ed. Samuel Joeckel and Thomas Chesnes (Abilene, Texas: Abilene Christian University Press, 2011), 181.
11. Samuel Schuman, *Seeing the Light: Religious Colleges in Twenty-First Century America* (Baltimore: Johns Hopkins University Press, 2010), 156.
12. Ringenberg, *Taylor University*, 149, 151–152; Eugene B. Habecker, "Academic Freedom in the Context of Mission," *Christian Scholars Review* xxi, no. 2 (1991): 176–177, 179–180; Eugene Habecker in discussion with the author, October 29, 2013.
13. Ted Grimsrud, "Is Academic Freedom a Mennonite Value?" *Anabaptist-Mennonite Scholars Network Newsletter* 1 (May, 2001): 4–5.
14. Ralph E. Enlow Jr., letter to author, October 31, 2013; Randall Bell in discussion with the author, November 12, 2013; Ronald C. Kroll in discussion with the author, November 15, 2013.

Chapter 16

1. McConnell, "Academic Freedom in Religious Colleges and Universities," 303–324.
2. Ibid., 306; Jan Crawford Greenburg, "White House Pares Picks for Top Court," *Chicago Tribune*, June 22, 2005, http://articles.chicagotribune.com/2005-06-22/news/0506220167_1_official-and-other-sources-chief-justice-william-rehnquist-gen-alberto-gonzales; Linda Greenhouse, "Chief Justice Rehnquist Dies at 80," *The New York Times*, September 4, 2005, http://www.nytimes.com/2005/09/04/politics/chief-justice-rehnquist-dies-at-80.html.
3. McConnell, "Academic Freedom in Religious Colleges and Universities," 303–311, 317–320.
4. Ibid., 324.
5. Schmidt, *Liberal Arts College*, 254–256; "A. Lawrence Lowell on Academic Freedom in Wartime, 1917" in *A Documentary History*, ed. Hofstadter and Smith, II, 878–882.
6. Robert C. Cloud, "Sweezy v. New Hampshire," *Law and Higher Education*, January 30, 2011, http://lawhighereducation.org/124-sweezy-v-new-hampshire.html; David M. Rabban, "A Functional Analysis of Individual and Institutional Academic Freedom Under the First Amendment," *Law and Contemporary Problems* 53, no. 3 (1990): 236–239.
7. Rabban, "A Functional Analysis," 240, 256.
8. Ibid., 256; "Grutter v. Bollinger," *Cornell University Law School*, 2003, http://www.law.cornell.edu/supct/html/02-241.ZS.html.
9. Scott Jaschik, "Academic Freedom after September 11," *Inside Higher Education*, March 7, 2006, http://app3.insidehighered.com/news/2006/03/07/acfree.
10. Scott Jaschik, "Ward Churchill Fired," *Inside Higher Education*, July 25, 2007, https://www.insidehighered.com/news/2007/07/25/churchill; "Ward Churchill vs. University of Colorado Boulder," *AAUP*, http://www.aaup.org/brief/ward-churchill-v-university-colorado-boulder-293-p3d16-61-app-2010-affd-285-p3d-986-col-2012; Ward Churchill, "The Myth of Academic Freedom: Experiencing the Application of Liberal Principle in a Neoconservative Era" in *Academic Freedom in the Post-9/11 Era*, ed. Edward J. Carvalho and David B. Downing (New York: Palgrave Macmillan, 2010), 65–113.
11. Vincent J. Schodolski, "Professors Learn Freedom of Expression Has Risks, Limits," *Chicago Tribune*, November 18, 2001, http://articles.chicagotribune.com/2001-11-18/news/0111180275_1_academic-freedom-tenured-professor-cold-war; Richard Berthold, "My Five Minutes of Infamy," *FIRE*, November 25, 2002, https://www.thefire.org/my-five-minutes-of-infamy/; "*FIRE*'s Letter to President Gordon," *FIRE*, October 23, 2001, https://www.thefire.org/fires-letter-to-president-gordon/.
12. "Wisconsin Lawmakers Want University Instructor Fired for Sept. 11 Comments," *Fox News*, July 22, 2006, http://www.foxnews.com/story/2006/07/22/wisconsin-lawmakers-want-university-instructor-fired-for-sept-11-comments/;

Gretchen Ruethling, "A Skeptic on 9/11 Prompts Questions on Academic Freedom," *The New York Times*, August 1, 2006, http://www.nytimes.com/2006/08/01/education/01madison.html?_r=0; Amanda Paulson, "Teacher's Radical 9/11 Views Raise Red Flags," *Christian Science Monitor*, August 18, 2006, http://www.csmonitor.com/2006/0818/p03s01-legn.html; Donald Downs, "Perspective: The Barrett Case and Academic Freedom at Wisconsin," *University of Wisconsin-Madison News*, July 13, 2006, http://www.news.wisc.edu/12709.

13. The 2007 Norman Finkelstein case at DePauw (IL) was remarkably similar to the Salaita one. Both professors were very critical of modern Israeli policies and practices with its immediate neighbors, and both lost a faculty position—or would-be position—when their related institutions ruled them severely deficient in professional civil discourse and collegiality. See Scott Jaschik, "DePaul Rejects Finkelstein," *Inside Higher Education*, June 11, 2007, https://www.insidehighered.com/news/2007/06/11/finkelstein; Patricia Cohen, "A Bitter Spat Over Ideas, Israel, and Tenure," *The New York Times*, April 12, 2007, http://www.nytimes.com/2007/04/12/arts/12tenu.html; Norman G. Finkelstein, "Civility and Academic life" in *Academic Freedom*, ed. Carvalho and Downing, 117–128.

14. Juan Perez Jr., "U. of I. Defends Pulling Job Offer Over Tweets Critical of Israel," *Chicago Tribune*, August 22, 2014, http://www.chicagotribune.com/news/local/breaking/chi-university-of-illinois-job-offer-tweet-israel-20140822-story.html; "AAUP Takes UIUC to Task for Apparent Summary Dismissal," *AAUP*, August 29, 2014, http://www.aaup.org/news/aaup-takes-uiuc-task-apparent-summary-dismissal; Jodi S. Cohen, "Steven Salaita Sues U. of I. Over Lost Job," *Chicago Tribune*, January 29, 2015, http://www.chicagotribune.com/news/local/breaking/ct-steven-salaita-university-of-illinois-lawsuit-0130-20150129-story.html.

Chapter 17

1. Hoye, "Religious Roots of Academic Freedom," 416.
2. Rudolph, *The American College and University*, 144; Ralph Waldo Emerson, James H. Woods, and James Elliot Cabot, *A Memoir of Ralph Waldo Emerson* (Charleston, South Carolina: Nabu Press, 2012), 615.
3. "Major Recommendations of Scranton Report on Campus Unrest," *Academe* 4, no. 4 (October, 1970).
4. William C. Ringenberg, "Quality in the Classroom," *Taylor University Magazine*, (Winter, 1979), 16; "Joint Statement on Rights and Freedoms of Students," *American Association for University Professors*, June, 1967, www.aaup.org/report/joint-statement-rights-and-freedoms-students.
5. "Academic Bill of Rights," *Students for Academic Freedom*, www.studentsforacademicfreedom.org/documents/1925/abor.html; "Academic Freedom and Educational Responsibility," *Association of American Colleges and Universities*,

January 6, 2006, www.aacu.org/about/statements/academic_freedom.cfm; Scott Jaschik, "Stop Blaming Professors," *Inside Higher Education*, June 10, 2014, https://www.insidehighered.com/news/2014/06/10/study-finds-students-themselves-not-professors-lead-some-become-more-liberal-college#sthash.bWA9dH8W.dpbs.

6. Ronald Mahurin in discussion with the author, 2013; "Top Conservative Colleges," *Young Americans for Freedom*, www.yaf./org/topconservativecolleges.aspx.

7. Billy Graham, *Just As I Am: The Autobiography of Billy Graham* (New York: HarperCollins, 1997), 39–41, 46–47.

8. Richard Hughes in discussion with the author, April 22, 2013.

9. In secular institutions the students are more interested in talking about religion than are the faculty. Even beyond the educational setting, legal scholar Stephen L. Carter found that "America is bursting with the desire to talk about religion but often afraid to do so." See Stephen L. Carter, *The Culture of Disbelief: How America Law and Politics Trivialize Religious Devotion* (New York: Doubleday, 1994), xiii.

10. Donna R. Euben, "Who Grades Students?" (address to the University of Michigan, AAUP chapter, November 13, 2001), www.umuch.edu/~aaupum/gradesrb.html; Lawrence White, "Does Academic Freedom Give a Professor the Final Say on Grades?" *Chronicle of Higher Education* 54, no. 33 (April 25, 2008): 39.

11. The *Hosty v. Carter* case (2005) in the federal Seventh Circuit Court cast some doubt on how broad this freedom is for public colleges. See "Hosty v. Carter: An Analysis," *Student Press Law Center (SPLC)*, 2005, http://www.splc.org/article/2005/09/hosty-v-carter-an-analysis.

12. "Legal Guide for the Private School Press," *Student Press Law Center*, 2002, www.splc.org/knowyourrights/legalresearch.asp?id=52.

13. Sarah Eekhoff Zylstra, "Breaking the Bubble," *Christianity Today* 53, no. 12 (December 9, 2009): 17–18; Donna Downs in discussion with the author, June 12, 2014.

14. For examples of such newspapers in Christian colleges, see Melita Marie Garza, "Controversy Splits Wheaton College," *Chicago Tribune*, May 16, 1990, http://articles.chicagotribune.com/1990-05-16/news/9002090345_1_christian-campus-students-billy-graham; Warren Throckmorton, "Underground Newspaper shut down at Cedarville," *Patheos*, April 23, 2014, http://www.patheos.com/blogs/warrenthrockmorton/2014/04/23/underground-newspaper-shut-down-at-cedarville-university/; Rachel Marie Stone, "Cedarville University Shuts Down Dissenting Newspaper," *Religion News Service*, April 24, 2014, http://rachelmariestone.religionnews.com/2014/04/24/cedarville-university-shuts-dissenting-student-newspaper/; *The Student Voice: The Unofficial Pensacola Christian College Information Site*, www.pensacolachristiancollege.acautionarytale.com.

15. Valerie Straus, "Christian College's Student Leader 'Comes Out' As Atheist," *Washington Post*, November 7, 2013, http://www.washingtonpost.com/blogs/answer-sheet/wp/2013/11/07/christian-colleges-student-leader-comes-out-as-atheist/.

Chapter 18

1. Jeff Denneed and Tom Dretler, "The Financially Sustainable University," *Bain and Company Insights*, July 6, 2012, http://www.bain.com/Images/BAIN_BRIEF_The_ financially_sustainable_university.pdf; Robert C. Andringa, "Keeping the Faith: Leadership Challenges Unique to Religiously Affiliated Colleges and Universities" in *Turnaround: Leading Stressed Colleges and Universities to Excellence*, ed. James Martin, James E. Samels and Associates (Baltimore: Johns Hopkins University Press, 2009), 168–171; Skip Trudeau in discussion with the author, November 13, 2013.

2. Kevin Riley, "The Cost of Values," *Inside Higher Education*, October 8, 2012; Rajashri Chakrabarti, Maricar Mabutas, and Basit Zafar, "Soaring Tuitions: Are Public Funding Cuts to Blame?" *Liberty Street Economics*, September 19, 2012, http://libertystreeteconomics.newyorkfed.org/2012/09/soaring-tuitions-are-public-funding-cuts-to-blame.html#.U_eVa7xdW9Y; Jordan Weissmann, "A Truly Devastating Graph on State Higher Education Spending," *The Atlantic*, March 20, 2013, http://www.theatlantic.com/business/archive/2013/03/a-truly-devastating-graph-on-state-higher-education-spending/274199/; Doug Lederman, "State Budgeters' View of Higher Ed," *Inside Higher Education*, March 27, 2013, https://www.insidehighered.com/news/2013/03/27/state-state-funding-higher-education.

3. Andy Thomason, "Student Loan Default Rates Continue Steady Climb," *Chronicle of Higher Education*, October 1, 2013, http://chronicle.com/article/Student-Loan-Default-Rates/142009/; "Federal Student Aid Portfolio Summary," *National Student Loan Data System*; "President Obama Takes Executive Action to Reform PAYE," *Educated Risk*, June 8, 2014, http://educatedrisk.org/news/president-obama-takes-executive-action-reform-paye-and-publicly-backs-senator-warrens-student; David Jesse, "Pay it Forward: Plan Would Allow Michigan Students to Attend College for 'Free,' " *Detroit Free Press*, March 19, 2014, http://www.freep.com/article/20140319/NEWS06/303190038/Pay-it-forward-Plan-would-allow-Michigan-students-to-attend-college-for-free-.

4. Lyndsey Layton, "High School Graduation Rates at Historic High," *Washington Post*, April 28, 2014, http://www.washingtonpost.com/local/education/high-school-graduation-rates-at-historic-high/2014/04/28/84eb0122-cee0-11e3-937f-d3026234b51c_story.html; *NCHEMS Information Center for Higher Education Policymaking and Analysis*, www.nchems.org; Sandy Baum and Kathleen Payea, "Trends in For-Profit Postsecondary Education," *College Board Advocacy & Policy Center*, 2011, trends.collegeboard.org/sites/default/files/trends-2011-for-profit-postsecondary-ed-outcomes-brief.pdf; Sandy Baum, Kathie Little, and Kathleen Payea, "Trends in Community College Education," *College Board Advocacy & Policy Center*, 2011, https://trends.collegeboard.org/sites/default/files/trends-2011-community-colleges-ed-enrollment-debt-brief.pdf; Eduardo Porter, "The Bane and the Boon of For-Profit Colleges," *New York Times*, February 25, 2014, http://www.nytimes.com/2014/02/26/business/economy/

the-bane-and-the-boon-of-for-profit-colleges.html?_r=0; Thomason, "Student Loan Default Rates."

5. Kevin Carey, "Into the Future with MOOCs," *Chronicle of Higher Education*, September 3, 2012, http://chronicle.com/article/Into-the-Future-With-MOOCs/134080/; Chris Parr, "Clinton: MOOCs May be a Key to a More Efficient U.S. System," *Times Higher Education*, April 11, 2013, http://www.improvingthestudentexperience.com/news/moocs-may-be-more-efficient/; "What You Need to Know about MOOCs," *Chronicle of Higher Education*, June 20, 2014, http://chronicle.com/article/What-You-Need-to-Know-About/133475/; Alan Finder, "A Surge of Growth for a New Kind of Online Course," *New York Times*, September 25, 2013, http://www.nytimes.com/2013/09/26/technology/personaltech/a-surge-in-growth-for-a-new-kind-of-online-course.html?pagewanted=all; Tamar Lewin, "After Setbacks, Online Courses Are Rethought," *New York Times*, December 10, 2013, http://www.nytimes.com/2013/12/11/us/after-setbacks-online-courses-are-rethought.html?pagewanted=all.

6. Carl Straumsheim, "Tempered Expectations," *Inside Higher Education*, January 15, 2014, https://www.insidehighered.com/news/2014/01/15/after-two-years-mooc-mania-enthusiasm-online-education-dips.

7. L. Richard Meeth, *Quality Education for Less Money* (San Francisco: Jossey-Bass, 1974), 163–164.

8. Donna M. Desrochers and Rita Kirshstein, "Labor Intensive or Labor Expensive?: Changing Staffing and Compensation Patterns in Higher Education," *American Institutes for Research*, February 2014, http://www.air.org/sites/default/files/downloads/report/DeltaCostAIR-Labor-Expensive-Higher-Education-Staffing-Brief-Feb2014.pdf; Scott Carlson, "Administrative Hiring Drove 28% Boom in Higher-Ed Work Force, Report Says," *Chronicle of Higher Education*, February 5, 2014, http://chronicle.com/article/Administrator-Hiring-Drove-28-/144519/.

9. Richard Vedder, *Going Broke by Degree: Why College Costs Too Much* (Washington, DC: AEI Press, 2004), 196–204. In 2006, Vedder founded the Center for College Affordability and Productivity (CCAP).

10. Eugene B. Habecker, John E. Brown III, and William Hasker, "The First Amendment, Private Religious Colleges, and the State," *Christian Scholar's Review* 10, no. 4 (1981): 295.

11. *Conrad Grebel University College*, uwaterloo.ca/grebel/node/1; *Consortium of Christian Study Centers*, studycentersonline.org.

12. Andringa, "Keeping the Faith," 178–183.

Chapter 19

1. Mark A. Noll and Carolyn Nystrom, *Is the Reformation Over?: An Evangelical Assessment of Contemporary Roman Catholicism* (Grand Rapids: Baker Academic, 2005), 18–24.

2. "Evangelicals and Catholics Together: The Christian Mission in the Third Millennium," *First Things*, May, 1994, http://www.firstthings.com/article/1994/05/evangelicals--catholics-together-the-christian-mission-in-the-third-millennium-2.

3. Graham, *Just As I Am*, 302; Alan Jacobs, *More Than 95 Theses*, ayjay.tumblr.com; "Cushing Praises Graham Crusade," *The New York Times*, October 8, 1964, http://www.nytimes.com/1964/10/08/cushing-praises-graham-crusade.html.

4. Paul Kengor, "A Tale of 2 Christian Colleges," *National Catholic Register*, July 8, 2011, http://www.ncregister.com/site/article/a-tale-of-2-christian-colleges/.

5. Philip Ryken and John Garvey, "An Evangelical-Catholic Stand on Liberty," *Wall Street Journal*, July 18, 2012, http://online.wsj.com/news/articles/SB10001424052 702303933704577533251292715324\; "HHS Mandate Information Central," *The Becket Fund for Religious Liberty*, December 16, 2014, http://www.becketfund.org/hhsinformationcentral/.

6. Thomas A. Howard, "A Timely and Important Conversation," *Stillpoint*, 2008, http://www.gordon.edu/article.cfm?iArticleID=563&iReferrerPageID=2114&iPrevCatID=94&bLive=1; Mark A. Noll and James Turner with Thomas Albert Howard, eds., *The Future of Christian Learning: An Evangelical and Catholic Dialogue* (Grand Rapids: Brazos Press, 2008).

7. Noll, Turner, and Howard, *Future of Christian Learning*, 43, 66–68.

8. Ibid., 84–87.

9. Kenneth Garcia, *Academic Freedom and the Telos of the Catholic University* (New York: Palgrave Macmillan, 2012), ix–xii, 1–4, 56, 148–149, 162–163.

10. Ibid., 17–19; Gregory Kalscheur, "Key Task for Catholic Higher Ed," *Inside Higher Education*, November 29, 2011, https://www.insidehighered.com/views/2011/11/29/essay-future-direction-catholic-colleges.

11. Thomas Howard tells his conversion story in *Evangelical Is Not Enough: Worship of God in Liturgy and Sacrament* (San Francisco: Ignatius Press, 1988) and *Lead Kindly Light: My Journey to Rome* (San Francisco: Ignatius Press, 2004).

12. Mark Galli, "The Confidence of the Evangelical," *Christianity Today*, November 17, 2011, http://www.christianitytoday.com/ct/2011/novemberweb-only/confidenceevangelical.html; Scott McKnight, "From Wheaton to Rome: Why Evangelicals Become Roman Catholic," *Journal of Evangelical Theological Society* 45, no. 3 (September, 2002): 451–472.

13. David E. Bjork, "Christian Discipleship and Diversity" (lecture, Taylor University's Ray Fitzgerald Lectureship, Upland, Indiana, September 24, 2013); David E. Bjork in discussion with the author, September 24, 2013; also see David E. Bjork, *Unfamiliar Paths: The Challenge of Recognizing the Work of Christ in Strange Clothing—A Case Study from France* (Pasadena, California: William Carey Library, 1997).

14. Bjork, "Christian Discipleship and Diversity," 14–15.

15. Daniel Godlen, "A Test of Faith," *Wall Street Journal*, January 7, 2006, http://online.wsj.com/news/articles/SB113659805227040466; Alan Jacobs, "To Be a Christian College," *First Things*, April, 2006, http://www.firstthings.com/article/2006/04/to-be-a-christian-college.

Chapter 20

1. Ringenberg, *The Christian College*, 117–119; James McCosh, "God Works Through Evolution" in *A Documentary History of American Thought and Society*, ed. Charles Crowe (Boston: Allyn and Bacon, 1968), 229.

2. Ronald L. Numbers, *The Creationists: The Evolution of Scientific Creationism* (Berkeley: University of California Press, 1992), 7–19; David N. Livingstone, *Darwin's Forgotten Defenders: The Encounter Between Evangelical Theology and Evolutionary Thought* (Grand Rapids: Eerdmans, 1987), 70–71, 76–77, 85.

3. Livingstone, *Darwin's Forgotten Defenders*, 140–145; Mark A. Noll and David N. Livingstone, *Evolution, Scripture, and Science: Selected Writings* (Grand Rapids: Baker Books, 2000), 13–15.

4. Edward B. Davis, "Science Falsely So Called: Fundamentalism and Science" in *The Blackwell Companion to Science and Christianity*, eds. J. B. Stump and Alan G. Padgett (Oxford, England: John Wiley and Sons, 2012), 49–50.

5. Louis W. Koenig, *Bryan* (New York: G.P. Putnam's Sons, 1971), 605–609, 612–615, 631; Michael Kazin, *A Godly Hero: The Life of William Jennings Bryan* (New York: Alfred A. Knopf, 2006), 263–264, 272–277.

6. The SDA Church associates seven 24-hour days of creation with the fourth commandment and its practice of worshiping on the seventh day.

7. Numbers, *The Creationists*, chapters 5, 9, 10; "Who Are We?" *The American Scientific Affiliation: A Network of Christians in the Sciences*, http://network.asa3.org/?page=ASAAbout#Who%20we%20are.

8. Deborah Haarsma, letter to author, September 3, 2013; Ted Davis, letter to author, July 26, 2013; "Creation Colleges," *Answers in Genesis*, 2011, https://answersingenesis.org/colleges/; Numbers, *The Creationists*, 290; Joeckel and Chesnes, *The Christian College Phenomenon*, 365, 388.

9. Philip E. Johnson, *Darwin on Trial* (Downers Grove, Illinois: InterVarsity Press, 1993), 158; Alvin Plantinga, *Where the Conflict Really Lies: Science, Religion, and Naturalism* (New York: Oxford University Press, 2011), ix–x.

10. S. O. Moshier, D. E. Maas, and J. K. Greenberg, "From the Beginning: Faith and Geology at Evangelical Wheaton College" in *Geology and Religion: A History of Harmony and Hostility*, ed. M. Kolbl-Ebert (London: Geological Society of London, 2009), 301–315; Numbers, *The Creationists*, 172–178; John H. Walton, *The Lost World of Genesis One: Ancient Cosmology and the Origins Debate* (Downers Grove, Illinois: InterVarsity Press Academic, 2009), 16–36, 163–166, 171.

11. Numbers, *The Creationists*, 116, 181–183; Moshier et al., "From the Beginning," 308; Beth McMurtrie, "Do Professors Lose Academic Freedom by Signing Statements of Faith?" *Chronicle of Higher Education*, May 24, 2002; Chignell, "Whither Wheaton"; John Owens, "Schools' Faith-Based Doctrines Raise Concerns, Risk Backlash," *Chicago Tribune*, October 6, 2002, http://articles.chicagotribune.com/2002-10-06/news/0210060223_1_faith-based-catholic-colleges-mandatums.

Chapter 21

1. Major writings in the ID movement include Michael Behe, *Darwin's Black Box: The Biochemical Challenge to Evolution* (New York: The Free Press, 1996); Stephen C. Meyer, *Signature in the Cell* (New York: HarperOne, 2010); William A. Demski, *Intelligent Design: The Bridge Between Science and Theology* (Downers Grove, Illinois: InterVarsity Press, 1999); and the aforementioned Phillip E. Johnson, *Darwin on Trial*. Evangelical critiques of ID include John Wilson, "Unintelligent Debate," *Christianity Today*, September 1, 2004, http://www.christianitytoday.com/ct/2004/september/24.62.html?paging=off; and Karl Giberson, "Find a Fertile Idea," *Christianity Today*, May 19, 2010, http://www.christianitytoday.com/ct/2010/may/20.50.html. Also critical of ID are "Kitzmiller v. Dover: Intelligent Design on Trial," *Nation Center for Science Education*, October 17, 2008, ncse.com/creationism/legal/intelligent-design-trial-kitzmiller-v-dover, and "Kitzmiller v. Dover," *United States District Court for the Middle District of Pennsylvania*, Document 342, 136, ncse.com/files/pub/legal/kitzmiller/2005-12-20_Kitzmiller_decision.pdf.

2. Tony Carnes, "Intelligent Design: Design Interference," *Christianity Today*, December 4, 2000, http://www.christianitytoday.com/ct/2000/december4/18.20.html?paging=off; Fred Heeren, "The Lynching of Bill Dembski: Scientists Say the Jury Is Out—So Let the Hanging Begin," *The American Spectator*, November 15, 2000, http://www.discovery.org/a/532; Elizabeth F. Farrell, "Baylor U. Removes a Web Page Associated with Intelligent Design from Its Site," *Chronicle of Higher Education*, September 4, 2007, http://chronicle.com/article/Baylor-U-Removes-a-Web-Pag/121996/; Clair St. Amant, "New Intelligent Design Conflict Hits BU," *The Baylor Lariat*, September 11, 2007, http://www.discovery.org/a/4217.

3. Francis S. Collins, *The Language of God* (New York: Free Press, 2006), 2, 133–134, 140–141; "Team Members," "Board of Directors," and "Advising Council," *BioLogos*, biologos.org; Richard Ostling, "The Search for the Historical Adam," *Christianity Today*, June 3, 2011, http://www.christianitytoday.com/ct/2011/june/historicaladam.html?paging=off.

4. Daniel C. Harlow, "After Adam: Reading Genesis in the Age of Evolutionary Science," *Perspectives on Science and Christian Faith* 62, no. 3 (September, 2010): 179; John R. Schneider, "Recent Genetic Science and Christian Theology on Human Origins: An Aesthetic Supralapsarianism," *American Scientific Affiliation*, August 5, 2010, http://www.asa3online.org/PSCF/2010/08/05/recent-genetic-science-and-christian-theology-on-human-origins-an-%E2%80%9Caesthetic-supralapsarianism%E2%80%9D/; Scott Jaschik, "Fall From Grace," *Inside Higher Education*, August 15, 2011, https://www.insidehighered.com/news/2011/08/15/a_professor_s_departure_raises_questions_about_freedom_of_scholarship_at_calvin_college; Napp Nazworth, "Calvin College Professor Claims Administration Not Truthful Over Colleague's Resignation," *The Christian Post*, August 17, 2011, http://www.christianpost.com/news/calvin-college-professor-claims-administration-not-truthful-over-colleagues-resignation-54046/; Howard J. Van Till, *The Fourth Day* (Grand Rapids: Eerdmans, 1986).

5. Ruth Moon, "Bryan College Faculty Vote 'No Confidence' in President Over Adam and Eve," *Christianity Today*, March 7, 2014, http://www.christianitytoday.com/gleanings/2014/march/bryan-college-faculty-vote-no-confidence-president-adam-eve.html?paging=off; Deborah Haarsma, "The Controversy at Bryan College," *The BioLogos Forum*, March 6, 2014, http://biologos.org/blog/the-controversy-at-bryan-college; Alan Blinder, "Bryan College Is Torn: Can Darwin and Eden Coexist?" *New York Times*, May 20, 2014, http://www.nytimes.com/2014/05/21/education/christian-college-faces-uproar-after-bolstering-its-view-on-evolution.html; Tim Omarzu, "Four Trustees Resign from Bryan College," *Chattanooga Times Press*, July 19, 2014, http://www.timesfreepress.com/news/2014/jul/19/four-trustees-resign-from-bryan-college/?breakingnews.

6. Scott Jaschik, "Faith, Science, and Academic Freedom," *Inside Higher Education*, January 15, 2009, https://www.insidehighered.com/news/2009/01/15/aaup; Richard G. Colling, "Evolution and Christian Faith" in *The Christian College Phenomenon*, ed. Joeckel and Chesnes, 313–314; Richard Colling, "Evolution and Faith: Communicating Compatibility in Christian Higher Education," *The BioLogos Forum: Science and Faith in Dialogue*, February 20, 2010, http://biologos.org/blog/evolution-and-faith; Scott Jaschik, "Believing in God and Evolution," *Inside Higher Education*, October 14, 2009, https://www.insidehighered.com/news/2009/10/14/evolution.

7. "Statement on Creation: The Bible's Worldview," *Seventh-Day Adventist Church*, www.adventist.org/beliefs/statements/bible-worldview; Jack Stripling, "Creating Controversy," *Inside Higher Education*, September 1, 2009, https://www.insidehighered.com/news/2009/09/01/evolution; Lee Greer, "Terminated LSU Biologist Lee Greer Issues Press Release," *Spectrum Magazine*, May 9, 2012, http://spectrummagazine.org/blog/2012/05/09/terminated-lsu-biologist-lee-greer-issues-press-release; David Olson, "La Sierra University: Employees' Case Dismissed," *Press Enterprise*, May 20, 2012, http://www.pe.com/articles/university-688936-church-sierra.html; Tim Standish in discussion with the author, July 15, 2014; Brian Bull, Fritz Guy, and Ervin Taylor, eds., *Understanding Genesis: Contemporary Adventist Perspectives* (Riverside, California: Adventist Today Foundation, 2006), vi; Nathaniel Jeanson and Brian Thomas, "The Resurrection of 'Junk DNA,'" *Institute of Creation Research*, March 20, 2013, http://www.icr.org/article/7383/; Fazale Rana, "Do Scientists Accept the Results of the Encode Project?" *Reasons to Believe*, September 12, 2013, http://www.reasons.org/articles/do-scientists-accept-the-results-of-the-encode-project; Kenneth Keathley, "Southern Baptist Voices: Expressing Our Concern, Part I," *The BioLogos Forum*, February 28, 2012, http://biologos.org/blog/southern-baptist-voices-expressing-our-concerns-part-1.

8. I Corinthians 13:12; Michael Polanyi, *Personal Knowledge: Towards a Post-Critical Philosophy* (Chicago: University of Chicago Press, 1958), vii; Walter R. Thorson, "The Biblical Insights of Michael Polanyi," *Journal of the American Scientific Affiliation*, September, 1981, http://www.asa3.org/ASA/PSCF/1981/JASA9-81Thorson.html.

Chapter 22

1. "Changing Attitudes on Gay Marriage," *The Pew Forum on Religion and Public Life*, June, 2013, http://www.pewforum.org/2014/09/24/graphics-slideshow-changing-attitudes-on-gay-marriage/.

2. "Wave III of the Baylor Religion Survey Examines How Religion Affects Individuals' Outlook and Well-Being in Tumultuous Times," *Baylor University*, September, 2011, http://www.baylor.edu/mediacommunications/news.php?action=story&story=100503; Corrie Mitchell, "Evangelical 'Messy Middle' More Accepting of Gays," *Sojourners: Faith in Action for Social Justice*, August 13, 2013, http://sojo.net/blogs/2013/08/13/study-evangelical -%E2%80%98messy-middle%E2%80%99-more-accepting-gays.

3. Rich Morin, "Opposition to Same-Sex Marriage May Be Understated in Public Opinion Polls," *Pew Research Center*, September 30, 2013, http://www.pewresearch.org/fact-tank/2013/09/30/opposition-to-same-sex-marriage-may-be-understated-in-public-opinion-polls/.

4. "Same-Sex Marriage State-by-State," *The Pew Forum*, November 20, 2014, http://www.pewforum.org/2014/11/20/same-sex-marriage-state-by-state/; "States," *Freedom to Marry*, www.freedomtomarry.org/states; Josh Earnest, "President Obama Supports Same-Sex Marriage," *The White House Blog*, May 10, 2012, http://www.whitehouse.gov/blog/2012/05/10/obama-supports-same-sex-marriage; "Supreme Court Strikes Down Defense of Marriage Act, Paves Way for Gay Marriage to Resume in California," *NBC Politics*, June 26, 2013, www.nbcnews.com/politics; Greg Stohr, "Gay Marriage Nears Supreme Court with Inevitability Tag," *Bloomberg*, July 31, 2014, http://www.bloomberg.com/news/2014-07-31/gay-marriage-nears-supreme-court-with-inevitability-tag.html.

5. "Religious Groups' Official Positions on Same-Sex Marriage," *The Pew Forum*, December 7, 2012, http://www.pewforum.org/2012/12/07/religious-groups-official-positions-on-same-sex-marriage/.

6. "A Survey of LGBT Americans: Attitudes, Experiences, and Values in Changing Times," *Pew Research Center*, June 13, 2013, http://www.pewsocialtrends.org/2013/06/13/a-survey-of-lgbt-americans/; "Open and Affirming in the UCC," *United Church of Christ*, http://www.ucc.org/lgbt/ona.html.

7. "History of MCC" and "Who We Are," *Metropolitan Community Churches*, mccchurch.org.

8. "Essay About Being a Gay Faculty Member at a Christian College," *Inside Higher Education*, March 18, 2013, https://www.insidehighered.com/advice/2013/03/18/essay-about-being-gay-faculty-member-christian-college; Stanton L. Jones, "Letter to a Gay Professor," *Inside Higher Education*, April 3, 2013, https://www.insidehighered.com/advice/2013/04/03/essay-responds-open-letter-gay-professor-christian-college.

9. Stanton L. Jones, "Same-Sex Science: The Social Sciences Cannot Settle the Moral Status of Homosexuality," *First Things*, February, 2012, http://www.firstthings.com/article/2012/02/same-sex-science; Stanton L. Jones and Mark

A. Yarhouse, *Homosexuality: The Use of Scientific Research in the Church's Moral Debate* (Downers Grove, Illinois: InterVarsity Press, 2000).

10. David G. Myers and Letha Dawson Scanzoni, *What God Has Joined Together?: A Christian Case for Gay Marriage* (San Francisco: Harper San Francisco, 2005), especially chapter 7, "What the Bible Does and Doesn't Say"; James V. Brownson, *Bible, Gender, Sexuality: Reframing the Church's Debate on Same-Sex Relationships* (Grand Rapids: Eerdmans, 2013); David G. Myers, "Accepting What Cannot Be Changed" in *Homosexuality and Christian Faith: Questions of Conscience for the Churches*, ed. Walter Wink (Minneapolis: Augsburg Fortress Publishers, 1999); Kym Reinstadler, "Hope College Stands by Homosexuality Statement," *Huffington Post*, May 25, 2011, http://www.huffingtonpost.com/religion/the-news/2010/05/10/; "Hope College Position Statement on Human Sexuality," *Hope College*, January 28, 2011, www.hope.edu/news/2011/01/28/hope-college-position-statement-on-human-sexuality.html; Ruth Graham, "Can the Evangelical Church Embrace Gay Couples?: A New Wave of Thinkers Says Yes—and Is Looking to Scripture for Support," *Boston Globe*, January 12, 2014, http://www.bostonglobe.com/ideas/2014/01/12/can-evangelical-church-embrace-gay-couples/5Tqq4n7xNZcsBtrAeszJBM/story.html.

11. Charles Honey, "The Litmus Test: Trustee Ban on 'Advocacy of Homosexual Practice and Same-Sex Marriage' Stirs Up Calvin Faculty," *Christianity Today*, October 28, 2009, http://www.christianitytoday.com/ct/2009/november/9.17.html; Libby A. Nelson, "Standing Their Ground," *Inside Higher Education*, February 3, 2012, https://www.insidehighered.com/news/2012/02/03/christian-college-presidents-discuss-what-do-about-sexuality.

12. Mel White, *Stranger at the Gate: To Be Gay and Christian in America* (New York: Simon and Schuster, 1994), see especially chapters 11–12; "Our Founders," *Soulforce*, http://soulforce.com/about/co-founders/; Sarah Pulliam, "Gay Rights Group Targets Christian Colleges," *Christianity Today*, March 9, 2006, http://www.christianitytoday.com/ct/2006/marchweb-only/110-42.0.html; Kristin Rudolph, "Evangelical Colleges Inching Toward Affirmation of Homosexuality," *Juicy Ecumenism: The Institute on Religion and Democracy's Blog*, http://juicyecumenism.com/2013/04/03/evangelical-colleges-inching-toward-affirmation-of-homosexuality/; Kathryn Joyce, "LGBT Christian College Students Fight for a Voice," *The Daily Beast*, February 14, 2014, http://www.thedailybeast.com/articles/2014/02/14/lgbt-christian-college-students-fight-for-a-voice.html.

13. Cherin Poovey, "Justin Lee ('00): Of Faith—and Finding Faith in One's Self: Founder of Gay Christian Network Publishes New Book about His Personal Journey," *Wake Forest Magazine*, February 4, 2013, http://magazine.wfu.edu/2013/02/04/justin-lee-00-of-faith-and-finding-faith-in-ones-self/; Stephanie Fairyington, "Virgin Marys," *Questia*, February, 2007, https://www.questia.com/magazine/1P3-1207607921/virgin-marys; *The Gay Christian Network*, gaychristian.net.

14. Jeannie Choi, "Changes in Attitude," *Sojourners*, July, 2012, http://sojo.net/magazine/2012/07/changes-attitude; Paul Southwick, "Is There Hope

for Queer Students at Conservative Christian Colleges?" *Huffington Post Gay Voices*, August 24, 2012, http://www.huffingtonpost.com/paul-southwick/ is-there-hope-for-queer-s_b_1829246.html; Libby A. Nelson, "No Longer a Silent Minority," *Inside Higher Education*, December 17, 2012, https://www. insidehighered.com/news/2012/12/17/gay-students-increasingly-vocal-evangelical-colleges; Joyce, "LGBT Students Fight for Voice"; Philip Francis and Mark Longhurst, "How LGBT Students Are Changing Christian Colleges," *The Atlantic*, July 23, 2014, http://www.theatlantic.com/education/archive/2014/ 07/gordon-college-the-new-frontier-of-gay-rights/374861/; *Haven, An Unofficial SPU Club*, spuhaven.blogspot.com; Allison J. Althoff, "Hope for the Gay Undergrad," *Christianity Today*, December 7, 2012, http://www.christianitytoday. com/ct/2013/january-february/hope-for-gay-undergrad.html; *Choros: Sexuality and Gender Discussion at Taylor University*, taylorchoros.wordpress.com; "Refuge: A Community for Wheaton's Same-Sex Attracted Students; Guiding Document," http://www.wheaton.edu/~/media/Files/Student-Life/Student-Activities/Student-Government/Refuge%20Guiding%20Document.pdf; Wesley Hill, *Washed and Waiting: Reflections on Christian Faithfulness and Homosexuality* (Grand Rapids: Zondervan, 2010); *Christopher Yuan*, christopheryuan.com.

Chapter 23

1. Bonnie Miller Rubin, "Lutheran College Opens the Door to Same-Sex Wedding," *Chicago Tribune*, January 14, 2013, http://articles.chicagotribune.com/ 2013-01-14/news/ct-met-gay-marriage-religious-colleges-20130114_1_elca-augustana-college-liberal-arts-college; Libby A. Nelson, "Going to the Chapel," *Inside Higher Education*, December 19, 2012, https://www.insidehighered.com/ news/2012/12/19/religious-colleges-deciding-whether-allow-blessings-gay-unions-their-chapels.

2. Sarah Pulliam Bailey, "Transgender Theology Professor Leaves Christian College," *Christianity Today*, September 23, 2013, http://www.christianitytoday. com/gleanings/2013/september/transgender-professor-azusa-pacific-heath-adam-ackley.html?paging=off; Scott Jaschik, "Freedom of Religion or Free to Discriminate?" *Inside Higher Education*, July 14, 2014, https://www.insidehighered.com/ news/2014/07/14/two-legal-cases-illustrate-growing-tensions-over-rights-transgender-students; "Partial Win for California Baptist in Transgender Case," *Baptist Press*, July 15, 2014, http://www.bpnews.net/42974/partial-win-for-cal-baptist-in-transgender-case; Kate Tracy, "Transgender Students Battle Christian Universities," *Christianity Today*, July 15, 2014, http://www.christianitytoday. com/gleanings/2014/july/transgender-students-battle-christian-universities.html? paging=off; Francis and Longhurst, "LGBT Students"; "Transgender Professor, Christian College Settle Sex-Discrimination Complaint," *Advocate*, March 14, 2007, http://www.advocate.com/news/2007/03/15/transgender-professor-christian-college-settle-sex-discrimination-complaint; "Transgender

Professor Runs Afoul of 'Ideals' at Christian University," *Chronicle of Higher Education*, February 6, 2007, http://chronicle.com/article/Transgender-Professor-Runs/38176.

3. Samuel G. Freedman, "'Griner Effect' May Change the Game at Baylor," *The New York Times*, May 18, 2013, http://www.nytimes.com/2013/05/18/us/griner-baylor-lesbian-college-sports.html?_r=0; Mike Chiari, "Brittney Griner Criticizes Baylor's Anti-Gay Policies in Memoir 'In My Skin,'" *Bleacher Report*, April 15, 2014, http://bleacherreport.com/articles/2030399-brittney-griner-criticizes-baylors-anti-gay-policies-in-memoir-in-my-skin; Bob Allen, "Baylor Keeps Homosexuality Ban," *Baptist News Global*, November 1, 2013, http://baptistnews.com/ministry/organizations/item/8981-baylor-keeps-homosexuality-ban/.

4. Mike Organ, "Belmont Disputes Gay Coach Was Fired: Sexuality Brought Ultimatum from School, Players Say," *The Tennessean*, December 3, 2010, http://archive.tennessean.com/article/20101203/SPORTS06/12030362/Belmont-disputes-gay-coach-fired; Campbell Robertson, "Lesbian Coach's Exit from Belmont U. Has Nashville Talking," *The New York Times*, December 17, 2010, http://www.nytimes.com/2010/12/18/education/18belmont.html; Scott Jaschik, "Change of Heart at Belmont," *Inside Higher Education*, January 27, 2011, https://www.insidehighered.com/news/2011/01/27/belmont_bars_discrimination_based_on_sexual_orientation.

5. Charles Honey, "Seven Passages: Play about Gay Christians Moves to World Stage," *Grand Rapids Press*, July 28, 2008, http://blog.mlive.com/grpress/2008/07/seven_passages_play_about_gay.html; Roxanne Van Farowe, "Play about Gay Christians Sells Out," *Banner*, January 2011, http://www.thebanner.org/news/2011/01/play-about-gay-christians-sells-out; Jim Harger, "Calvin College Faculty Senate Asks College to Drop Order on Teaching about Homosexuality and Same-Sex Marriage," *MLive Media Group*, October 1, 2009, http://www.mlive.com/news/grand-rapids/index.ssf/2009/10/calvin_college_faculty_senate.html; Christian Bell, "Calvin College Statement about Homosexuality Draws Fire," *Banner*, January 18, 2011, http://www.thebanner.org/news/2011/01/calvin-college-statement-about-homosexuality-draws-fire; Brian McVicar, "Calvin College Alumni Using the Web to Push for More Welcoming Environment for LGBT Students," *MLive Media Group*, October 18, 2012, http://www.mlive.com/news/grand-rapids/index.ssf/2012/10/alumni_say_calvin_college_must.html.

6. "Homosexuality," Position Statements, *Christian Reformed Church*, 2002, http://www.crcna.org/welcome/beliefs/position-statements/homosexuality.

7. *Christ Evangelical Bible Institute*, cebiaz.com.

8. Lawn Griffiths, "Peggy Campolo," *Scottsdale Tribune*, October 4, 2003, http://www.nolongersilent.org/TribuneArticleOct2003.html; "Building Bridges of Understanding: Tony and Peggy Campolo on Homosexuality," *The Gay Christian Network*, https://www.gaychristian.net/campolos.php; Peggy Campolo, "In God's House There Are Many Closets" in *Homosexuality and Christian Faith*, ed. Walter Wink (Minneapolis: Fortune Press, 1999), 100–104.

9. Kate Tracy, "CCCU School Permits Professors in Same-Sex Relationships (At Least for Six Months)," *Christianity Today*, November 27, 2013, http://www.christianitytoday.com/gleanings/2013/november/eastern-mennonite-university-professors-same-sex-cccu-emu.html?paging=off; Ruth Moon, "Eastern Mennonite University Delays Decision on Same-Sex Relationships," *Christianity Today*, June 23, 2014, http://www.christianitytoday.com/gleanings/2014/june/eastern-mennonite-university-delays-decision-on-same-sex-re.html?paging=off; Bob Smietana, "Two CCCU Colleges to Allow Same-Sex Married Faculty," *Christianity Today*, July 20, 2015.

10. Jeff Brady, "College Course Lumps Homosexuality, Rape, and Murder," *US & World*, September 11, 2012, http://www.scpr.org/news/2012/09/10/34219/college-course-lumps-homosexuality-rape-murder/.

11. Rosaria Champagne Butterfield, *The Secret Thoughts of an Unlikely Convert: An English Professor's Journey into the Christian Faith* (Pittsburg: Crown and Covenant Publications, 2012); Rosaria Champagne Butterfield, "My Train Wreck Conversion," *Christianity Today*, February 7, 2013, http://www.christianitytoday.com/ct/2013/january-february/my-train-wreck-conversion.html; also note Rosaria Champagne, *The Politics of Survivorship: Incest, Women's Literature, and Feminist Theory* (New York: New York University Press, 1998).

12. Francis and Longhurst, "LGBT Students"; Mary Moore, "Accreditation Board Gives Gordon College a Year to Review Policy on Homosexuality," *Boston Business Journal*, September 25, 2014, http://www.bizjournals.com/boston/news/2014/09/25/accreditation-board-gives-gordon-college-a-year-to.html?page=all; "An Explanation of Gordon College's Policy on Homosexuality," *Gordon College*, http://www.gordon.edu/download/galleries/HomosexualityPolicy.pdf.

13. "Christian College in Omaha Expels Lesbian," *USA Today*, June 14, 2013, http://www.usatoday.com/story/news/nation/2013/06/14/grace-university-omaha-christian-college-lesbian/2425467/.

14. Peter J. Smith, "Notre Dame's Plan for Homosexual Outreach: University Says Church Teaching Will Be Addressed, But Skepticism Remains," *National Catholic Register*, January 7, 2013, http://www.ncregister.com/site/article/notre-dames-plan-for-homosexual-outreach/.

15. David Gibson, "Notre Dame Signals Welcome to Gay Athletes in New Campaign," *The Washington Post*, May 8, 2014, http://www.washingtonpost.com/national/religion/notre-dame-signals-welcome-to-gay-athletes-in-new-campaign/2014/05/08/5a15494a-d6eb-11e3-8f7d-7786660fff7c_story.html; *You Can Play*, youcanplayproject.org.

16. "Academic Freedom and Tenure Report: Nyack College," *Academe*, September–October, 1994, http://www.aaup.org/NR/rdonlyres/08117260-1AA8-46A4-B987-B74A31CFEE70/0/nyack.pdf; Scott Jaschik, "Shrinking Censure List," *Inside Higher Education*, June 12, 2006, https://www.insidehighered.com/news/2006/06/12/aaup.

17. Sunnivie Brydum, "Pepperdine University Introduces LGBT Scholarship," *Advocate*, February 14, 2013, http://www.advocate.com/society/education/2013/

02/14/pepperdine-introduces-lgbt-scholarship; Olivia Damavandi, "Professor's Defense of Prop 8 Puts Pepperdine in Crossfires," *The Malibu Times*, August 28, 2012, http://www.malibutimes.com/news/article_e2dd01d9-41c7-53eb-bfc3-7fe54cb1dace.html.

18. Jennie Choi, "Changes in Attitude," *Sojourners*, July, 2012, http://www.sojo.net/magazine/2012/07/changes-attitude; *Union Theological Seminary*, utsnyc.edu; also see Todd Clayton's many articles in *Huffington Post* including Todd Clayton, "Coming Out at a Christian College," *Huffington Post*, January 30, 2012, http://www.huffingtonpost.com/todd-clayton/coming-out-at-christian-universities_b_1242404.html; and Todd Clayton, "Why I Haven't Dropped Out of Seminary," *Huffington Post*, November 13, 2012, http://www.huffingtonpost.com/todd-clayton/why-i-havent-dropped-out-of-union-theological-seminary_b_2109218.html.

19. Libby A. Nelson, "Banned," *Inside Higher Education*, December 1, 2011, https://www.insidehighered.com/news/2011/12/01/controversy-shorter-over-faith-statements; Libby A. Nelson, "Shorter's Exodus, A Year Later," *Inside Higher Education*, November 14, 2012, https://www.insidehighered.com/news/2012/11/14/cultural-change-tears-georgia-baptist-college-apart.

20. Joyce, "LGBT Christian College Students"; "Former SWU staffer, son discuss transgender issues," *Thomaston Times*, July 31, 2013, http://thomastontimes.com/apps/pbcs.dll/article?AID=/20130731/news/307319967.

21. Steve Chawkins, "Gay Alumni Question Policy of Christian College in Montecito," *Los Angeles Times*, February 16, 2011, http://articles.latimes.com/2011/feb/16/local/la-me-gay-westmont-20110216; Artie Van Why, "Living as a Homosexual Christian," *The Horizon*, November 16, 2010, http://blogs.westmont.edu/horizon/2010/11/16/living-as-a-homosexual-christian/.

22. *Gay Straight Association* (see also *Pirate PRIDE*), *Associated Students of Whitworth University*, whitworthclubs.com; Julia K. Stronks, "Discrimination and Pluralism," *Journal of Higher Education*, July 22, 2014, https://www.insidehighered.com/views/2014/07/22/essay-push-christian-colleges-and-others-be-exempt-federal-civil-rights; Shawn Vestal, "Evangelicalism Shouldn't Close Hearts," *The Spokesman Review*, April 18, 2014, http://www.spokesman.com/stories/2014/apr/18/evangelicalism-shouldnt-close-hearts/; "Guest Post from Board Member Richard Cizik," *Evangelicals for Marriage Equality*, September 7, 2014, https://www.evangelicals4equality.com/guest-post-richard-cizik/; "Statement of Belief," *Evangelicals for Marriage Equality*, https://www.evangelicals4equality.com/the-statement/.

Chapter 24

1. Anthony Diekema in discussion with the author, October 9, 2013.

2. Barry Hankins in discussion with the author, November 26, 2013; "Colleges and Universities," *Southern Baptist Convention*, www.sbc.net/colleges.asp.

3. Barry Hankins in discussion with the author; Barry Hankins, *Uneasy in Babylon: Southern Baptist Conservatives and American Culture* (Tuscaloosa: University of

Alabama Press, 2002), 3–10, 200ff; Arthur Emery Farnsley II, *Southern Baptist Politics: Authority and Power in the Restructuring of an American Denomination* (University Park: Pennsylvania State University Press, 1994), 18–29; Gregory A. Willis, "Progressive Theology and Southern Baptist Controversies of the 1950s and 1960s," *Southern Baptist Journal of Theology*, July 2010, http://www.sbts. edu/resources/files/2010/07/sbjt_071_spr03_wills.pdf; "The Baptist Faith and Message," *Southern Baptist Convention*, 2000, www.sbc.net/bfm/bfm2000.asp.

4. David Treadwell, "Fundamentalist Baptists Suffer Major Defeat in Georgia," *Los Angeles Times*, November 12, 1987, http://articles.latimes.com/1987-11-12/news/mn-20469_1_georgia-baptists; Gerald Harris, "Georgia Baptists Vote to End Relationship with Mercer University after 172 Years," *The Christian Index*, November 24, 2005, http://www.christianindex.org/1759.article; R. Kirby Godsey, "To Whom Are Baptist Colleges and Universities Accountable?" in *The Future of Baptist Higher Education*, ed. Donald D. Schmeltekopf and Dianna M. Vitanza (Waco, Texas: Baylor University Press, 2006), 177–185.

5. Nelson, "Shorter's Exodus."

6. Gerald Harris, "Truett-McConnell Makes Historic Decision," *The Christian Index*, December 17, 2009, http://www.christianindex.org/6041.article.

7. Scott Jaschik, "Difficult Separation for Belmont," *Inside Higher Education*, May 11, 2006, https://m.insidehighered.com/news/2006/05/11/belmont; "Belmont Names First Non-Baptists to Board as Controversy Continues," *Baptist News Global*, December 28, 2006, http://baptistnews.com/archives/item/1700-belmont-names-first-non-baptists-to-board-as-controversy-continues; "Tennessee Baptists Drop Challenge to Belmont University," *Christian Century*, December 11, 2007, http://www.christiancentury.org/article/2007-12/tennessee-baptists-drop-challenge-belmont-university.

8. "Official Report of Findings: Baptist College and University Accountability Subcommittee, Strategic Relationships Committee, Tennessee Baptist Convention Executive Board," *Baptist Reflector*, October 3, 2012, http://www.tnbaptist. org/BRARticle.asp?ID=4483; "Carson-Newman University Vision, Mission, and Faith Statements," *Carson-Newman University*, http://www.cn.edu/about-c-n/vision-mission-faith-statements.

9. "David S. Dockery, 15th President of Union University," *Union University*, http://www.uu.edu/president/dockery/; Todd Ream in discussion with the author, August 12, 2014.

10. Justin Taylor, "An Interview with David Dockery on the Identity and Future of the Southern Baptist Convention," *The Gospel Coalition*, June 2, 2009, http://www.thegospelcoalition.org/blogs/justintaylor/2012/06/19/reclaiming-the-christian-intellectual-tradition-an-interview-with-david-dockery/.

11. Eileen W. Lindner, *Yearbook of American and Canadian Churches, 2012* (Nashville: Abingdon Press, 2012), 12, 378; Robert Benne, "The Trials of American Lutheranism: The Torments That the Two Major American Lutheran Churches Have Visited On Themselves," *First Things*, May, 2011, http://www.firstthings.com/article/2011/05/the-trials-of-american-lutheranism; Lawrence Rast, "Lutheran Church-Missouri Synod," and Robert

Kolb, "Lutheranism," in *The Encyclopedia of Protestantism*, ed. Hans J. Hillerbrand (New York: Routledge, 2004), vol. 3, 1124–1126, 1130–1136; "Academic Freedom and Tenure: Concordia Seminary," *AAUP Bulletin*, Spring 1975, http://www.aaup.org/report/academic-freedom-and-tenure-concordia-seminary; James Nuechterlein, "The Idol of Academic Freedom," *First Things*, December, 1993, http://www.firstthings.com/article/1993/12/001-the-idol-of-academic-freedom; "Seminary Head to Stay in Post Pending Rulings," *Los Angeles Times*, August 26, 1989, http://articles.latimes.com/1989-08-26/local/me-891_1_seminary-pending-ruling.

12. Ted Olson, "Valparaiso Repents for Holding Interfaith 9/11 Service," *Christianity Today*, September 1, 2003, http://www.christianitytoday.com/ct/2003/septemberweb-only/9-29-31.0.html; Tim Townsend, "Newtown Interfaith Prayer by Lutheran Missouri Synod Pastor Reopens Old Wounds," *Huffington Post*, March 26, 2013, http://www.huffingtonpost.com/2013/02/13/lcms-newtown-interfaith-prayers-reopens-old-wounds-for-missouri-synod_n_268 1340.html.

13. Terry L. Miethe, "Christian Church (Disciples of Christ)" and "Christian Churches/Churches of Christ (Independent)" in *Dictionary of Christianity*, ed. Daniel G. Reid, Robert D. Linder, Bruce L. Shelley, and Harry S. Stout (Downers Grove, Illinois: InterVarsity Press, 1990), 253–255; also see Michael W. Casey and Douglas A. Foster, eds., *The Stone-Campbell Movement: An International Religious Movement* (Knoxville: University of Tennessee Press, 2002).

14. "When Ideology and Indoctrination Are More Important Than Education: The Bizarre Firing of Anthony Le Donne," Zwingli Redivivus, https://zwingliusredivivus.wordpress.com/2012/04/30/when-ideology-and-indoctrination-are-more-important-than-education-the-bizarre-firing-of-anthony-le-donne/; Chris Keith, *Jesus Against the Scribal Elite* (Grand Rapids: Baker Publishing Group, 2014), xi–xii.

15. James F. McGrath, "In Support of Christopher Rollston," *Exploring Our Matrix* (blog), http://www.patheos.com/blogs/exploringourmatrix/2012/10/in-support-of-christopher-rollston.html; Christopher Rollston, "The Marginalization of Women: A Biblical Value We Don't Like to Talk About," *Huffington Post*, August 31, 2012, http://www.huffingtonpost.com/christopher-rollston/the-marginalization-of-women-biblical-value-we-dont-like-to-talk-about_b_183 3648.html; Robert Cargill, "Winners and Losers in the Emmanuel Christian Seminary Scandal," *KV8R* (blog), http://robertcargill.com/2012/12/31/winners-and-losers-in-the-emmanuel-christian-seminary-scandal/; Libby A. Nelson, "Tenure vs. Donors," *Inside Higher Education*, October 15, 2012, https://www.insidehighered.com/news/2012/10/15/seminary-threatens-discipline-professor-offending-prospective-students-donors.

16. Floyd Greenleaf, "Seventh Day Adventists" in *Encyclopedia of Protestantism*, ed. Hillerbrand, vol. 4, 1714–1719; Raymond F. Cottrell, "The 'Sanctuary Doctrine'—Asset or Liability? Part I," *Truth or Fables*, http://truthorfables.com/Sanctuary_Cottrell.htm; Dennis Priebe, "Evangelicals and Adventists Together?"

Dennis Priebe Seminars, http://www.dennispriebe.com/new/node/12; Gerard Damsteegt, "How Our Pioneers Discovered the Heavenly Sanctuary," *Adventist Affirm*, Fall, 1992, http://www.andrews.edu/~damsteeg/pion.html; Alita Byrd, "Prophetess of Health Reappears: Interview with Ronald Numbers," *The Spectrum*, August 10, 2008, http://spectrummagazine.org/article/interviews/2008/08/10/prophetess-health-reappears.

17. Cottrell, "The 'Sanctuary Doctrine,' Part I"; "A Statement on Theological and Academic Freedom and Accountability," *Seventh Day Adventist Church*, www.adventist.org/beliefs/statements/mainstat36.html; "28 Fundamental Beliefs," *Seventh Day Adventist Church*, http://www.adventistarchives.org/fundamental-beliefs-of-seventh-day-adventists.pdf.

Chapter 25

1. See Mark A. Noll, ed., *The Princeton Theology 1812–1921: Scripture, Science, and Theological Method from Archibald Alexander to Benjamin Breckenridge Warfield* (Grand Rapids: Baker Academic, 2001); George M. Marsden, *Fundamentalism and American Culture: The Shaping of Twentieth-Century Evangelicalism, 1870–1925* (New York: Oxford University Press, 1980); and Gary Dorrien, *The Remaking of Evangelical Theology* (Louisville: Westminster John Knox Press, 1998).

2. Dorrien, *Remaking Evangelical Theology*, 22–28, 95–101, 160–169; Molly Worthen, *Apostles of Reason: The Crisis of Authority in American Evangelicalism* (New York: Oxford University Press, 2014), 52.

3. Harold Lindsell, *The Battle for the Bible* (Grand Rapids: Zondervan, 1978), chapters 4–5; Dorrien, *Remaking Evangelical Theology*, 118–119. Also see George Marsden, *Reforming Fundamentalism: Fuller Seminary and the New Evangelicalism* (Grand Rapids: Eerdmans, 1995); "Chicago Statement on Biblical Inerrancy with Exposition," Fall, 1978, http://www.bible-researcher.com/chicago1.html.

4. Worthen, *Apostles of Reason*, 52–53; Dorrien, *Remaking Evangelical Theology*, 119–120, 161; Robert T. Sandin, *The Search for Excellence: The Christian College in an Age of Educational Competition* (Macon, Georgia: Mercer University Press, 1982), 22.

5. Roger E. Olson, "Why Inerrancy Doesn't Matter," *Patheos*, August 19, 2010, http://www.patheos.com/blogs/rogereolson/2010/08/why-inerrancy-doesnt-matter/; Christian Smith, *The Bible Made Impossible: Why Biblicism is not a Truly Evangelical Reading of Scripture* (Grand Rapids: Baker Brazos, 2011), viii, 14–19, 173.

6. George Marsden, "Moving up the Slippery Slope" in *Christian College Phenomenon*, ed. Joeckel and Chesnes, 330–333.

7. Dorrien, *Remaking Evangelical Theology*, 120; Justin Taylor, "J. I. Packer's Critique of Harold Lindsell on Inerrancy and Interpretation," *The Gospel Coalition*, August 7, 2014, http://www.thegospelcoalition.org/blogs/justintaylor/2014/08/

07/j-i-packers-critique-of-harold-lindsell-on-inerrancy-and-interpretation/; Jay Kesler in discussion with the author, Summer, 2013; Marcus Borg, "Does the Bible Matter?: Progressive Christians and Scripture," *Patheos*, June 18, 2014, http://www.patheos.com/blogs/marcusborg/2014/06/does-the-bible-matter-progressive-christians-and-scripture/.

8. Richard Rice, *The Openness of God: the Relationship of Divine Foreknowledge and Human Freewill* (Hagerstown, Maryland: Review and Herald Publishing Association, 1980); Clark Pinnock, Richard Rice, John Sanders, William Hasker, and David Basinger, *The Openness of God: A Biblical Challenge to the Traditional Understanding of God* (Downers Grove, Illinois: InterVarsity Press, 1994); Fisher Humphreys, "Open Theism and Theology Today," *The Center for Baptist Studies*, Mercer University, www.centerforbaptiststudies.org/conference/humphreys2005/opentheism.htm.

9. Dorrien, *Remaking Evangelical Theology*, 129–146; also see Barry Callen, *Clark H. Pinnock: Journey Toward Renewal* (Nappanee, Indiana: Evangel Publishing House, 2000); Doug Koop, "Clark Pinnock Dies at 73," *Christianity Today*, August 17, 2010, http://www.christianitytoday.com/ct/2010/augustweb-only/43-22.0.html.

10. Humphreys, "Open Theism and Theology Today"; Russell D. Moore, "The Openness of God Rejected by the E.T.S.," *Banner of Truth*, December 17, 2001, http://banneroftruth.org/us/resources/articles/2001/the-openness-of-god-rejected-by-the-ets/; Stan Guthrie, "Open or Closed Case?" *Christianity Today*, December 1, 2004, http://www.christianitytoday.com/ct/2004/decemberweb-only/12-20-32.0.html.

11. Humphreys, "Open Theism and Theology Today."

12. "Committee for Review of Dr. Gregory Boyd's View of God," *Bethel College and Seminary*, http://www.libraryoftheology.com/writings/opentheism/Committee_Review_Greg_Boyd%27s_Open_View.pdf.

13. "The 2000 Baptist Faith and Message," *Southern Baptist Convention*, http://www.sbc.net/bfm2000/bfm2000.asp.

14. J. Murray Murdoch with Thomas S. Mach, *Cedarville University: Inspiring Greatness for 125 Years* (Virginia Beach, Virginia: Donning Company Publishers, 2012), 13–21, 219–227; J. Murray Murdoch in discussion with the author, April 11, 2014; Mark Weinstein in discussion with the author, April 11, 2014; "Academic Freedom and Tenure: Cedarville University," *AAUP*, January-February, 2009, http://www.aaup.org/report/academic-freedom-and-tenure-cedarville-university.

15. Libby A. Nelson, "A Campus in Turmoil," *Inside Higher Education*, January 22, 2013, https://www.insidehighered.com/news/2013/01/22/several-controversies-converge-ohio-baptist-college; Melissa Steffan, "Administrators' Resignations Fuel Fears at Cedarville University," *Christianity Today*, January 23, 2013, http://www.christianitytoday.com/ct/2013/january-web-only/resignations-of-top-administrators-fuel-fears-at-cedarville.html; Mark Oppenheimer, "An Ohio Christian College Struggles to Further Define Itself," *The*

New York Times, February 15, 2013, http://www.nytimes.com/2013/02/16/us/a-christian-college-struggles-to-define-itself.html?_r=0; Sarah Pulliam Bailey, "Cedarville University 'Faculty Shakeup' Appears to Indicate Southern Baptist Future," *Huffington Post,* January 23, 2014, http://www.huffingtonpost.com/2013/12/22/cedarville-university-faculty_n_4469241.html.

16. Jenna Ross, "An Identity Crisis for a Christian College," *Star Tribune,* January 21, 2010, http://www.startribune.com/local/east/82213892.html; Randy W. Nelson in discussion with the author, Winter, 2010; also see William V. Trollinger, *God's Empire: William Bell Riley and Midwestern Fundamentalism* (Madison: University of Wisconsin Press, 1991).

17. Peter Enns, *Inspiration and Incarnation: Evangelicals and the Problem of the Old Testament* (Grand Rapids: Baker Academic, 2005); Sarah Pulliam, "Westminster Theological Suspension," *Christianity Today,* April 1, 2008, http://www.christianitytoday.com/ct/2008/aprilweb-only/114-24.0.html; Trevin Wax, "The Peter Enns Controversy," *The Gospel Coalition,* March 29, 2008, http://www.thegospelcoalition.org/blogs/trevinwax/2008/03/29/the-peter-enns-controversy/; Brandon G. Withrow, "How Westminster Theological Seminary Came to Define Fundamentalism For Me," *Huffington Post,* July 29, 2014, http://www.huffingtonpost.com/brandon-g-withrow/how-westminster-theologic_b_5624650.html; Peter Enns, "The Ten Commandments of How Jesus Wants You to Fire a Colleague," *Patheos,* May 2, 2012, http://www.patheos.com/blogs/peterenns/2012/05/the-ten-commandments-of-how-jesus-wants-you-to-fire-a-colleague/.

18. The recent ongoing trauma at Erskine College can best be followed in the series of *Inside Higher Education* articles, primarily by Scott Jaschik; note the following issues: March 4, 8, 11, 17, April 7, May 26, June 28, 2010; September 8, 2011, February 20, 2012, and June 2, 2014. Also see Ken Pierce, "No New Battles—the Inerrancy Controversy Strikes Again on the Erskine Campus," *The Aquila Report,* February 24, 2011, http://theaquilareport.com/no-new-battles-the-inerrancy-controversy-strikes-again-on-the-erskine-campus/; and Richard E. Burnett, "Has Erskine 'gone secular'?" *The Aquila Report,* March 18, 2010, http://theaquilareport.com/has-erskine-gone-secular/.

Chapter 26

1. Galatians 3:28.

2. M. Elizabeth Hall, "Finding Home in Academia: Gender Equality at CCCU Institutions" in *The Christian College Phenomenon,* ed. Joeckel and Chesnes, 240; Jennifer McKinney, "Holding on to the Tradition of Men: Christianity, Gender, and the Academy" in *The Christian College Phenomenon,* ed. Joeckel and Chesnes, 277; Jolyn E. Dahlvig, "A Narrative Study of Women Leading within the Council for Christian Colleges and Universities," *Christian Higher Education* 12, no. 1–2 (January-April 2013): 93–94; Karen Longman and Patricia S. Anderson, "Gender Trends in Senior-Level Leadership: A 12-Year Analysis of the CCCU U.S. Member Institutions," *Christian Higher*

Education 10, no. 5 (2011): 422–443; Joeckel and Chesnes, *Christian College Phenomenon*, 390; Sally K. Gallagher, "Symbolic Traditionalism and Pragmatic Egalitarianism: Contemporary Evangelicals, Families, and Gender," *Hartford Institute for Religion Research*, 1996, http://hirr.hartsem.edu/research/evangelicalroles_report.html; Christian Smith and Melinda Lundquist, "Male Headship and Gender Equality" in *Christian America?: What Evangelicals Really Want*, ed. Christian Smith (Berkeley, California: University of California Press, 2005), 190.

3. Bernard Weisberger, *They Gathered at the River: The Story of the Great Revivalists and Their Impact Upon Religion in America* (Chicago: Quadrangle Paperbacks, 1958), 110; Rebecca M. Groothuis, *Women Caught in the Conflict: The Culture War between Traditionalism and Feminism* (Eugene, Oregon: Wipf and Stock Publishers, 1997), 56–57; Janette Hassey, *No Time for Silence* (Grand Rapids: Zondervan, 1986), 31, 44–45.

4. Groothuis, *Women Caught in the Conflict*, 39, 55; Hassey, *No Time for Silence*, 20–22; Jessica L. Rousselow and Alan Winquist, *God's Ordinary People: No Ordinary Heritage* (Upland, Indiana: Taylor University Press, 1996), 102–106; Robert F. Lay, "Holiness and Higher Education at Taylor University: A Double Cure?" in *Called to Unite Knowledge and Vital Piety: Indiana's Wesleyan-Related Universities*, ed. Michael G. Cartwright and Merle D. Strege (Indianapolis: University of Indianapolis Press, 2012), 91–100.

5. Page Smith, *Daughters of the Promised Land: Women in American History* (Boston: Little Brown and Company, 1970), 191.

6. Hassey, *No Time for Silence*, 16.

7. Ibid., 23–25; Groothuis, *Women Caught in the Conflict*, 54, 57–58, 67.

8. Patricia Gundry, *Woman Be Free* (Grand Rapids: Zondervan, 1977); Stan Gundry, "From *Bobbed Hair, Bossy Wives, and Women Preachers* to *Woman Be Free*: My Story," *Christians for Biblical Equality*, http://www.cbeinternational.org/resources/bobbed-hair-bossy-wives-and-women-preachers-woman-be-free.

9. "The 2000 Baptist Faith and Message," *Southern Baptist Convention*, sbc.net; "Professor: Seminary Ousted Her Over Gender," *NBC News*, January 26, 2007, www.nbcnews.com/id/16828466; Sheri Klouda in discussion with the author, November 19, 2013.

10. "Academic Freedom and Tenure: Brigham Young University," *Academe* 83, no. 5 (September-October, 1997): 52–71; Edward Carter, "BYU Disagrees with Report on Academic Freedom," *Desert News*, September 15, 1997, http://www.deseretnews.com/article/583111/BYU-disagrees-with-report-on-academic-freedom.html?pg=all.

11. Mary Stewart Van Leeuwen, ed., *After Eden: Facing Challenges of Gender Reconciliation* (Grand Rapids: Eerdmans, 1993), xiv–xv, 200–209; Gayla R. Postma, "Women in Ministry: 15 Years Later," *Banner*, October 22, 2011, http://www.thebanner.org/features/2011/10/women-in-ministry-15-years-later.

12. Mary Todd, *Authority Vested: A Story of Identity and Change in the Lutheran Church—Missouri Synod* (Grand Rapids: Eerdmans, 1999); "Belief and Practice:

The Ordination of Women to the Pastoral Office," *The Lutheran Church— Missouri Synod*, http://www.lcms.org/belief-and-practice.

13. *Christian Feminism Today*, 2014, eewc.com; "About Virginia Ramey Mollenkott," *Virginia Ramey Mollenkott webpage*, 2010, www.virginiamollenkott.com/about. html; *Christians for Biblical Equality*, 2014, www.cbeinternational.org; Mimi Haddad in discussion with the author, Summer, 2014; *The Council on Biblical Manhood and Womanhood*, 2014, cbmw.org; Ruth A. Tucker, *Women in the Maze: Questions and Answers in Biblical Equality* (Downers Grove, Illinois: InterVarsity Press, 1992), 7; Jennifer McKinley, letter to author, September 4, 2014.

14. "Bob Jones v. United States" *FindLaw*, 1983, http://caselaw.lp.findlaw.com/ scripts/getcase.pl?court=US&vol=461&invol=574; "Bob Jones Univ. Apologizes for Racist Policies," *NBC News*, November 21, 2008, http://www.nbcnews.com/ id/27845030/ns/us_news-life/t/bob-jones-univ-apologizes-racist-policies/#.U_ fldrywKAY.

15. Sarah Eekhoff Zylstra, "Values Clash," *Christianity Today* 52, no. 1 (January 2008): 20; "Calvin Says Prof Must Choose between School, Church," *Banner*, January 18, 2011, http://www.thebanner.org/news/2011/01/calvin-says-prof-must-choose-between-school-church; Elizabeth Redden, "When Identity Trumps Diversity," *Inside Higher Education*, January 4, 2008, https://www. insidehighered.com/news/2008/01/04/calvin.

16. Elizabeth Redden, "Christian Colleges Grow More Diverse," *Inside Higher Education*, August 15, 2008, https://www.insidehighered.com/news/2008/08/15/ christian.

17. Marcy Jane Knopf-Newman, *The Politics of Teaching Palestine to America* (New York: Palgrave Macmillan, 2011), xxi; Stephen Sizer, *Christian Zionism: Road Map to Armageddon?* (Leister, England: InterVarsity Press, 2004), 7–8, 119, 171, 248; Jonathan Brenneman in discussion with the author, April 24, 2014; Omar Barghouti, "On Academic Freedom and the BDS Movement," *The Nation*, December 14, 2013, http://www.thenation.com/ article/177596/academic-freedom-and-bds-movement; David Kuttab, "Israel Irked by Pro-Palestinian Evangelicals Christian Conference," *Almonitor*, March 10, 2014, http://www.al-monitor.com/pulse/originals/2014/03/christ-conference-evangelical-christian-palestine.html#; Timothy C. Morgan, "Evangelicals Defend 'Christ at the Checkpoint' From Israeli Critics," *Christianity Today*, March 12, 2014, http://www.christianitytoday.com/gleanings/2014/march/ israel-blasts-evangelical-bethlehem-christ-at-checkpoint.html; Sarah Pulliam Bailey, "Is Support for Israel Waning Among Evangelicals?" *Washington Post*, April 8, 2014, http://www.washingtonpost.com/national/religion/is-support-for-israel-waning-among-evangelicals/2014/04/09/a75ead8c-bff7-11e3-9ee7-02c1e1 0a03f0_story.html.

18. David Brog, "The End of Evangelical Support for Israel?" *The Middle East Quarterly*, Spring, 2014, http://www.meforum.org/3769/israel-evangelical-support;

also see Gary Burge, *Whose Lord? Whose Promise? What Christians Are Not Being Told About Israel and the Palestinians* (Cleveland: Pilgrim Press, 2013).

19. Joeckel and Chesnes, *The Christian College Phenomenon*, 353, 379.

Chapter 27

1. "Christian Legal Society Chapter v. Martinez," *Legal Information Institute*, 2010, http://www.law.cornell.edu/supct/html/08-1371.ZS.html; Ted Olsen and Trevor Persaud, "Christian Legal Society Loses in Supreme Court Case," *Christianity Today*, June 28, 2010, http://www.christianitytoday.com/ct/2010/juneweb-only/christian-legal-society-loses-supreme-court.html; Leigh Jones, "Supreme Court Declines Religious Liberty Case," *World on Campus*, March 19, 2012, http://www.worldoncampus.com/2012/03/supreme_court_declines_religious_liberty_case; Kimberly Winston, "Christian Group Sanctioned at Two Dozen College Campuses," *Religion News Service*, September 8, 2014, http://www.washingtonpost.com/national/religion/christian-group-sanctioned-at-two-dozen-college-campuses/2014/09/08/ecda6b1c-379d-11e4-a023-1d61f7f31a05_story.html.

2. Gordon Govier, "Campus Faith: A Civil Rights Issue," *InterVarsity*, February 28, 2013, http://www.intervarsity.org/news/campus-faith-%E2%80%93-civil-rights-issue; Doug Erickson, "Madison-Based InterVarsity Christian Fellowship Reaches Almost 600 College Campuses," *Wisconsin State Journal*, October 7, 2012, http://host.madison.com/news/local/madison-based-intervarsity-christian-fellowship-reaches-almost-college-campuses/article_dbc5c90a-1087-11e2-a119-001a4bcf887a.html.

3. Adelle M. Banks, "Supreme Court Decision on Religion Upends Campus Religious Groups," *Christianity Today*, May 10, 2012, http://www.christianitytoday.com/ct/2012/mayweb-only/supreme-court-decision-upends-religious-groups.html; Robert Shibley, "The Fallout from *Christian Legal Society*: Vanderbilt Launches an Offensive Against Religious Freedom," *The National Review*, February 6, 2012, http://www.nationalreview.com/articles/290199/fallout-ichristian-legal-societyi-robert-shibley; Gordon Govier, "U.S. Commission on Civil Rights Briefing Report," *InterVarsity*, March 26, 2013, http://www.intervarsity.org/news/us-commission-civil-rights-briefing-report.

4. Armando Montaño, "Christian Group Accused of Discrimination Loses Student Group Status, Splits in Two," *Scarlet and Black*, September 3, 2011, http://www.thesandb.com/news/christian-group-accused-of-discrimination-loses-student-group-status-splits-into-two.html.

5. See John D. Inazu, "Religious Freedom vs. LGBT Rights? It's More Complicated," *Christianity Today*, July 16, 2014, http://www.christianitytoday.com/ct/2014/july-web-only/religious-freedom-vs-lgbt-rights-its-more-complicated.html.

6. "On Freedom of Expression and Campus Speech Codes," *AAUP*, November 1994, aaup.org.

7. "Hate Speech on Campus," *American Civil Liberties Union*, December 31, 1994, https://www.aclu.org/free-speech/hate-speech-campus.

8. Greg Lukianoff, "Feigning Free Speech on Campus," *New York Times*, October 24, 2012, http://www.nytimes.com/2012/10/25/opinion/feigning-free-speech-on-campus.html; Alan Kors and Harvey Silverglate, *The Shadow University: The Betrayal of Liberty on America's Campuses* (New York: The Free Press, 1998), 153.

9. "Spotlight on Speech Codes 2014: The State of Free Speech on Our Nation's Campuses," *FIRE*, http://www.thefire.org/spotlight/reports/.

10. "Doe v. University of Michigan," *United States District Court for the Eastern District of Michigan*, September 22, 1989, http://www.bc.edu/bc_org/avp/cas/comm/free_speech/doe.html; David L. Hudson, "Hate Speech and Campus Speech Codes," *First Amendment Center*, September 13, 2002, firstamemdmentcenter.org.

11. Greg Lukianoff, "Federal Government Mandates Unconstitutional Speech Codes at Colleges and Universities Nationwide," *FIRE*, May 17, 2013, http://www.thefire.org/federal-government-mandates-unconstitutional-speech-codes-at-colleges-and-universities-nationwide-3/.

Chapter 28

1. Rudolph, *American College and University*, 42, 247–252.

2. Ringenberg, *Christian College*, 202–203.

3. Max Fisher, "Here's a Map of the Countries that Provide Universal Health Care (America's Still Not on It)," *The Atlantic*, June 28, 2012, http://www.theatlantic.com/international/archive/2012/06/heres-a-map-of-the-countries-that-provide-universal-health-care-americas-still-not-on-it/259153/; Mike Patton, "Obamacare: Seven Major Provisions and How They Affect You," *Forbes Magazine*, November 27, 2013, http://www.forbes.com/sites/mikepatton/2013/11/27/how-obamacare-will-change-the-american-health-system/; "Becket Fund's HHS Mandate Challenge," *The Becket Fund for Religious Liberty*, http://www.becketfund.org/hhs/.

4. Joe Carter, "Supreme Court to Decide Obamacare Contraceptive-Abortifacient Mandate," *Acton Institute Power Blog*, November 26, 2013, http://blog.acton.org/archives/tag/emergency-contraception; Ariane DeVogue, "Hobby Lobby Wins Contraceptive Ruling in Supreme Court," January 30, 2014, http://abcnews.go.com/politics/hobby-lobby-wins-contraceptive-ruling-supreme-court/story?id=24364311; Jess Bravin, "Administration Points to Hobby Lobby Ruling in Wheaton College Case," *Wall Street Journal*, July 2, 2014, http://www.wsj.com/articles/administration-points-to-hobby-lobby-ruling-in-wheaton-college-case-1404331673.

5. Joshua Wood, "What's Next? How Hobby Lobby Affects Wheaton College and Nearly 100 Other Cases," *Christianity Today*, July 2, 2004, http://www.christianitytoday.com/gleanings/2014/july/supreme-court-ruled-hobby-lobby-

wheaton-college-healthcare.html?paging=off; David Lawder, "Supreme Court Awards Wheaton College Temporary Exemption on Obamacare Birth Control," *Chicago Tribune*, July 3, 2014, http://articles.chicagotribune.com/2014-07-03/news/chi-supreme-court-wheaton-college-birth-control-20140703_1_wheaton-college-contraception-coverage-supreme-court; Vinnie Rotondaro, "HHS Tries New Modifications to Contraceptive Coverage Rules," *National Catholic Reporter*, September 8, 2014, http://ncronline.org/news/politics/hhs-tries-new-modifications-contraceptive-coverage-rules.

6. "Text of the Employment Non-Discrimination Act of 2013," s. 815, Section 6a, https://www.govtrack.us/congress/bills/113/s815/text; Leigh Ann Caldwell, "Senate Passes LGBT Anti-Discrimination Bill," *CNN Politics*, November 8, 2013, http://www.cnn.com/2013/11/07/politics/senate-lgbt-workplace-discrimination/.

7. Colin Daileda, "A Short History of Obama's Evolving Stance on Gay Marriage," *Mashable*, April 16, 2014, http://mashable.com/2014/04/16/history-obama-gay-marriage/; Brett Snider, "Obama Bars Anti-Gay Discrimination by Federal Contractors," *Findlaw* (blog), July 21, 2004, http://blogs.findlaw.com/free_enterprise/2014/07/obama-bars-anti-gay-discrimination-by-federal-contractors.html.

8. Melissa Rogers, "Letter to the President on Executive Order," *National Association of Evangelicals*, June 25, 2014, http://www.nae.net/resources/news/1140-letter-to-the-president-on-lgbt-nondiscrimination.

9. Melissa Rogers, "Religious Exemption Letter to President Obama," *Scribed*, July 1, 2014, http://www.scribd.com/doc/232327567/Religious-Exemption-Letter-to-President-Obama#scribd; Evan Allen, "Gordon College Leader Joins Request for Exemption to Hiring Rule," *Boston Globe*, July 4, 2014, http://www.bostonglobe.com/metro/2014/07/03/gordon-college-president-signs-letter-asking-for-religious-exemption-from-order-banning-anti-gay-discrimination/79cgrbFOuUg7lxH2rKXOgO/story.html; Billy Hallowell, "Is a Christian College's Ban on 'Homosexual Practice' Landing It in Major Hot Water?" *The Blaze*, October 6, 2014, http://www.theblaze.com/stories/2014/10/06/is-this-christian-college-going-to-lose-its-accreditation-over-its-ban-on-homosexual-practice/; Shapri LoMaglio in discussion with the author, October 14, 2014.

10. Motoko Rich, " 'No Child' Law Whittled Down by White House," *The New York Times*, July 6, 2012, http://www.nytimes.com/2012/07/06/education/no-child-left-behind-whittled-down-under-obama.html?pagewanted=all&_r=0; Joy Resmovits, "George W. Bush's Education Law, No Child Left Behind, Abandoned by Texas," *Huffington Post Politics*, September 30, 2013, http://www.huffingtonpost.com/2013/09/30/bush-education-law-texas_n_4018971.html; Joy Resmovits, "States Escaping No Child Left Behind Can Get More Time on Teacher Evaluations," *Huffington Post*, August 21, 2014, http://www.huffingtonpost.com/2014/08/21/obama-teacher-evaluations_n_5697616.html.

11. "AAUP Statement on Spellings Commission Report," *AAUP*, http://www.aaup.org/our-work/government-relations/GRarchive/Spellings/Statement; Robert

Zemsky, "The Unwitting Damage Done by the Spellings Commission," *Chronicle of Higher Education*, September 18, 2011, http://m.chronicle.com/article/The-Unwitting-Damage-Done-by/129051/.

12. "College Cost Reduction Act of 2007," *Open Congress*, http://www.opencongress.org/wiki/College_Cost_Reduction_Act_of_2007#External_articles; "ACE Analysis of Higher Education Act Reauthorization," *American Council on Education*, August, 2008, http://www.acenet.edu/news-room/Documents/ACE-Analysis-of-2008-Higher-Education-Act-Reauthorization.pdf; Judith S. Eaton, "Accreditation and the Federal Future of Higher Education," *AAUP*, September–October, 2010, http://www.aaup.org/article/accreditation-and-federal-future-higher-education#.VL_wmUfF98E; Judith S. Eaton, "Federalizing Accreditation: A Quandary for Higher Education," *Inside Accreditation*, February 16, 2011, http://www.chea.org/ia/IA_2011.01.18.html.

13. Naomi Schaefer Riley, "New Rules Worry Christian Colleges," *Christianity Today*, November 1, 2010, http://www.christianitytoday.com/ct/2010/november web-only/53.11.0.html; Morgan Feddes, "Christian Colleges Hope House Bill Will Repeal New Rules," *Christianity Today*, June 30, 2011, http://www.christianitytoday.com/ct/2011/juneweb-only/christiancollegesrules.html.

14. "Senate Unveils Bill to Reauthorize the Higher Education Act," *ACE*, June 25, 2014, http://www.acenet.edu/news-room/Pages/Senate-Unveils-Bill-to-Reauthorize-the-Higher-Education-Act-House-Plan-Would-Take-Incremental-Approach.aspx; "Recommendations from 39 Higher Education Associations for the Reauthorization of the Higher Education Act," *ACE*, August 2, 2013, http://www.acenet.edu/news-room/Documents/HEA-Reauthorization-Recs-080213.pdf.

15. Jason Mandryk, *Operation World* (Colorado Springs, Colorado: Biblica Publishing, 2010), 194–195; "Christian Higher Education Canada Showcases and Celebrates Collaboration," *Christian Higher Education Canada*, http://www.checanada.ca/news/christian-higher-education-canada-showcases-and-celebrates-collaboration/.

16. "Universities That Impose a Faith or Ideological Test," *Canada Association of University Teachers*, http://www.caut.ca/issues-and-campaigns/academic-freedom/faith-ideological-test.

17. "History of Trinity Western University," *Trinity Western University*, http://twu.ca/undergraduate/about/twu-history.html; Harro Van Brummelen and Kevin Sawatsky, "Colliding Rights in Schools: Trinity Western University v. the British Columbia College of Teachers," *Journal of Educational Thought* 36, no. 3 (December 2001): 207–28; Samuel Smith, "Canadian Law Society Rejects Christian School Over Biblical Homosexuality Stance," *CP Politics*, November 4, 2014, http://m.christianpost.com/news/canadian-law-society-rejects-christian-school-over-biblical-homosexuality-stance-129115/.

18. "Accreditation of Canadian and U.S. Universities," *Universities in the USA and Canada*, http://www.universitiesintheusa.com/university-accreditation.html; Charles Honey, "Confession Clash," *Christianity Today*, May 25, 2010, http://www.christianitytoday.com/ct/2010/april/5.15.html.

19. Inazu, "Religious Freedom v. LGBT Rights"; Shapri LoMaglio in discussion with the author, October 14, 2014; Paul Lowell Haines in discussion with the author, October 14, 2014.

20. Adam Liptak, "Supreme Court Ruling Makes Same-Sex Marriage a Right Nationwide," June 26, 2015; Scott Jaschik, "Will Supreme Court Decision on Same-Sex Marriage Challenge or Change Christian Colleges?" *Inside Higher Education*, June 29, 2015.

Chapter 29

1. George M. Marsden, "The Ambiguities of Academic Freedom," *Church History* 62, no. 2 (June, 1993): 221–236.

2. Nicholas Wolterstorff, "Academic Freedom in Religiously Based Colleges and Universities" in *Educating for Shalom: Essays on Christian Higher Education*, ed. Nicholas Wolterstorff, Clarence W. Joldersma, and Gloria Goris Stronks (Grand Rapids: Eerdmans, 2004), 252–253.

3. Diekema, *Academic Freedom and Christian Scholarship*, 135–138, 141.

4. "Academic Freedom and Tenure: Bethune-Cookman University," *AAUP Bulletin*, 2011, http://www.aaup.org/NR/rdonlyres/4EE9AC2E-A49B-4BA0-A449-F130A9BBC5A9/0/bethunecookmanreport.pdf.

5. "Academic Freedom and Tenure: Cedarville University," *AAUP*, January–February, 2009, http://www.aaup.org/report/academic-freedom-and-tenure-cedarville-university.

6. "Academic Freedom and Tenure: Charleston Southern University," *Academe*, January–February, 2001, 63–77.

7. In January 2005, the institution changed its name from Cumberland College to the University of the Cumberlands. The incidents described herein took place before the name change while the AAUP published its report afterward. In this report I will use the current name except for this one occasion involving a direct quotation.

8. "Academic Freedom and Tenure: University of the Cumberlands," *Academe*, March–April, 2005, 99–113.

9. "Academic Freedom and Tenure: Greenville College," *Academe*, May–June, 2006, 71–90.

10. "Academic Freedom and Tenure: Grove City College," *AAUP*, Spring, 1963, 15–24; David M. Lascell, "Grove City v. Bell: What the Case Means Today," *The Grove City Journal of Law and Public Policy* 1, no. 1, 1–6.

11. "Academic Freedom and Tenure: Loma Linda University," *AAUP*, May–June, 1992, http://www.aaup.org/report/academic-freedom-and-tenure-charleston-southern-university.

12. Bethany Broida, "Top Louisiana College Leaders Resign as Trustees Consider Conservative Policies," *Chronicle of Higher Education*, April 16, 2004; "Louisiana College Placed on Probation," *Christian Century*, January 11,

2005, http://www.christiancentury.org/article/2005-01/louisiana-college-placed-probation; Andy Guess, "Explaining an Exodus," *Inside Higher Education*, April 25, 2007, https://www.insidehighered.com/news/2007/04/25/louisiana; Kevin Kiley, "Fundamental Disagreements," *Insider Higher Education*, May 12, 2011, https://www.insidehighered.com/news/2011/05/12/professor_s_lawsuit_against_louisiana_college_suggest_suppression_of_dissent_by_administrators; Joe Aguillard, "President's Pen," *Louisiana College*, January 17, 2013, http://www.lacollege.edu/reformedtheology; Thomas Kidd, "Calvinist Controversy at Louisiana College," *First Things*, February 26, 2013, http://www.firstthings.com/blogs/firstthoughts/2013/02/calvinist-controversy-at-louisiana-college; Bob Allen, "Louisiana College to Seek New President," *The Baptist Standard*, April 21, 2014, https://www.baptiststandard.com/news/baptist/16356-louisiana-college-to-seek-new-president; Ruth Moon, "Three Controversial Christian Colleges Learn Their Accreditation Fate," *Christianity Today*, June 24, 2014, http://www.christianitytoday.com/gleanings/2014/june/accreditation-decisions-handed-down-controversial-southern-.html?paging=off.

13. Beth McMurtrie, "Do Professors Lose Academic Freedom by Signing Statements of Faith?" *Chronicle of Higher Education*, May 24, 2002.

14. Thomas Bartlett, "5 Departures on Patrick Henry Faculty Pose Question: Are Christianity and Liberal Arts Contradictory Missions?" *Chronicle of Higher Education*, May 12, 2006; Sheryl Henderson Blunt, "Shakeup at Patrick Henry College," *Christianity Today*, May 15, 2006, http://www.christianitytoday.com/ct/2006/mayweb-only/120–12.0.html; Michael Alison Chandler, "5 Professors Quit Religious School," *The Washington Post*, May 19, 2006, http://www.washingtonpost.com/wp-dyn/content/article/2006/05/18/AR2006051801995.html; Naomi Schaeffer Riley, "The Press and Patrick Henry College," naomiriley.com, http://naomiriley.com/wp-content/uploads/2010/07/press.pdf.

Bibliography

"28 Fundamental Beliefs." *Seventh Day Adventist Church.* http://www.adventistarchives.org/fundamental-beliefs-of-seventh-day-adventists.pdf.

"A Statement on Theological and Academic Freedom and Accountability." *Seventh Day Adventist Church.* www.adventist.org/beliefs/statements/mainstat36.html.

"A Survey of LGBT Americans: Attitudes, Experiences, and Values in Changing Times." *Pew Research Center.* June 13, 2013. http://www.pewsocialtrends.org/2013/06/13/a-survey-of-lgbt-americans/.

"A. Lawrence Lowell on Academic Freedom in Wartime, 1917." In *A Documentary History,* edited by Hofstadter and Smith, II, 878–882.

"AAUP 1915 Declaration of Principles on Academic Freedom and Tenure." *American Association of University Professors.* 1915. http://www.aaup.org/NR/rdonlyres/A6520A9D-0A9A-47B3-B550-C006B5B224E7/0/1915Declaration.pdf.

"AAUP 1940 State of Principles on Academic Freedom and Tenure." *American Association of University Professors.* 1940. http://www.aaup.org/report/1940-statement-principles-academic-freedom-and-tenure.

"AAUP Statement on Spellings Commission Report." *American Association of University Professors.* http://www.aaup.org/our-work/government-relations/GRarchive/Spellings/Statement.

"AAUP Takes UIUC to Task for Apparent Summary Dismissal." *American Association of University Professors.* August 29, 2014. http://www.aaup.org/news/aaup-takes-uiuc-task-apparent-summary-dismissal.

"AAUP: The Limitations Clause in the 1940 Statement of Principles on Academic Freedom and Tenure: Some Operating Guidelines." *American Association of University Professors.* 1940. http://www.aaup.org/report/1940-statement-principles-academic-freedom-and-tenure.

"About Virginia Ramey Mollenkott." *Virginia Ramey Mollenkott Webpage.* 2010. www.virginiamollenkott.com/about.html.

"Academic Bill of Rights." *Students for Academic Freedom.* www.studentsforacademicfreedom.org/documents/1925/abor.html.

"Academic Freedom and Educational Responsibility." *Association of American Colleges and Universities.* January 6, 2006. www.aacu.org/about/statements/academic_freedom.cfm.

"Academic Freedom and Tenure Report: Nyack College." *Academe*. September–October 1994. http://www.aaup.org/NR/rdonlyres/08117260-1AA8-46A4-B987-B74A31CFEE70/0/nyack.pdf.

"Academic Freedom and Tenure: Bethune-Cookman University." *AAUP Bulletin*. 2011. http://www.aaup.org/NR/rdonlyres/4EE9AC2E-A49B-4BA0-A449-F130A9BBC5A9/0/bethunecookmanreport.pdf.

"Academic Freedom and Tenure: Brigham Young University." *Academe* 83, no. 5 (September–October 1997): 52–71.

"Academic Freedom and Tenure: Cedarville University." *American Association of University Professors*. January–February 2009. http://www.aaup.org/report/academic-freedom-and-tenure-cedarville-university.

"Academic Freedom and Tenure: Charleston Southern University." *Academe*. January–February 2001, 63–77.

"Academic Freedom and Tenure: Concordia Seminary." *American Association of University Professors Bulletin*. Spring 1975. http://www.aaup.org/report/academic-freedom-and-tenure-concordia-seminary.

"Academic Freedom and Tenure: Greenville College." *Academe*. May–June 2006, 71–90.

"Academic Freedom and Tenure: Loma Linda University." *American Association of University Professors*. May–June 1992. http://www.aaup.org/report/academic-freedom-and-tenure-charleston-southern-university.

"Academic Freedom and Tenure: University of the Cumberlands." *Academe*. March–April 2005, 99–113.

"Accreditation of Canadian and U.S. Universities." *Universities in the USA and Canada*. http://www.universitiesintheusa.com/university-accreditation.html.

"ACE Analysis of Higher Education Act Reauthorization." *American Council on Education*. August 2008. http://www.acenet.edu/news-room/Documents/ACE-Analysis-of-2008-Higher-Education-Act-Reauthorization.pdf.

"An Explanation of Gordon College's Policy on Homosexuality." *Gordon College*. http://www.gordon.edu/download/galleries/HomosexualityPolicy.pdf.

"Becket Fund's HHS Mandate Challenge." *The Becket Fund for Religious Liberty*. http://www.becketfund.org/hhs/.

"Belief and Practice: The Ordination of Women to the Pastoral Office." *The Lutheran Church—Missouri Synod*. http://www.lcms.org/belief-and-practice.

"Belmont Names First Non-Baptists to Board as Controversy Continues." *Baptist News Global*. December 28, 2006. http://baptistnews.com/archives/item/1700-belmont-names-first-non-baptists-to-board-as-controversy-continues.

"Bob Jones Univ. Apologizes for Racist Policies." *NBC News*. November 21, 2008. http://www.nbcnews.com/id/27845030/ns/us_news-life/t/bob-jones-univ-apologizes-racist-policies/#.U_fldrywKAY.

"Bob Jones v. United States." *FindLaw*. 1983. http://caselaw.lp.findlaw.com/scripts/getcase.pl?court=US&vol=461&invol=574.

"Building Bridges of Understanding: Tony and Peggy Campolo on Homosexuality." *The Gay Christian Network*. https://www.gaychristian.net/campolos.php.

"Calvin Says Prof Must Choose between School, Church." *Banner*. January 18, 2011. http://www.thebanner.org/news/2011/01/calvin-says-prof-must-choose-between-school-church.

"Carson-Newman University Vision, Mission, and Faith Statements." *Carson-Newman University*. http://www.cn.edu/about-c-n/vision-mission-faith-statements.

"Changing Attitudes on Gay Marriage." *The Pew Forum on Religion and Public Life*. June 2013. http://www.pewforum.org/2014/09/24/graphics-slideshow-changing-attitudes-on-gay-marriage/.

"Christian College in Omaha Expels Lesbian." *USA Today*. June 14, 2013. http://www.usatoday.com/story/news/nation/2013/06/14/grace-university-omaha-christian-college-lesbian/2425467/.

"Christian Higher Education Canada Showcases and Celebrates Collaboration." *Christian Higher Education Canada*. http://www.checanada.ca/news/christian-higher-education-canada-showcases-and-celebrates-collaboration/.

"Christian Legal Society Chapter v. Martinez." *Legal Information Institute*. 2010. http://www.law.cornell.edu/supct/html/08-1371.ZS.html.

"College Cost Reduction Act of 2007." *Open Congress*. http://www.opencongress.org/wiki/College_Cost_Reduction_Act_of_2007#External_articles.

"Colleges and Universities." *Southern Baptist Convention*. www.sbc.net/colleges.asp.

"Committee for Review of Dr. Gregory Boyd's View of God." *Bethel College and Seminary*. http://www.libraryoftheology.com/writings/opentheism/Committee_Review_Greg_Boyd%27s_Open_View.pdf.

"Creation Colleges." *Answers in Genesis*. 2011. https://answersingenesis.org/colleges/.

"Cushing Praises Graham Crusade." *The New York Times*. October 8, 1964. http://www.nytimes.com/1964/10/08/cushing-praises-graham-crusade.html.

"David S. Dockery, 15th President of Union University." *Union University*. August 12, 2014. http://www.uu.edu/president/dockery/.

"Doe v. University of Michigan." *United States District Court for the Eastern District of Michigan*. September 22, 1989. http://www.bc.edu/bc_org/avp/cas/comm/free_speech/doe.html.

"Essay About Being a Gay Faculty Member at a Christian College." *Inside Higher Education*. March 18, 2013. https://www.insidehighered.com/advice/2013/03/18/essay-about-being-gay-faculty-member-christian-college.

"Evangelicals and Catholics Together: The Christian Mission in the Third Millennium." *First Things*. May 1994. http://www.firstthings.com/article/1994/05/evangelicals--catholics-together-the-christian-mission-in-the-third-millennium-2.

"Federal Student Aid Portfolio Summary." *National Student Loan Data System*.

"*FIRE's* Letter to President Gordon." *FIRE*. October 23, 2001. https://www.thefire.org/fires-letter-to-president-gordon/.

"Former SWU Staffer, Son Discuss Transgender Issues." *Thomaston Times*. July 31, 2013. http://thomastontimes.com/apps/pbcs.dll/article?AID=/20130731/news/307319967.

"Grutter v. Bollinger." *Cornell University Law School*. 2003. http://www.law.cornell.edu/supct/html/02-241.ZS.html.

"Guest Post from Board Member Richard Cizik." *Evangelicals for Marriage Equality*. September 7, 2014. https://www.evangelicals4equality.com/guest-post-richard-cizik/.

"Hate Speech on Campus." *American Civil Liberties Union*. December 31, 1994. https://www.aclu.org/free-speech/hate-speech-campus.

"HHS Mandate Information Central." *The Becket Fund for Religious Liberty*. December 16, 2014. http://www.becketfund.org/hhsinformationcentral/.

"History of MCC" and "Who We Are." *Metropolitan Community Churches*. mcc-church.org.

"History of Trinity Western University." *Trinity Western University*. http://twu.ca/undergraduate/about/twu-history.html.

"Homosexuality." Position Statements. *Christian Reformed Church*. 2002. http://www.crcna.org/welcome/beliefs/position-statements/homosexuality.

"Hope College Position Statement on Human Sexuality." *Hope College*. Jaunary 28, 2011. www.hope.edu/news/2011/01/28/hope-college-position-statement-on-human-sexuality.html.

"Joint Statement on Rights and Freedoms of Students." *American Association for University Professors*. June 1967. www.aaup.org/report/joint-statement-rights-and-freedoms-students.

"Legal Guide for the Private School Press." *Student Press Law Center*. 2002. www.splc.org/knowyourrights/legalresearch.asp?id=52.

"Louisiana College Placed on Probation." *Christian Century*. January 11, 2005. http://www.christiancentury.org/article/2005-01/louisiana-college-placed-probation.

"Major Recommendations of Scranton Report on Campus Unrest." *Academe* 4, no. 4 (October 1970).

"Official Report of Findings: Baptist College and University Accountability Subcommittee, Strategic Relationships Committee, Tennessee Baptist Convention Executive Board." *Baptist Reflector*. October 3, 2012. http://www.tnbaptist.org/BRARticle.asp?ID=4483.

"On Freedom of Expression and Campus Speech Codes." *American Association for University Professors*. November 1994, aaup.org.

"Open and Affirming in the UCC." *United Church of Christ*. http://www.ucc.org/lgbt/ona.html.

"Our Founders." *Soulforce*. http://soulforce.com/about/co-founders/.

"Partial Win for California Baptist in Transgender Case." *Baptist Press*. July 15, 2014. http://www.bpnews.net/42974/partial-win-for-cal-baptist-in-transgender-case.

Daniel Webster, "Peroration, The Dartmouth College Case." *Dartmouth College*. 2014. https://www.dartmouth.edu/~dwebster/speeches/dartmouth-peroration.html.

"President Obama Takes Executive Action to Reform PAYE." *Educated Risk*. June 8, 2014. http://educatedrisk.org/news/president-obama-takes-executive-action-reform-paye-and-publicly-backs-senator-warrens-student.

"Professor: Seminary Ousted Her Over Gender." *NBC News*. January 26, 2007. www.nbcnews.com/id/16828466.

"Recommendations from 39 Higher Education Associations for the Reauthorization of the Higher Education Act." *ACE*. August 2, 2013. http://www.acenet.edu/news-room/Documents/HEA-Reauthorization-Recs-080213.pdf.

"Refuge: A Community for Wheaton's Same-Sex Attracted Students; Guiding Document." http://www.wheaton.edu/~/media/Files/Student-Life/Student-Activities/Student-Government/Refuge%20Guiding%20Document.pdf

"Religious Groups' Official Positions on Same-Sex Marriage." *The Pew Forum*. December 7, 2012. http://www.pewforum.org/2012/12/07/religious-groups-official-positions-on-same-sex-marriage/.

"Same-Sex Marriage State-by-State." *The Pew Forum*. November 20, 2014. http://www.pewforum.org/2014/11/20/same-sex-marriage-state-by-state/.

"School District of Abington Township v. Schempp." *Legal Information Institute*. http://www.law.cornell.edu/supremecourt/text/374/203.

"Seeking Truth: Three Views on the Calvin Approach to Academic Freedom." *The Calvin Spark*. Winter 2009. http://www.calvin.edu/publications/spark/2009/winter/truth.htm.

"Seminary Head to Stay in Post Pending Rulings." *Los Angeles Times*. August 26, 1989. http://articles.latimes.com/1989-08-26/local/me-891_1_seminary-pending-ruling.

"Senate Unveils Bill to Reauthorize the Higher Education Act." *ACE*. June 25, 2014. http://www.acenet.edu/news-room/Pages/Senate-Unveils-Bill-to-Reauthorize-the-Higher-Education-Act-House-Plan-Would-Take-Incremental-Approach.aspx.

"Spotlight on Speech Codes 2014: The State of Free Speech on Our Nation's Campuses." *FIRE*. http://www.thefire.org/spotlight/reports/.

"Statement of Belief." *Evangelicals for Marriage Equality*. https://www.evangelicals4equality.com/the-statement/.

"Statement on Academic Rights and Responsibilities." *American Council on Education*. http://www.chea.org/pdf/ACE__Statement_on_Academic_Rights_and_Responsibilities_(6_23_2005).pdf.

"Statement on Creation: The Bible's Worldview." *Seventh-Day Adventist Church*. www.adventist.org/beliefs/statements/bible-worldview.

"States." *Freedom to Marry*. www.freedomtomarry.org/states.

"Supreme Court Strikes Down Defense of Marriage Act, Paves Way for Gay Marriage to Resume in California." *NBC Politics*. June 26, 2013. www.nbcnews.com/politics.

"Tennessee Baptists Drop Challenge to Belmont University." *Christian Century*. December 11, 2007. http://www.christiancentury.org/article/2007-12/tennessee-baptists-drop-challenge-belmont-university.

"Text of the Employment Non-Discrimination Act of 2013." s. 815, Section 6a. https://www.govtrack.us/congress/bills/113/s815/text.

"The 2000 Baptist Faith and Message." *Southern Baptist Convention*. http://www.sbc.net/bfm2000/bfm2000.asp.

"The 2000 Baptist Faith and Message." *Southern Baptist Convention*. http://www.sbc.net.

"The Baptist Faith and Message." *Southern Baptist Convention*. 2000. www.sbc.net/bfm/bfm2000.asp.

"The Westminster Shorter Catechism." *The Orthodox Presbyterian Church*. http://www.opc.org/sc.html.

"Top Conservative Colleges." *Young Americans for Freedom*. www.yaf./org/topconservativecolleges.aspx.

"Transgender Professor Runs Afoul of 'Ideals' at Christian University." *Chronicle of Higher Education*. February 6, 2007. http://chronicle.com/article/Transgender-Professor-Runs/38176.

"Transgender Professor, Christian College Settle Sex-Discrimination Complaint." *Advocate*. March 14, 2007. http://www.advocate.com/news/2007/03/15/transgender-professor-christian-college-settle-sex-discrimination-complaint.

"Universities That Impose a Faith or Ideological Test." *Canada Association of University Teachers*. http://www.caut.ca/issues-and-campaigns/academic-freedom/faith-ideological-test.

"Ward Churchill vs. University of Colorado Boulder." *American Association for University Professors*. http://www.aaup.org/brief/ward-churchill-v-university-colorado-boulder-293-p3d16-61-app-2010-affd-285-p3d-986-col-2012.

"Wave III of the Baylor Religion Survey Examines How Religion Affects Individuals' Outlook and Well-Being in Tumultuous Times." *Baylor University*. September 2011. http://www.baylor.edu/mediacommunications/news.php?action=story&story=100503.

"What You Need to Know About MOOCs." *Chronicle of Higher Education*. June 20, 2014. http://chronicle.com/article/What-You-Need-to-Know-About/133475/.

"When Ideology and Indoctrination Are More Important Than Education: The Bizarre Firing of Anthony Le Donne." Zwingli Redivivus. https://zwingliusredivivus.wordpress.com/2012/04/30/when-ideology-and-indoctrination-are-more-important-than-education-the-bizarre-firing-of-anthony-le-donne/.

"Who Are We?" *The American Scientific Affiliation: A Network of Christians in the Sciences*. http://network.asa3.org/?page=ASAAbout#Who%20we%20are.

"William Smith (1727–1803)." *Penn University Records and Archives*. www.archives.upenn.edu/people/1700s/smith_wm.html.

"Wisconsin Lawmakers Want University Instructor Fired for Sept. 11 Comments." *Fox News*. July 22, 2006. http://www.foxnews.com/story/2006/07/22/wisconsin-lawmakers-want-university-instructor-fired-for-sept-11-comments/.

"Woodrow Wilson on a University's Use." In *Wilson Papers*, edited by Arthur S. Link, vol. 14, 283–284. Princeton: Princeton University Press, 1966–1994.

Adrian, William. "Perils of the Life of the Mind: Lessons from the German University." *Christian Higher Education* 2, no. 2 (2003): 169–185.

Aguillard, Joe. "President's Pen." *Louisiana College*. January 17, 2013. http://www.lacollege.edu/reformedtheology.

Allen, Bob. "Baylor Keeps Homosexuality Ban." *Baptist News Global*. November 1, 2013. http://baptistnews.com/ministry/organizations/item/8981-baylor-keeps-homosexuality-ban/.

Allen, Evan. "Gordon College Leader Joins Request for Exemption to Hiring Rule." *Boston Globe.* July 4, 2014. http://www.bostonglobe.com/metro/2014/07/03/gordon-college-president-signs-letter-asking-for-religious-exemption-from-order-banning-anti-gay-discrimination/79cgrbFOuUg7lxH2rKXOgO/story.html.

Allison J. Althoff, "Hope for the Gay Undergrad." *Christianity Today.* December 7, 2012. http://www.christianitytoday.com/ct/2013/january-february/hope-for-gay-undergrad.html.

American Academy of Religion. "The Religious Study Major and Liberal Education." *Liberal Education* 95, no. 2 (2009): 48–55.

Andringa, Robert C. "Keeping the Faith: Leadership Challenges Unique to Religiously Affiliated Colleges and Universities." In *Turnaround: Leading Stressed Colleges and Universities to Excellence*, edited by James Martin, James E. Samels and Associates, 168–171. Baltimore: Johns Hopkins University Press, 2009.

Augustine, *Confessions*, book 1, chapter 1, in *Great Books of the Western World*, ed. Robert Maynard Hutchins (Chicago: Encyclopedia Britannica, 1952), vol. 18, 1.

—— In *12,000 Religious Quotations*, edited by Frank S. Mead. Grand Rapids: Baker Book House, 2000.

Banks, Adelle M. "Supreme Court Decision on Religion Upends Campus Religious Groups." *Christianity Today.* May 10, 2012. http://www.christianitytoday.com/ct/2012/mayweb-only/supreme-court-decision-upends-religious-groups.html.

Barclay, William. *And Jesus Said*. Philadelphia: The Westminster Press, 1970.

Barghouti, Omar. "On Academic Freedom and the BDS Movement." *The Nation.* December 14, 2013. http://www.thenation.com/article/177596/academic-freedom-and-bds-movement.

Barrett, David B. and Todd M. Johnson. *World Christian Trends, A.D. 30–A.D. 2200.* Pasadena, CA: William Carey Library, 2001.

Barrett, William. *Irrational Man: A Study in Existential Philosophy*. Garden City, NY: Doubleday and Company, 1962.

Bartlett, Thomas. "5 Departures on Patrick Henry Faculty Pose Question: Are Christianity and Liberal Arts Contradictory Missions?" *Chronicle of Higher Education.* May 12, 2006.

Baum, Sandy and Kathleen Payea. "Trends in For-Profit Postsecondary Education." *College Board Advocacy & Policy Center.* 2011. http://trends.collegeboard.org/sites/default/files/trends-2011-for-profit-postsecondary-ed-outcomes-brief.pdf.

Baum, Sandy, Kathie Little, and Kathleen Payea. "Trends in Community College Education." *College Board Advocacy & Policy Center.* 2011. https://trends.collegeboard.org/sites/default/files/trends-2011-community-colleges-ed-enrollment-debt-brief.pdf.

Bebbington, D. W. "Christian Higher Education in Europe: A Historical Analysis." *Christian Higher Education* 10, no. 1 (2011): 10–24.

Bell, Christian. "Calvin College Statement about Homosexuality Draws Fire." *Banner.* January 18, 2011. http://www.thebanner.org/news/2011/01/calvin-college-statement-about-homosexuality-draws-fire.

Benne, Robert. "The Trials of American Lutheranism: The Torments That the Two Major American Lutheran Churches Have Visited On Themselves." *First Things*. May 2011. http://www.firstthings.com/article/2011/05/the-trials-of-american-lutheranism.

Berthold, Richard. "My Five Minutes of Infamy." *FIRE*. November 25, 2002. https://www.thefire.org/my-five-minutes-of-infamy/.

BioLogos. biologos.org.

Bixler, William G. "How the Early Church Viewed Martyrs." *Christian History* IX, no. 3 (1990): 28–30.

Blinder, Alan. "Bryan College Is Torn: Can Darwin and Eden Coexist?" *New York Times*. May 20, 2014. http://www.nytimes.com/2014/05/21/education/christian-college-faces-uproar-after-bolstering-its-view-on-evolution.html.

Borg, Marcus. "Does the Bible Matter?: Progressive Christians and Scripture." *Patheos*. June 18, 2014. http://www.patheos.com/blogs/marcusborg/2014/06/does-the-bible-matter-progressive-christians-and-scripture/.

Brady, Jeff. "College Course Lumps Homosexuality, Rape, and Murder." *US & World*. September 11, 2012. http://www.scpr.org/news/2012/09/10/34219/college-course-lumps-homosexuality-rape-murder/.

Bravin, Jess. "Administration Points to Hobby Lobby Ruling in Wheaton College Case." *Wall Street Journal*. July 2, 2014. http://www.wsj.com/articles/adminis tration-points-to-hobby-lobby-ruling-in-wheaton-college-case-1404331673.

Brog, David. "The End of Evangelical Support for Israel?" *The Middle East Quarterly*. Spring 2014. http://www.meforum.org/3769/israel-evangelical-support.

Broida, Bethany. "Top Louisiana College Leaders Resign as Trustees Consider Conservative Policies." *Chronicle of Higher Education*. April 16, 2004.

Brownson, James V. *Bible, Gender, Sexuality: Reframing the Church's Debate on Same-Sex Relationships*. Grand Rapids: Eerdmans, 2013.

Brydum, Sunnivie. "Pepperdine University Introduces LGBT Scholarship." *Advocate*. February 14, 2013. http://www.advocate.com/society/education/2013/02/14/pepperdine-introduces-lgbt-scholarship.

Buechner, Frederick. *Telling the Truth: The Gospel as Tragedy, Comedy, and Fairy Tale*. New York: HarperCollins, 1977.

Bull, Brian, Fritz Guy, and Er vin Taylor, editors. *Understanding Genesis: Contemporary Adventist Perspectives*. Riverside, CA: Adventist Today Foundation, 2006.

Byrd, Alita. "Prophetess of Health Reappears: Interview with Ronald Numbers," *The Spectrum*, August 10, 2008. http://spectrummagazine.org/article/interviews/2008/08/10/prophetess-health-reappears.

Caldwell, Leigh Ann. "Senate Passes LGBT Anti-Discrimination Bill." *CNN Politics*. November 8, 2013. http://www.cnn.com/2013/11/07/politics/senate-lgbt-workplace-discrimination/.

Campolo, Peggy. "In God's House There Are Many Closets." In *Homosexuality and Christian Faith*, edited by Walter Wink, 100–104. Minneapolis: Fortune Press, 1999.

Carey, Kevin. "Into the Future with MOOCs." *Chronicle of Higher Education.* September 3, 2012. http://chronicle.com/article/Into-the-Future-With-MOOCs/134080/.

Cargill, Robert. "Winners and Losers in the Emmanuel Christian Seminary Scandal." *KV8R* (blog). http://robertcargill.com/2012/12/31/winners-and-losers-in-the-emmanuel-christian-seminary-scandal/.

Carlson, Scott. "Administrative Hiring Drove 28% Boom in Higher-Ed Work Force, Report Says." *Chronicle of Higher Education.* February 5, 2014. http://chronicle.com/article/Administrator-Hiring-Drove-28-/144519/.

Carnes, Tony. "Intelligent Design: Design Interference." *Christianity Today.* December 4, 2000. http://www.christianitytoday.com/ct/2000/december4/18.20.html?paging=off.

Carter, Edward. "BYU Disagrees with Report on Academic Freedom." *Desert News.* September 15, 1997. http://www.deseretnews.com/article/583111/BYU-disagrees-with-report-on-academic-freedom.html?pg=all.

Carter, Joe. "Supreme Court to Decide Obamacare Contraceptive-Abortifacient Mandate." *Acton Institute Power Blog.* November 26, 2013. http://blog.acton.org/archives/tag/emergency-contraception.

Chakrabarti, Rajashri, Maricar Mabutas, and Basit Zafar. "Soaring Tuitions: Are Public Funding Cuts to Blame?" *Liberty Street Economics.* September 19, 2012. http://libertystreeteconomics.newyorkfed.org/2012/09/soaring-tuitions-are-public-funding-cuts-to-blame.html#.U_eVa7xdW9Y.

Champagne Butterfield, Rosaria. "My Train Wreck Conversion." *Christianity Today.* February 7, 2013. http://www.christianitytoday.com/ct/2013/january-february/my-train-wreck-conversion.html.

—— *The Secret Thoughts of an Unlikely Convert: An English Professor's Journey into the Christian Faith.* Pittsburg: Crown and Covenant Publications, 2012.

Chandler, Michael Alison. "5 Professors Quit Religious School." *The Washington Post.* May 19, 2006. http://www.washingtonpost.com/wp-dyn/content/article/2006/05/18/AR2006051801995.html.

Charles Honey, "Seven Passages: Play about Gay Christians Moves to World Stage," *Grand Rapids Press*, July 28, 2008. http://blog.mlive.com/grpress/2008/07/seven_passages_play_about_gay.html

Chawkins, Steve. "Gay Alumni Question Policy of Christian College in Montecito." *Los Angeles Times.* February 16, 2011. http://articles.latimes.com/2011/feb/16/local/la-me-gay-westmont-20110216.

Chiari, Mike. "Brittney Griner Criticizes Baylor's Anti-Gay Policies in Memoir 'In My Skin.'" *Bleacher Report.* April 15, 2014. http://bleacherreport.com/articles/2030399-brittney-griner-criticizes-baylors-anti-gay-policies-in-memoir-in-my-skin.

Chignell, Andrew. "Whither Wheaton." *Soma: A Review of Religion and Culture.* January 13, 2010. http://www.somareview.com/whitherwheaton.cfm.

Choi, Jeannie. "Changes in Attitude." *Sojourners.* July 2012. http://sojo.net/magazine/2012/07/changes-attitude.

Choros: Sexuality and Gender Discussion at Taylor University. taylorchoros.wordpress. com.

Christ Evangelical Bible Institute. cebiaz.com.

Christian Feminism Today. 2014. eewc.com.

Christians for Biblical Equality. 2014. www.cbeinternational.org.

Christopher Yuan. christopheryuan.com.

Churchill, Ward. "The Myth of Academic Freedom: Experiencing the Application of Liberal Principle in a Neoconservative Era." In *Academic Freedom in the Post-9/11 Era,* edited by Edward J. Carvalho and David B. Downing, 65–113. New York: Palgrave Macmillan, 2010.

Clark, Thomas. *Indiana University.* Bloomington: Indiana University Press, 1970.

Cloud, Robert C. "Sweezy v. New Hampshire." *Law and Higher Education.* January 30, 2011. http://lawhighereducation.org/124-sweezy-v-new-hampshire. html.

Cohen, Jodi S. "Steven Salaita Sues U. of I. Over Lost Job." *Chicago Tribune.* January 29, 2015. http://www.chicagotribune.com/news/local/breaking/ct-steven-salaita-university-of-illinois-lawsuit-0130-20150129-story.html.

Colling, Richard. "Evolution and Faith: Communicating Compatibility in Christian Higher Education." *The Biologos Forum: Science and Faith in Dialogue.* February 20, 2010. http://biologos.org/blog/evolution-and-faith.

Collins, Francis S. *The Language of God.* New York: Free Press, 2006.

Conrad Grebel University College, uwaterloo.ca/grebel/node/1.

Consortium of Christian Study Centers, studycentersonline.org.

Cottrell, Raymond F. "The 'Sanctuary Doctrine'—Asset or Liability?, Part I." *Truth or Fables.* http://truthorfables.com/Sanctuary_Cottrell.htm.

Courtenay, William J. "Inquiry and Inquisition: Academic Freedom in Medieval Universities." *Church History* 58, no. 2 (June 1989): 169–173, 180–181.

Dahlvig, Jolyn E. "A Narrative Study of Women Leading Within the Council for Christian Colleges and Universities." *Christian Higher Education* 12, no. 1–2 (January–April 2013): 93–94.

Daileda, Colin. "A Short History of Obama's Evolving Stance on Gay Marriage." *Mashable.* April 16, 2014. http://mashable.com/2014/04/16/history-obama-gay-marriage/.

Damavandi, Olivia. "Professor's Defense of Prop 8 Puts Pepperdine in Crossfires." *The Malibu Times.* August 28, 2012. http://www.malibutimes.com/news/article_e2dd01d9-41c7-53eb-bfc3-7fe54cb1dace.html.

Damsteegt, Gerard. "How Our Pioneers Discovered the Heavenly Sanctuary." *Adventist Affirm.* Fall 1992. http://www.andrews.edu/~damsteeg/pion.html.

David C. Humphrey, "Colonial Colleges and English Dissenting Academics: A Study in Transatlantic Culture," *History of Education Quarterly* 12, no. 2 (Summer 1972): 184–197.

Davis, Edward B. "Science Falsely So Called: Fundamentalism and Science." In *The Blackwell Companion to Science and Christianity,* edited by J.B. Stump and Alan G. Padgett, 49–50. Oxford, England: John Wiley and Sons, 2012.

Davis, James Calvin. "Resisting Politics as Usual: Civility as Christian Witness." *Colombia Theological Seminary*. 2012. http://www.atthispoint.net/articles/resisting-politics-as-usual-civility-as-christian-witness/225/

Denneed, Jeff and Tom Dretler. "The Financially Sustainable University." *Bain and Company Insights*. July 6, 2012. http://www.bain.com/Images/BAIN_BRIEF_ The_ financially_sustainable_university.pdf.

Desrochers, Donna M. and Rita Kirshstein. "Labor Intensive or Labor Expensive?: Changing Staffing and Compensation Patterns in Higher Education." *American Institutes for Research*. February 2014. http://www.air.org/sites/default/files/ downloads/report/DeltaCostAIR-Labor-Expensive-Higher-Education-Staffing-Brief-Feb2014.pdf.

DeVogue, Ariane. "Hobby Lobby Wins Contraceptive Ruling in Supreme Court." January 30, 2014. http://abcnews.go.com/politics/hobby-lobby-wins-contraceptive-ruling-supreme-court/story?id=24364311.

Diekema, Anthony. *Academic Freedom and Christian Scholarship*. Grand Rapids: Eerdmans, 2000.

Downs, Donald. "Perspective: The Barrett Case and Academic Freedom at Wisconsin." *University of Wisconsin-Madison News*. July 13, 2006. http://www. news.wisc.edu/12709.

Earnest, Josh. "President Obama Supports Same-Sex Marriage." *The White House Blog*. May 10, 2012. http://www.whitehouse.gov/blog/2012/05/10/obama-supports-same-sex-marriage.

Eaton, Judith S. "Accreditation and the Federal Future of Higher Education." *American Association for University Professors*. September–October 2010. http:// www.aaup.org/article/accreditation-and-federal-future-higher-education#.VL_ wmUfF98E.

——— "Federalizing Accreditation: A Quandary for Higher Education." *Inside Accreditation*. February 16, 2011. http://www.chea.org/ia/IA_2011.01.18. html.

Edwards, David L. *Christian England*. Grand Rapids: Eerdmans, 1984.

Eekhoff Zylstra, Sarah. "Breaking the Bubble." *Christianity Today* 53, no. 12 (December 9, 2009): 17–18.

——— "Values Clash." *Christianity Today* 52, no. 1 (January 2008): 20.

Ellul, Jacques. *The Ethics of Freedom*. Grand Rapids: Eerdmans, 1976.

Emerson, Ralph Waldo, James H. Woods, and James Elliot Cabot. *A Memoir of Ralph Waldo Emerson*. Charleston, South Carolina: Nabu Press, 2012.

Emrich, Richard S. *Earth Might Be Fair*. New York: Harper and Brothers, 1945.

Enns, Peter. "The Ten Commandments of How Jesus Wants You to Fire a Colleague." *Patheos*. May 2, 2012. http://www.patheos.com/blogs/peterenns/2012/05/the-ten-commandments-of-how-jesus-wants-you-to-fire-a-colleague/.

——— *Inspiration and Incarnation: Evangelicals and the Problem of the Old Testament*. Grand Rapids: Baker Academic, 2005.

Erickson, Doug. "Madison-Based InterVarsity Christian Fellowship Reaches Almost 600 College Campuses." *Wisconsin State Journal*. October 7, 2012. http://host.

madison.com/news/local/madison-based-intervarsity-christian-fellowship-reaches-almost-college-campuses/article_dbc5c90a-1087-11e2-a119-001a4bcf887a.html.

Euben, Donna R. "Who Grades Students?" Address to the University of Michigan, *American Association for University Professors* chapter, November 13, 2001. www.umuch.edu/~aaupum/gradesrb.html.

Fairyington, Stephanie. "Virgin Marys." *Questia*. February 2007. https://www.questia.com/magazine/1P3-1207607921/virgin-marys; *The Gay Christian Network*, gaychristian.net.

Falon, Daniel. "German Influences on American Education." In *The German-American Encounter: Conflict and Cooperation Between Two Cultures, 1800–2000*, edited by Frank Trommler and Elliott Shore, 83. New York: Berghahn Publishers, 2001.

Farnsley II, Arthur Emery. *Southern Baptist Politics: Authority and Power in the Restructuring of an American Denomination*. University Park: Pennsylvania State University Press, 1994.

Farrell, Elizabeth F. "Baylor U. Removes a Web Page Associated with Intelligent Design from Its Site." *Chronicle of Higher Education*. September 4, 2007. http://chronicle.com/article/Baylor-U-Removes-a-Web-Pag/121996/.

Feddes, Morgan. "Christian Colleges Hope House Bill Will Repeal New Rules." *Christianity Today*. June 30, 2011. http://www.christianitytoday.com/ct/2011/juneweb-only/christiancollegesrules.html.

Finch, Jeremiah S. "Preceptorial Method." *Princeton University*. http://etcweb.princeton.edu/CampusWWW/Companion/preceptorial_method.html.

Finder, Alan. "A Surge of Growth for a New Kind of Online Course." *New York Times*. September 25, 2013. http://www.nytimes.com/2013/09/26/technology/personaltech/a-surge-in-growth-for-a-new-kind-of-online-course.html?pagewanted=all.

Fisher, Max. "Here's a Map of the Countries That Provide Universal Health Care (America's Still Not on It)." *The Atlantic*. June 28, 2012. http://www.theatlantic.com/international/archive/2012/06/heres-a-map-of-the-countries-that-provide-universal-health-care-americas-still-not-on-it/259153/.

Flexner, Abraham. *Universities: American, English, German*. New York: Oxford University Press, 1968.

Fogleman, Lori Scott. "Baylor Hosts National Conference on Academic Freedom." *Baylor Media Communications*. April 6, 2000. http://www.baylor.edu/mediacommunications/news.php?action=story&story=3697.

Fowler, James. *Stages of Faith: The Psychology of Human Development and the Quest for Meaning*. San Francisco: Harper and Row, 1981.

Francis, Philip and Mark Longhurst. "How LGBT Students Are Changing Christian Colleges." *The Atlantic*. July 23, 2014. http://www.theatlantic.com/education/archive/2014/07/gordon-college-the-new-frontier-of-gay-rights/374861/.

Franklin, Benjamin. "Proposals Relating to the Education of Youth in Pennsylvania." *Penn University Records and Archives*. 1749. http://www.archives.upenn.edu/primdocs/1749proposals.html.

Freedman, Samuel G. "'Griner Effect' May Change the Game at Baylor." *The New York Times*. May 18, 2013. http://www.nytimes.com/2013/05/18/us/griner-baylor-lesbian-college-sports.html?_r=0.

Frend, William H. C. "Persecution in the Early Church." *Christian History* IX, no. 3 (1990): 5–11.

—— "When Christianity Triumphed." *Christian History* IX, no. 3 (1990): 11.

Gallagher, Sally K. "Symbolic Traditionalism and Pragmatic Egalitarianism: Contemporary Evangelicals, Families, and Gender." *Hartford Institute for Religion Research*. 1996. http://hirr.hartsem.edu/research/evangelicalroles_report.html.

Galli, Mark. "The Confidence of the Evangelical." *Christianity Today*. November 17, 2011. http://www.christianitytoday.com/ct/2011/novemberweb-only/confidenceevangelical.html.

Garcia, Kenneth. *Academic Freedom and the Telos of the Catholic University*. New York: Palgrave Macmillan, 2012.

Gaustad, Edward S. "Thomas Jefferson." In *The Encyclopedia of Protestantism*, edited by Hans J. Hillerbrand, volume 2, 975–977. New York: Routledge, 2004.

—— *Sworn on the Altar of God: A Religious Biography of Thomas Jefferson*. Grand Rapids: Eerdmans, 1996.

Gay Straight Association (see also *Pirate PRIDE*), Associated Students of Whitworth University. whitworthclubs.com.

Gibson, David. "Notre Dame Signals Welcome to Gay Athletes in New Campaign." *The Washington Post*. May 8, 2014. http://www.washingtonpost.com/national/religion/notre-dame-signals-welcome-to-gay-athletes-in-new-campaign/2014/05/08/5a15494a-d6eb-11e3-8f7d-7786660fff7c_story.html.

Godlen, Daniel. "A Test of Faith." *Wall Street Journal*. January 7, 2006. http://online.wsj.com/news/articles/SB113659805227040466.

Godsey, R. Kirby. "To Whom Are Baptist Colleges and Universities Accountable?" In *The Future of Baptist Higher Education*, edited by Donald D. Schmeltekopf and Dianna M. Vitanza, 177–185. Waco: Baylor University Press, 2006.

Gooch, John O. "Cowards Among the Christians." *Christian History* IX, no. 3 (1990): 34–36.

Govier, Gordon. "Campus Faith: A Civil Rights Issue." *InterVarsity*. February 28, 2013. http://www.intervarsity.org/news/campus-faith-%E2%80%93-civil-rights-issue.

—— "U.S. Commission on Civil Rights Briefing Report." *InterVarsity*. March 26, 2013. http://www.intervarsity.org/news/us-commission-civil-rights-briefing-report.

Graham, Billy. *Just As I Am: The Autobiography of Billy Graham*. New York: HarperCollins, 1997.

Graham, Ruth. "Can the Evangelical Church Embrace Gay Couples?: A New Wave of Thinkers Says Yes—and Is Looking to Scripture for Support." *Boston Globe*. January 12, 2014. http://www.bostonglobe.com/ideas/2014/01/12/can-evangelical-church-embrace-gay-couples/5Tqq4n7xNZcsBtrAeszJBM/story.html.

Greenburg, Jan Crawford. "White House Pares Picks for Top Court." *Chicago Tribune*. June 22, 2005. http://articles.chicagotribune.com/2005-06-22/news/

0506220167_1_official-and-other-sources-chief-justice-william-rehnquist-gen-alberto-gonzales.

Greenhouse, Linda. "Chief Justice Rehnquist Dies at 80." *The New York Times.* September 4, 2005. http://www.nytimes.com/2005/09/04/politics/chief-justice-rehnquist-dies-at-80.html.

Greer, Lee. "Terminated LSU Biologist Lee Greer Issues Press Release." *Spectrum Magazine.* May 9, 2012. http://spectrummagazine.org/blog/2012/05/09/terminated-lsu-biologist-lee-greer-issues-press-release.

Griffiths, Lawn. "Peggy Campolo." *Scottsdale Tribune.* October 4, 2003. http://www.nolongersilent.org/TribuneArticleOct2003.html.

Grimsrud, Ted. "Is Academic Freedom a Mennonite Value?" *Anabaptist-Mennonite Scholars Network Newsletter.* May 2001.

Groothuis, Rebecca M. *Women Caught in the Conflict: The Culture War Between Traditionalism and Feminism.* Eugene, OR: Wipf and Stock Publishers, 1997.

Gross, Neil and Solon Simmons. "How Religious Are America's College and University Professors?" *Social Science Research Council.* February 6, 2007. religion.ssrc.org/reforum/Gross_Simmons.pdf.

Guess, Andy. "Explaining an Exodus." *Inside Higher Education.* April 25, 2007. https://www.insidehighered.com/news/2007/04/25/louisiana.

Gundry, Patricia. *Woman Be Free.* Grand Rapids: Zondervan, 1977.

Gundry, Stan. "From *Bobbed Hair, Bossy Wives, and Women Preachers* to *Woman Be Free*: My Story." *Christians for Biblical Equality.* http://www.cbeinternational.org/resources/bobbed-hair-bossy-wives-and-women-preachers-woman-be-free.

Haarsma, Deborah. "The Controversy at Bryan College." *The BioLogos Forum.* March 6, 2014. http://biologos.org/blog/the-controversy-at-bryan-college.

Habecker, Eugene B. "Academic Freedom in the Context of Mission." *Christian Scholars Review* 21, no. 2 (1991): 175–181.

———, John E. Brown III, and William Hasker. "The First Amendment, Private Religious Colleges, and the State." *Christian Scholar's Review* 10, no. 4 (1981): 279–295.

Hallowell, Billy. "Is a Christian College's Ban on 'Homosexual Practice' Landing It in Major Hot Water?" *The Blaze.* October 6, 2014. http://www.theblaze.com/stories/2014/10/06/is-this-christian-college-going-to-lose-its-accreditation-over-its-ban-on-homosexual-practice/.

Hamilton, Michael S. "The Fundamentalist Harvard: Wheaton College and the Continuing Vitality of American Evangelicalism, 1919–1965." Doctoral dissertation, Notre Dame University, 1994.

Hankins, Barry. *Uneasy in Babylon: Southern Baptist Conservatives and American Culture.* Tuscaloosa: University of Alabama Press, 2002.

Hardon, John A. "History of Religious Life: St. Dominic and the Apostolate of Teaching the Word of God." *The Real Presence Association.* http://www.therealpresence.org/archives/Religious_Life/Religious_Life_020.htm.

Hardy, Lee. "The Value of Limitations." *Academe* 92, no. 1 (2006): 23–27.

Harger, Jim. "Calvin College Faculty Senate Asks College to Drop Order on Teaching about Homosexuality and Same-Sex Marriage." *MLive Media Group.*

October 1, 2009. http://www.mlive.com/news/grand-rapids/index.ssf/2009/10/calvin_college_faculty_senate.html.

Harlow, Daniel C. "After Adam: Reading Genesis in the Age of Evolutionary Science." *Perspectives on Science and Christian Faith* 62, no. 3 (September 2010): 179–195.

Harris, Gerald. "Georgia Baptists Vote to End Relationship with Mercer University after 172 Years." *The Christian Index.* November 24, 2005. http://www.christianindex.org/1759.article.

—— "Truett-McConnell Makes Historic Decision." *The Christian Index.* December 17, 2009. http://www.christianindex.org/6041.article.

Hart, James Morgan. "The German University and the American College During the 1860s." In *American Higher Education: A Documentary History*, edited by Richard Hofstadter and Wilson Smith, 2 vols, II, 569, 573, 577 (Chicago: University of Chicago Press, 1961).

Hassey, Janette. *No Time for Silence.* Grand Rapids: Zondervan, 1986.

Hatch, Nathan. *The Democratization of American Christianity.* New Haven: Yale University Press, 1989.

Haven, An Unofficial SPU Club. spuhaven.blogspot.com.

Healy, Robert M. *Jefferson on Religion in Public Education.* New Haven: Yale University Press, 1962.

Heeren, Fred. "The Lynching of Bill Dembski: Scientists Say the Jury Is Out—So Let the Hanging Begin." *The American Spectator.* November 15, 2000. http://www.discovery.org/a/532.

Henderson Blunt, Sheryl. "Shakeup at Patrick Henry College." *Christianity Today.* May 15, 2006. http://www.christianitytoday.com/ct/2006/mayweb-only/120-12.0.html.

Hill, Wesley. *Washed and Waiting: Reflections on Christian Faithfulness and Homosexuality.* Grand Rapids: Zondervan, 2010.

Hofstadter, Richard and Wilson Smith, editors. *American Higher Education: A Documentary History.* Chicago: University of Chicago Press, 1961.

—— *The Development of Academic Freedom in the Age of the College.* New York: Colombia University Press, 1961.

Holmes, Arthur F. *The Idea of a Christian College.* Grand Rapids: Eerdmans, 1975.

Honey, Charles. "Confession Clash." *Christianity Today.* May 25, 2010. http://www.christianitytoday.com/ct/2010/april/5.15.html.

—— "The Litmus Test: Trustee ban on 'Advocacy of Homosexual Practice and Same-Sex Marriage' Stirs Up Calvin Faculty." *Christianity Today.* October 28, 2009. http://www.christianitytoday.com/ct/2009/november/9.17.html.

Howard, Thomas A. "A Timely and Important Conversation." *Stillpoint.* 2008. http://www.gordon.edu/article.cfm?iArticleID=563&iReferrerPageID=2114&iPrevCatID=94&bLive=1.

Hoye, William J. "The Religious Roots of Academic Freedom." *Theological Studies* 58, no. 3 (1997): 409–428.

Hudson, David L. "Hate Speech and Campus Speech Codes." *First Amendment Center.* September 13, 2002. firstamemdmentcenter.org.

Humphreys, Fisher. "Open Theism and Theology Today." *The Center for Baptist Studies*. Mercer University. http://conterforbaptiststudies.org/conference/humphreys2005/opentheism.

Jacobs, Alan. "To Be a Christian College." *First Things*. April 2006. http://www.firstthings.com/article/2006/04/to-be-a-christian-college.

—— *More Than 95 Theses*. ayjay.tumblr.com.

Jacobsen, Douglas and Rhonda. *No Longer Invisible: Religion in University Education*. New York: Oxford University Press, 2012.

Jaschik, Scott. "Academic and Publishing Freedom." *Inside Higher Education*. January 20, 2010. www.insidehighed.com/news/2010/01/20/wheaton.

—— "Academic Freedom after September 11." *Inside Higher Education*. March 7, 2006. http://app3.insidehighered.com/news/2006/03/07/acfree.

—— "Believing in God and Evolution." *Inside Higher Education*. October 14, 2009. https://www.insidehighered.com/news/2009/10/14/evolution.

—— "Change of Heart at Belmont." *Inside Higher Education*. January 27, 2011. https://www.insidehighered.com/news/2011/01/27/belmont_bars_discrimination_based_on_sexual_orientation.

—— "Détente with David Horowitz." *Inside Higher Education*. June 23, 2005. https://www.insidehighered.com/news/2005/06/23/statement.

—— "Difficult Separation for Belmont." *Inside Higher Education*. May 11, 2006. https://m.insidehighered.com/news/2006/05/11/belmont.

—— "Faith, Science, and Academic Freedom." *Inside Higher Education*. January 15, 2009. https://www.insidehighered.com/news/2009/01/15/aaup.

—— "Fall from Grace." *Inside Higher Education*. August 15, 2011. https://www.insidehighered.com/news/2011/08/15/a_professor_s_departure_raises_questions_about_freedom_of_scholarship_at_calvin_college.

—— "Freedom of Religion or Free to Discriminate?" *Inside Higher Education*. July 14, 2014. https://www.insidehighered.com/news/2014/07/14/two-legal-cases-illustrate-growing-tensions-over-rights-transgender-students.

—— "Shrinking Censure List." *Inside Higher Education*. June 12, 2006. https://www.insidehighered.com/news/2006/06/12/aaup.

—— "Stop Blaming Professors." *Inside Higher Education*. June 10, 2014. https://www.insidehighered.com/news/2014/06/10/study-finds-students-themselves-not-professors-lead-some-become-more-liberal-college#sthash.bWA9dH8W.dpbs.

—— "Ward Churchill Fired." *Inside Higher Education*. July 25, 2007. https://www.insidehighered.com/news/2007/07/25/churchill.

Jeanson, Nathaniel and Brian Thomas. "The Resurrection of 'Junk DNA.'" *Institute of Creation Research*. March 20, 2013. http://www.icr.org/article/7383/.

Jefferson, Thomas. Letter to H. D. Tiffin, 1807 in "Government Founders Speak Out." *Free Republic*. http://www.freerepublic.com/focus/news/670189/posts.

—— *Writings*, edited by Merrill D. Peterson. New York: Library of America, 1984.

Jeffrey, David L. "Biblical Literacy, Academic Freedom, and Christian Liberty." In *The Bible and the University*, edited by David L. Jeffrey and C. Stephen Evans. Grand Rapids: Zondervan, 2007.

Jennie Choi, "Changes in Attitude." *Sojourners*. July 2012. http://www.sojo.net/magazine/2012/07/changes-attitude.

Jesse, David. "Pay It Forward: Plan Would Allow Michigan Students to Attend College for 'Free.'" *Detroit Free Press*. March 19, 2014. http://www.freep.com/article/20140319/NEWS06/303190038/Pay-it-forward-Plan-would-allow-Michigan-students-to-attend-college-for-free-.

Johnson, Philip E. *Darwin on Trial*. Downers Grove, IL: InterVarsity Press, 1993.

Jones, Leigh. "Supreme Court Declines Religious Liberty Case." *World on Campus*. March 19, 2012. http://www.worldoncampus.com/2012/03/supreme_court_declines_religious_liberty_case.

Jones, Stanton L. "Letter to a Gay Professor." *Inside Higher Education*. April 3, 2013. https://www.insidehighered.com/advice/2013/04/03/essay-responds-open-letter-gay-professor-christian-college.

—— "Same-Sex Science: The Social Sciences Cannot Settle the Moral Status of Homosexuality." *First Things*. February 2012. http://www.firstthings.com/article/2012/02/same-sex-science.

Jones, Stanton L. and Mark A. Yarhouse. *Homosexuality: The Use of Scientific Research in the Church's Moral Debate*. Downers Grove, IL: InterVarsity Press, 2000.

Joyce, Kathryn. "LGBT Christian College Students Fight for a Voice." *The Daily Beast*. February 14, 2014. http://www.thedailybeast.com/articles/2014/02/14/lgbt-christian-college-students-fight-for-a-voice.html.

Justin Taylor. "An Interview with David Dockery on the Identity and Future of the Southern Baptist Convention." *The Gospel Coalition*. June 2, 2009. http://www.thegospelcoalition.org/blogs/justintaylor/2012/06/19/reclaiming-the-christian-intellectual-tradition-an-interview-with-david-dockery/.

Kafka, Franz. "World." In *A Treasury of Jewish Quotations*, edited by Joseph L. Baron, 554. New York: Crown Publishers, 1956.

Kalscheur, Gregory. "Key Task for Catholic Higher Ed." *Inside Higher Education*. November 29, 2011. https://www.insidehighered.com/views/2011/11/29/essay-future-direction-catholic-colleges.

Karran, Terence. "Academic Freedom in Europe: A Preliminary Comparative Analysis." *Higher Education Policy* 34, no. 3 (September 1, 2009).

Kazin, Michael. *A Godly Hero: The Life of William Jennings Bryan*. New York: Alfred A. Knopf, 2006.

Keathley, Kenneth. "Southern Baptist Voices: Expressing Our Concern, Part I." *The Biologos Forum*. February 28, 2012. http://biologos.org/blog/southern-baptist-voices-expressing-our-concerns-part-1.

Keith, Chris. *Jesus Against the Scribal Elite*. Grand Rapids: Baker Publishing Group, 2014.

Kelley, Brooks Mather. *Yale: A History*. New Haven: Yale University Press, 1974.

Kempis, Thomas á. *The Imitation of Christ*. New York: Hurst and Company, 1843.

Kengor, Paul. "A Tale of 2 Christian Colleges." *National Catholic Register*. July 8, 2011. http://www.ncregister.com/site/article/a-tale-of-2-christian-colleges/.

Kidd, Thomas. "Calvinist Controversy at Louisiana College." *First Things*. February 26, 2013. http://www.firstthings.com/blogs/firstthoughts/2013/02/calvinist-controversy-at-louisiana-college.

Kiley, Kevin. "Fundamental Disagreements." *Insider Higher Education*. May 12, 2011. https://www.insidehighered.com/news/2011/05/12/professor_s_lawsuit_against_louisiana_college_suggest_suppression_of_dissent_by_administrators.

Knopf-Newman, Marcy Jane. *The Politics of Teaching Palestine to America*. New York: Palgrave Macmillan, 2011.

Koenig, Louis W. *Bryan*. New York: G.P. Putnam's Sons, 1971.

Kors, Alan and Harvey Silverglate. *The Shadow University: The Betrayal of Liberty on America's Campuses*. New York: The Free Press, 1998.

Kreeft, Peter. *Heaven: The Heart's Deepest Longing*. San Francisco: Ignatius Press, 1989.

Kuttab, David. "Israel Irked by Pro-Palestinian Evangelical Christian Conference." *Almonitor*. March 10, 2014. http://www.al-monitor.com/pulse/originals/2014/03/christ-conference-evangelical-christian-palestine.html#.

Lascell, David M. "Grove City v. Bell: What the Case Means Today." *The Grove City Journal of Law and Public Policy* 1, no. 1 (2010): 1–6.

Latourette, Kenneth Scott. *A History of Christianity*, vol. 1. New York: Harper and Row, 1975.

Lawder, David. "Supreme Court Awards Wheaton College Temporary Exemption on Obamacare Birth Control." *Chicago Tribune*. July 3, 2014. http://articles.chicagotribune.com/2014-07-03/news/chi-supreme-court-wheaton-college-birth-control-20140703_1_wheaton-college-contraception-coverage-supreme-court.

Lay, Robert F. "Holiness and Higher Education at Taylor University: A Double Cure?" In *Called to Unite Knowledge and Vital Piety: Indiana's Wesleyan-Related Universities*, edited by Michael G. Cartwright and Merle D. Strege, 91–100. Indianapolis: University of Indianapolis Press, 2012.

Layton, Lyndsey. "High School Graduation Rates at Historic High." *Washington Post*. April 28, 2014. http://www.washingtonpost.com/local/education/high-school-graduation-rates-at-historic-high/2014/04/28/84eb0122-cee0-11e3-937f-d3026234b51c_story.html.

Lederman, Doug. "State Budgeters' View of Higher Ed." *Inside Higher Education*. March 27, 2013. https://www.insidehighered.com/news/2013/03/27/state-state-funding-higher-education.

Lewin, Tamar. "After Setbacks, Online Courses Are Rethought." *New York Times*. December 10, 2013. http://www.nytimes.com/2013/12/11/us/after-setbacks-online-courses-are-rethought.html?pagewanted=all.

Lewis, C. S. "The Inner Ring." *The Weight of Glory*. New York: Simon and Schuster, 1980.

—— *Mere Christianity*. New York: Macmillan, 1952.

Lindner, Eileen W. *Yearbook of American and Canadian Churches, 2012*. Nashville: Abingdon Press, 2012.

Lindsay, Michael D. "Evangelicalism Rebounds in Academe." *Chronicle of Higher Education* 54, no. 35 (May 2008): 12–14.

Livingstone, David N. *Darwin's Forgotten Defenders: The Encounter Between Evangelical Theology and Evolutionary Thought*. Grand Rapids: Eerdmans, 1987.

Longman, Karen and Patricia S. Anderson. "Gender Trends in Senior-Level Leadership: A 12-Year Analysis of the CCCU U.S. Member Institutions." *Christian Higher Education* 10, no. 5 (2011): 422–443.

Lukianoff, Greg. "Federal Government Mandates Unconstitutional Speech Codes at Colleges and Universities Nationwide." *FIRE*. May 17, 2013. http://www.thefire.org/federal-government-mandates-unconstitutional-speech-codes-at-colleges-and-universities-nationwide-3/.

——— "Feigning Free Speech on Campus." *New York Times*. October 24, 2012. http://www.nytimes.com/2012/10/25/opinion/feigning-free-speech-on-campus.html.

Madawar, Jean and David Pyke. *Hitler's Gift*. New York: Arcade Publishing, 2000.

Mandryk, Jason. *Operation World*. Colorado Springs: Biblica Publishing, 2010.

Manning, Brennan. *Lion and Lamb: The Relentless Tenderness of Jesus*. Grand Rapids: Baker Book House, 1993.

Markoe, Lauren. "Religious Leaders Seek to Overcome Polarization." *Religion News Service*. May 16, 2013. http://www.religionnews.com/2013/05/15/christian-leaders-seek-to-overcome-polarization/.

Marsden, George M. "The Ambiguities of Academic Freedom." *Church History* 62, no. 2 (June 1993): 221–236.

——— "Liberating Academic Freedom." *First Things*. 1998. http://www.firstthings.com/article/1998/12/liberating-academic-freedom.

——— *The Soul of the American University: From Protestant Establishment to Established Nonbelief*. New York: Oxford University Press, 1994.

McConnell, Michael W. "Academic Freedom in Religious Colleges and Universities." *Law and Contemporary Problems* 53, no. 3 (1990): 303–324.

McCosh, James. "God Works Through Evolution." In *A Documentary History of American Thought and Society*, edited by Charles Crowe, 229. Boston: Allyn and Bacon, 1968.

McCutcheon, Russell T. "What Is the Academic Study of Religion?" University of Alabama. http://rel.as.ua.edu/pdf/rel100introhandout.pdf.

McGrath, James F. "In Support of Christopher Rollston." *Exploring Our Matrix* (blog). http://www.patheos.com/blogs/exploringourmatrix/2012/10/in-support-of-christopher-rollston.html.

McKnight, Scott. "From Wheaton to Rome: Why Evangelicals Become Roman Catholic." *Journal of Evangelical Theological Society* 45, no. 3 (September 2002): 451–472.

McMurtrie, Beth. "Do Professors Lose Academic Freedom by Signing Statements of Faith?" *Chronicle of Higher Education*. May 24, 2002.

McVicar, Brian. "Calvin College Alumni Using the Web to Push for More Welcoming Environment for LGBT Students." *MLive Media Group*. October 18, 2012. http://www.mlive.com/news/grand-rapids/index.ssf/2012/10/alumni_say_calvin_college_must.html.

Meeth, L. Richard. *Quality Education for Less Money*. San Francisco: Jossey-Bass, 1974.

Mello, Anthony de. *The Way to Love*. New York: Doubleday, 1995.

Merton, Thomas. *New Seeds of Contemplation*. New York: New Directions Publishing, 1961.

—— *No Man Is an Island*. San Diego: Harcourt Brace, 1983.

Metzger, Walter P. *Academic Freedom in the Age of the University*. New York: Columbia University Press, 1964.

Miethe, Terry L. "Christian Church (Disciples of Christ)" and "Christian Churches/Churches of Christ (Independent)." In *Dictionary of Christianity*, edited by Daniel G. Reid, Robert D. Linder, Bruce L. Shelley, and Harry S. Stout, 253–255. Downers Grove, IL: InterVarsity Press, 1990.

Mill, John Stuart. *On Liberty*. New York: W. W. Norton and Company, 1975.

Miller Rubin, Bonnie. "Lutheran College Opens the Door to Same-Sex Wedding." *Chicago Tribune*. January 14, 2013. http://articles.chicagotribune.com/2013-01-14/news/ct-met-gay-marriage-religious-colleges-20130114_1_elca-augustana-college-liberal-arts-college.

Miller, Lisa. "Why Harvard Students Should Study More Religion." *Newsweek*. February 10, 2010. http://www.newsweek.com/why-harvard-students-should-study-more-religion-75231.

Mitchell, Corrie. "Evangelical 'Messy Middle' More Accepting of Gays." *Sojourners: Faith in Action for Social Justice*. August 13, 2013. http://sojo.net/blogs/2013/08/13/study-evangelical-%E2%80%98messy-middle%E2%80%99-more-accepting-gays.

Monsma Jr., George N. "Faith and Faculty Autonomy at Calvin College." *Academe* 87, no. 1 (2001): 43–47.

Montaño, Armando. "Christian Group Accused of Discrimination Loses Student Group Status, Splits in Two." *Scarlet and Black*. September 3, 2011. http://www.thesandb.com/news/christian-group-accused-of-discrimination-loses-student-group-status-splits-into-two.html.

Moody Jr., Raymond A. *Life After Life*. New York: Bantam Books, 1976.

Moon, Ruth. "Bryan College Faculty Vote 'No Confidence' in President Over Adam and Eve." *Christianity Today*. March 7, 2014. http://www.christianitytoday.com/gleanings/2014/march/bryan-college-faculty-vote-no-confidence-president-adam-eve.html?paging=off.

—— "Eastern Mennonite University Delays Decision on Same-Sex Relationships." *Christianity Today*. June 23, 2014. http://www.christianitytoday.com/gleanings/2014/june/eastern-mennonite-university-delays-decision-on-same-sex-re.html?paging=off.

—— "Three Controversial Christian Colleges Learn Their Accreditation Fate." *Christianity Today*. June 24, 2014. http://www.christianitytoday.com/gleanings/2014/june/accreditation-decisions-handed-down-controversial-southern-.html?paging=off.

Moore, Mary. "Accreditation Board Gives Gordon College a Year to Review Policy on Homosexuality." *Boston Business Journal*. September 25, 2014. http://www.bizj

ournals.com/boston/news/2014/09/25/accreditation-board-gives-gordon-college-a-year-to.html?page=all.

Morgan, Timothy C. "Evangelicals Defend 'Christ at the Checkpoint' from Israeli Critics." *Christianity Today*. March 12, 2014. http://www.christianitytoday.com/gleanings/2014/march/israel-blasts-evangelical-bethlehem-christ-at-checkpoint.html.

Morin, Rich. "Opposition to Same-Sex Marriage May Be Understated in Public Opinion Polls." *Pew Research Center*. September 30, 2013. http://www.pewresearch.org/fact-tank/2013/09/30/opposition-to-same-sex-marriage-may-be-understated-in-public-opinion-polls/.

Moshier, S. O., D. E. Maas, and J. K. Greenberg. "From the Beginning: Faith and Geology at Evangelical Wheaton College." In *Geology and Religion: A History of Harmony and Hostility*, edited by M. Kolbl-Ebert, 301–315. London: Geological Society of London, 2009.

Murdoch, J. Murray with Thomas S. Mach. *Cedarville University: Inspiring Greatness for 125 Years*. Virginia Beach: Donning Company Publishers, 2012.

Myers, David G. "Accepting What Cannot Be Changed." In *Homosexuality and Christian Faith: Questions of Conscience for the Churches*, edited by Walter Wink, 67–70. Minneapolis: Augsburg Fortress Publishers, 1999.

Myers, David G. and Letha Dawson Scanzoni. *What God Has Joined Together?: A Christian Case for Gay Marriage*. San Francisco: Harper San Francisco, 2005.

National Research Council. "Doctoral Programs by the Numbers: Religion." *The Chronicle of Higher Education*. 2010. http://chronicle.com/article/nrc-religion/124664/.

Nazworth, Napp. "Calvin College Professor Claims Administration Not Truthful Over Colleague's Resignation." *The Christian Post*. August 17, 2011. http://www.christianpost.com/news/calvin-college-professor-claims-administration-not-truthful-over-colleagues-resignation-54046/.

NCHEMS Information Center for Higher Education Policymaking and Analysis. www.nchems.org.

Nelson, Cary. *No University Is an Island: Saving Academic Freedom*. New York: New York University Press, 2010.

Nelson, Libby A. "A Campus in Turmoil." *Inside Higher Education*. January 22, 2013. https://www.insidehighered.com/news/2013/01/22/several-controversies-converge-ohio-baptist-college.

—— "Banned." *Inside Higher Education*. December 1, 2011. https://www.insidehighered.com/news/2011/12/01/controversy-shorter-over-faith-statements.

—— "Shorter's Exodus, A Year Later." *Inside Higher Education*. November 14, 2012. https://www.insidehighered.com/news/2012/11/14/cultural-change-tears-georgia-baptist-college-apart.

—— "Standing Their Ground." *Inside Higher Education*. February 3, 2012. https://www.insidehighered.com/news/2012/02/03/christian-college-presidents-discuss-what-do-about-sexuality.

—— "Tenure vs. Donors." *Inside Higher Education.* October 15, 2012. https://www.insidehighered.com/news/2012/10/15/seminary-threatens-discipline-professor-offending-prospective-students-donors.

—— "Going to the Chapel." *Inside Higher Education.* December 19, 2012. https://www.insidehighered.com/news/2012/12/19/religious-colleges-deciding-whether-allow-blessings-gay-unions-their-chapels.

—— "No Longer a Silent Minority." *Inside Higher Education.* December 17, 2012. https://www.insidehighered.com/news/2012/12/17/gay-students-increasingly-vocal-evangelical-colleges.

Newman, John Henry. *The Idea of a University.* Notre Dame: University of Notre Dame Press, 1982.

Noll, Mark A. *America's God.* New York: Oxford University Press, 2002.

—— *Between Faith and Criticism: Evangelicals, Scholarship, and the Bible in America.* San Francisco: Harper and Row, 1986.

—— and Carolyn Nystrom. *Is the Reformation Over?: An Evangelical Assessment of Contemporary Roman Catholicism.* Grand Rapids: Baker Academic, 2005.

—— and David N. Livingstone. *Evolution, Scripture, and Science: Selected Writings.* Grand Rapids: Baker Books, 2000.

——, James Turner, Thomas Albert Howard, editors. *The Future of Christian Learning: An Evangelical and Catholic Dialogue.* Grand Rapids: Brazos Press, 2008.

Nord, Warren. *Does God Make a Difference? Taking God Seriously in Our Schools and Universities.* New York: Oxford University Press, 2010.

Notestein, Wallace. *The English People on the Eve of Colonization.* New York: Harper and Row, 1962.

Nuechterlein, James. "The Idol of Academic Freedom." *First Things.* December 1993. http://www.firstthings.com/article/1993/12/001-the-idol-of-academic-freedom.

Numbers, Ronald L. *The Creationists: The Evolution of Scientific Creationism.* Berkeley: University of California Press, 1992.

Olson, Ted. "Valparaiso Repents for Holding Interfaith 9/11 Service." *Christianity Today.* September 1, 2003. http://www.christianitytoday.com/ct/2003/septemberweb-only/9-29-31.0.html.

—— and Trevor Persaud. "Christian Legal Society Loses in Supreme Court Case." *Christianity Today.* June 28, 2010. http://www.christianitytoday.com/ct/2010/juneweb-only/christian-legal-society-loses-supreme-court.html.

Olson, David. "La Sierra University: Employees' Case Dismissed." *Press Enterprise.* May 20, 2012. http://www.pe.com/articles/university-688936-church-sierra.html.

Olson, Roger E. "Why Inerrancy Doesn't Matter." *Patheos.* August 19, 2010. http://www.patheos.com/blogs/rogereolson/2010/08/why-inerrancy-doesnt-matter/.

Omarzu, Tim. "Four Trustees Resign from Bryan College." *Chattanooga Times Press.* July 19, 2014. http://www.timesfreepress.com/news/2014/jul/19/four-trustees-resign-from-bryan-college/?breakingnews.

Organ, Mike. "Belmont Disputes Gay Coach Was Fired: Sexuality Brought Ultimatum from school, Players Say." *The Tennessean.* December 3, 2010. http://archive.tennessean.com/article/20101203/SPORTS06/12030362/Belmont-disputes-gay-coach-fired.

Ostling, Richard. "The Search for the Historical Adam." *Christianity Today*. June 3, 2011. http://www.christianitytoday.com/ct/2011/june/historicaladam.html?paging=off.

Owens, John. "Schools' Faith-Based Doctrines Raise Concerns, Risk Backlash." *Chicago Tribune*. October 6, 2002. http://articles.chicagotribune.com/2002-10-06/news/0210060223_1_faith-based-catholic-colleges-mandatums.

Parr, Chris. "Clinton: MOOCs May Be a Key to a More Efficient U.S. System." *Times Higher Education*. April 11, 2013. http://www.improvingthestudentexperience.com/news/moocs-may-be-more-efficient/.

Paton, Alan. *Cry, the Beloved Country*. New York: Macmillan, 1987.

Patton, Mike. "Obamacare: Seven Major Provisions and How They Affect You." *Forbes Magazine*. November 27, 2013. http://www.forbes.com/sites/mikepatton/2013/11/27/how-obamacare-will-change-the-american-health-system/

Paulsen, Friedrich. *The German Universities: Their Character and Historical Development*. New York: Macmillan, 1895.

Paulson, Amanda. "Teacher's Radical 9/11 Views Raise Red Flags." *Christian Science Monitor*. August 18, 2006. http://www.csmonitor.com/2006/0818/p03s01-legn.html.

Peck, M. Scott. *People of the Lie: The Hope for Healing Human Evil*. New York: Simon and Schuster, 1983.

—— *The Different Drum: Community Making and Peace*. New York: Simon and Schuster, 1988.

Perez Jr., Juan. "U. of I. Defends Pulling Job Offer Over Tweets Critical of Israel." *Chicago Tribune*. August 22, 2014. http://www.chicagotribune.com/news/local/breaking/chi-university-of-illinois-job-offer-tweet-israel-20140822-story.html.

Pinnock, Clark et al. *The Openness of God: A Biblical Challenge to the Traditional Understanding of God*. Downers Grove, IL: InterVarsity Press, 1994.

Plantinga, Alvin. *Where the Conflict Really Lies: Science, Religion, and Naturalism*. New York: Oxford University Press, 2011.

Poch, Robert K. *Academic Freedom in American Higher Education: Rights, Responsibilities and Limitations*. Washington, DC: School of Education and Human Development, George Washington University, 1993.

Polanyi, Michael. *Personal Knowledge: Towards a Post-Critical Philosophy*. Chicago: University of Chicago Press, 1958.

Poovey, Cherin. "Justin Lee ('00): Of Faith—and Finding Faith in One's Self: Founder of Gay Christian Network Publishes New Book about His Personal Journey." *Wake Forest Magazine*. February 4, 2013. http://magazine.wfu.edu/2013/02/04/justin-lee-00-of-faith-and-finding-faith-in-ones-self/.

Porter, Eduardo. "The Bane and the Boon of For-Profit Colleges." *New York Times*. February 25, 2014. http://www.nytimes.com/2014/02/26/business/economy/the-bane-and-the-boon-of-for-profit-colleges.html?_r=0.

Postma, Gayla R. "Women in Ministry: 15 Years Later." *Banner*. October 22, 2011. http://www.thebanner.org/features/2011/10/women-in-ministry-15-years-later.

Priebe, Dennis. "Evangelicals and Adventists Together?" *Dennis Priebe Seminars*. http://www.dennispriebe.com/new/node/12.

Prothero, Stephen. *Religious Literacy: What Every American Needs to Know—and Doesn't.* New York: HarperCollins, 2008.

Pulliam Bailey, Sarah. "Cedarville University 'Faculty Shakeup' Appears to Indicate Southern Baptist Future." *Huffington Post.* January 23, 2014. http://www.huffingtonpost.com/2013/12/22/cedarville-university-faculty_n_4469241.html.

—— "Is Support for Israel Waning Among Evangelicals?" *Washington Post.* April 8, 2014. http://www.washingtonpost.com/national/religion/is-support-for-israel-waning-among-evangelicals/2014/04/09/a75ead8c-bff7-11e3-9ee7-02c1e10a03f0_story.html.

—— "Transgender Theology Professor Leaves Christian College." *Christianity Today.* September 23, 2013. http://www.christianitytoday.com/gleanings/2013/september/transgender-professor-azusa-pacific-heath-adam-ackley.html?paging=off.

—— "Gay Rights Group Targets Christian Colleges." *Christianity Today.* March 9, 2006. http://www.christianitytoday.com/ct/2006/marchweb-only/110-42.0.html.

—— "Westminster Theological Suspension." *Christianity Today.* April 1, 2008. http://www.christianitytoday.com/ct/2008/aprilweb-only/114-24.0.html.

Rabban, David M. "A Functional Analysis of Individual and Institutional Academic Freedom Under the First Amendment." *Law and Contemporary Problems* 53, no. 3 (1990): 236–239.

Rana, Fazale. "Do Scientists Accept the Results of the Encode Project?" *Reasons to Believe.* September 12, 2013. http://www.reasons.org/articles/do-scientists-accept-the-results-of-the-encode-project.

Rast, Lawrence. "Lutheran Church-Missouri Synod." and Robert Kolb. "Lutheranism." In *The Encyclopedia of Protestantism,* edited by Hans J. Hillerbrand, 1124–1126, 1130–1136. New York: Routledge, 2004.

Redden, Elizabeth. "Christian Colleges Grow More Diverse." *Inside Higher Education.* August 15, 2008. https://www.insidehighered.com/news/2008/08/15/christian.

—— "When Identity Trumps Diversity." *Inside Higher Education.* January 4, 2008. https://www.insidehighered.com/news/2008/01/04/calvin.

Reinstadler, Kym. "Hope College Stands by Homosexuality Statement." *Huffington Post.* May 25, 2011. http://www.huffingtonpost.com/religion/the-news/2010/05/10/.

Resmovits, Joy. "George W. Bush's Education Law, No Child Left Behind, Abandoned by Texas." *Huffington Post Politics.* September 30, 2013. http://www.huffingtonpost.com/2013/09/30/bush-education-law-texas_n_4018971.html.

—— "States Escaping No Child Left Behind Can Get More Time on Teacher Evaluations." *Huffington Post.* August 21, 2014. http://www.huffingtonpost.com/2014/08/21/obama-teacher-evaluations_n_5697616.html.

Rice, Richard. *The Openness of God: the Relationship of Divine Foreknowledge and Human Freewill.* Hagerstown, MD: Review and Herald Publishing Association, 1980.

Rich, Motoko. " 'No Child' Law Whittled Down by White House." *The New York Times.* July 6, 2012. http://www.nytimes.com/2012/07/06/education/no-child-left-behind-whittled-down-under-obama.html?pagewanted=all&_r=0.

Riley, Kevin. "The Cost of Values." *Inside Higher Education.* October 8, 2012. https://www.insidehighered.com/news/2012/10/08/changes-funding-sources-shifting-public-university-admissions.

Ringenberg, William C. "Quality in the Classroom." *Taylor University Magazine* (Winter 1979).

—— *Taylor University: The First 150 Years.* Grand Rapids: Eerdmans, 1996.

—— *The Christian College: A History of Protestant Higher Education in America.* Grand Rapids: Baker Academic, 2006.

Roberts, Jon and James Turner. *The Sacred and the Secular University.* Princeton: University of Princeton Press, 2000.

Roberts, Robert C. "What Is It to Be Intellectually Humble?" *Big Questions Online.* June 21, 2012. https://www.bigquestionsonline.com/content/what-it-be-intellectually-humble.

Robertson, "Lesbian Coach's Exit from Belmont U. Has Nashville Talking." *The New York Times.* December 17, 2010. http://www.nytimes.com/2010/12/18/education/18belmont.html.

Rockwell, Leo L. "Academic Freedom: German Origins and American Development." *Bulletin of the American Association of University Professors* 36, no. 2 (Summer 1950): 225–236.

Rogers, Melissa. "Letter to the President on Executive Order." *National Association of Evangelicals.* June 25, 2014. http://www.nae.net/resources/news/1140-letter-to-the-president-on-lgbt-nondiscrimination.

—— "Religious Exemption Letter to President Obama." *Scribd.* July 1, 2014. http://www.scribd.com/doc/232327567/Religious-Exemption-Letter-to-President-Obama#scribd.

Rollston, Christopher. "The Marginalization of Women: A Biblical Value We Don't Like to Talk About." *Huffington Post.* August 31, 2012. http://www.huffingtonpost.com/christopher-rollston/the-marginalization-of-women-biblical-value-we-dont-like-to-talk-about_b_1833648.html.

Ross, Jenna. "An Identity Crisis for a Christian College." *Star Tribune.* January 21, 2010. http://www.startribune.com/local/east/82213892.html.

Rotondaro, Vinnie. "HHS Tries New Modifications to Contraceptive Coverage Rules." *National Catholic Reporter.* September 8, 2014. http://ncronline.org/news/politics/hhs-tries-new-modifications-contraceptive-coverage-rules.

Rousselow, Jessica L. and Alan Winquist. *God's Ordinary People: No Ordinary Heritage.* Upland, IN: Taylor University Press, 1996.

Rudolph, Frederick. *Curriculum: A History of the American Undergraduate Course of Study.* San Francisco: Jossey-Bass, 1977.

—— *The American College and University: A History.* New York: Random House, 1965.

Rudolph, Kristin. "Evangelical Colleges Inching Toward Affirmation of Homosexuality." *Juicy Ecumenism: The Institute on Religion and Democracy's Blog.* http://juicyecumenism.com/2013/04/03/evangelical-colleges-inching-toward-affirmation-of-homosexuality/.

Ruethling, Gretchen. "A Skeptic on 9/11 Prompts Questions on Academic Freedom." *The New York Times*. August 1, 2006. http://www.nytimes.com/2006/08/01/education/01madison.html?_r=0.

Russ, Dan. "Fear Not: Security, Risk, and Academic Freedom." In *The Christian College Phenomenon: Inside America's Fastest Growing Institutions*, edited by Samuel Joeckel and Thomas Chesnes, 181. Abilene, TX: Abilene Christian University Press, 2011.

Ryken, Philip and John Garvey. "An Evangelical-Catholic Stand on Liberty." *Wall Street Journal*. July 18, 2012. http://online.wsj.com/news/articles/SB10001424052702303933704577533251292715324/.

Sandin, Robert T. *The Search for Excellence: The Christian College in an Age of Educational Competition*. Macon, GA: Mercer University Press, 1982.

Schaefer Riley, Naomi. "New Rules Worry Christian Colleges." *Christianity Today*. November 1, 2010. http://www.christianitytoday.com/ct/2010/novemberwebonly/53.11.0.html.

——— "The Press and Patrick Henry College." *naomiriley.com*. http://naomiriley.com/wp-content/uploads/2010/07/press.pdf.

Schmalzbauer, John and Kathleen Mahoney. "Religion and Knowledge in the Post-Secular Academy." In *The Post-Secular Question: Religion in Contemporary Society*, edited by John Torpey, David Kyoman, and Jonathan Van Antwerpen, 216ff. New York: New York University Press, 2012.

Schmidt, George P. *The Liberal Arts College*. New Brunswick: Rutgers University Press, 1957.

Schneider, John R. "Recent Genetic Science and Christian Theology on Human Origins: An Aesthetic Supralapsarianism." *American Scientific Affiliation*. August 5, 2010. http://www.asa3online.org/PSCF/2010/08/05/recent-genetic-science-and-christian-theology-on-human-origins-an-%E2%80%9Caesthetic-supralapsarianism%E2%80%9D/.

Schodolski, Vincent J. "Professors Learn Freedom of Expression Has Risks, Limits." *Chicago Tribune*. November 18, 2001. http://articles.chicagotribune.com/2001-11-18/news/0111180275_1_academic-freedom-tenured-professor-cold-war.

Schuman, Samuel. *Seeing the Light: Religious Colleges in Twenty-First Century America*. Baltimore: Johns Hopkins University Press, 2010.

Seldes, George, editor. *The Great Thoughts*. New York: Ballantine Books, 1996.

Shakespeare, William. *Hamlet*, Act 1, Scene 3.

Shibley, Robert. "The Fallout from *Christian Legal Society*: Vanderbilt Launches an Offensive Against Religious Freedom." *The National Review*. February 6, 2012. http://www.nationalreview.com/articles/290199/fallout-ichristian-legal-societyi-robert-shibley.

Sizer, Stephen. *Christian Zionism: Road Map to Armageddon?* Leister, England: InterVarsity Press, 2004.

Smith, Christian. *Christian America?: What Evangelicals Really Want*. Berkeley: University of California Press, 2005.

—— *The Bible Made Impossible: Why Biblicism Is Not a Truly Evangelical Reading of Scripture*. Grand Rapids: Baker Brazos, 2011.

Smith, Page. *Daughters of the Promised Land: Women in American History*. Boston: Little Brown and Company, 1970.

—— *Killing the Spirit: Higher Education in America*. New York: Viking Penguin, 1990.

Smith, Peter J. "Notre Dame's Plan for Homosexual Outreach: University Says Church Teaching Will Be Addressed, But Skepticism Remains." *National Catholic Register*. January 7, 2013. http://www.ncregister.com/site/article/notre-dames-plan-for-homosexual-outreach/.

Smith, Samuel. "Canadian Law Society Rejects Christian School Over Biblical Homosexuality Stance." *CP Politics*. November 4, 2014. http://m.christianpost.com/news/canadian-law-society-rejects-christian-school-over-biblical-homosexuality-stance-129115/.

Snider, Brett. "Obama Bars Anti-Gay Discrimination by Federal Contractors." *Findlaw* (blog). July 21, 2004. http://blogs.findlaw.com/free_enterprise/2014/07/obama-bars-anti-gay-discrimination-by-federal-contractors.html.

Sommerville, C. John. *The Decline of the Secular University*. New York: Oxford University Press, 2006.

Southwick, Paul. "Is There Hope for Queer Students at Conservative Christian Colleges?" *Huffington Post Gay Voices*. August 24, 2012. http://www.huffingtonpost.com/paul-southwick/is-there-hope-for-queer-s_b_1829246.html.

St. Amant, Clair. "New Intelligent Design Conflict Hits BU." *The Baylor Lariat*. September 11, 2007. http://www.discovery.org/a/4217.

Steffan, Melissa. "Administrators' Resignations Fuel Fears at Cedarville University." *Christianity Today*. January 23, 2013. http://www.christianitytoday.com/ct/2013/january-web-only/resignations-of-top-administrators-fuel-fears-at-cedarville.html.

Stewart Van Leeuwen, Mary, editor. *After Eden: Facing Challenges of Gender Reconciliation*. Grand Rapids: Eerdmans, 1993.

Stohr, Greg. "Gay Marriage Nears Supreme Court with Inevitability Tag." *Bloomberg*. July 31, 2014. http://www.bloomberg.com/news/2014-07-31/gay-marriage-nears-supreme-court-with-inevitability-tag.html.

Stone, Lawrence. "The Educational Revolution in England, 1560–1640." *Past and Present* 28, no. 1 (July 1964): 41–80.

Straumsheim, Carl. "Tempered Expectations." *Inside Higher Education*. January 15, 2014. https://www.insidehighered.com/news/2014/01/15/after-two-years-mooc-mania-enthusiasm-online-education-dips.

Straus, Valerie. "Christian College's Student Leader 'Comes Out' as Atheist." *Washington Post*. November 7, 2013. http://www.washingtonpost.com/blogs/answer-sheet/wp/2013/11/07/christian-colleges-student-leader-comes-out-as-atheist/.

Stripling, Jack. "Creating Controversy." *Inside Higher Education*. September 1, 2009. https://www.insidehighered.com/news/2009/09/01/evolution.

Stronks, Julia K. "Discrimination and Pluralism." *Journal of Higher Education.* July 22, 2014. https://www.insidehighered.com/views/2014/07/22/essay-push-christian-colleges-and-others-be-exempt-federal-civil-rights.

Taylor, Justin. "J. I. Packer's Critique of Harold Lindsell on Inerrancy and Interpretation." *The Gospel Coalition.* August 7, 2014. http://www.thegospelcoalition.org/blogs/justintaylor/2014/08/07/j-i-packers-critique-of-harold-lindsell-on-inerrancy-and-interpretation/.

Tewksbury, Donald G. *The Founding of the American Colleges and Universities Before the Civil War.* New York: Columbia University, 1932.

The Council on Biblical Manhood and Womanhood. 2014. cbmw.org.

Thelin, John. *A History of American Higher Education.* Baltimore: Johns Hopkins University Press, 2004.

Thomason, Andy. "Student Loan Default Rates Continue Steady Climb." *Chronicle of Higher Education.* October 1, 2013. http://chronicle.com/article/Student-Loan-Default-Rates/142009/.

Thorson, Walter R. "The Biblical Insights of Michael Polanyi." *Journal of the American Scientific Affiliation.* September 1981. http://www.asa3.org/ASA/PSCF/1981/JASA9-81Thorson.html.

Tournier, Paul. *Learn to Grow Old.* New York: Harper and Row, 1971.

Townsend, Tim. "Newtown Interfaith Prayer By Lutheran Missouri Synod Pastor Reopens Old Wounds." *Huffington Post.* March 26, 2013. http://www.huffingtonpost.com/2013/02/13/lcms-newtown-interfaith-prayers-reopens-old-wounds-for-missouri-synod_n_2681340.html.

Tracy, Kate. "CCCU School Permits Professors in Same-Sex Relationships (At Least for Six Months)." *Christianity Today.* November 27, 2013. http://www.christianitytoday.com/gleanings/2013/november/eastern-mennonite-university-professors-same-sex-cccu-emu.html?paging=off.

——— "Transgender Students Battle Christian Universities." *Christianity Today.* July 15, 2014. http://www.christianitytoday.com/gleanings/2014/july/transgender-students-battle-christian-universities.html?paging=off.

Treadwell, David. "Fundamentalist Baptists Suffer Major Defeat in Georgia." *Los Angeles Times.* November 12, 1987. http://articles.latimes.com/1987-11-12/news/mn-20469_1_georgia-baptists/.

Trueblood, Elton. *The Common Ventures of Life: Marriage, Birth, Work, and Death.* New York: Harper and Brothers, 1949.

Tucker, Ruth A. *Women in the Maze: Questions and Answers in Biblical Equality.* Downers Grove, IL: InterVarsity Press, 1992.

Union Theological Seminary. utsnyc.edu

United States Holocaust Memorial Museum, www.ushmm.org.

Van Brummelen, Harro and Kevin Sawatsky. "Colliding Rights in Schools: Trinity Western University v. the British Columbia College of Teachers." *Journal of Educational Thought* 36, no. 3 (December 2001).

Van Farowe, Roxanne. "Play about Gay Christians Sells Out." *Banner.* January 2011. http://www.thebanner.org/news/2011/01/play-about-gay-christians-sells-out.

Van Why, Artie. "Living as a Homosexual Christian." *The Horizon.* November 16, 2010. http://blogs.westmont.edu/horizon/2010/11/16/living-as-a-homosexual-christian/.

VanTill, Howard J. *The Fourth Day.* Grand Rapids: Eerdmans, 1986.

Vedder, Richard. *Going Broke by Degree: Why College Costs Too Much.* Washington, DC: AEI Press, 2004.

Vestal, Shawn. "Evangelicalism Shouldn't Close Hearts." *The Spokesman Review.* April 18, 2014. http://www.spokesman.com/stories/2014/apr/18/evangelicalism-shouldnt-close-hearts/.

Veysey, Laurence R. *The Emergence of the American University.* Chicago: University of Chicago Press, 1965.

Walton, John H. *The Lost World of Genesis One: Ancient Cosmology and the Origins Debate.* Downers Grove, IL: InterVarsity Press Academic, 2009.

Warch, Richard. *School of the Prophets: Yale College, 1701–1740.* New Haven: Yale University Press, 1973.

Wax, Trevin. "The Peter Enns Controversy." *The Gospel Coalition.* March 29, 2008. http://www.thegospelcoalition.org/blogs/trevinwax/2008/03/29/the-peter-enns-controversy/.

Weisberger, Bernard. *They Gathered at the River: The Story of the Great Revivalists and Their Impact Upon Religion in America.* Chicago: Quadrangle Paperbacks, 1958.

Weissmann, Jordan. "A Truly Devastating Graph on State Higher Education Spending." *The Atlantic.* March 20, 2013. http://www.theatlantic.com/business/archive/2013/03/a-truly-devastating-graph-on-state-higher-education-spending/274199/.

White, Lawrence. "Does Academic Freedom Give a Professor the Final Say on Grades?" *Chronicle of Higher Education* 54, no. 33 (April 25, 2008): 39.

White, Mel. *Stranger at the Gate: To Be Gay and Christian in America.* New York: Simon and Schuster, 1994.

Whitehead, Alfred North. *Science and the Modern World.* New York: Macmillan, 1950.

Whittier, John Greenleaf. "Dear Lord and Father of Mankind." *NetHymnal.* http://www.cyberhymnal.org/htm/d/e/dearlord.htm.

Wilken, Robert L. "The Piety of the Persecutors." *Christian History* IX, no. 3 (1990): 16–19.

Wilkinson, Kate B. "May the Mind of Christ, My Savior." *NetHymnal.* 1925. http://cyberhymnal.org/htm/m/a/maytmind.htm.

Willimon, Will. *A Peculiar Prophet* (blog). willimon.blogspot.com.

Willis, Gregory A. "Progressive Theology and Southern Baptist Controversies of the 1950s and 1960s." *Southern Baptist Journal of Theology.* July 2010. http://www.sbts.edu/resources/files/2010/07/sbjt_071_spr03_wills.pdf.

Wilson, Robin. "The AAUP, 92 and Ailing." *Chronicle of Higher Education.* June 8, 2007. http://www.csun.edu/pubrels/clips/June07/06-05-07A.pdf.

Winston, Kimberly. "Christian Group Sanctioned at Two Dozen College Campuses." *Religion News Service.* September 8, 2014. http://www.washingtonpost.com/national/religion/christian-group-sanctioned-at-two-dozen-college-campuses/2014/09/08/ecda6b1c-379d-11e4-a023-1d61f7f31a05_story.html.

Withrow, Brandon G. "How Westminster Theological Seminary Came to Define Fundamentalism For Me." *Huffington Post*. July 29, 2014. http://www.huffingtonpost.com/brandon-g-withrow/how-westminster-theologic_b_5624650.html.

Wolterstorff, Nicholas. "Academic Freedom in Religiously Based Colleges and Universities." In *Educating for Shalom: Essays on Christian Higher Education*, edited by Nicholas Wolterstorff, Clarence W. Joldersma, and Gloria Goris Stronks, 252–253. Grand Rapids: Eerdmans, 2004.

—— "Ivory Tower or Holy Mountain?: Faith and Academic Freedom." *Academe* 87, no. 1 (2001): 17–22.

—— *Thomas Reid and the Story of Epistemology*. Cambridge, England: Cambridge University Press, 2001.

Wood, Joshua. "What's Next? How Hobby Lobby Affects Wheaton College and Nearly 100 Other Cases." *Christianity Today*. July 2, 2004. http://www.christianitytoday.com/gleanings/2014/july/supreme-court-ruled-hobby-lobby-wheaton-college-healthcare.html?paging=off.

Wood, W. Jay. "How Might Intellectual Humility Lead to Scientific Insight?" *Big Questions Online*. December 10, 2012. https://www.bigquestionsonline.com/content/how-might-intellectual-humility-lead-scientific-insight.

Worthen, Molly. *Apostles of Reason: The Crisis of Authority in American Evangelicalism*. New York: Oxford University Press, 2014.

You Can Play. youcanplayproject.org.

Zemsky, Robert. "The Unwitting Damage Done by the Spellings Commission." *Chronicle of Higher Education*. September 18, 2011. http://m.chronicle.com/article/The-Unwitting-Damage-Done-by/129051/.

Index

CPSIA information can be obtained
at www.ICGtesting.com
Printed in the USA
LVOW04*1803310116

473073LV00004B/14/P